SEX PLUS

⋟• LEARNING, LOVING, AND ENJOYING YOUR BODY •⋞

WITHDRAWN

by LACI GREEN

HARPER

An Imprint of HarperCollinsPublishers

Library of Congress Control Number: 2018943100
ISBN 978-0-06-256097-1 — ISBN 978-0-06-288929-4 (special edition)

Typography by Lori S. Malkin
18 19 20 21 22   PC/LSCC   10 9 8 7 6 5 4 3 2 1
❖

First Edition

CONTENTS

CLITICAL THINKING

I CAN'T REMEMBER THE EXACT MOMENT "sex" became a dirty word to me. It certainly didn't start out that way. One of my earliest memories is staring in fascination at my mom's very large belly when she was pregnant with my brother. Supposedly, she had a *freaking human* growing inside there. And like most kids, I was curious about bodies, especially naked ones. I wanted to know what was underneath people's clothes, and why boys and girls had different stuff down there.

On rainy school nights in Portland, Oregon, my dad would take me to the public library downtown. The library felt huge and enchanting, full of secrets waiting to be set free. During one memorable visit, as I was strolling through the maze of towering bookshelves, I stumbled on a small shelf of human anatomy books. I picked out the one with a naked person on the front (of course) and hid it behind the pages of a children's book so that I could sneak a read. I was about eight at the time, and while I clearly had an inkling that I was doing something forbidden, I didn't feel much shame about it.

From then on, the anatomy section became a regular pit stop at the library. Through books with blunt descriptions and colorful diagrams, I learned that females can produce milk because of their mammary glands and that penises contain a spongy tissue that fills with blood.

This is also how I learned where babies come from. I learned that human females have eggs while males have sperm, and sex is how you put those two together to make a baby. I was riveted by human sexuality from the start.

By age ten, I had declared that I wanted to be a doctor when I grew up. My family was very supportive of my interest in the human body, and they offered me books and computer games to learn about biology. My room was cluttered with diagrams of the human cell and plastic models of body parts. I was as curious as I was precocious.

But as my body awkwardly hurled toward pubescence, things started to change.

EVERY MORNING IN JUNIOR HIGH, I would slip my sterling silver ring onto my pointer finger. It was etched with flowers and a purple shield marked "C.T.R."—a reminder to Choose the Right. I had received the ring after being baptized into the Mormon church a few years earlier. I took pride in wearing it and didn't think much about it. Until I realized its significance.

One weeknight during youth group in my early teens, me and the other girls my age from church sat cross-legged on the floor of the church's gym. Sister Thompson, our group leader, placed a tray of cookies in the center of the circle and opened up the first conversation I had ever had out loud about sexuality. She told us that as we grew from girls into women, boys would soon find our bodies tempting. Heck, we might even be tempted ourselves. As she spoke, she passed a plastic baggie of abstinence rings around the circle. When she noticed I was already wearing one, she stopped and praised me. I felt my cheeks flush, and the ring suddenly felt hot around my fingers . . . the very fingers I had used to masturbate that morning. While it hadn't even occurred to me to have *actual sex* until that very conversation, I sure had been having some sexy thoughts. A lot of them. Mostly about cute boys at school.

Now, to be fair, I'd *tried* to push these thoughts down.

All the way down.

Further.

Resist the thoughts!

KEEP PUSHING!!!!

The trouble was, the more I tried not to think about it, the more I thought about it. Not only did I start having *more* sexual thoughts after that lesson on abstinence, but they were surfacing in ever more creative and spectacular detail. Great.

In ninth grade, similar messages were repeated in PE health class, just with some sexier packaging. During our week-long unit on sex, our

teacher warned us that teenage boys have a hard time controlling their sexual urges. Girls, he said, gotta keep boys in line. If a boy is getting handsy—and they will get handsy— it's a girl's job to tell him "no." In order to prevent disease, heartbreak, "loose vaginas," pregnancy, and a whole grab bag of consequences, sex had to be avoided. The only other thing I remember from that class was a horrific birthing video that featured a woman screaming her lungs out for ninety minutes. I still see that video in my nightmares.

Notably, the class did very little to address the actual issues I was dealing with at that point in my life. I was questioning my sexuality, wondering if my occasional attraction to girls meant I was a little gay or perhaps a little broken. I was having some very sexual feelings for my first boyfriend, and we were finding it nearly impossible to keep our hands off each other. I was struggling with self-hatred about my body and all the weird things it had started doing. I was also increasingly fed up with the idiocy at school: how girls who wore a lot of makeup were branded "sluts"; how boys in gym class were infected with paranoia about being gay ("no homo, bro"); how men in public had taken to hollering sexual profanities at me while I was simply walking down the street; how a boy in theater class had taken to touching me without my permission.

It was difficult to make sense of this world I found myself in as a teenager. It felt like I was being crushed by the weight of my own sexuality. The thought of talking to my parents about it filled me with shame. Faith leaders, who once offered answers, now rejected my questions. Teachers, who once guided me, now turned a blind eye to bullying and bad behavior. My body, a place I used to feel at home in, now felt like it belonged to everyone but me.

One frustrated night, I flipped on my webcam to vent about it all on a budding video website called YouTube. YouTube was one of the first places where I was free to say what I wanted, to ask questions openly, and to be who I wanted to be. It offered me a space to discuss issues in sexuality when nobody else was. And although it was much more public than church or school, it somehow felt safer.

AFTER I FINISHED MY DEGREE IN legal studies and education at UC Berkeley, I went on to research and create over three hundred videos dispensing health and wellness information about sexuality to young adults. In an epic plot twist, it turns out a lot of other people were seeking the same information that I was. Which is what brought me here, to you. And to this book. And to the adventure we're about to go on.

So, hi! I'm Laci. Pleased to meet you, fellow human.

Perhaps you, too, have had moments of strain surrounding your sexuality. Perhaps you've also encountered a tidal wave of misinformation, confusion, shame, fear, guilt, self-doubt, or self-hatred. For too many of us, these negative feelings color our world of sexuality.

But I promise you: there is another way of doing things.

sex: positive

TOWARD THE END OF COLLEGE, I finally managed to reclaim the curiosity about sexuality that had come naturally to me as a kid. This was in part because I started thinking about my experiences and beliefs more critically. Over time, I wound up incorporating a more sex-positive philosophy into my life. This philosophy acts as the undercurrent of all my work in sex education.

Sex positivity can be thought of as a tool to help people develop a healthier relationship with their sexuality and to create a healthier sexual culture in general. At its core, sex positivity presents a loose set of guiding principles based on the assumption that sexuality is a normal part of life. It asserts that sexuality is diverse, expansive, and worth celebrating. I'd loosely chalk being sex positive up to: "Who cares? Just don't be a jerk." (I know—pretty wild stuff.)

As I put myself in a more sex-positive mindset, it helped me unlearn some of my shame and better understand my sexuality. I am a healthier, happier person for it. And I think the world could be, too!

Here's the definition of sex positivity put forth by sexologist Carol Queen in her book *Real Live Nude Girl: Chronicles of Sex-Positive Culture*:

Sex-positive, a term that's coming into cultural awareness, isn't a dippy love-child celebration of orgone—it's a simple yet radical affirmation that we each grow our own passions on a different medium, that instead of having two or three or even half a dozen sexual orientations, we should be thinking in terms of millions. "Sex-positive" respects each of our unique sexual profiles, even as we acknowledge that some of us have been damaged by a culture that tries to eradicate sexual difference and possibility. Even so, we grow like weeds.

Here's a little more about what sex positivity means to me personally:

1 Do No Harm.

Consent and safety are the central tenets of ethical sexuality. All the people involved in a sexual situation must consent to it. There is simply no room, and no tolerance, for sexual behavior that is forceful or coercive. Sexuality must also be approached safely. Efforts to make it easier to stay safe during sex are great for society—they promote public health and safety.

2 Sexuality Is a Normal Part of Life.

For the vast majority of us, sexuality is part of who we are. It is part of how we relate and connect with each other, and it is how our species reproduces to survive. Sexuality is a part of life. No need for hysterics or fearmongering.

3 Your Body Belongs to You.

You are the owner, sole proprietor, boss lady/man/person of your bits. As adults, we have the right to make decisions about our bodies and must respect other peoples' right to make decisions about theirs.

4 Withhold Judgment.

We should try to be aware of our own judgy impulses and do our best to correct them in order to become more loving, accepting, and nonjudgmental about ethical sexuality. You have a right to your own sexuality, no matter your sexual orientation, gender, body type or ability, race, religion, age, and so on. All are welcome here.

5 *It's Okay to Say No.*

There is no "should." No is a powerful word, and you are always allowed to use it.

6 *Pleasure Is Part of Sexual Health.*

Experiencing sexual pleasure and intimacy with our partners is part of having a healthy and fulfilling sex life. It brings connection and vitality to our sexual relationships. Pleasure is not a dirty or shameful experience. Our understanding of sex should not be limited to reproduction alone.

7 *Learning Is Lifelong.*

Curiosity is worth celebrating. Wherever possible, we should seek a nuanced understanding of issues in sexuality that are informed by the scientific method, a diversity of experiences and cultures, and open minds.

8 *Think Critically.*

Ask questions. When you think you're done digging, dig deeper.

9 *Fight for Sexual Equality.*

Humans have been subjected to myriad sexual injustices throughout history because of their gender, sexual orientation, race, age, and ability, among others. The fight for a sexually healthy society goes hand in hand with the fight for broader social equality.

10 Set Information Free.

Everyone has a right to information about their body and to the resources they need to stay safe and healthy. This information should never be censored, hidden, or distorted. Knowledge is essential to freedom.

SO, WHAT *ISN'T* SEX POSITIVITY? SEX positivity isn't "pro sex." It's not a belief that everybody should have sex, that more sex is better, or that some types of sex are "enlightened." These attitudes are at odds with sex positivity because they still tell people what to do and who to be.

Sex positivity can be juxtaposed against what is sometimes called *sex negativity*. Sex negativity is a disposition toward sexuality that regards it as a dirty, dangerous, harmful, or shameful impulse that needs to be repressed. Information about sexuality is censored, hidden, or distorted in sex-negative cultures. Misinformation is common. Natural sexual feelings are met with shame and fear. It is no coincidence that sexuality is then expressed in unhealthy ways: violation and exploitation lurk under the surface, and with no logical ethical compass, people tend to turn a blind eye to such injustices. Our sexual culture in the United States has both positive and negative dispositions toward sexuality, with wide variations depending on our geographic location, the values of the community, or the particular school, church, government, or institutions we are a part of.

The power of sex positivity is in its ability to guide us toward a healthier relationship with sexuality and a sexually healthier culture in general. It challenges us to reflect more deeply, to react thoughtfully, to love ourselves and others a little bit more, and to challenge the elements of our sexual culture that are harmful or unjust. Which is why, within these pages, you'll find a whole lot of sex positivity! *Sex Plus*, the title of my YouTube series and this book, is a decided nod toward a sex-positivity philosophy. It's also a nod toward the fact that sexuality intersects with many other aspects of our lives, like body image, gender, and relationships.

how to use this book

I WROTE THIS GUIDE WITH MY younger self in mind. What information did I need that I didn't have back then? What problems was I dealing with that I could have used a wee bit more guidance on? And what are the coolest, most helpful things I've learned about sexuality along the way? I also wrote this with *you* in mind. Those of you who have emailed me or left me comments on YouTube and tweets on Twitter—I think about the stories you've told me, and how our stories are connected.

As you read on, you'll find a ton of sex info narrated by *moi*, which has been fact-checked and reviewed by experts. I've included bits and pieces of cool sexuality research, as well as some broader commentary about our sexual culture. My hope is you will discover passages that are practical and useful, and that help you put some pieces together. Since you may encounter topics in this book in a different order IRL than they're presented here, you're invited to skip around. However, reading it cover to cover will provide ~maximum impact~. Even if a passage doesn't pertain to you, it may pertain to a partner or a friend at some point! Should you come across information that doesn't feel useful to you or doesn't speak to your experience, feel free to leave it behind. I've often struggled to figure out how to speak to as many experiences as possible, given that sexuality is simultaneously vast and personal. The reality is: ya just can't. So, where I was able to, I've brought in loved ones and friends to share their perspectives. I hope you'll enjoy reading their advice and stories as much as I did.

Lastly, you'll find that this book is a little vulva-centric and that I tend to center female experiences. This is because female sexuality has historically been left out of conversations and research about sex, and female bodies are the site of so much confusion and fear. Plus, hi, vulva owner here! But that's not to say this book is only for vulva owners or women—there's lots of stuff for everyone. Not only that, but anybody who dates or loves women (sexually or platonically) will benefit tremendously from knowing this stuff.

I also write from the perspective of someone who was raised devoutly religious. I was heavily influenced by Mormonism growing up and, to a slightly lesser extent, by my family's roots in the Middle East. I move through the world as white, bisexual, and cisgender. While I don't feel any single identity defines me, together they influence my experiences and perspectives in sexuality. If you are just beginning your journey exploring your sexuality, reflect on where you're coming from, and make sure to explore the perspectives of others who may differ from you (whether within this book or beyond)! There are so many more stories than I could hope to capture within these pages.

A few other notes before you dive in:

- ♥ You can find my suggested resources at the back of the book, and at lacigreen.tv. I will keep an updated list on my website with more information, books, websites, videos, and perspectives to consider!
- ♥ You will find the sources for each section in the bibliography in the back.
- ♥ Most of the research discussed in this book was conducted on straight folks, because most of the research about sex is conducted on straight folks. I just want to point out that this doesn't necessarily represent the whole spectrum of sexual experiences. I tried to include relevant studies on smaller populations wherever possible!

♥ This book was fact-checked and reviewed by two doctors and a leading expert on human sexuality.

♥ I have aimed to use the most inclusive and scientifically accurate language to describe concepts without being vague or confusing. Should any of the language in this book not resonate with your experience, please know this is not meant to confuse or invalidate anyone, and whatever language feels best to you is 100% valid.

♥ This book has content warnings before sections that may be sensitive to some readers, marked with a ⚠.

Ready? Let's get this party started.

ONE

YOUR GENITALS

IN MY EXPERIENCE, ONE OF THE MOST HELPFUL foundations for sex positivity is to understand a bit about how our bodies work. I mean, what the heck is going on down there, anyway? Although we live our lives in these bodies, for many of us, they are kind of a mystery. And that, combined with taboos about sex—well, it's no wonder that there's so much misinformation about genitals.

To kick things off right, first we gotta get a little scientific. We'll start with an overview of all the anatomical bits and pieces that you'll *definitely* want to know about. Along the way, we'll bust several common myths and misconceptions about vulvas, penises, and lots of bits in between.

IN THIS CHAPTER WE'LL COVER

The vulva (and other bits)
The penis (and other bits)
Sex, beyond male and female

the vulva (and other bits)

AROUND AGE NINETEEN, IT OCCURRED TO me that I'd never actually seen my own vulva. I had certainly seen vulvas in porn. I had observed their hairlessness, their lack of moles and squish and folds that I knew mine had. One night, I Googled a diagram of the vulva on my laptop and grabbed a mirror to follow along. Using the mirror, I explored the folds of my labia, the wispy hairs on the outer lips, the smooth but uneven edges of the inner ones. At the top of the inner lips, I spotted my clitoris. It was small and hidden away, tucked back in a little hood. It felt disrespectful that I was only then seeing what it looked like, after all we'd been through together.

Though I was nearly twenty years old, I had never seen the clitoris on an anatomical diagram, never heard about it in health class or from a teacher. The clitoris was never mentioned in the erotica I read on the internet in secret at night. I had never seen or heard the clitoris mentioned in porn. The word "clitoris" had never been uttered by either of the two partners I'd had by that point, and for all our nonstop joking about sex, I'd never heard any of my friends reference it either. At first I was amused at this little secret. Then . . . I was troubled. For half of the entire planet, this little nub is where sexual pleasure begins. And yet, it has so often been ignored.

WHERE IN THE WORLD IS THE CLITORIS?

RIGHT HERE!

For all these reasons and more, the first stop on our adventure is the clitoris. The clitoris is the pleasure center of the vulva. It is responsible for the vast majority of female orgasms. You can find it at the top of the labia minora (inner lips), above the entrance to the vagina.

Everybody's clitoris is a little different in terms of shape, size, color, and sensitivity. It is relatively small and can usually be found hiding out behind a protective hood (a.k.a. the clitoral hood). What we can see on the outside—the head of the clitoris—is just the tip of the iceberg. There's an entire clitoral organ inside that extends back into the body. It looks something like this.

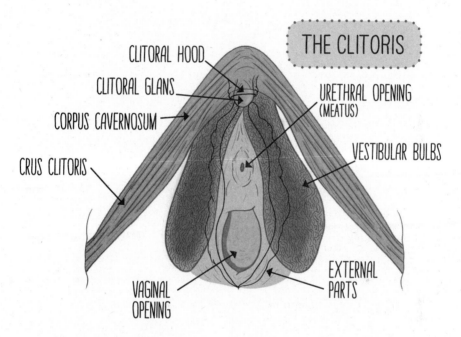

THE CLITORIS

CLITORAL HOOD

CLITORAL GLANS

CORPUS CAVERNOSUM

CRUS CLITORIS

URETHRAL OPENING (MEATUS)

VESTIBULAR BULBS

EXTERNAL PARTS

VAGINAL OPENING

The clitoris is the *only* organ in the human body that exists *solely* for pleasure. *The only one!* Wild, right? But it's obviously not the only body part that can play a role in pleasure—not by a long shot.

The vulva refers to all the parts on the outside of female genitals. The vagina, on the other hand, refers to a specific organ on the inside of the body. The vagina is the oh-so-magical pleasure pocket and birth canal. Strangely, the vulva is incorrectly called the vagina all the time. I've seen the vulva wrongly called a vagina in art, in politics, even in classrooms. It's madness, I tell you! So, yell it from the mountaintops: it's a vulva, not a vagina! And no two are exactly the same.

Here are some highlights of the vulva's lovely parts. This symbol ♡ means that the part produces pleasure for most people.

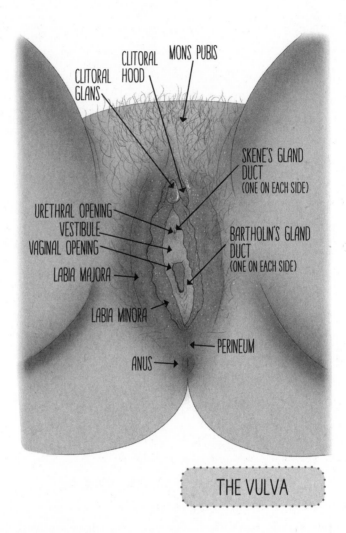

THE VULVA

♡ *The Mons*

The mons pubis—or just the "mons" if we're being casual—is the soft, fleshy triangle that is often covered by pubic hair. It's soft and squishy because there's a layer of fat there. The fat on the mons pubis provides a cushion when you're having sex; that way you're not grinding your bones together. The mons divides into the labia majora at the pudendal cleft (the vertical divide that begins near the clitoris).

Pubic Hair

Pubic hair grows on the mons and down along the labia majora, the inner thighs, around the anus, and up the pelvis, sometimes connecting to the hair by the belly button (a.k.a. the happy trail!). Pubic hair comes in lots of textures, thicknesses, and colors. It may differ from the hair on your head.

♡ The Labia

The labia are the lips of the vulva. There are two sets: the inner lips (labia minora) and the outer lips (labia majora). The inner lips contain oil glands. The outer lips contain fatty tissue and grow hair. Their inner surface is smooth and hairless, and has oil glands. There are relatively few pleasurable nerve endings in the labia, but the labia majora do fill with blood during sexual arousal. #LabiaBoner

• •

MYTH BUSTED:
Nope, sex doesn't change your labia!

When I was younger, I worried a lot about what my vulva looked like. Boys at school joked about girls with dreaded "roast beef curtains" and how their vaginas were "gross." Supposedly, having longer labia meant a girl was a slut who had a lot of sex. Which, of course, is pure bollocks. If sex made the labia longer, grannies would be rolling theirs up every morning before putting on their undies.

The truth is that labia lips come in a million different

shapes and sizes. The inner or outer labia is typically anywhere from less than a centimeter to twelve centimeters long. The outer labia may be longer than the inner labia, or the inner may be longer than the outer. One side may be longer than the other. The inner and outer labia may be the same color, or they may be different colors. Normal, normal, normal! So why do so many of us feel like we aren't?

Obviously, peer shaming plays a role. But I also blame mainstream porn for planting a lot of the needless insecurities and concerns I've had about how my vulva looks. Millennials are the first generation to grow up under the influence of internet porn and, as a result, from a relatively young age we've been fed a pretty steady stream of imagery conveying what's attractive and acceptable. In mainstream porn, female performers' genitals typically look pretty much the same: very short labia that are completely hairless. In some places, this standard is even legally enforced. In Australia, labia in porn magazines (and any media) are required to be "discreet," with only a single crease. Basically: no inner labia are allowed. As of this writing, Australian magazines are required to airbrush female genitals, lest they be hit with a higher obscenity rating, which affects their distribution and sales. Unsurprisingly, cosmetic surgeries are on the rise, with more than 1,200 women getting a labiaplasty per year in Australia alone.

Growing up in a world that tells us our bodies are obscene and offensive, it's no wonder that so many of us have a tenuous relationship with our bits. ♥

• •

♡ The Clitoris

My bae. At the top of the inner labia, the lips conjoin to form the clitoral hood. The clitoral hood protects the glans (head) of the clitoris when you're not having sex.

Under the clitoral hood is the tip of the clitoris (glans) and part of the shaft. Clitorises vary in size and are densely packed with nerve endings—around 8,000! That's about twice the number of nerve endings on the head of the penis. When the clitoris becomes erect with blood during arousal, it may poke out of the clitoral hood and becomes even more sensitive. For many women, the clitoris is central to orgasm.

Vaginal Corona (a.k.a. the Hymen)

The vaginal corona is a thin membrane at the opening of the vagina. You can think of it like a cuticle, but for the vagina. It's a fairly insignificant remnant from when the vagina was being formed in the womb.

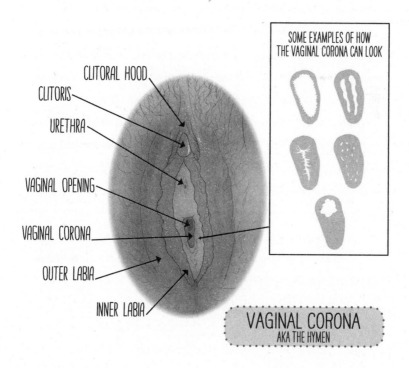

SOME EXAMPLES OF HOW THE VAGINAL CORONA CAN LOOK

CLITORAL HOOD
CLITORIS
URETHRA
VAGINAL OPENING
VAGINAL CORONA
OUTER LABIA
INNER LABIA

VAGINAL CORONA
AKA THE HYMEN

The vaginal corona does not pop or break, it shouldn't bleed, and it does not usually cover the vagina. Like all body stuff, it can come in lots of different shapes and sizes! The majority of women (approximately 97%) have hymens that are open in the middle. They may have a ring that wraps all the way around the vaginal opening, a small crescent moon band along one side, or any other number of appearances. Rarely, women may have a "septum" or band of tissue that crosses through the opening.

• •

MYTH BUSTED:
You can't "pop your cherry."

When I was growing up, I somehow caught word about the mysterious hymen. Friends whispered tales about how the hymen covered the vagina, hinting at the horror that lay ahead when a girl lost her virginity. Naturally, I anticipated that my first time would be a gory mess. Imagine my shock when my first time came and . . . it wasn't. To this day, this myth about the hymen is taught in classrooms across the USA.

Let's set the record straight: the vaginal corona (a.k.a. the hymen) does not typically completely cover the vagina. It is not popped or broken when you put something up there—whether that be tampons, fingers, dildos, or penises. However, if the hymen is stretched too quickly, play is too rough, or there is not enough lubricant, the membrane can get a little tear in it that hurts, and can bleed if it's severe. It is important to be gentle and careful during sexual play, and not to rush penetration. We'll talk a whole lot more about this later in this book! It's also worth noting that less than 1% of women have a hymen that completely covers the vaginal opening, or an imperforate hymen. This is a medical condition that causes menstrual blood to back up and fill the vagina (or even the uterus) and usually requires surgery. For everyone else, the hymen is simply a small, stretchy membrane that sits at the entrance to the vagina. While the hymen is thought to indicate virginity, the truth is that the hymen is pretty insignificant medically—its shape varies greatly by person, and it cannot reliably indicate whether someone has had sex or not. ♥

Urinary Meatus

The urinary meatus is a fancy name for the opening to your pee hole. It is the teensy hole that sits above the entrance to the vagina and about an inch below the clitoris. It can have a number of appearances, from a small but visible hole to a tiny slit with raised borders.

The Vulvar Vestibule

"Vestibule" is a grand term for an entrance. When you part the labia minora, you are looking at the vulvar vestibule. The urinary meatus, the vaginal opening, and the Skene's and Bartholin's ducts all encompass the vestibule. It's basically all the pinkish slippery parts right outside of the vagina.

♡ Perineum

The small, sensitive patch of skin between the vagina and the anus.

♡ Anus

The anus is the small patch of skin that is the entrance to the rectum (inside your butt). The skin is densely packed with nerve endings and can be a very pleasurable area.

Of course, the female reproductive anatomy doesn't end with the vulva. Here's what's going on inside.

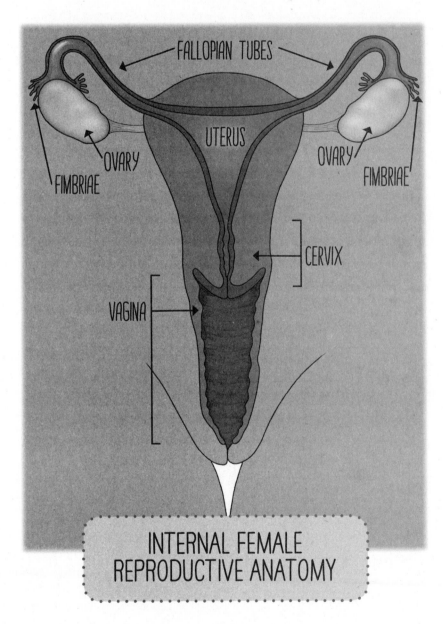

INTERNAL FEMALE
REPRODUCTIVE ANATOMY

♡ The Vagina

The infamous vagina is a canal made up of folds of soft mucous membrane and muscle. It is 4 to 7 inches long on average and lengthens when you are turned on. That's right—vaginas get erections where the vaginal tissues engorge with blood. It's also tilted; it sits at about a 45-degree angle up toward your belly if you're lying down. At rest, the vagina has approximately the shape of the letter "W," but vaginas conform to the shape of whatever is inside of it, like a freakin' shape-shifter.

While the vagina is considered to be *the* pleasure organ for females, in reality, for most women that organ is the clitoris. Meanwhile, the vagina remains significant for reproduction: it is the canal that sperm must swim through to fertilize the egg, and it's the birth canal that babies are delivered through.

♡ The "G-spot"

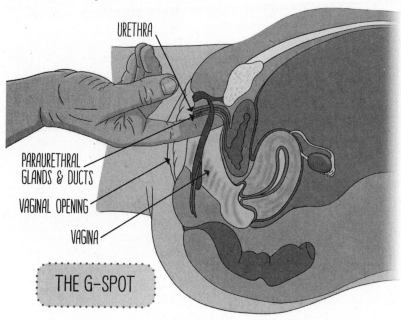

URETHRA

PARAURETHRAL
GLANDS & DUCTS

VAGINAL OPENING

VAGINA

THE G-SPOT

The g-spot is less of a ~spot~ and more of an ~area~ on the front wall of the vagina—about two inches inside. Stimulation of this area is highly pleasurable for some people, because it is essentially a massage for the back of the clitoris; it's the area where the front vaginal wall, the wishbone-like legs of the clitoris, and the urethra intersect in a bundle of nerves, vessels, and glands. Massaging this area also stimulates the urethral sponge, which is tissue that surrounds the pee tube and fills with blood when you're aroused. The urethral sponge includes a network of small paraurethral glands (which literally means "around-urethra glands"). These glands produce fluid that drains out of the urethra or the Skene's ducts. The largest of these paraurethral glands are called the Skene's glands.

PSSST. YOU GET ALL THAT? YOU'RE definitely gonna want to know the rest of these bits to understand things like squirting, orgasms, and periods down the road.

FULL SPEED AHEAD, VAGINA EXPLORERS.

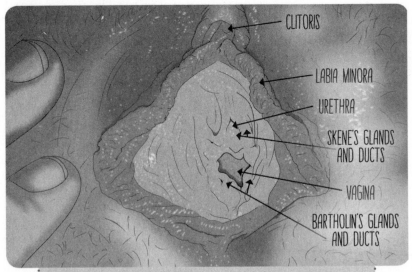

BARTHOLIN'S AND SKENE'S GLANDS AND DUCTS

Skene's Glands

The Skene's glands are paraurethral glands that wrap around your pee tube and produce a milky fluid when they're stimulated. Let's talk about glands for a sec. Glands are groups of cells that work together to secrete various substances (like mucus, hormones, oils, or other fluids) throughout the body. *Endocrine glands*—like those found in the ovaries or testes—secrete their hormones into the bloodstream to be used inside the body. But the Skene's glands, Bartholin's glands, and the prostate are *exocrine glands*. Exocrine glands pool their products into little sacs and secrete them to nearby places, like out to the skin or into the gut, using small chutes called ducts. Other examples of exocrine glands are sweat glands and salivary glands.

In the case of female ejaculation, the milky fluid produced by the Skene's glands drains out of two Skene's ducts to the left and right of the pee hole, and into the urethra itself. Scientists have found that some people's Skene's are bigger than others—and in fact, some people don't appear to have them at all (in the "Who's Afraid of the G-Spot?" study in the *Journal of Sexual Medicine*, 15% of women showed no trace, though it's possible they were just too itty bitty to detect).

Bartholin's Glands

Bartholin's glands are two small, spherical glands that produce a few drops of natural lubrication when you're turned on. This lubrication travels to the surface of the vulva through the Bartholin's ducts, which sit at the bottom of the vestibule to the left and right of the vagina.

Urethra

A short (around 1.5-inch) tube that leads to the bladder.

♡ Clitoral Body

Once the clitoral shaft recedes behind the pubic bone, it splits into a wishbone shape with two crura (legs). These crura are about 5 to 9 centimeters long and engorge with blood before orgasm. The clitoral body interacts with over fifteen thousand nerve endings throughout the pelvis. Its pleasurable superpowers shouldn't be underestimated.

Vestibular Bulbs

The vestibular bulbs are two bulbs of erectile tissue that hang out between the crura of the clitoris and wrap around the urethra and vagina. These bulbs engorge with blood when aroused. They are surrounded by muscle tissue that contracts during orgasm.

♡ Cervix

The cervix is a doughnut-shaped little nub that sits at the top of the vagina, between the uterus and the vagina. Unfortunately, it's not as delicious as doughnuts and has no chocolate frosting. The surface of the cervix contains very few nerve endings, but it can definitely hurt like hell if you ram into it too hard with . . . whatever you're putting up there. In the center of the cervix is a teensy hole (called the cervical os) that leads into the uterus. The cervical os allows menstrual blood to come out of the uterus and allows sperm to come in. The cervix is far too small to get a finger, penis, tampon, dildo, or anything else through on your average day, so no need to worry about things getting lost in the vagina. BUT, in preparation for birth, the cervical os will dilate up to ten centimeters. Pretty hardcore.

Uterus

The uterus is where period blood comes from (the lining sheds itself every month) and where a fertilized egg can implant itself to carry a pregnancy. Normally, the uterus is about 3×2×1 inches in size. However, during pregnancy, the uterus can stretch to accommodate up to 500 times its normal capacity.

Fallopian Tubes

The fallopian tubes are the egg's pathway from the ovaries to the uterus. The fallopian tube is where the egg and sperm meet before traveling down together into the uterus. The little hairs—called cilia—that line the fallopian tubes are incredibly neat. As the sperm swim toward the egg, the cilia beat together in synchrony to create a current toward the egg/ovary. After the egg and sperm meet, the cilia beat toward the uterus to help the zygote (egg and sperm) travel down to the womb.

Ovaries

The two ovaries usually take turns releasing an egg every month (in rarer cases, one ovary will release an egg for multiple months in a row). More specifically, the egg is released from little follicles (water-filled sacs) in the ovaries. The ovaries are smooth and almond sized.

♡ Rectum

The inside of your butt. To pass through the anus into the rectum, you'll encounter two sphincters: external and internal. These sphincters regulate when poop comes out.

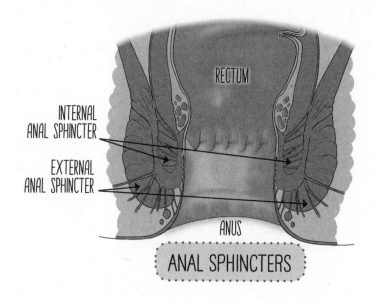

the penis (and other bits)

THROUGHOUT HISTORY, THE PENIS HAS BEEN a pretty visible symbol of sexuality—if not *the* symbol. When I was growing up, the teen dramas I watched on TV often had a plot line about a young guy who starts getting random boners (I mean, it happens), and dicks are definitely a favored subject for graffiti art and notebook doodles. Our obsession with dicks isn't anything new. In fact, penis drawings have been found on cave walls dating back at least 9,000 years. So, you could say us humans kind of have a thing for peen. But when you look beyond the dick drawings, the penis is actually a pretty cool organ with some interesting bits and quirky functions.

So, let's talk peen. Most of us get the hint early on that the penis is a soft dangly bit of flesh that gets hard when you're turned on. As boys in puberty often discover, the penis sometimes becomes erect even when

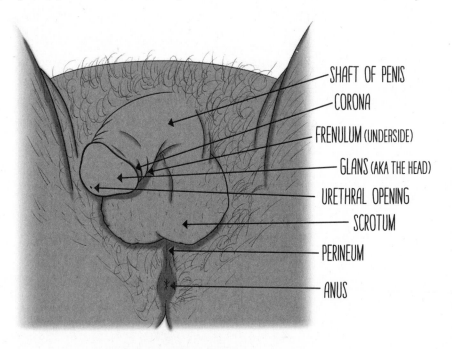

SHAFT OF PENIS
CORONA
FRENULUM (UNDERSIDE)
GLANS (AKA THE HEAD)
URETHRAL OPENING
SCROTUM
PERINEUM
ANUS

you're not turned on. This is especially common during puberty, and scientists believe it's caused in part by fluctuating testosterone levels. Testosterone peaks in the morning, which also helps explain the good ol' "morning wood." Morning wood (which is an erection when you first wake up) is more common before age forty, when testosterone levels are at their highest in males. But random boners can also be the result of subtle nonsexual stimulation—like the penis brushing your jeans just the right way. Guys I've talked to have dealt with random erections by thinking about something else, by shifting it upward under the waistband of his pants to disguise it, or by covering it with a jacket.

But hey, there's obviously a lot more to penises than surprise erections! Let's go over the outer bits first, and then we'll explore what's going on inside.

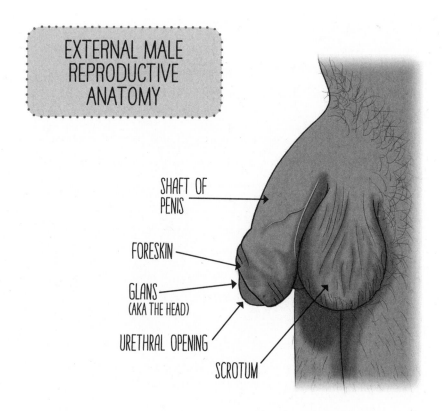

EXTERNAL MALE REPRODUCTIVE ANATOMY

SHAFT OF PENIS

FORESKIN

GLANS (AKA THE HEAD)

URETHRAL OPENING

SCROTUM

♡ The Glans (a.k.a. the Head)

The head at the top of the penis is smooth, moist, and sensitive. It may be slightly darker in pigment and contains about 4,000 nerve endings. At birth, the head is covered by the foreskin.

♡ The Shaft

The shaft refers to the body of the penis. It's made up of spongy erectile tissue, causing the shaft to become erect during sexual arousal. When you're turned on, nerve signals in the brain tell the penis muscles to relax, allowing the shaft to fill with blood. While erect, the blood vessels close to hold the blood in, and they reopen as arousal decreases to let blood out. Penises are typically about 1–3 inches while flaccid, and 4–6 inches while erect.

● ●

MYTH BUSTED:
Size doesn't matter very much.

In scientific studies, men consistently list penis size as one of their top concerns about their body (alongside height and weight). Does size matter when it comes to pleasing a partner? The truth is: not really. Research on heterosexual couples suggests that the vast majority of men's partners don't care about penis size nearly as much as the man does. For the small group of women who reported that they prefer a larger penis size, they were more likely to orgasm from vaginal penetration. If you ask me, hype about penis size is somewhat overblown. Anybody of any genital size can have pleasurable sex, and having a big dick doesn't translate to good sex on its own.

As a society, we also tend to put way too much pressure on guys to be physically large—not just in penis size, but also in height, musculature, shoe size, and so on. This expectation is wrapped up in our cultural ideas of masculinity and what it means to be a "real man." But given that penis size doesn't mean much for pleasure, it's hard to see the size question as much more than a preoccupation that shames (or rewards) people for something that's out of their control. ♥

♡ Corona

The ridge around the head. This ridge is densely packed with nerve endings.

♡ Frenulum

Sometimes called the frenum, the frenulum is the V-shaped underside of the head of the penis. Some folks say that this area (and the underside of the penis in general) is the most pleasurable part of the penis.

Urinary Meatus

The pee hole. Woo.

♡ Foreskin

The foreskin is a retractable bit of skin that protects the shaft and head of the penis. It serves three critical functions: it helps distribute lubrication, which helps with masturbation and sex. It provides pleasure through a network of more than twenty thousand nerve endings. It also covers the head of the penis, keeping the delicate membranes from chafing and desensitizing over time (a process called keratinization).

● ●

MYTH BUSTED:
Foreskin isn't "dirty."

While the foreskin serves several important functions for male sexuality and pleasure, there is a slightly-too-popular belief that foreskin is "dirty" and should thus be removed with circumcision. This is simply not true. Uncircumcised penises aren't any more dirty than circumcised penises. (I mean, unless you don't shower regularly—but that goes for anyone!) On the contrary, foreskin helps keep irritants away from the urethra, offering an extra layer of protection to keep you healthy. To clean the foreskin, gently pull back and rinse with mild soap and warm water. This method of cleaning is far less cumbersome and damaging to pleasurable nerve endings than simply cutting the foreskin off. It is also more ethical in the case of routine infant circumcision, which permanently alters the genitals of male infants without medical necessity before they are able to consent. ♥

♡ *Scrotum*

The scrotum is a bag of skin that holds the testes (a.k.a. balls). It is lined with smooth muscle, including a wall of muscle running down the center separating the testes. Inside the scrotum, the testes are connected to the rest of the body by the spermatic cord, which is largely composed of the cremaster muscle, which helps to maintain the temperature of the testes for optimal sperm production. Believe it or not, the spermatic cord is a direct extension of the oblique muscles, which contract and pull the testes into the body when it's too cold and relax to allow the testes to hang down lower when it's too warm. (The ideal temperature for sperm production is 2.5 to 3 degrees Celsius below average body temperature, which is 37 degrees Celsius). Pretty neat when you think about it! The scrotum is *very* sensitive to pressure, so be careful with those babies. But hey, their sensitivity can be a source of pleasure as well.

♡ Perineum

Also lovingly known as the "taint" or the "gooch," the perineum is the sensitive area between the base of the penis and the anus.

♡ Anus

Just like the female anus, the male anus is densely packed with nerve endings. More so than any other part of your butt.

Phew, that's a whole lot of peen!
But there are even more secrets on the inside.
Let's go over the internal bits—which are key in understanding how sperm is made and how ejaculation happens.

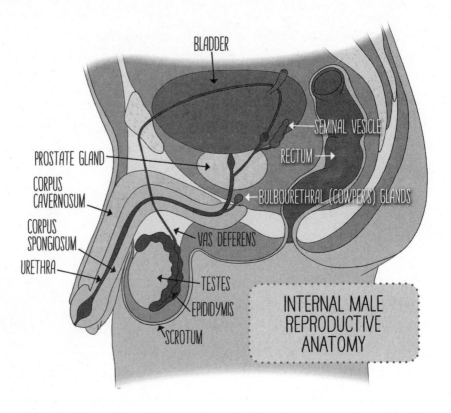

BLADDER

SEMINAL VESICLE

PROSTATE GLAND

RECTUM

CORPUS CAVERNOSUM

BULBOURETHRAL (COWPER'S) GLANDS

CORPUS SPONGIOSUM

VAS DEFERENS

URETHRA

TESTES

EPIDIDYMIS

SCROTUM

INTERNAL MALE REPRODUCTIVE ANATOMY

Testes

The testes produce testosterone and sperm. They are roughly the size and shape of a jumbo olive . . . or, ahem, a walnut. Typically, one will hang a little lower than the other.

● ●

MYTH BUSTED:
Blue balls aren't really a thing.

Could not having an orgasm when you're turned on actually turn your balls . . . blue? Nah! During sexual arousal, blood flows into the penis and testicles through the arteries, while the veins (which carry blood away from the genitals) slightly restrict. This is called vasocongestion. The term "blue balls" may be a reference to the bluish tint of our blood vessels. However, this process doesn't turn the balls blue—and it should not last long or be painful. Vasocongestion can cause a slightly uncomfortable feeling though. It may feel like a heaviness in the genitals and pelvis that is relieved once you become less aroused or achieve orgasm. It can happen to everyone, not just penis owners. ♥

Epididymis

The epididymis is a small, tightly coiled tube on top of the testes. This is where sperm go to mature after being produced in the testes. Without ejaculation, they can hang out there for up to 6 weeks (!!!) before they die. The dead sperm are then reabsorbed by the body. That's some magic, man.

Vas Deferens

During sexual arousal, sperm move from the epididymis to the vas deferens and into the seminal vesicles. The vas deferens is about the width of spaghetti.

Seminal Vesicle

The seminal vesicle produces most of the fluid that is in ejaculate. It's also a sort of mixing pot. Sperm flows in from the vas deferens to mix with other fluids to make up the semen. Sperm only makes up 2 to 5% of the semen, but it still works out to about 280,000,000 sperm per ejaculation!

♡ Prostate (a.k.a. "the Male G-spot")

The prostate is perhaps the most underrated body part in males. This bit is a walnut-sized gland that sits beneath the bladder and surrounds the urethra. It produces 15 to 30% of the fluid that ends up in semen. The prostate can produce pleasurable sensations, and even orgasm, when it is gently stimulated (more on that in chapter 13).

Cowper's Glands

The Cowper's glands make pre-cum. These pea-sized glands sit below the prostate and produce a thick, clear fluid that flushes out the urethra before ejaculation. Some of the fluid also drains into the seminal vesicle to become part of semen. Pre-cum makes it easier for the sperm to survive. It does not contain any sperm of its own, but it may come into contact with sperm hanging out in shared ducts. To lower the odds of sperm lurking in pre-cum, pee before having sex.

● ●

MYTH BUSTED:
Wet dreams are totally normal.

Studies have found that about 83% of men will have a wet dream, a.k.a. a nocturnal emission, at some point in their life. This is basically when someone releases ejaculate in their sleep, and folks usually notice it when they wake up to a wet spot on their undies. These emissions sometimes happen on their own, and sometimes they happen with an orgasm as well. As it turns out, women have nocturnal emissions too at approximately the same rate, and 37% even have an orgasm in their sleep at some point.

While some people worry that wet dreams mean they

are unhealthy or becoming a sexual deviant of some kind, rest assured that sexual arousal during sleep is totally normal. Wet dreams typically kick in around puberty and have been connected to fluctuating testosterone levels, stimulation during sleep (like rubbing against sheets, grinding, or self-touching during sleep), and ejaculation frequency. If you go for a while without an orgasm, you are more likely to have a wet dream. The more ya know. ♥

· ·

Urethra

The tube that transports pee and semen to the outside of the body.

♡ Rectum

The rectum is the inside of the butt. To pass through the anus into the rectum, you'll encounter two sphincters: external and internal (see the diagram on page 15).

YOU GET ALL THAT? NICE WORK! Knowing these parts will come in handy as we talk about sexual health and having sex later on.

sex, beyond male and female

SEXUAL ANATOMY IS OFTEN TALKED ABOUT in terms of penises and vaginas. When a baby is born, their sex is usually determined and marked down based on their genitals. Vulva = female, and penis = male. As a shortcut, it tends to do the trick, but if you want to get geeky about it (which I always do), there's more to biological sex than genitals alone.

There are four basic determinants of sex:

- Chromosomes
- Hormones
- Primary sex characteristics
- Secondary sex characteristics

	Female	Male	Intersex
Human Prevalence	About 50%	About 50%	About 1%
Sex Chromosomes Part of your DNA. Sex chromosomes designate the developmental pathway of a fetus's sex.	XX	XY	Variable
Sex Hormones Sex hormones are secreted by glands into your blood. They guide the development of sex characteristics.	More estrogen Less MIS (Mullerian inhibiting substance)	More testosterone More MIS (Mullerian inhibiting substance)	Variable
Primary Sex Characteristics Reproductive parts you are born with.	Ovaries, vulva, vagina	Testes, penis	Variable
Secondary sex characteristics Traits that develop during puberty.	Relatively larger breasts, wider hips, more fat, higher voice, rounded features, shorter height	Relatively more facial hair, larger larynx/ deeper voice, more muscle, taller height	Variable

While male (XY) and female (XX) are the most common developmental pathways for biological sex, when an infant is born with some combination of *both*, they are intersex. Intersex traits are anatomical, hormonal, or chromosomal variations that are different than what's typically expected of males or females. It goes something like this:

Intersex

In the beginning, all our anatomy looks the same. For the first six weeks in the womb, females and males are almost identical. But around week seven, sex differentiation begins.

Clitoris ◄ Genital Tubercle ► Penis

Labia majora ◄ Labioscrotal Area ► Scrotum

Labia minora ◄ Urogenital Fold ► Urethra and underside of the penis

Ovaries ◄ Gonads ► Testes

Bartholin's Glands ◄ Accessory Glands ► Cowper's Glands

Because a lot of intersex variations happen inside the body, it's not always obvious when a baby is intersex. For example, someone might have XY (typically male) chromosomes but be unresponsive to testosterone and thus be born with a vulva and vagina and eventually develop breasts. Someone else might have XX chromosomes (typically female) and an adrenal condition that leads to overproduction of testosterone during development and thus develops a larger than expected clitoris with fused labia. Sometimes people don't find out they're intersex until puberty, until they try to have a baby, or . . . ever. Which is A-okay. As long as it's not bringing harm to the person's life, why should it matter? Intersex is yet another example of the wonderful diversity of sex.

All that said, for reasons that are complex and also dumb, intersex has been highly stigmatized throughout history. Beginning in the Victorian era and until only recently, doctors referred to intersex folks as "hermaphrodites," after the Greek mythological character Hermaphrodite, who possessed both sets of genitals. The public was led to believe that being intersex meant being born with fully formed female *and* male genitalia, though this is anatomically impossible. Today, intersex stigma often manifests as nonconsensual surgeries on intersex infants' genitals to make them appear "more normal." But who gets to define what's "normal"? Though it is rapidly falling out of favor in the medical community, these surgeries unfortunately continue to happen. In most cases, they are purely cosmetic. Rarely is there a medical need for surgery—and actually, there are plenty of reasons not to operate. Among them: no medical need, children (especially infants) can't consent, and altering their body without permission can compromise a person's sense of ownership of their body down the line. Many intersex folks experience psychological trauma at the hands of their healthcare providers. Plus, surgery itself comes with its own health risks and can cause devastating physical complications like chronic pain, decreased sensation, inability to orgasm, and infertility.

Many human rights organizations, including the United Nations, Human Rights Watch, and the World Health Organization, have spoken out against medically unnecessary, nonconsensual surgeries on an infant's intersex genitals. It's a violation of people's human rights to bodily integrity and choice—rights that intersex people deserve just as much as everyone else. Leave people be!

Parents of intersex children often find themselves with many questions and pressure to make difficult decisions regarding how to care for their intersex child. The organization interACT: Advocates for Intersex Youth has the following recommendations for parents:

- Parental distress about the sex characteristics of their infant should be addressed by psychological support, not surgery, which is a violation of a person's human rights when performed without their consent.

- It is essential to maintain an open atmosphere with the family and child about their condition. Healthy differences are natural and should be celebrated rather than treated as something shameful. Positive and affirming support from clinicians should be coupled with peer support via other intersex individuals and intersex support groups.

- As is the case with any child, an intersex infant can be raised as a boy or a girl without being forced to undergo unnecessary surgery. Decisions around surgery that are not life-threatening should be delayed until they can participate in the decision.

There are many conditions that can lead to a person being diagnosed as intersex, and there are even more intersex traits (where part of the body has intersex characteristics even though the individual does not identify as intersex). Here are a few of them.

Congenital Adrenal Hyperplasia (CAH) causes the body to produce more androgens (male sex hormones) than is typical. For females it may cause facial hair, closure of the vaginal opening, or an enlarged clitoris. For males, it may mean earlier onset of puberty, a deepened voice, or more body hair. As infants, people with CAH can sometimes get extremely sick at birth from dysregulation of the adrenal hormones.

Mayer-Rokitansky-Küster-Hauser syndrome (Müllerian agenesis or MRKH) is when a female has no uterus or vagina, or if it's differently shaped, or very small. People with MRKH have no period, which is often how a person detects the condition. They are also unable to carry a pregnancy themselves (although their ovaries work fine) and some seek out a surrogate for childbearing.

Androgen insensitivity syndrome (AIS) is when the body is completely or partially resistant to androgens. Those with AIS are born with typically male chromosomes (XY) but appear typically female when the androgen resistance is complete. If androgen resistance is partial, their appearance may be less clear. A person with AIS typically has no uterus, fallopian tubes, or cervix; internal testes instead of ovaries; sometimes a short or nonexistent vaginal canal; very little body hair; and no period.

Klinefelter's syndrome refers to the presence of one or more extra sex chromosomes (Xs) in some or all of the cells. The most common form of Klinefelter's is XXY, but there's also XXXY and XXXXY. More Xs typically means more severe symptoms, including hindered development. Klinefelter's alters the functioning of the testes and reduces testosterone production.

BEING INTERSEXY
Kimberly Zieselman

To me, being sexy means being confident, owning your body, and feeling entitled to love. This isn't easy for lots of people for many different reasons. Confidence and self-worth are things we all deserve but don't necessarily have. For some intersex people, it can be particularly challenging. Not because intersex bodies are any less attractive or worthy of love—of course they are attractive and worthy! But for many intersex people, whether they identify as male, female, nonbinary, or gender fluid, messages of shame and taboo about their bodies have been prevalent their entire life. Take it from me. I am intersex.

From the time we are babies, our parents are told that our bodies aren't "normal" and should be "fixed." This message transfers down to us as children in both direct and profound ways as we grow up. Sometimes this negative feedback starts as soon as an intersex baby is born—in the delivery room. Instead of "congratulations you have a healthy child," parents instead see panicked looks on the faces of the doctors and nurses in the room as they quickly try to explain why they are taking the baby away for further tests. In other cases, a child's intersex traits are not known until later in life, such as adolescence, when they don't experience puberty in the way their friends do.

That's what happened to me. At age fifteen, I still hadn't had my period despite my younger sister getting hers a year earlier—so it was off to the doctor to determine what was wrong with me. I wanted to be just like all the other girls who were talking about their periods and starting to date. But instead I ended up in the operating room over summer break to have my healthy and essential hormone-producing undescended testes removed. But that's not what they told me—instead I was told I had partially formed "ovaries" that needed to be removed so they did not become cancerous. (It wasn't until many years later when I got my medical records that I discovered the truth—that I had XY or typically "male" chromosomes and undescended testes instead of ovaries and a uterus.)

The doctors also tried to convince me and my parents that I should get a vaginoplasty because the length of my vaginal canal was "too short" to have "successful" intercourse (apparently they discovered this while I was under anesthesia!). This diagnosis seemed to rely on the assumption that I am straight, and, more generally, that penetration was necessary for me to have good sex. Thankfully I escaped that unwanted, unnecessary, and harmful surgery. Other intersex people I know have not been so lucky.

Since the 1950s, the medical profession has been classifying intersex as a disorder, and doctors have been developing surgical and hormonal interventions to change our bodies to fit the binary boxes of what they think should be a typical "male" or "female" body. These interventions, especially irreversible cosmetic surgeries, have caused way more harm than good. First of all, they are performed on an infant or child well before they are old enough to give full informed consent. In many cases, before a child is even old enough to speak, not to mention establish a gender identity. Many intersex adults today talk about the trauma they suffered as children as a result of medical intervention. Repeated physical exams, genital photography, multiple doctors lifting up the sheet to inspect "their work" and discussing it as if the child isn't even there. On top of feeling violated and powerless, the intervention sends a message to the child that they are broken, bad, and need to be fixed in order to be loved. In order to be lovable. These messages of shame combined with the experiences of medical trauma often translate into mental health issues resulting in difficulties with trust and intimacy, body image, and self-worth. That can make it very difficult to feel . . . sexy.

But thankfully, not impossible! Intersex people can also learn to be confident, own your body, and feel entitled to love and affection just like anyone else. You can be intersexy! The path to being intersexy will be different for everyone, but there are some contributing factors. For example, connecting with other intersex people and sharing common experiences, fears, and even laughs is perhaps the best medicine available to build confidence. It challenges those lurking feelings of being alone and "different." Learning not only about your body, but about the diversity of human bodies in nature generally, can also help you internalize the fact that bodily diversity is actually the norm! No two vaginas or penises look alike. Finally, having kind, generous, and loving friends and partners who are aware of your struggles can help create a safe and loving space.

Being sexy is a state of mind. And sometimes intersex people need a little extra emotional support to counteract the negative messaging and medical trauma they've been subjected to. Thankfully, a number of human rights organizations, activists, legal organizations, and even medical associations are now speaking out against these harmful practices. More and more people are finally realizing the negative physical and psychological impact these practices have had on generations of intersex people. A new level of awareness has surfaced in the last few years with intersex characters being portrayed in books and on TV, and celebs like internationally renowned fashion model Hanne Gaby Odiele coming out and sharing her pride about being intersex. Now that's intersexy! 🍑

Constructing Sex

Intersex sheds light on the ways that our understanding of sex has changed over time. Back in the day, the scientific view touted by the ancient Greeks was that there was only one sex. Females and males were considered to be one and the same, with females merely having inverted male genitals. In the late 1700s, scientists started to think about male and female reproductive differences as significant, shifting away from a one-sex model to the two-sex model of today. This evolution in how we think about sex is to be expected as our understanding of the wacky world of human biology deepens and expands.

What we do know for sure is that sex is not always as straightforward as it appears. Secondary sex characteristics (which are usually the most obvious aspects of a person's sex to a stranger) are especially diverse. For example:

- Some males have a large amount of breast tissue.
- Some females have facial hair.
- Some males are shorter than the average female.
- Some females are more muscular than the average male.

Because our understanding of sex comes along with a number of exceptions and generalizations, I find it helpful to think of sex as more a matter of degree, rather than stark black-and-white categories. The vast majority of humans follow one of two developmental pathways (XX or XY), but along those pathways, there is a whole lot of variation and diversity.

What can I say? Sex is a messy and nuanced world, my friends. And we're just getting started.

TWO

PERIODS

THE FEMALE ANATOMY IS MAGICAL FOR a lot of reasons, but two reasons in particular stand out. The first we already discussed: it is equipped with the only human body part that exists purely for pleasure (that clitoris!). The second is that females can create ACTUAL HUMAN BEINGS INSIDE OF THEM. For every human in existence, there is a uterus that nurtured them before they came into the world. Goddess #bless.

Here's the DL on the menstrual cycle and all the pesky hormones involved.

IN THIS CHAPTER WE'LL COVER

Phases of the menstrual cycle

Am I bloody normal?

Period products

PMS

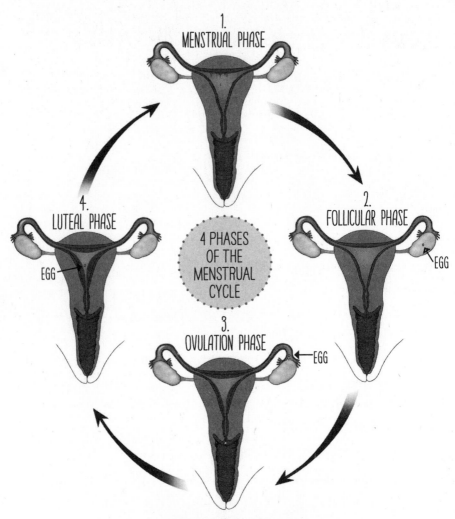

1. MENSTRUAL PHASE: LINING SHEDS
2. FOLLICULAR PHASE: OVARY FOLLICLES MATURE
3. OVULATION PHASE: EGG IS RELEASED AND TRAVELS THROUGH THE FALLOPIAN TUBE
4. LUTEAL PHASE: EGG IN UTERUS; IF EGG ISN'T FERTILIZED,
THE CYCLE WILL BEGIN AGAIN WITH THE MENSTRUAL PHASE

phases of the menstrual cycle

THE FIRST TIME YOU GET YOUR period is called menarche. The menstrual cycle is the biological process that makes it possible to get pregnant. It lasts twenty-one to thirty-five days on average, and it has four phases. Each phase is guided by different hormones that are released by the ovaries, the hypothalamus, and the pituitary gland.

Phase 1: Menstruation (Lasts 4 to 10 Days on Average)

The first day of the menstrual cycle is when bleeding begins. When you're on your period, the tissue that lines the uterus sheds and makes an exit through the cervix and out of the vagina. The uterus shedding its lining means there's no fertilized egg, and you're not pregnant. . . . :)

What we typically call "period blood" isn't just blood, it's also mucus and tissue. Basically, a uterus smoothie. Mmmmm. And the uterus isn't the only place where action is happening. During your period, the pituitary gland also begins to produce follicle-stimulating hormone, which stimulates the follicles inside the ovaries. A follicle is a small sac of fluid lined with cells surrounding one oocyte (egg). This signals the next phase!

Phase 2: Follicular Phase (Lasts ~7 Days)

With the help of follicle-stimulating hormone, the follicles inside the ovaries begin to mature. Several follicles will begin to develop, but only one follicle will fully mature each cycle. That, my friend, is the Chosen Follicle. (Okay, it's actually the dominant follicle, but the Chosen Follicle sounds cooler.)

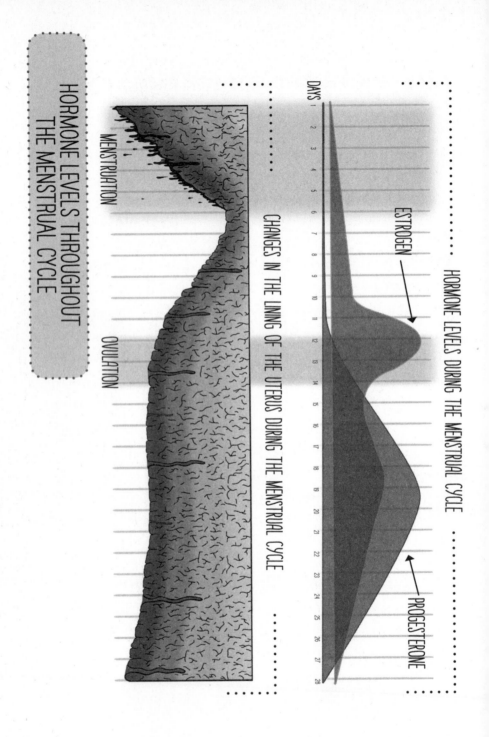

HORMONE LEVELS THROUGHOUT THE MENSTRUAL CYCLE

MENSTRUATION

OVULATION

CHANGES IN THE LINING OF THE UTERUS DURING THE MENSTRUAL CYCLE

DAYS 1 2 3 4 5 6 7 8 9 10 11 12 13 14 15 16 17 18 19 20 21 22 23 24 25 26 27 28

ESTROGEN

PROGESTERONE

HORMONE LEVELS DURING THE MENSTRUAL CYCLE

The ovaries also begin producing more estrogen, which is another hormone. Estrogen tells the lining of the uterus to get nice and thick and cushy. If the egg is fertilized, it's going to need a soft bed of tissue to rest on. When estrogen is at its peak, the pituitary gland slows down on the follicle-stimulating hormone and starts releasing luteinizing hormone instead. Luteinizing hormone signals the matured Chosen Follicle to rupture and release an egg. Bam. Ovulation has begun.

Phase 3: Ovulation (Lasts 24 Hours—PREGNANCY ALERT)

Ovulation is the most fertile point of the menstrual cycle, and the only phase when you can get pregnant. It occurs about halfway through the menstrual cycle, around fourteen days after you start your period. During ovulation, the egg takes its journey through the fallopian tubes. What happens next depends on whether or not a sperm finds the egg.

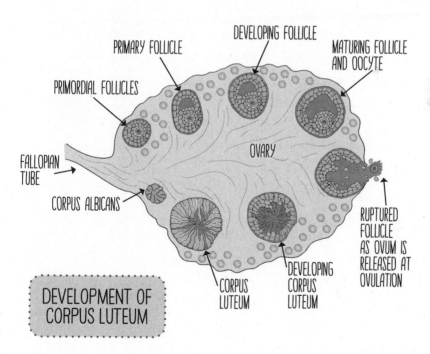

DEVELOPING FOLLICLE

PRIMARY FOLLICLE

MATURING FOLLICLE AND OOCYTE

PRIMORDIAL FOLLICLES

FALLOPIAN TUBE

OVARY

CORPUS ALBICANS

RUPTURED FOLLICLE AS OVUM IS RELEASED AT OVULATION

CORPUS LUTEUM

DEVELOPING CORPUS LUTEUM

DEVELOPMENT OF CORPUS LUTEUM

Phase 4: Luteal Phase (Lasts ~14 Days)

During the luteal phase, luteinizing hormone prompts the now rup-tured follicle to become the corpus luteum. Corpus luteum translates to "yellow body" in Latin, which is fitting, because it's yellowish. The corpus luteum releases progesterone.

Estrogen levels remain elevated and progesterone is now at its peak for the whole, preparing for an egg to implant if it's fertilized by sperm.

▶ **If the egg is fertilized by the sperm:** the corpus luteum continues to produce progesterone, which keeps the lining of the uterus thick and nour-ished for a healthy pregnancy. The corpus luteum will continue doing this until the placenta takes over, around ten weeks into a pregnancy.

▶ **If the egg is not fertilized:** the corpus luteum waits for a sign of human chorionic gonado-tropin (also known as hCG, it's a pregnancy hormone which is produced by the placenta) from a fertilized egg for twenty-four hours. This is the same hormone that pregnancy tests look for. If there is no hCG, our bubbly, yellow corpus luteum slowly dies. It takes about ten days for the corpus luteum to completely degener-ate. Estrogen and progesterone levels drop back down, which signals the uterus lining to shed—and we're back at the beginning of the cycle.

am i bloody normal?

WHEN IT COMES TO PERIODS, THERE'S a big range of what's considered "normal." On average, bleeding lasts four to seven days. The color of the blood and tissue will change throughout a period, from a brighter red to dark brown. These color changes indicate how old the blood is, and it's nothing to worry about—except if your menstrual blood is black or gray, which may indicate infection or miscarriage and may require medical attention.

In terms of volume, blood loss during a period really varies. Researchers have found that the average blood loss during menstruation is around 30 mL, or two tablespoons of blood. For about one in ten menstruating folks, the fluid loss during periods is a little more intense than that. Heavy periods, or "menorrhagia," are officially defined as 80 mL or more—about sixteen completely soaked tampons or pads. Scientists don't fully understand yet why some people have heavier periods than others. In some cases, heavy bleeding may be caused by an underlying health issue, like uterine fibroids (which are common, noncancerous growths in the uterus).

Stress, exercise, or dramatic changes in diet can cause your period to get heavier or lighter, and come a little sooner or later. If you are a heavy bleeder, it's important to stay hydrated. Water can seem inconsequential, but it helps your body replace the blood. Upping your iron intake in your diet is also a good idea. Lentils, broccoli, spinach, beef, and dark chocolate are all higher in iron. If at any point a heavy period becomes a burden, talk to your healthcare provider about it. Don't worry, your doctor won't make you bring in a bag of soaked tampons—a diagnosis is usually made when bleeding is significant enough to impact your daily life. There are contraceptives and other treatments that can help.

It's also fairly common to find a few spots of blood in your underwear between periods. This is called spotting, or breakthrough bleeding, and it has a whole lot of possible causes:

- Sex that was a liiiittle too rough
- Side effect of hormonal birth control
- Missing a birth control pill
- Taking emergency contraception
- Contracting an STI
- Yeast infection or other vaginal/cervical irritation
- Pregnancy
- Cervical cancer

Most of the time spotting is no big deal, but sometimes it can be a hint that something else is going on. If you have concerns, talk to your healthcare provider!

DISCHARGE

When you're not on your period, you may have noticed that sometimes there's white stuff in your underwear or when you wipe. That's discharge. It's normal to have discharge that is clear or white throughout your cycle. Discharge is how the vagina expels cells and fluids from the uterus, cervix, and vagina. It is part of the vagina's natural self-cleaning process, and the color and consistency changes a little depending on what part of your cycle you're in.

Here's what discharge is typically like throughout the menstrual cycle!

During your period: you won't notice discharge because it's mixed in with your period.

Right after your period: little to no discharge.

Leading up to ovulation: whitish, pale yellowish, or cloudy discharge. Feels a little sticky/tacky. Hangs out at the opening of your vag (you might notice it when you wipe).

Before and during ovulation: the most discharge! Wet, clear, and slippery. Consistency may be similar to egg whites, and can be stretched between your fingers. You are at your most fertile when your discharge is like this.

After ovulation: less discharge, which gets a little thicker, cloudy, and tacky again.

Right before period: little to no discharge.

In general, healthy discharge is clear or cloudy white. It might leave a white or yellowish tinge in your underwear. It may have a slight odor, but shouldn't smell strong.

Discharge can be the first sign of infection if it is yellow/greenish (like snot during a cold), if it's clumpy, cottage cheese–like, or has a strong odor. Other signs of possible infection are an itchy vulva, itchy entrance of the vagina, pain and swelling, or soreness.

period products

SO, UH, PERIODS CAN GET A little messy. We've all left the accidental drip (or five) on the bathroom floor, there may be some new smells going on down there, and sheets or undies could end up stained casualties. It happens.

There are so many period products available out there: tampons, pads, cups, sponges, absorbent undies, and so on. Which is the best? The answer to that question is almost entirely a matter of personal taste. Check out the chart below for some pros and cons to consider.

Product	PROS	CONS
Pads (Disposable)	Worn outside of the body, which is more comfortable sometimes Easy to use Portable Safe to use for longer periods of time Easy to find at the store	Can feel bulky, like wearing a diaper Can't wear them in water Can feel goopy on the vulva during heavy days Those with sensitive skin may have vulvar irritation from disposable pads Not great for the environment May contain additives
Pads (Reusable)	Worn outside of the body, which is more comfortable sometimes Easy to use Portable Safe to use for longer periods of time Washable/reusable and eco-friendly!	Can feel bulky, like wearing a diaper Can't wear them in water Can feel goopy on the vulva during heavy days Higher up-front investment Typically need to be bought online You have to wash them
Tampons	Small Internal/unnoticeable Portable Easy to find at the store Can wear in water	Limited wear time Increased risk of TSS Takes practice to insert, which can be uncomfortable for some Not great for environment

Product	PROS	CONS
Tampons (continued)		May contain additives Can be uncomfortable for some
Menstrual Cups (Reusable)	You can use it for years, making it the cheapest option Environmentally friendly No additives	Removal can be messy Takes practice to insert/remove Can't always be found at the store (may need to order online) Can be uncomfortable for some
Menstrual Cups (Disposable)	Flexible cup that has soft plastic, making it a great option for period sex No additives Stays put for a long time	Individual cups can be $1.00 or more each! Spendy Not great for environment Takes practice to insert Harder to find Removal can be messy Can be uncomfortable for some
Menstrual Undies	Reusable, just throw in the laundry Convenient; built right into your undies!	Expensive Typically for lighter days only Some brands can have a swampy feeling due to the material not breathing well

Whatever your personal favorite period products are, here are a few relatively minor but also important-to-know safety notes:

Chemicals in Menstrual Products

In the United States, period products exist in a legal gray area because they're classified as "medical devices." That means manufacturers don't have to tell consumers what they're putting in them. Tampons, in particular, are put inside the body next to the highly absorbent mucous membranes of the vagina for hours at a time. If you ask me, we deserve to know what exactly is in them (and some laws have been proposed to make the ingredients transparent). What we do know is that bleaching agents are typically used to disinfect the rayon and cotton, which turns tampons a bright white color. We also know that cotton is a crop that is typically sprayed with pesticides while it is being grown. The effects of these various chemicals in our hygiene products haven't been studied extensively, but as far as we know, there is no cause for alarm. The word "chemical" can be scary, but it's important to remember that literally everything is chemicals! Chemicals aren't bad in and of themselves. That said, it's something to be aware of. For those who want an alternative, reusable menstrual cups are made of silicone, which is body-safe.

Toxic Shock Syndrome

Toxic shock syndrome, or TSS, was once a big, scary acronym that has since become a condition people are only vaguely aware of. TSS is caused by an overgrowth of bacteria that can produce toxins that infect the bloodstream. It causes feelings of dizziness or nausea, and can give you a fever, rash, or make you vomit. In the 1970s and '80s, there were a slew of TSS cases caused by tampons. As medical professionals advised that people change their tampons more regularly and superabsorbent tampons were pulled from store shelves, TSS cases dropped off dramatically. These days, TSS from tampons is very rare (1 in 100,000), but it can still happen. It's not clear what it is about tampons that can cause TSS. One theory is that tampons offer a breeding ground for bacteria like staph and strep. The bacteria get into the bloodstream through tiny micro-tears caused by tampon insertion, particularly when the tampon is too big or dry for your flow.

If you ever find yourself feeling dizziness, fatigue, nausea, headache, muscle pain, or developing a rash while wearing a tampon—take it out and call a doctor right away. If it's after hours, head to the emergency room. TSS is a medical emergency, and it can be fatal if it's not treated immediately.

pms

AROUND 15-20% OF FOLKS ARE #BLESSED with easy, symptom-free periods. If that's you, congrats! What a gift. If that's NOT you . . . welcome to the club. We don't have jackets (because they're not comfortable for moping), but we do have chocolate and Netflix.

Symptoms that kick in right before your period starts are sometimes referred to as premenstrual syndrome or PMS. These symptoms are thought to be caused by how our bodies respond to the hormonal fluctuations that happen during the luteal phase of menstruation. Everyone's response is a little different.

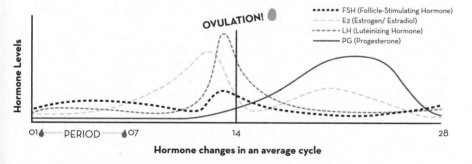

Hormone changes in an average cycle

Here's a handy chart about common symptoms that can pop up before menstruation, their causes, and some tried-and-true remedies from yours truly:

Symptom	What It's Caused By	Remedies
Cramps	To help shed the lining of the uterus, the uterus undergoes a number of contractions. Prostaglandins help aid these contractions. Cramps are caused by these contractions, and are worse with high levels of prostaglandins.	Taking ibuprofen when your symptoms hit (and for as long as they last) can make a huge difference. Heat also helps, and will bring more blood to the area. Try an electric heating pad. You can also make a heating pad by sewing a cloth bag full of dry rice and microwaving it a couple minutes. And of course, nothing beats a hot bath.
Sleepiness	The research is inconclusive on what can cause increased fatigue during menstruation. Likely culprits are hormonal shifts, diet changes, or blood loss.	SLEEEEEEEEPPPP!!! It's normal to need more sleep on your period. Caffeine can help you power through the day, but it can also make cramps and aching worse. So . . . pick your poison.
Acne	Hormones!! Specifically, the drop in progesterone and estrogen that happens before your period, which can result in an excess of DHT, or dihydrotestosterone. When testosterone increases, so can sebum production. Sebum is an oily substance that lubricates your skin. But when there's too much of it, it can clog	Acne related to menstruation is *not* caused by bad hygiene. All the creams and gels and special brushes sold at makeup stores won't stop menstrual acne entirely. You can apply some topical creams to help soothe it, but for the most part, you just gotta ride it out. My go-to topical aid is a few dabs of tea tree oil.

Symptom	What It's Caused By	Remedies
Acne (continued)	your follicles and cause pimples.	It soothes the pimple, reduces redness, and helps it heal faster. There are treatments for acne, like hormonal birth control, but they can come with side effects.
Irritability & unexplained sads	Hormones being assholes.	Make time for awesome people and activities that bring you joy for a mood boost. Writing in a journal or blog can help get thoughts on paper, which can be therapeutic. Period blahs typically pass as soon as your period starts.
Achy boobs	Likely caused by hormonal shifts, but the cause hasn't been definitively identified.	Achy boobies are a perfect excuse to wear your comfiest bra (not that you needed one). Some people feel that evening primrose oil helps with breast soreness.
Period poops	High levels of prostaglandins can affect your bowels, causing contractions where they shouldn't be.	Not much can be done except to eat a balanced diet that isn't too hard on your tummy. Avoid junk food the best you can to avoid further indigestion.
Bloating	High levels of prostaglandins can affect your bowels, causing gas and water retention.	Eating right can help, but won't eliminate bloating. Try deep stretches and get some exercise to help relieve gas pains.

One of my favorite period hacks is to use a period tracking app. I use an app to track my symptoms and better understand my cycle and how it affects me. Most apps will let you track when you start and stop bleeding, the volume, as well as any symptoms you experience, like cramping or mood changes. Keeping a consistent diary can help you predict when you're ovulating, when you'll start your period, and it can help get ahead of your symptoms. For instance, if you find yourself feeling extra fatigue three days before your period starts each month, you may benefit from lightening up your schedule right before your period when you are able to.

PMDD: MORE THAN THE BLUES

Around the time I had my first period, I also started experiencing bouts of depression. The week or two before my period sucked the life out of me, leaving me feeling like a hollow shell of myself. It made work and school almost impossible to manage, and it put a heavy strain on my relationships. It wasn't until I began tracking my cycles that I realized my symptoms corresponded with my cycle, which prompted me to talk to my doctor.

About 2-8% of menstruators out there will have a somewhat similar experience. Pre-menstrual dysphoric disorder (PMDD) is a type of depressive disorder where symptoms worsen during the luteal phase of the menstrual cycle, and then clear up once bleeding begins.

Symptoms include:

- Depression (hopelessness, lack of interest, loss of energy)
- Irritability and lashing out
- Increased interpersonal conflicts
- Severe anxiety
- Feeling overwhelmed and out of control
- Suicidal thoughts

Though the majority of women with PMDD have a normal hormonal profile, research indicates that for some, hormonal fluctuations during the menstrual cycle can cause serotonin deficiency. Folks with personal or family histories of depression, postpartum depression, or other mood disorders are more likely to be affected. PMDD can be a painfully dark and isolating experience. If you're ever experiencing symptoms like these, whether it's period related or not, please reach out to a healthcare provider who can help you feel yourself again. Take care of yourself, bb.

MENSTRUAL STIGMA: A BLOODY BURDEN

Periods can be a pain (literally) but they're a part of life, so we figure out how to deal with them, and life keeps marching on. And hey! At least our society is super chill and supportive about menstruation.

Oh wait. Lol. No, it isn't.

Social attitudes about menstruation are spotted with oddities, not unlike my favorite period undies. Twelve-year-old me was so horrified when I got my first period, I actually hid it from my mom for six entire months. I wasn't scared because I was effectively shitting blood out of my vagina, but because of what I thought getting my period *meant*. It was the ultimate symbol of womanhood, which my preteen self was desperately trying to run away from. I hated that menstruation was going to happen whether I liked it or not. It felt like a mark of fragility, weakness, and inescapable femininity. Based purely on the number of That Time of the Month jokes I've heard in the years since, I can't blame my pubescent self for having some reservations.

Some people have decidedly odd conclusions about periods and what they say about womanhood. We learn that women are "emotional creatures." Women are thought of as oversensitive, irrational, and illogical because of our periods. Strong displays of emotion, regardless of whether it's related to periods or not, are chalked up to "PMS." There's something particularly sinister about this cultural tale we tell, in part because it operates to delegitimize a woman's aptitude and abilities. During Hillary Clinton's first presidential run in 2008, Bill O'Reilly asked Marc Rudov during a television program about the downside of a female president. Rudov replied, "You mean besides the PMS and the mood swings, right?" Rudov, a master of female biology, must have forgotten that the vast majority of women no longer menstruate when they're sixty years old. But Rudov's jab comes with another telling implication: that men are never irrational or emotional. Obviously, no male president has ever had a mood swing or been irrational. No male sports fan has ever had a meltdown after a disappointing loss. No man has ever lashed out at a bar over the wrong look. Nope. No, sir. Nothing to see here.

In this way, menstrual misogyny slyly casts an emotional double standard. When a man expresses strong negative emotions, he probably has a reason to. But should a woman do the same, she is hysterical, she's PMSing, she's irrational. To be heard, to be seen as equally competent, to be taken seriously, a woman must remain calm and collected, and never flinch. She must not fly off the handle, raise her voice, or appear angry, lest she be dismissed. Women in powerful positions are tasked with the impossible expectation of not appearing too emotional (signaling she is unfit for a "man's job") but also appearing emotional enough (signaling she is not a robot or an ice queen).

Another strange menstrual stigma manifests as the unspoken expectation that periods be kept neatly out of sight. Monthly bleeding is considered not only gross and impolite, but somehow "unladylike" (?). So, girls are told to hide it, to do our best to pretend it's not happening, and to try to stealthily pass as nonbleeders. To meet that goal, modern-day tampon and pad commercials offer discreet wrapping, ever-tinier packaging, and other fun features that ensure that nobody will ever find out menstruation is happening. Shhhh.

If you think I'm kidding about this hide-your-period, hide-your-pads business, know that I am dead serious, y'all. In 2012, a rumor circulated that pop diva Christina Aguilera had the audacity to menstruate in public. During a performance, a stream of reddish liquid had run down her leg, leading people to believe she was having her *frickin' period* on stage. In reality, sweat had caused her spray tan to start running down her leg—but a drip was all it took for a media frenzy to ensue. The incident ultimately catalogued nearly one million Google results, with people going completely nuts about the public display of supposed menstruation. For that level of hubbub, you'd have thought Aguilera gave birth live on television while belting out "Lady Marmalade" in perfect pitch. But nope, just some period blood that wasn't even period blood.

This is all odd, of course, because menstruation is a part of life. Menstruating can come with its own set of challenges, but this should not be confused with weakness. I mean, I may be bleeding, but I will still kick several asses. Menstruation doesn't say anything about women's personalities, abilities, or competence as a whole. The only traits shared by people who menstruate are the physical cycle itself, the equipment to make babies, and the shared experience of stigmas that can come with menstruation.

All told, I think periods are pretty freaking cool. Hopefully one day people will find their chill about them.

THREE

THE CARE AND KEEPING OF VAGINAS

NOW THAT WE'RE ALL ACQUAINTED WITH periods, what else is going on down there? Turns out . . . a lot.

IN THIS CHAPTER WE'LL TALK ABOUT

4 easy ways to keep your vagina healthy
Pap smears
Common vagina problems and infections
Boobs and bras

---

4 easy ways to keep your vagina healthy

1 *Ditch the Douche.*

Next to the tampons and pads at department stores, you'll find an array of special soaps, wipes, and douches that claim to promote "feminine hygiene." The truth is, most of this stuff is crap and can actually *cause* infections.

Douches and vaginal soaps in particular are basically evil. The threat of a squeeze bottle full of foreign chemicals is enough to make any hot pocket want to run for the hills. When it comes to vaginal hygiene, it's important to remember that the vagina is an independent ecosystem. Soaps and douches tamper with your natural pH, which acts as a defense system against harmful bacteria. If your vaginal pH is off, it makes it easier to get an infection. These products also kill off the vagina's good bacteria, known as lactobacilli. Good bacteria are like little soldiers, and wiping them out can cause increased susceptibility to yeast infections, sexually transmitted infections, and non-sexually transmitted bacterial infections. There is some evidence to suggest an abnormal vaginal microbiome may even lead to difficulty getting pregnant. I have heard stories from folks who didn't like the smell of their vulva, started douching to try to fix it, and then found the smell got stronger. This is a pretty classic tale of infection, usually bacterial vaginosis or a yeast infection, and it's easily avoided. The reality is, vaginas don't smell like flowers and rainbows—and they're not supposed to. A healthy vagina has a light scent that (to me) smells slightly musky. To me, vaginas smell similar to penises (though there are strangely no shelves at Target dedicated to helping penises smell better). You may notice a stronger scent around your period. Any other strong scents may be an infection, so hit up your nurse or doctor.

Instead of douching and soaps, if you're feeling a little funky, gently rub the folds of the labia with your hand in the shower, or use a washcloth with warm water. That's it! You don't even need soap, which can be irritating to mucous membranes and the urethra. Baby wipes can be irritating as well, and often contain ingredients that increase your risk of infection (like glycerin) or be very drying (like citric acid). If you must use soap, opt for something like Cetaphil or any other completely scentless non-soap cleanser. A good rule of thumb is if you wouldn't wash your eyes with it, you shouldn't wash your vulva with it. If you want to make sure you smell nice, perhaps because you're expecting a visitor between your legs, just place a small dab of perfume between your thighs. No harm to the vag and works like a charm.

I'll admit to being a little salty that "feminine products" like douches, vaginal soaps, sprays, and whatever-the-hell even exist. Somehow, they remain a lucrative industry in the United States, despite being widely denounced by doctors and sexual health experts. IMO, these companies promote misinformation and cash in on women's insecurity about their vaginas. It's just another force telling girls that their vaginas are gross and that they should be ashamed. As a solution (to the problem they help create), they sell their products with ads and commercials that promise to freshen up your gross/stale/fishy vagina. Yeah, can we not? There's nothing wrong with vaginas. They are not gross or icky. They don't need special cleansers. They actually clean themselves. But then again, if that was their message, these douchebags would be outta business.

2 *Cotton Undies Are Your Friend. Thongs Are Not.*

As far as underwear goes, cotton is easily the best material for vulvas because it wicks moisture away, letting your vag breathe easy. Materials like nylon and Lycra can do the opposite, trapping moisture and heat in (sweaty vag, anyone?). Trapped moisture can make it easier for yeast to grow.

Thongs can also cause problems, especially if they're worn while working out. Because thongs are tight fitting and also slide back and forth, it makes it easier for bacteria like *E. coli* to make it from your butt to your vagina or urethra. This can cause bacterial infections like urinary tract infections, or UTIs. The effect is exaggerated during exercise because you're moving a bunch. Obviously it's not gonna kill you to wear a thong from time to time, but vaginal healthwise, it's best not to wear them every day.

3 Take a Daily Probiotic—Especially if You've Taken Antibiotics.

Our bodies are full of bacteria that perform critical functions throughout the body, including the vagina. There's a growing pile of compelling evidence that a good probiotic helps keep the vagina healthy, and that it can help prevent bacterial and yeast infections. Having a healthy vaginal flora helps the tissues maintain a healthy pH level, which is between 3.8 to 4.5. If you've taken a chem class, you know that's pretty darn acidic. When the vagina becomes too basic, it creates an environment that allows bad bacteria and yeast to flourish. As with many things in life, it's generally bad to be too basic. Probiotics are especially important to take during and after antibiotic treatment, since antibiotics kill off good bacteria along with bad bacteria. Things like birth control, menopause, unmanaged diabetes, and hormone replacement therapy can also take a toll on beneficial bacteria.

Which kind of probiotic should you take? There are a bunch on the market these days. Many experts say to look for a probiotic that contains a broad spectrum of *Lactobacillus* and has at least 5 billion CFU (colony forming units). Specifically, formulations that contain *Lactobacillus rhamnosus* (GR-1) and *Lactobacillus reuteri* (RC-14). You can find probiotics refrigerated at health food stores like Whole Foods. If you buy them online, make sure they are shipped with refrigeration, or the bacteria may die before they get to you. Ask your nurse or doctor for recommendations if you're unsure. The quality and benefits of different probiotic brands can vary enormously. You can also give the good bacteria in your vagina a hand by regularly eating probiotic-rich foods, like yogurt, kefir, kombucha, miso, kim-chi, tempeh, and sauerkraut.

4 *Get Vaccinated for HPV.*

HPV, or human papillomavirus, is a family of viruses that causes warts and other changes that could lead to cancer. It has more than 200 different strains, 40 of which are known to wreak havoc on the genitals. Every year, nearly 30,000 people in the US get cancer caused by HPV. Only a dozen or so high-risk strains cause the majority of problems. Types 16 and 18 are especially harmful. According to the National Cancer Institute, high-risk strains of HPV cause:

- Virtually all cervical cancer cases
- 95% of anal cancer cases (male and female)
- 70% of oropharyngeal cancers (throat and mouth, male and female)
- 50% of vulvar cancer cases
- 65% of vaginal cancer cases
- 35% of penile cancer cases

Yikes! The good news is that there are vaccines that protect against cancers caused by HPV. The CDC recommends that children get vaccinated at age eleven or twelve, before they have a chance to be exposed to the virus. This is the same age that preteens need to get Tdap and meningococcal vaccines. It is critical to get it early on, since about 50% of new HPV infections are contracted by fifteen- to twenty-four-year-olds. The earlier you get the HPV vaccine, the more cancer protection it will offer you! The CDC recommends the HPV vaccine up through age twenty-four. (For more information about HPV, check out the HPV section in chapter 10, "Safer Sex.")

pap smears

THOUGH THE NAME MIGHT SOUND A little . . . intimidating, pap smears are just routine screenings for cervical cancer. The American Cancer Society recommends that pap smears begin at age twenty-one, and then every three years after if the results are normal (so ages twenty-one, twenty-four, twenty-seven, and thirty). Women over thirty can have pap smears and HPV testing ("co-testing") every five years. It is critical to stay up-to-date on screenings to protect your health! Combined with vaccinations for HPV, these health measures have saved thousands of lives.

So, what's a pap smear like? During a pap smear, your nurse or doc will take a swab of your cervix to examine the cells and make sure they look normal. The screening is fast and relatively painless, but does require you to be naked. Your healthcare provider will ask you to take off your pants/skirt/undies and put your legs in footrests to get a cervical swab. They will give you a paper gown to cover yourself so you feel more comfortable. During a pap, don't forget to relax your muscles and breathe deeply—it will take no more than five minutes. First, they will gently insert a lubricated speculum into the vagina to reach the cervix. Then, they will swab the cervix with a small plastic brush, or a teensy spatula. Sometimes, a cotton swab is used to test for gonorrhea, chlamydia, or trichomoniasis at the same time. When they're done, they'll gently pull out the speculum—and you're all set!

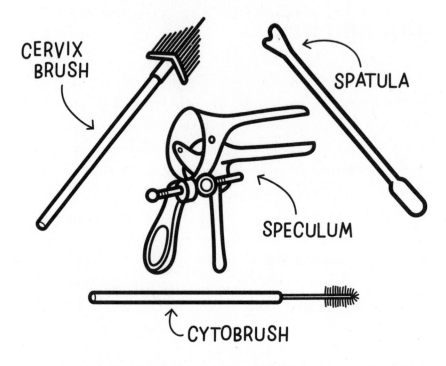

CERVIX
BRUSH

SPATULA

SPECULUM

CYTOBRUSH

It's normal to feel a little awk about your first (or second, or third) pap, but it's best to try not to stress. Remember, your practitioner has seen hundreds of vulvas, and the screening is there to keep you healthy. If you are a survivor of sexual trauma and are having anxiety about the screening, talk to your practitioner ahead of time. If you are too nervous to bring it up in person, email them before your appointment. They are there to take care of you and can suggest some ways to make the screening more comfortable. For instance, some people prefer to sit up a little more, to put the speculum in themselves, or to leave their bra/shirt on during the screening. These are all accommodations your provider should be open to. You can also let your practitioner know what language feels affirming and comfortable to you when discussing your anatomy. If you'd feel more comfortable with a friend or partner there, that can be done, too. If you have a practitioner who is not willing to accommodate your needs, find a different doctor or nurse practitioner!

If you have an abnormal pap result, don't panic. It does not necessarily mean you have cervical cancer, and in fact the likelihood of cancer—especially if you are up-to-date on screenings—is very low. The point of routine pap smears is to catch abnormal cells *before* they have the chance to become cancerous. Depending on your results, you may need a follow-up pap in six months to a year. They may test for HPV with the sample that was sent from your pap. Or the nurse or doc may need to do a colposcopy, which is a fancy word for looking at the vagina and cervix with a lighted magnifying tool. They may also do a biopsy, which is taking a tiny tissue sample to look at under a microscope. If they find harmful cells, your nurse or doc will do a follow-up to remove them before the cells can spread or become cancerous. These procedures are lifesaving. Thank you, science.

common vagina problems and infections

Yeast Infections 101

The vast majority of women will get at least one yeast infection in their lifetime. Men get them, too, though they are less common because male anatomy is less susceptible. So, what's the deal with yeasties? Yeast, a.k.a. *Candida albicans*, is a normal part of the vaginal flora. But if it's given the opportunity, yeast can get a little rambunctious and start to take over. Yeast infections are not dangerous to your health, and they are typically not sexually transmitted. They're just annoying. And painful. They can ITCH like mad and make sex hurt like hell, so it's best to abstain until it's treated.

Here are common symptoms of a yeast infection:
- Thick, white discharge that may be clumpy and cottage cheese–like
- ITCHY! Itchy vulva (clitoris, labia, entrance to vagina) and itching inside the vagina
- Red, irritated, or swollen vulva
- Pain using tampons or during vaginal sex
- Pain while peeing

The risk of yeast infections increases with:
- Douching
- Antibiotics
- Too much moisture in the genital area (made worse by undies, clothing, or pantyhose that don't breathe well, or sitting around in a wet bathing suit)
- Poor diet, especially one high in sugar and simple carbohydrates
- Sexually transmitted infections
- Poorly controlled diabetes
- Being immunocompromised (like being HIV+ or on cancer treatment)
- Elevated estrogen levels (during pregnancy and using some oral contraceptives)

If you suspect you have a yeast infection, and it's your first time getting one, it's best to see your nurse or doc to make sure. If you have any doubts it's a yeast infection and are sexually active, it's also a good idea to see your nurse or doc, since a lot of the yeast infection symptoms are similar to sexually transmitted infections. It's also important to see a healthcare provider if you are getting infections often, as it may be a sign that there's an underlying immune system issue. A nurse or doctor may prescribe an antifungal pill, like fluconazole. However, yeast infections are most often treated with over-the-counter suppository creams that are put into the vagina. You can buy treatments at the pharmacy (usually next to the tampons or condoms), which may come with a cream you can apply to the vulva for itch relief. If you can swing it, the longer treatments (seven-day) tend to be a little less harsh on the body than the shorter ones. It's ideal to use over-the-counter treatments at night and sleep with a disposable cotton panty liner or pad to protect your undies (there may be spillage). Plastic lined pads can be irritating for some when they have a yeast infection. Don't use tampons or have sex until you're feeling better.

To help prevent yeast infections, you can also:
- Eats lots of unsweetened yogurt
- Take a probiotic
- Avoid tight, non-cotton underwear
- Avoid pantyhose
- Avoid antibacterial soaps on the vulva
- Change out of wet swimsuits immediately
- Eat a healthy diet low in sugar and simple carbohydrates

UTIs 101

Bladder infections, a.k.a. urinary tract infections or UTIs, are the most common type of bacterial infection in the United States. And my god, do they hurt. Major ouch. UTIs are not sexually transmitted, nor are they contagious. While both males and females can get UTIs, females are about eight times more susceptible to them. EIGHT. TIMES. Damnit! This is because of female anatomy; we have shorter urethras, which means a shorter pathway for bacteria from the anus to the urethra. *Escherichia coli (E. coli)* causes 75-95% of uncomplicated UTIs, although they can be caused by several types of bacteria.

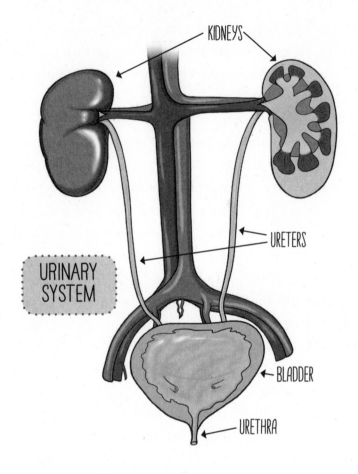

KIDNEYS

URETERS

URINARY
SYSTEM

BLADDER

URETHRA

Symptoms of a UTI:

- Feeling like you have to pee all the time, even when your bladder is empty
- Feeling like you have to go RIGHT NOW or you'll pee yourself (a.k.a. urgency)
- Burning while peeing
- Pelvic pain or lower back pain
- Cloudy urine, or blood in urine
- Incontinence or wetting the bed
- May also have no symptoms

The risk of UTIs increases with:

- If you are female, sex is the most common culprit. The motions of sex make it easier for bacteria to travel to the urethra. UTIs triggered by sex are sometimes referred to as *honeymoon cystitis.*
- Holding it and dehydration. When you don't pee enough and there's not enough fluid flushing through, it makes it easier for bacteria to survive and multiply.
- Birth control. Hormonal birth control and spermicides can alter the vaginal flora. Diaphragms can make it hard to fully empty the bladder. This allows bacteria to multiply.
- Constipation. Similar to diaphragms, constipation can make it hard to fully empty the bladder, allowing bacteria to multiply.
- Nonbreathable undies and thongs. These can trap bacteria and give it a ride to the urethra.
- Pregnancy
- Diabetes

Contrary to popular belief, UTIs usually aren't caused by poor hygiene, and better hygiene won't resolve chronic UTIs. It's an anatomy issue.

If you have a UTI, it needs to be treated by your healthcare provider! Otherwise, it will most likely get worse. If you've had symptoms for more than a week, it should be treated ASAP. Bacteria can move up into the kidneys and even the bloodstream, wreaking havoc in there. UTIs are treated with antibiotics prescribed by your nurse practitioner or doctor. It's important to take the entire prescription according to your healthcare provider's directions to make sure the infection is fully cleared. You'll likely feel better in the first few days—but continue taking the antibiotic until it's finished.

While antibiotics can treat a UTI once you have it, ideally we are able to prevent UTIs in the first place. Antibiotics aren't exactly easy on the body, and they kill off beneficial bacteria along with the bad guys. There is also a burgeoning antibiotic resistance crisis due to overuse of antibiotics. Bacteria are pretty sneaky—they rapidly evolve and adapt to avoid being killed. Preventing infections in the first place is key.

FORTUNATELY, THERE ARE MANY STRATEGIES TO help prevent UTIs:

- Stay hydrated and drink plenty of water.
- Ditch thongs, opt for cotton undies.
- Pee immediately after sex.
- Take a daily probiotic.
- Take a daily cranberry pill or drink cranberry juice without added sugar. (Avoid sugary "cranberry cocktail" beverages.)
- Take D-Mannose supplements daily and/or after sex (D-Mannose is the sugar found in cranberries that binds to *E. coli* to help flush the bacteria).
- Take proanthocyanidin (PAC) supplements daily and/or after sex. (PAC is found in supplements like ellura. It works together with D-Mannose.)
- Avoid hormonal birth control, spermicides, and diaphragms if possible.
- Avoid lubes that contain sugars, glycerin, or propylene glycol. If you find yourself getting UTIs from sex, make sure to try a different lube. Many UTI sufferers enjoy coconut oil. Preliminary studies show it has antibacterial and antifungal properties, which may protect against UTIs. The bad news is that coconut oil can break latex condoms, so only use it with nonlatex varieties (like polyisoprene or polyurethane). We

will talk more about coconut oil in chapter 10, "Safer Sex"!

- Ask your doctor about a low prophylactic dose of antibiotic after sex.

As someone who gets UTIs chronically, I actually do . . . all these things. It may seem like overkill, but it's the only regime that has ever prevented UTIs for me. There's a lot of new research about what causes chronic UTIs and how to prevent them. Probiotics, D-Mannose, and PAC are among those discoveries—but preventing UTIs may also begin with diet.

While conventional wisdom and intuition might suggest that acidic urine could prevent the growth of bacteria, preliminary research suggests that a more neutral or basic pH may actually be the ticket. Researchers at Washington University School of Medicine found that a protein called siderocalin helps fight UTIs by depriving the bacteria of iron, which they need to grow and multiply. The siderocalin protein was more successful at depriving the bacteria in neutral pH environments. This suggests that consuming a more alkaline diet *might* help to inhibit bacterial growth. Meals that contain sugar, grains, meat, and alcohol acidify urine, while whole fruits (not juice), nuts, legumes, and vegetables can help alkalize it.

If UTIs are turning your life upside down, finding yourself a good urogynecologist—especially one who specializes in chronic UTIs—can make a huge difference in identifying root causes and effective treatment. Sometimes painful bladder syndrome, also called interstitial cystitis (IC), is mistaken for chronic UTIs. Those with IC often benefit from bladder instillations (like pain killers put into the bladder) because their pain isn't from an infection, but from chronic inflammation.

Bacterial Vaginosis (BV) 101

The mother of all female bacterial infections is bacterial vaginosis, or BV. It's the most common vaginal bacterial infection among women, and the most common cause of abnormal discharge. BV is simply an overgrowth of bacteria. The vaginal flora contains lots of bacteria—mostly good, some bad. The good guys should be in charge. But when the bad bacteria are able to take over, it causes BV. BV is not thought to be sexually transmitted, but it is sexually associated. Getting BV without being sexually active is rare. Males don't contract BV in the conventional sense and so they don't need to be treated, but they can harbor bacteria that are involved in it.

Symptoms of BV:
- Usually no symptoms
- Thin white or gray discharge
- Strong, "fishy"-smelling discharge, especially after sex

Fortunately, mild BV sometimes clears up on its own and doesn't need to be treated. But if you're having symptoms, it's best to see a healthcare provider. Because bacterial vaginosis is a bacterial infection, it can be treated with antibiotics. Unfortunately, it can still come back. It is important to take your entire dose of antibiotics according to your doctor's directions, otherwise the infection may not be entirely wiped out. If BV is left untreated, it increases the risk of contracting STIs and pelvic inflammatory disease, and of having a preterm birth (for those who are pregnant).

It's unclear what, exactly, causes BV to develop. Given how common it is, there are likely a lot of different potential causes. Either way, maintaining a healthy vaginal flora can help prevent BV. To help support your vaginal flora:

- Avoid douching.
- Eat a healthy diet full of fruits and vegetables.
- Take a daily probiotic.

Gynecologic cancers

Okay, so cancer isn't a routine vagina issue, thank goodness. But it's still important to be in the loop about it. Unfortunately, pap smears do not screen for most gynecologic cancers, only cervical cancer. The best way to protect yourself against the range of cancers that can affect the cervix, vagina, and vulva is to get the HPV vaccine. It's also important to be in touch with your body and know what's normal for you. See a healthcare provider if you notice any changes that last more than two weeks.

One symptom shared by most gynecologic cancers is abnormal discharge (typically watery or blood tinged). Here are other potential symptoms to be aware of for each type of cancer:

- **Endometrial cancer:** pelvic pain or pressure, noticing your abdomen looks or feels much larger without being pregnant
- **Ovarian cancer:** pelvic pain or pressure, feeling full too quickly or difficulty eating, more frequent need to urinate, constipation, bloating, abdominal or back pain, unexplained weight loss
- **Vaginal cancer:** almost always has no symptoms. Less commonly, a mass may be felt. More frequent need to urinate, constipation
- **Vulvar cancer:** itching, burning, pain, or tenderness of the vulva as well as changes in vulva color or skin such as a rash, sores, or new moles

boobs and bras

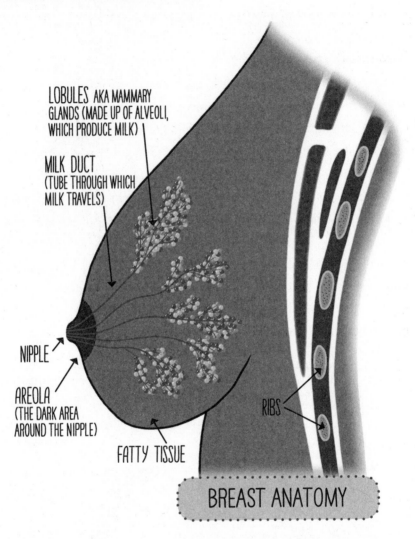

LOBULES AKA MAMMARY GLANDS (MADE UP OF ALVEOLI, WHICH PRODUCE MILK)

MILK DUCT (TUBE THROUGH WHICH MILK TRAVELS)

NIPPLE

AREOLA (THE DARK AREA AROUND THE NIPPLE)

FATTY TISSUE

RIBS

BREAST ANATOMY

TAKING A SMALL DIVERSION FROM ALL the vagina talk, I'm sure I don't need to tell you that breasts are magic. I don't think I've met a single human being in my life that has claimed not to like boobs. Makes sense. Boobs are pretty, they're squishy, they feel nice. What's not to like? Breasts are also the reason that humans are mammals.

Mammary glands that produce milk are the one characteristic all mammals share. Breast milk is highly nutritious, and a landslide of studies show that a mother's nutritious milk is the perfect food for babies, and may help babies develop a strong microbiome and immune system. In most species, mammary glands enlarge during pregnancy and lactation, and then deflate afterward. But in humans, for reasons that are not fully understood, the mammary glands are perpetually enlarged.

Both males and females have mammary glands, which means everyone has the equipment to produce breast milk. The reason males usually don't is because of genetics, and more specifically, because it requires hormones produced by the female body. Estrogen and prolactin cause the mammary glands in females to fully mature, making it easier to lactate.

Breasts serve a pleasurable function too, of course. They are an erogenous zone that are highly sensitive for a lot of people; male, female, and everyone in-between! The nipples in particular are densely packed with nerve endings. For some, nipple stimulation can even cause orgasm. Recent research has found that nipple stimulation activates the same areas of the brain as genital stimulation.

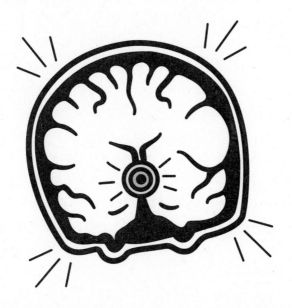

Are My Boobs Normal?

Good news: your boobs are totally normal. Whatever they look like is perfectly okay! Boobs come in so many shapes and sizes. Boobs might be large, small, or in-between. They might sit low or high on your chest. Your nipples may point upward or downward or inward or out to the sides. The areola (the round patch your nipple sits in the middle of) may be large or small, dark or light, bumpy or smooth. One breast is usually a little bigger than the other, too. Asymmetry is normal. Natural breasts come in a wide variety, and they're all lovely.

While females have the most prominent breast growth during puberty, about half of all males experience some breast growth as well. Excess breast growth in males is called gynecomastia. Gynecomastia is usually caused by the hormone cocktail being whipped up in the body during puberty (specifically, a boost in estrogen). Breast growth in males usually goes away on its own within a few months or years as hormones level out. Gynecomastia can cause self-consciousness because boobs are typically thought of as a "girl thing." In reality, secondary sex characteristics are somewhat flexible, and hey, there's nothing wrong with female stuff anyway. Every body is different, and it's normal for bodies to change sometimes. Wear clothing and undies that feel comfortable to you, and keep doing your thing.

Growing up, my breasts were the main source of my self-consciousness. My shame was fueled in part by the influence of porn, and in part how people have treated me because of my breasts. In mainstream porn, it's typical to find large breasts that are perfectly circular, barely bounce, and sit high up on the chest with nipples dead center. Let's get real: this just isn't how boobs are in the wild. Best you can, try not to compare natural breasts to porn stars. Another source of insecurity was how people treated me when my breasts came in. In high school, people treated my breasts as a source of casual conversation;

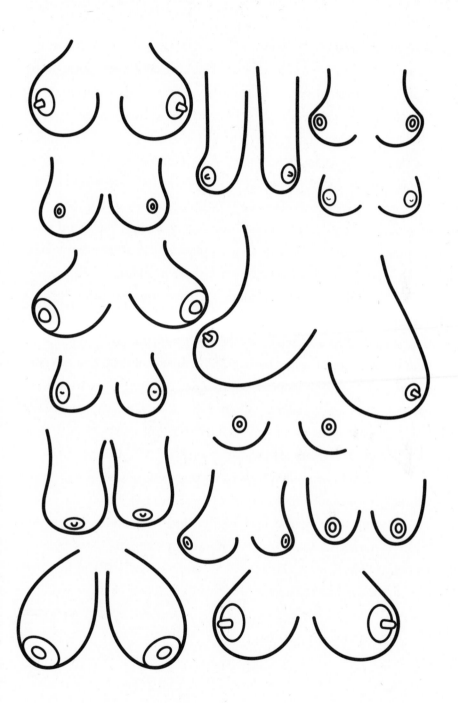

they would have full conversations about them in front of me as if I wasn't there. I was mocked and teased and sexualized to a degree that fourteen-year-old me did not know how to deal with. Some people even thought that it was okay to grope my breasts without my permission, just because they're big? I guess?

My experiences echoed some of the behaviors I had grown up seeing on TV and in movies. From time to time, a female character's breast size would come up in a show, usually as the butt of a joke or to discuss how hot she was. Women across the world have emailed me stories of being sexualized or mocked because of their boobs. "Big boobs? She must be a sex kitten! Small breasts? Eh, maybe get implants?" It should go without saying that a woman's value and sexuality is not determined by her breast size. And our breasts are only sexual in the contexts that *we* want them to be. Not when random dudes on the street want them to be, or people at school, or on TV, or anywhere else. I anxiously await the day that women are treated as more than their body parts.

Finding a Good Bra

So, yeah, have I mentioned I have big boobs? Besides dealing with jerks, this has also meant being painfully aware of just how important a good bra is. I spent years wearing bras that dug into my shoulders and breasts and underarms, with my breasts spilling out of cups and hurting after exercise. THE STRUGGLE IS REAL. But my first time getting fitted for a bra was a game changer.

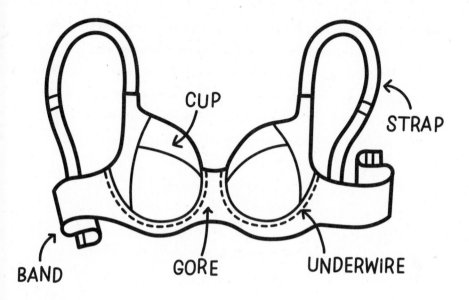

CUP

STRAP

BAND

GORE

UNDERWIRE

When it comes to booby comfort, it helps a ton to wear a bra that fits. Upper-end department stores and boutique underwear shops will typically fit you for a bra for free—but you can also do it yourself. To find your size, use a flexible measuring tape to measure around your rib cage, underneath your breasts. The number of inches is your band size. No matter what brand you try on, your band size will remain constant. However, your cup size may not be consistent, and sometimes varies by brand. Cup size also goes up with band size. So, for instance, a 32DD and a 38DD are not the same cup size—the DD on a 38 is larger than the 32. This is why a 30DD might be roughly the same cup size as a 38A. Using your band size as your anchor, try on different cups for fit.

Here's how to get the right fit on each part of the bra:

THE BAND

Your bra should feel comfortably snug on the *loosest* band setting when you buy it. As you break it in and the fibers stretch out, you then have some leeway to tighten the band up a bit. The band should sit straight across your back, not riding up (too big) or squeezing your rib cage (too small). The right band size is critical because it offers the majority of the support of a bra. It will take some of the strap pressure off your shoulders. A little strap digging is par for the course if you have heavy breasts, but the right band size and thick, soft straps will help distribute the weight.

UNDERWIRE

If there's a center gore between the cups, make sure that it sits flat against your chest. If it won't sit flat, the cup size is too small. Same with the underwire: you shouldn't feel it. If the wire is poking you or digging into your underarms, the cup size is too small.

THE CUP

When you're trying on a bra, do some jumping jacks or run in place for thirty seconds with the bra on. If you start spilling out the sides or the top, the cup is too small. If there's gapping or puckering at the top of the cup, the cup size is too big. Think Goldilocks: the cup should fit juuuust right. The cup should lie smooth and flat against the breast without empty space for gapping.

There are a few great brands that make bras beyond a DD cup size for large-chested people. A few of my personal favorites are Fantasie, Panache, Chantelle, and Brooks Running for sports bras. You can find these at bra stores online. If you live in the United States, I have found some of these brands at Nordstrom (they'll also do a bra fitting for you).

I like to have a few bras to rotate and to fit different occasions. But when it comes to sleep, it's best to take that baby off. Worth mentioning because when I first started wearing bras, I used to sleep in them. I'm not sure why. I think part of it was that I hated how unwieldy my breasts felt without a bra on. And in my bra, they felt more secure. When I got a little older and got more comfortable with my breasts, I discovered that the *real* magic is in taking my bra off for sleep. It's now the best part of my whole darn day. Ahhh, freedom. That said, there's nothing especially dangerous about sleeping with your bra on. It's slightly better for your circulation to sleep with it off, and it gives your skin and tissue a chance to stretch and breathe. But if you're more comfortable with it on, it's not gonna kill you; just opt for a bra that is stretchy and soft. No point in torturing yourself.

In a similar vein, it's okay to not wear a bra, too. I see bras as a utilitarian piece of underwear—it serves the purpose of keeping my boobs from moving all over the place. But for folks with smaller breasts, bras may not serve as much purpose. Run with whatever works best for you.

Breast Cancer Prevention

Not that long ago, healthcare providers recommended that everybody check their own breasts for lumps every few months. More recently, leading organizations have been saying, eh, it's probably not as important as we thought. Research has shown little to no benefit to self-screenings, and they may cause unnecessary distress when people find lumps in their breasts. Healthy breasts can actually be pretty lumpy, especially before your period.

What healthcare providers *do* recommend is "breast self-awareness," which is basically just being familiar with your breasts. Get to know how they look and feel throughout the different phases of your cycle. This is another instance where a period tracking app can be useful. If you notice something unusual, talk to your healthcare provider.

Beyond that, patients should talk with their healthcare provider about the proper time and frequency for screening. The American College of Obstetricians and Gynecologists suggests that those with average breast cancer risk get mammograms every one to two years, starting at age forty. Those who are at a higher risk for breast cancer (for instance, if a family member had it) may start getting screenings earlier under the guidance of a healthcare provider. However, there is some medical controversy about getting mammograms starting at age forty because it has resulted in a lot of overdiagnosis and overtreatment. The best course is to educate yourself, talk to your doctor, and choose what makes sense for you given your personal risk factors.

It should go without saying that staying up-to-date with breast cancer screenings saves lives. The research is clear: getting regular mammograms catches breast cancer earlier, which means less aggressive treatments and a higher chance of beating cancer. Take care of yourself! Don't neglect your breasts. Get screened on time.

FOUR

⋛° SEXUAL IDENTITY °⋚

NOW THAT WE'RE ACQUAINTED WITH THE equipment down below, how do you experience your sexuality upstairs, in your brain? *Sexual identity* refers to who you are as a sexual (or asexual) being and who you're attracted to, which is shaped by a number of cultural and biological forces. Sexual orientation, romantic orientation, and gender identity are three key aspects of sexual identity—and in the next couple chapters, we'll discuss 'em all. No matter who you are or where you come from, reflecting on your sexuality can be a deeply rewarding experience that helps you better understand yourself and others. So, let's hop to it!

IN THIS CHAPTER WE'LL TALK ABOUT

Sexual orientation
Questioning
Comin' out
Fighting discrimination

---

sexual orientation

WHO MAKES YOUR HEART BEAT FASTER and gives you tingly feelings in your pants? Figuring out the answer to that question is part of Finding Yourself and Figuring It All Out. For some, their sexual orientation is obvious to them from the get-go. Others have to do a little more soul-searching.

Sexual orientation can be thought of as having two pieces: *who* you're attracted to and *how* you're attracted to them.

Who Are You Attracted To?

Sexual orientation describes *who* you are sexually attracted to. Here is some basic terminology to get us started.

- A person who is attracted to the same sex or gender is **homosexual**, a.k.a. gay or lesbian.
- A person who is attracted to another sex or gender is **heterosexual**, a.k.a. straight.
- A person who is attracted to more than one sex or gender is **bisexual**.
- A person who is attracted to all sexes or genders is **pansexual**.
- A person who does not experience sexual attraction is **asexual**.

While these are the most common and recognizable terms used in society, other terms are used too. Notice that the definitions above require you to define your own sex or gender in relation to those you're attracted to. Alternatively, the following terms describe sexual attraction without requiring self-identification. These labels define attraction in terms of someone's femininity or masculinity (gender expression).

- A person who is attracted to masculine traits and appearance is **androsexual**.
- A person who is attracted to feminine traits and appearance is **gynesexual**.
- A person who is attracted to androgynous or genderqueer people is **skoliosexual**.

How Do You Experience Attraction?

Another big piece of sexual orientation is *how* you are attracted to someone. As you reflect on your sexuality, you may discover that you experience lots of different types of attraction. At its most basic, *sexual attraction* refers to the desire to be sexual with someone. Personally, I feel it pretty immediately when I see or meet someone hot ("love at first sight," as they call it). But attraction can also develop over time. Have you ever met someone you weren't attracted to at first, but somehow they grew magically sexier as you got to know them? Yup, that's totally a thing. Sexual attraction often develops alongside *emotional attraction*. I think of emotional attraction as being attracted to someone's ~spirit~, which is their personality, humor, skills, quirks, and how they make you feel. Emotional attraction isn't necessarily romantic; many of us experience platonic emotional attraction to friends and family. This is all slightly different from what you might describe as *romantic attraction*. Romantic attraction refers to the desire for emotional intimacy along-side companionship, and often, physical intimacy. Physical intimacy may be sexual or nonsexual, like hugging, hand-holding, cuddling, and sleeping together (and I do mean literally sleeping together).

The nuances of attraction are often felt distinctly by people who are asexual. Many asexual people, who do not experience sexual attraction, *do* experience romantic attraction and want companionship.

A few decades ago, there wasn't really a term to describe this experience, but now there is: romantic orientation! While sexual orientation describes attraction in a sexual context, romantic orientation describes attraction in a romantic context. To describe romantic orientation, the suffix "-romantic" is sometimes affixed instead of "-sexual" (i.e., **homoromantic**, **heteroromantic**, **biromantic**, etc.).

The Strengths and Limits of Language

Language is a pretty big part of how we express and understand sexual identities. Acronyms are often used to refer to sexual identity groups as a whole. LGBT is the most commonly recognized acronym to describe the entire lesbian, gay, bisexual, and transgender community. Other popular acronyms include:

- LGBTQ (Lesbian, Gay, Bisexual, Transgender, Queer)
- LGBTQIA (Lesbian, Gay, Bisexual, Transgender, Queer, Intersex, and Asexual)

Some acronyms get even more specific, like LGBTTQQIAAP (Lesbian, Gay, Bisexual, Transgender, Transsexual, Queer, Questioning, Intersex, Asexual, Ally, and Pansexual). Or, perhaps my favorite: QUILTBAG (Queer, Undecided, Intersex, Lesbian, Transgender, Bisexual, Asexual, Gay). I will use LGBTQ+ for inclusivity and simplicity.

Perhaps you are thinking to yourself: holy moly, that is a lot of words! That it is. A brief stroll through Google reveals hundreds of labels and definitions, many of which are relatively obscure. If the terminology overwhelms you, cast your eye to the bigger picture: sexual identity is diverse and personal, so people use lots of different words to describe those experiences. It's not that there are so many new sexual orientations or genders now, it's that people are finally finding language to describe experiences that have always existed. I take these evolutions in our language as a sign of growing awareness of sexual diversity. New terminologies can make it easier to express ourselves, to communicate our desires to others, and to be seen. These are basic human needs, and language is a tool for achieving them.

It's important to remember that language is there to serve us—not to create stress. My philosophy is that sexuality language should be accessible to everyone. In the quest for greater freedom and fluidity in our language, I also try to respect commonly held definitions to make it easier to communicate. On a personal level, I've found that identity labels can create stress when it increases the pressure to define myself—or others—in very specific terms. Labels are there to help us be seen and heard, not to force us into smaller boxes with more restrictions and requirements. So if you find a particular label is useful to you, use it! If it's not useful . . . then don't. If you feel there are no labels that accurately describe your sexual orientation, find a word that fits as a generalization, or you can forgo labels all together. For instance, when I was younger and questioning my sexual orientation, I described my sexual orientation as simply "sexual" for a while.

questioning

WHILE SEXUAL ORIENTATION IS SOMETIMES THOUGHT of as a black-and-white issue, in reality it may end up being a little messier than that. Like all things in the world of sexuality, it's all about the spectrum. Questioning is a way to reflect upon and unpack our experiences to better understand those gray areas.

The process of questioning is different for everyone—and in some cases can be quite difficult or painful. For most heterosexual people, sexual orientation is pretty STRAIGHTforward (hehe). This is because heterosexual people usually aren't prompted to question their sexuality in order to navigate crushes, dating, and sex. Being straight is the assumed default in our society. But this assumption makes questioning more difficult than it needs to be. These assumptions happen on an individual level, among family and friends, but also on a cultural level. The tendency to center heterosexuality in the law, media, religion, etc., to the exclusion of others, is called *heteronormativity*. Heteronormativity acts as a backdrop against which many LGBTQ+ people learn about their sexual identities and have sexual experiences. Another cultural backdrop is the belief that being straight is "normal" while being LGBTQ+ is not. This is also known as *heterosexism*. In a similar vein, the belief that homosexuality is deviant, sinful, or wrong is called *homophobia*. The takeaway here is that while we've come a very long way toward accepting LGBTQ+ folks, our culture is not an always a validating or safe place for young LGBTQ+ people to grow up in. We'll talk more about discrimination shortly, but given the huge role it plays in so many of our lives, it bears repeating: whoever you are is okay. Questioning is okay. Living your truth is okay.

LIKE MANY STRAIGHT FOLKS, MANY LGBTQ+ folks instinctively know how they feel from a young age. As children become young adults, most develop crushes and have their first experiences of attraction. This leads many young adults to question their sexuality as teenagers, but hey—it's never too late! Not everyone is given the right headspace or a supportive environment to safely question and explore how they feel as a teenager, and it's not uncommon for people to come out as adults. Question on your own time, and on your own terms.

"Feel" is a key word in the process of questioning. *What do you feel? Who do you find yourself having crushes on? Who do you fantasize about? Who sexually excites you? Who could you see yourself having a relationship with, if only maybe or someday?* For some, asking these questions means confronting feelings of shame and fear. Be patient and kind with yourself in your journey.

At some point, you may decide to explore your feelings by initiating new sexual or romantic relationships. As you explore, keep an open mind and heart, and pay attention to the discoveries, feelings, or needs that come up along the way. Also bear in mind that exploration is a self-discovery process—exploring certain relationships or sexual acts doesn't "make you" any particular sexual orientation. For instance, kissing someone of the same sex doesn't "make" someone gay any more than kissing the opposite sex "makes" someone straight. Sexual orientation is about how you identify; it's about the big picture, not a particular experience.

Eventually, most people ease into what feels right for them. It's normal to feel confused, frustrated, or even angry sometimes along the way. Build out your support system and let the process ride as little or as long as it takes. You will get there. Promise.

Here are a few tools to help you in your questioning process.

Sexual Orientation Scales

Sexual orientation scales can be a helpful tool to explore your sexual orientation. Throughout the history of sexuality studies, researchers have used hundreds of different scales to "measure" sexual orientation. Three of these scales are particularly popular: the Kinsey Scale, the Storm Scale, and the Klein Sexual Orientation Grid. Perhaps the most well-known is the earliest: the Kinsey Scale, which emerged in the 1940s. It is a linear, numerical scale from 0 to 6, with 0 representing "total heterosexuality" and 6 representing "total homosexuality." After 6, an "X" was later added to represent asexuality.

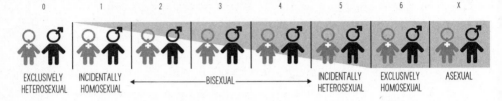

The Kinsey Scale was revolutionary for its time because it proposed that sexual orientation was a spectrum, rather than a binary. It also put bisexuality squarely on the map. In his book *Sexual Behavior in the Human Male*, Dr. Alfred Kinsey wrote:

Males do not represent two discrete populations, heterosexual and homosexual. The world is not to be divided into sheep and goats. It is a fundamental of taxonomy that nature rarely deals with discrete categories . . . The living world is a continuum in each and every one of its aspects.

Continuums are one of the themes that run throughout virtually all sexuality research. Though Kinsey's scale openly acknowledged bisexuality, he was later criticized for presenting bisexuality as a sort of "in-between" sexuality, a conglomeration of gay and straight, rather than a distinct orientation of its own.

IN LATER YEARS, THE STORM SCALE continued to develop and expand on Kinsey's ideas. Dr. Michael Storm added a y-axis to the scale, and made three key changes.

- He defined sexual orientation as "primarily an erotic fantasy orientation."
- The Storm Scale more overtly acknowledged asexuality as a sexual orientation.

- It reframed bisexuality as the simultaneous expression (rather than split expression) of homo- and heteroeroticism.

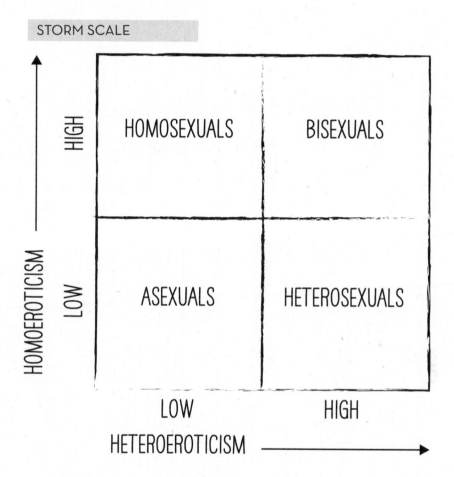

Five years later, in 1985, an even more comprehensive scale was published by Dr. Fritz Klein. The Klein Sexual Orientation Grid (a.k.a. the "KSOG") evaluates seven different dimensions of sexual orientation throughout the lifetime, all on a 1 to 7 Kinsey-style scale.

KLEIN SEXUAL ORIENTATION GRID

VARIABLE		PAST	PRESENT	IDEAL
A	Sexual Attraction			
B	Sexual Behavior			
C	Sexual Fantasies			
D	Emotional Preference			
E	Social Preference			
F	Heterosexual/Homosexual Lifestyle			
G	Self-Identification			

For Variables A to E

1 = Other sex only
2 = Other sex mostly
3 = Other sex somewhat more
4 = Both sexes
5 = Same sex somewhat more
6 = Same sex mostly
7 = Same sex only

For Variables F to G

1 = Heterosexual only
2 = Heterosexual mostly
3 = Heterosexual somewhat more
4 = Hetero/Gay-Lesbian equally
5 = Gay/Lesbian somewhat more
6 = Gay/Lesbian mostly
7 = Gay/Lesbian only

The KSOG has been praised for its multidimensional approach to sexuality, as well as for explicitly acknowledging that sexual orientation can develop or change over time.

So hey, where do you hang out on these scales?

comin' out

COMING OUT IS PERHAPS ONE OF the most visible experiences that there is regarding sexual orientation. All over social media, and occasionally TV or movies, the process of coming out draws a spectacle. On YouTube, coming out videos amass millions of views and comments expressing their love and support—or their hatred and rejection. While "coming out" is often thought of as a single, grand event, for many people it ends up being a lifelong process of recognizing, accepting, and sharing who you are with the outside world. Being out and at ease with your sexuality is something that you, and everybody, deserves! It's messed up for society to expect LGBTQ+ people to hide who they are, to stay quiet and in fear, for the comfort of small-minded people. Coming out is your right, when and if you are ready.

Let's talk about what to expect when you come out. Like questioning, the experience of coming out is different for everyone. It is inevitably influenced by how much support you have beforehand, the reactions of family and friends, the state of LGBTQ+ rights where you live, where you go to school or work, or what religion you/your family belong to.

My own experience coming out as bisexual was fairly nonchalant, in large part because I was still figuring things out when I lived at my parents' house. I first recognized my feelings in high school. My girl friends were what I'd describe as "boy crazy." VERY boy crazy. Boys were all they talked about, and we obsessed about cute movie stars and artists. But as hormone-laden infatuations swirled around me with my girlfriends, I occasionally found myself having crushes on . . . them. It was something I quietly pushed to the back of my mind, and because I still had crushes on boys, I knew I wasn't gay. Yet I didn't feel straight, either. My introduction to bisexuality wasn't very positive. It wasn't until college that bisexuality was treated as valid and legitimate. Kids in high school discussed bisexuality as something girls do to get a guy's attention and show off. Bisexuality wasn't thought of as a real orientation by my peers. It was treated as a performance for dudes. Women who were bi were thought to be either straight and pretending not to be for sex appeal—or they were secretly gay. Men who claimed to be bi were thought to be denying that they're really gay, a "pit stop" to gayness, if you will. And to top it off, anybody who was bi was assumed to be an untrustworthy "slut" who would sleep with anyone. Privately, I knew this was wrong, but I continued to doubt myself well into college. Why was it so hard to believe that attraction could take many shapes and forms? I didn't feel like bisexuality was something I could comfortably claim until after graduating college, when I had a sex-positive community around me. It didn't strike any of my new crew as weird or "slutty" or a phase. It just was. Knowing they wouldn't reduce my feelings to a stereotype or dismiss me made it easier to accept myself.

I feel privileged to have avoided a big "coming out" moment in an unaccepting environment. Through experimentation and exploration, I slowly eased into and accepted who I was in early adulthood. I've always felt pretty private about my sexuality, and I don't feel that my internal feelings are anybody else's business. I don't owe anyone an explanation. I'll do what I want, date who I want, discuss it with who I want—and that's that. Part of growing into my identity has been accepting that other people's ignorance doesn't define me, and it won't put me in a box. Bisexual people exist. It isn't a phase, an "in-between" sexuality, indecisiveness, "sluttiness," or whatever other crap is out there. We are who we are.

There are a few takeaways from my own experience. For me, coming out was largely an internal experience that I think of as a lifelong process rather than a one-time event. Coming out is a conversation I have with lovers and friends and family. And while those conversations are occasionally awkward or difficult, on the whole, my experience has been much more positive than some of my gay and lesbian friends'. The importance of supportive community cannot be understated. Find your people; it will make things much easier. Surround yourself with those friends and family who don't make a huge deal out of it. These things made my journey so much less trying.

While everybody's coming-out experience is different, researchers have found that there are some commonalities. Researcher Vivienne Cass breaks down common experiences of coming out into six basic stages. It's called the Cass Model.

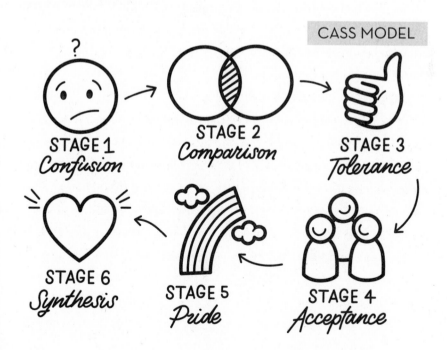

CASS MODEL

STAGE 1
Confusion

STAGE 2
Comparison

STAGE 3
Tolerance

STAGE 6
Synthesis

STAGE 5
Pride

STAGE 4
Acceptance

Stage 1: Confusion

One of the earliest stops on the coming-out journey is questioning. This is usually prompted by crushes and attractions that feel confusing.

Stage 2: Comparison

In stage 2, many people realize that they might, in fact, be lesbian/gay/bi/etc. This means dealing with the feelings of alienation that come with the possibility. You may grapple with what it means for your life and your future. Many people separate their sexuality and their identity label, and live in dissonance for a while (i.e., a person may still think of themselves as a heterosexual despite experiencing mostly homosexual attraction).

Stage 3: Tolerance

As a person's tolerance for their own sexual orientation increases, they are less likely to see themselves as heterosexual. It gets easier to acknowledge their own social, emotional, and sexual needs. As you start to think about what your needs are, you may decide to seek out other members of the LGBTQ+ community for support.

Stage 4: Acceptance

Tolerance turns into acceptance when a person is able to let go of society's expectations and establish harmony between the private and public self. This is made easier by spending time in LGBTQ+ communities. At the same time, this can increase pressure to fit in and perform your gayness, lesbianism, etc., the "right way." You may also find yourself more deeply exploring personal feelings of shame, internalized homophobia, and loss of heterosexual expectations for your future.

Stage 5: Pride

In stage 5, a person not only accepts, but begins to take pride in who they are. Commence all the rainbow parades! Identity pride is often marked by full immersion in gay and lesbian culture, development of a shared group identity, and less contact with predominantly hetero social communities. It can also come with feelings of resentment, defensiveness, and anger about heterosexism and homophobia from the world and people in your life. An "Us vs. Them" mentality is a common coping mechanism.

Try This: Positive Affirmations

Feeling a little defeated today? Taking a few minutes to practice affirming yourself can inject a little positivity into the day. You can practice self-affirmations in the morning while you're getting ready, during a meditation, or before falling asleep in bed. Think up one of your own affirmations that means something to you personally, or use one of mine:

- I deserve love, and I will allow myself to be loved.
- I will love and accept who I am.
- This, too, shall pass. My strength knows no bounds.
- I am calling on my kindness, my resilience, and my faith in humanity to make it through today.
- I am who I am, and who I am is okay.

Stage 6: Synthesis

When a person's identity is synthesized, the whole self comes into view. Your sexual orientation can be more actively worked into other facets of who you are. In this sense, being LGBTQ+ is synthesized as one aspect of multiple identities. Resentments may remain so long as there is inequality and marginalization, but the intensity may decrease as trust increases. More time is spent in the larger community of non-LGBTQ+s in the last stage.

The Cass Model can offer a loose guide on what kinds of feelings are common and what to expect. But as usual, take it with a grain of salt. If your journey is different, that's okay, too. People may move back and forth between these experiences, and linger in some longer than others. The model was also developed based on the experiences of white gay men, which cannot capture the full spectrum of identity development, particularly for people who are struggling with other aspects of their identity at the same time (e.g., ethnicity, race, gender, etc.). For a more in-depth guide to coming out, particularly in a hostile environment, check out the next chapter. It focuses on gender identity, but applies to sexual orientation as well.

HOW TO SUPPORT SOMEONE WHO COMES OUT TO YOU

One way to make the world a healthier, happier, and more sex-positive place is to increase the available support network for LGBTQ+ people, especially youth (who are more vulnerable to homelessness and abuse). Who makes up that network? Why, that would be . . . us! No matter who you are, each of us can work to become better allies and fighters for equality. Being an ally to LGBTQ+ people is an active role and a process; you will quickly find there is always more to learn. Here are a few ways to support someone you love.

1 *Respond with Love and Support.*

Coming out to a friend or family member can be a vulnerable and challenging experience. When someone chooses to come out to you, it is a sign of their trust in you. Take that seriously. Listen, affirm, and make yourself a safe harbor. Let them know that you love and support them.

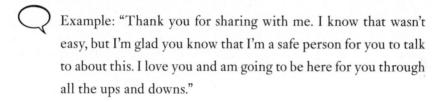

Example: "Thank you for sharing with me. I know that wasn't easy, but I'm glad you know that I'm a safe person for you to talk to about this. I love you and am going to be here for you through all the ups and downs."

2 *Keep the Conversation Open.*

You can learn a lot by asking open-ended, respectful questions. Be considerate and thoughtful in keeping the conversation going. Active listening can be therapeutic and affirming for them, and help you to learn more as well.

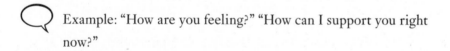

Example: "How are you feeling?" "How can I support you right now?"

3 *Be Honest.*

If you feel uncomfortable, it's okay to say so in a respectful way. Let them know that even though this is unfamiliar territory for you, you are committed to working through it and being supportive. Don't put the onus on them to help you deal with your feelings—they are already dealing with their own.

Example: "I'm sorry if I'm awkward about this. It's new to me. I want to be here for you. Give me time to process, and let me know how I can be supportive."

4 Self-educate.

If there is something you don't understand, don't leave it to your loved one to teach you. With all the people in their life that they have to have taxing conversations with to come out, it can quickly become overwhelming. Do your part by reading up. My resources list is a great place to start!

5 Walk the Walk.

When someone discloses their sexuality to us, it is a gentle nudge to self-reflect on our own biases and behaviors, and hopefully become better people in the process. This may include phasing out demeaning language, becoming more familiar with LGBTQ+ issues, or becoming more outspoken in supporting related causes. It's never too late to speak up and get involved.

MYTHS ABOUT SEXUAL ORIENTATION

Now that we're all comfortably in touch with our slightly (or hella) gay side, let's talk about common myths.

MYTH BUSTED:
You can't tell someone's sexual orientation by looking at them.

I've heard the sentiment many a time: "My gaydar is tingling!" Can you tell if someone is gay by looking at them? Unless you are the mind-reading Professor X from the X-Men, then . . . probably not. Strangely, people often assume that men who are feminine are gay while women who are masculine are lesbians. This is a common stereotype, perhaps even *the* most common stereotype of them all. Two of my friends, both gay men, have told me tales about how these stereotypes affected them when they were younger. As teenagers, both were under the impression that they had to be "flamboyant and sassy" to be gay. Several of my YouTube viewers have also expressed feelings of not being the "right type of lesbian" or not being "gay enough." Obviously, some gender nonconforming people *are* gay! But some aren't. Being gay isn't a personality type or a gender expression, it only refers to experiencing same-sex attraction. That's it. Gay doesn't have a special look or haircut, it isn't a manner of speaking, and it has nothing to do with what someone wears. (Unless, perhaps, they're wearing a shirt that says "I'M GAY.") ♥

MYTH BUSTED:
It's an orientation, not a phase.

More like "It's just a phrase!" One of the most common arguments dismissing LGBTQ+s is the idea that it's "just a phase"; that nonstraight sexuality is something people will just outgrow. Remember when we were talking about heterosexism and how it makes it harder for people to question and come out? This myth is a great example of that. While sexuality can certainly evolve throughout the lifetime, that does not make it a phase, abnormal, or less real.

That goes for bisexuality, too. The process of casting bisexuality to the realm of unicorns, fairies, and other things that aren't real is sometimes called *bisexual erasure*. Bisexual erasure is embodied in the idea that bisexuality is something you grow out of, or that bisexuals must "pick a side"—you are either straight or gay. Ultimately, there's no way to escape this type of accusation. If a woman is with a woman, she is accused of being gay. If she's with a man, she's accused of being straight. What's a bisexual lady (or man or human) to do? ♥

MYTH BUSTED:
You don't choose your sexual orientation.

Lady Gaga famously exclaimed: "Baby, I was born this way!" You'd probably agree that your sexual orientation isn't something you *chose*. It's not just you, me, and Lady Gaga who feel this way; the American Psychological Association holds that biology plays a significant role in who we are attracted to, and that it is largely out of our control. Here's a brief overview of what scientists have found:

- In identical twins, if one is gay, the other has a 20% chance of being gay as well. This is much higher than the natural incidence of homosexuality in the general population (which is about 3.5%, according to the Williams Institute at UCLA).
- There's a possible genetic influence on sexual orientation in males on the X chromosome (Xq28).
- Higher exposure to male hormones (androgens) in the womb creates a greater likelihood of a baby being homosexual.
- Pro-social homosexual behavior has been observed in over 1,500 species in the animal kingdom, and documented in over 500.

• •

THE IDEA THAT SEXUAL ORIENTATION IS a choice has been hotly debated for decades, and research on the topic has become politicized. The significance being: if sexual orientation is indeed a choice, the argument goes that gays and lesbians could instead *choose* to be straight. The "choice" argument of sexuality has been weaponized by those who believe that homosexuality is a sin, a mental illness, or a moral failure. The belief that sexual orientation is a "choice" underlies antigay regimes and the violence of religious groups and governments around the world.

The Heterosexuality Questionnaire

Is heterosexuality a choice? This is what it might sound like if we treated straight people like LGBTQ+s.

1. What do you think caused you to be straight?

2. When and how did you first decide you were straight?

3. Is it possible that your heterosexuality is just a phase you may grow out of?

4. Is it possible that you're straight because you're scared of people of your same sex?

5. If you have never slept with a member of your own sex, how can you know you're not gay?

6. Why do you straight people try to seduce others into your lifestyle?

7. Why do you flaunt your straightness? Can't you just be who you are and keep it discreet?

8. Would you want your children to be straight, knowing the problems they would face, such as heartbreak, disease, and divorce?

These silly questions were adapted from Dr. Martin Rochlin's
Heterosexuality Questionnaire (1977)

Even though the science generally points toward "not a choice," in my mind it really shouldn't matter. Again, I find myself back at my sex-positive mantra of, "Uhhhh, so long as nobody's harmed—who cares?" What does it matter what someone's sexual orientation is? And why should their sexual orientation say anything in particular about them? Sexual diversity is well documented in all species, throughout all of time.

You'd think we'd have gotten over it by now.

fighting discrimination

WHILE THE PAST FEW DECADES HAVE seen enormous leaps and gains for gender and sexual minorities, the fight is far from over and the struggle continues. For many young adults in the US who were too young to remember the AIDS epidemic, the Westboro Baptist Church's funeral protests were a first glimpse at the discrimination and hostility that LGBTQ+ people still face in our world. In fact, the WBC is the reason I first started making YouTube videos as a teenager. In the early 2000s, the church gained notoriety for protesting gay veterans' funerals with "God Hates Fags" signs. While many organizations avoid saying it so bluntly, the WBC was up front about their belief that homosexuality is an abominable sin. So abominable, in fact, that they believe gays and lesbians should be put to death. In a 2012 interview on "The David Pakman Show," Jonathon Phelps, son of WBC founder Fred Phelps, was asked, "You believe that based on what the Bible says, we should have the death penalty for homosexuality?" Phelps responded, "Absolutely." He is likely referring to Leviticus 20:13:

> *If a man lies with a male as with a woman, both of them have committed an abomination; they shall surely be put to death; their blood is upon them.* —The Holy Bible, King James Version

While other antigay religious regimes in the United States may not be nearly as extreme as the WBC, there is a shared theme: being gay is sinful, a moral abomination, and also kind of icky. Therefore, if you "choose" to be gay, you deserve to be punished and abused for it. These homophobic abuses take many forms in modern-day society.

In the United States, "conversion therapy," occasionally referred to as "pray the gay away" programs, are sometimes used to force queer youth to turn straight or cisgender. In conversion therapy, being gay is regarded as a destructive addiction, akin to alcoholism or drug abuse. To turn them straight/cisgender, LGBTQ+ kids undergo prayer, shaming, rehab, physical isolation, and electroshock therapy. There is no evidence these therapies work, and they have been rejected by every major medical and mental health organization in the United States for decades. Worse, the techniques that are used leave kids much worse off than they were coming in. According to research at San Francisco State University, LGBTQ+ youth who undergo high levels of sexual orientation rejection are three times more likely to struggle with drug addiction, six times more likely to experience major depression, and eight times more likely to commit suicide. In recent years, there have been several high-profile suicides attributed to conversion therapy. Nevertheless, for some reason, conversion therapy remains legal in the vast majority of states.

For LGBTQ+ youth who aren't subjected to abuse in a therapeutic setting, they are likely to encounter it at school. Bullying against kids who are seen as different is far too common, and many LGBTQ+ kids suffer daily humiliation and fear at school. According to the 2015 National School Climate Survey of LGBTQ students:

- 85% were verbally harassed because of their sexual orientation
- 60% were sexually harassed because of their sexual orientation
- 58% felt unsafe at school

While one might hope that teachers and administrators are intervening to make school safer for LGBTQ+ youth, 64 of the students reported that even the staff did not act when they witnessed bullying. While the 2015 survey shows a slight improvement since 2003, educators must work harder to address homophobia at school. There are a number of ways to improve the environment:

- Require professional development for staff members.
- Support student clubs like the Gay Straight Alliance.
- Create (and enforce) antibullying and harassment policies.
- Review school policies for discrimination.
- Use inclusive curriculum.

At schools where an inclusive curriculum is used, the report found that 75% of LGBTQ+ students said their peers are accepting. When we compare that to schools *without* an inclusive curriculum, the number drops to 40%. The consequences of hostile environments are real: LGBTQ+ youth experience higher levels of depression and suicide, social withdrawal, lower academic performance, and lowered self-esteem—just to name a few. Addressing homophobia at school makes it a safer and healthier environment for everyone. Furthermore, stopping violence in its tracks at school can help prevent hateful attitudes and behaviors from escalating.

Hate crimes against those who are gay, or are even perceived to be gay, are another disturbing consequence of homophobia. Back in 2014, the *New York Times* reported that FBI data for that year indicated that LGBT individuals were the most likely of any marginalized group to be targeted for hate crimes in the USA. The statistics may be even more grave than they appear; to avoid outing themselves and putting themselves in further danger, LGBTQ+ folks often don't report hate crimes directed against them. The majority of LGBTQ+ hate groups identified by the FBI were affiliated with religious extremism.

While we are slowly moving toward greater equality, progressive victories are often met with violent backlash. After marriage equality became federal law in the United States in 2015, violent crimes against

LGBTQ+ individuals spiked. The National Coalition of Anti-Violence Programs documented a 17% rise in LGBTQ+ hate killings in 2016, making it one of the deadliest years on record. Hate crime experts note that as society increases its acceptance of LGBTQ+s, those who hold prejudices appear to become radicalized in response. Less than a year after marriage equality became law, one of the deadliest mass murders in decades was carried out at Pulse Nightclub in Orlando, Florida. The gunman killed forty-nine people, most of whom were queer. After the tragedy, UC Davis psychology professor David Herek theorized about the attack in the *New York Times*: "[Anti-gay radicals] may feel that the way they see the world is threatened, which motivates them to strike out in some way, and for some people, that way could be in violent attacks."

You gotta wonder: what, exactly, is so threatening about someone's sexual orientation or gender identity that a completely unaffected stranger is compelled to become violent? To end discrimination, we must understand where it comes from. Studies have found some common characteristics among those with homophobic attitudes. PBS reports that people with homophobic attitudes:

1. *are less likely to have had personal contact with lesbians or gays;*
2. *are less likely to identify as lesbian or gay;*
3. *see their peers as similarly homophobic, especially among men;*
4. *are more likely to have resided in areas where negative attitudes toward gays are the norm, especially during adolescence;*
5. *are more likely to be older and less educated;*
6. *are more likely to be religious, to attend church frequently, and to subscribe to a conservative religious ideology;*
7. *are more likely to express traditional, restrictive attitudes about gender roles;*
8. *are less permissive sexually or manifest more guilt or negativity about sexuality;*

9. are more likely to manifest high levels of authoritarianism and related personality characteristics;

10. tend to have more negative attitudes toward homosexuals of their own sex than of the opposite sex.

—PBS Frontline, *"Hating Gays: An Overview of Scientific Studies"*

From this list, we get a few basic clues about reducing discrimination and violence:

- It helps alleviate homophobia if people know someone who is LGBTQ+, perhaps because it alleviates a "fear of the unknown" with a friendly face.
- It helps if they are in an environment where their peers are accepting and don't tolerate homophobia.
- It helps if their church and religion are accepting.
- It helps if they are encouraged to keep an open mind about gender roles and sexuality.

WHERE DO HOMOPHOBIA AND TRANSPHOBIA COME from? The suffix "-phobia" means "an irrational fear." While discrimination and violence are often thought of as being rooted in hatred, research suggests that it goes deeper than that. In many cases, hatred is the byproduct of feeling afraid. Here are some of the leading theories about why some people are homo- or transphobic.

Violation of Gender Roles

With a poetic frankness, the very existence of homosexuality challenges gender roles within relationships. A same-sex relationship means there are no clear roles about who-does-what based on reproductive sex. Which causes some anxiety sometimes—I mean, "who wears the pants?!" When you boil it down, this is often an anxiety about who is in charge and holds the dominant role in a relationship. In a healthy relationship, the answer is neither partner is in charge—partnership is built on equality. Gender roles aren't even required.

This theory of homophobia also offers some insight into why gay men are demeaned with insults like "sissy," "fairy," "pussy." All these terms are references to femininity, which is implied to be inferior. Gay males are shamed for pursuing men or having receptive sex, two behaviors that are associated with female sexuality. Gay men also face higher levels of stigma than lesbian women—which may also be explained by this theory. Gay men are perceived as "degrading" themselves to the status of women through their sexual orientation, whereas lesbians are "elevating" themselves with masculinity. Because women are more likely to be sexualized, lesbian relationships in the media are often portrayed through the lens of entertainment or sexual titillation for a straight male audience. The tendency to view women through a sexualized lens in the media is sometimes called "the male gaze." Remember Katy Perry's popular song "I Kissed a Girl," a sexy salute to girls kissing girls? In pop culture, lesbianism and female bisexuality are more comfortably accepted as a sexual spectacle—meanwhile, bisexual and gay male sexuality are regarded as "icky." In this sense, sexism and homophobia are deeply intertwined with each other; to end homophobia, we must also end sexism. This is also true for transphobia.

Gender role violation is at the very heart of transphobia. We'll talk a whole lot more about what transgender is shortly—but the very existence of people who don't conform to strict views of gender has ruffled many feathers. In a world that says "this is what a real woman is" or "this is what a real man is," gender nonconformity challenges us to think outside the box, and turns those understandings on their head. For some, this may prove uncomfortable. Too often, bullying and violence are used in response to that discomfort, in an attempt to police people's gender and how they express themselves. Violent retaliation is a way to punish and intimidate others into conforming.

Masculinity Threat

On average, straight men tend to have more homophobic attitudes than straight women. This lends credit to the theory that homophobia arises in response to what is called *masculinity threat*, which is thought to motivate violent outbursts against gay men (known as "gay bashing"). Michael Kimmel, a leading expert on American masculinity, writes:

> *Homophobia is more than the irrational fear of gay men, more than the fear that we might be perceived as gay. Homophobia is the fear that other men will unmask us, reveal to us and the world that we do not measure up, that we are not real men.*
> —*"Masculinity as Homophobia" in* Sex, Gender, and Sexuality:
> The New Basics: An Anthology

In Kimmel's analysis, two facets of masculinity collide: the need to express power over others and a fear of being emasculated. Masculinity differs from femininity in this way; to be straight is to be masculine. Failing to measure up to those standards of masculinity is more aggressively shamed in men than a lack of femininity in women is. This may help explain gender differences in homophobia.

Sexual Identity Threat

One of the oldest theories about homophobia is that it's the result of secret homosexual urges within a person who has a lot of fear about being (or "becoming") gay. Our old pal Sigmund Freud called this "reaction formation"; a person has a private experience of stressful homosexual thoughts, and they respond by outwardly trying to prove to themselves and others that they are definitely not gay. This theory is supported by some research and may help explain some situations. But that shouldn't be taken to mean that all homophobic people are secretly gay. It's complicated.

Perhaps some of the highest-profile (and most befuddling) examples of this situation are the slew of antigay politicians who have been outed as being gay themselves. It's a sad situation all around—that someone would feel such shame and hatred of themselves that they hide it, that someone would weaponize that shame to target fellow gays and lesbians with laws and policies, and that when outed, the outside world's first instinct is usually to mock them. When it comes to closeted antigay public figures, their actions aren't excusable—but shame can help us contextualize it and respond accordingly. If there are people who strongly oppose homosexuality but are themselves struggling with shame and fear, it suggests that *we must fight homophobia with love and compassion.* This starts at home, with parents creating an accepting place for their children. As a society, we must also work to help each other feel accepted and loved for who we are, regardless of sexual orientation.

Masculinity threat and sexual identity threat may also help us understand the phenomenon of violent retaliation against transgender people in sexual settings. Those who are heavily invested in their identity as "straight" are more likely to feel threatened when they discover they are attracted to someone who is transgender. This asks people to question their sexuality in a way that they may not be open to. Some people shut down and internalize their shame—but abusive people externalize it and go on to resolve their discomfort with violence. Through physical violence or sexual assault, the abuser reestablishes their identity and sense of power. It is not a coincidence that transgender women experience exceptionally high rates of violence, abuse, and homicide.

Religious Values Violation

What if being gay or transgender is at odds with a person's spiritual beliefs? Some feel that their aversion isn't homophobia; it's just a matter of faith. This is obviously pretty complicated. For one, biblical condemnation of homosexuality is often recited and enforced while other controversial passages are ignored (Leviticus notably also bans polyester, the consumption of bacon and shellfish, bowl cuts, tattoos, and a slew of other things). It is also nearly impossible to separate out religion from the influence of other cultural factors that cause homophobia. This tension between faith and sexual orientation can be a source of incredible suffering for many families and LGBTQ+ folks of faith.

There are no simple solutions to this conundrum, except to open our hearts and accept people for who they are. Among those who are LGBTQ+ and wish to hold on to their faith, different people take a variety of approaches. Here are some things to consider:

- Some denominations are LGBTQ+ inclusive. If yours is not, it might be worth looking into a similar congregation that is. If your congregation *is* inclusive, then yay!

- Religious texts, like the Bible, have been interpreted in many ways throughout history. Study their history and how they have been used to both harm and uplift people throughout history. Opt for interpretations that call for us to embrace one another.

- Challenge yourself and your faith leaders to make your congregation an even more supportive place to be. You, and your faith, can only grow from it.

FIVE

﹥° GENDER IDENTITY °﹤

WITH PROMINENT TRANSGENDER FIGURES MORE VISIBLE in the media now than ever before, the United States—and the world— is having a robust conversation about gender. If terms like "transgender," "gender identity," or "nonbinary" have you a bit confused, that's okay! Lemme just say: gender is complicated. In fact, gender might be one of the most complicated topics in sex ed. It's also one of the most debated. I suspect this is true for a few reasons: firstly, because the meaning of gender is a matter of both science and philosophy, and philosophy never provides clear-cut answers. Secondly, because the meaning of gender has a big effect on how we see ourselves and each other, with both personal and political implications.

In my time on YouTube, I have frequently found myself caught in the crosshairs of debates about gender. A few years ago, a video of mine where I discussed parts of the world where there are more than two genders went viral. I hadn't noticed that the video was gaining so much attention until my teen brother came crashing downstairs hysterically laughing, "Sis, you're a meme!!" Great. Just what I always wanted! On a regular basis, people still email me essays on why they feel there are only two genders. And actually, I quite enjoy reading them. It's interesting to hear how different people think about gender.

For those who see gender as the same thing as sex, one will conclude that there are, basically, only two genders and that this entire conversation isn't really necessary. However, lived experiences; the available research in biology, psychology, neurology, and anthropology; as well as a brief look at other parts of the world paint a more complicated picture of gender. In this section, we'll wade in and explore.

> **IN THIS CHAPTER WE'LL DISCUSS**
> ───♡───
> What is gender, anyway?
> Gender dysphoria
> Transitioning
> Supporting transgender loved ones

what is gender, anyway?

LET'S START WITH SOME BASIC DEFINITIONS. According to the American Psychological Association, "gender refers to the attitudes, feelings, and behaviors that a given culture associates with a person's biological sex." That is to say, gender is the way a person's sex is interpreted and understood in our social world. In the sex-edusphere, we have a popular saying: "Sex is between your legs, and gender is between your ears." Sex and gender refer to two different aspects of the self. Sex is physical and refers to body parts and our genes (see also chapter 1: "Your Genitals"). Gender, on the other hand, is not physical; it is the cultural and psychological facets of the sex. Gender is how I'm expected to behave in my culture because I am female. Gender is the clothes I'm expected to wear, the hobbies I'm supposed to enjoy, the careers I am supposed to pursue—because of my genitals. For some, gender is part of how we see ourselves within our culture. While sex and gender are different, they intertwine to inform our sexual identities.

Gender can be broken down into three basic pieces:
- **Gender roles:** how we're expected to behave based on our perceived sex
- **Gender expression:** how we express our gender to others
- **Gender identity:** how we see ourselves

Gender Roles

Gender roles are the behaviors, attitudes, and personality traits we are expected to have based on our perceived sex. If you look female, you are expected to be feminine. If you look male, you're expected to be masculine. Here's a nonexhaustive list of what "feminine" and "masculine" are typically thought to mean in American society:

Traditional Gender Roles

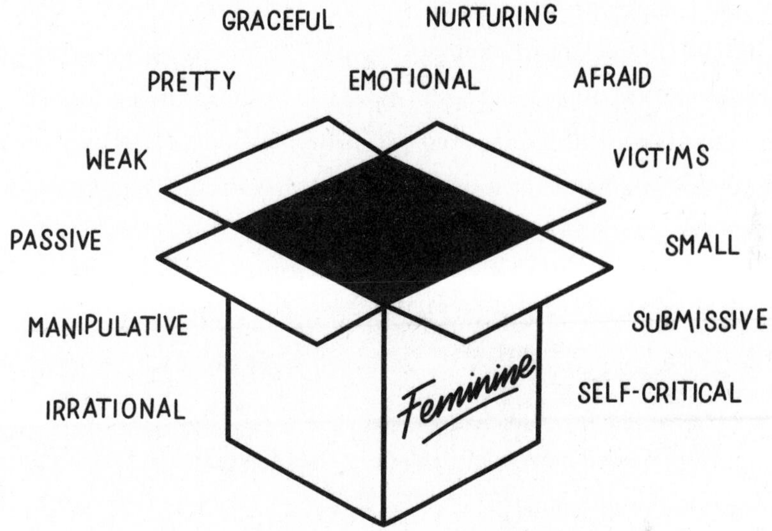

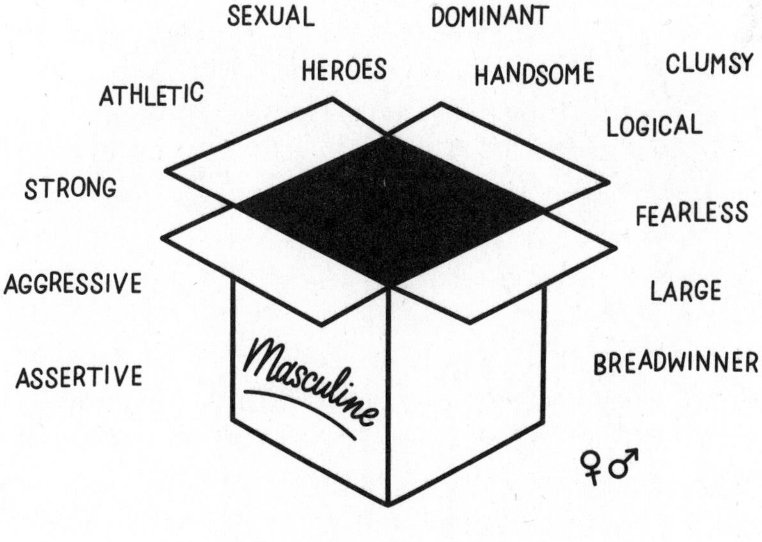

GRACEFUL   NURTURING

PRETTY   EMOTIONAL   AFRAID

WEAK   VICTIMS

PASSIVE   SMALL

MANIPULATIVE   SUBMISSIVE

IRRATIONAL   *Feminine*   SELF-CRITICAL

SEXUAL   DOMINANT

HEROES   HANDSOME   CLUMSY

ATHLETIC   LOGICAL

STRONG   FEARLESS

AGGRESSIVE   LARGE

ASSERTIVE   *Masculine*   BREADWINNER

If you take a look around, messages about who men and women are supposed to be are pretty much everywhere. They are found at home, work, school, church, and in the media. When we behave in ways that affirm our gender roles, we gain social approval. But should we break the rules, there are often social consequences. A woman who chooses not to have children is selfish and cold-hearted; a man who is soft spoken and sensitive is a "pussy."

It's all silly, of course. People are more than a list of masculine or feminine traits based on what's in their pants; we are individuals, with individual personalities and traits. In reality, nobody conforms to their gender role 100% of the time, and we all have traits from both lists. There are plenty of rough-'n'-tumble girls who love trucks and baseball, as well as boys who love to play dress-up or do ballet. As adults, there are assertive boss-ladies who run a tight ship, and gentle dads who are committed to raising strong, compassionate kids. Exceptions to traditional gender roles are everywhere—but their grip on us runs deep. All of us will experience the pressure of gender role expectations at one point or another.

Life is hard enough as it is without having to follow a list of arbitrary rules. So . . . can we not? People should be free to be who they are, regardless of their sex. There's no need to shame, blame, or freak out if someone breaks gender roles. People are people, not "ladylike" or "manly" gender robots. It's just not a big deal. Women and men can be whoever and whatever they want to be, regardless of their sex. Just do you!

Gender Expression

Gender expression refers to how people communicate their gender to those around them. Gender expression may match a person's gender role, or not. Gender expression may be physical stuff, like hairstyle, makeup, nail polish, clothing choice, or accessories. But it can also go beyond physical appearance and encompass masculine or feminine social expectations regarding manner of speaking, walking, talking, or even how we sit. There are a variety of terms to describe gender expression, such as femme, butch, or androgynous.

Gender expression is slightly different from gender roles and gender identity. How someone dresses doesn't necessarily indicate their gender. A man who enjoys wearing nail polish is still a man, a woman who likes to wear a suit and tie is still a woman—that's the beauty of gender expression.

One of America's most visible groups pushing the boundaries of gender expression are drag queens. A "drag queen" is usually a man dressing up as an extreme caricature of a woman or femininity. On the flip side, drag kings are (usually) women who dress up as men. Similar to drag, some people prefer to wear clothing that is different than their gender role. This is called cross-dressing. People cross-dress for a variety of reasons. For some, it's a practical matter. I mean, a flowy dress, with its convenient genital breezes, can be very comfortable on a warm day. Some folks might cross-dress to explore their gender identity.

Others like glam and fashion and enjoy dressing up. Some might even find it erotic. Either way, it isn't a big deal. (Noticing a theme here?) They're just clothes; it's just nail polish; it's just makeup. Whatever.

Gender Identity

While gender roles refer to behaviors that are expected in our social world, gender identity blossoms from within. Gender identity refers to how we perceive and experience our own gender. Psychologists are still researching the nature of gender identity, but there are a few things that we know: it's normal for children to become aware of their gender at an early age, a child's understanding of their gender sometimes shifts during puberty, and gender identity is likely informed by both biology (nature) and environment or culture (nurture).

When a person's gender matches their birth sex, they are *cisgender*, or cis for short. *Cis* is Latin for "on this side of."

- Cisgender woman: Born female ➤ and is a woman!
- Cisgender man: Born male ➤ and is a man!

But sometimes, a person's gender identity simply doesn't match the one that is expected because of their sex. *Trans* is Latin for "on the other side of." People who are *transgender* experience incongruence between their sex and gender. Put simply:

- Transgender woman: Born male ➤ and is a woman!
- Transgender man: Born female ➤ and is a man!

♡ Folks who fall under the transgender umbrella include:

GENDER FLUID

GENDER EXPANSIVE

GENDERQUEER

PEOPLE WHO TRANSITION THEIR SEX

NONBINARY GENDERS
(AGENDER, BIGENDER)

3RD GENDERS
(TWO-SPIRIT, HIJRA, ETC.)

Population surveys by the Williams Institute at UCLA found that .6% of adults in the United States are transgender. While .6% might not sound like a lot, that's still at least 1.4 million people in the USA alone! And the true number may be even higher—the number really varies by area (for instance, .3% of people in North Dakota describe themselves as transgender while 2.8% of people in DC are), as well as age (younger people are more likely to be transgender). These differences may be related to how accepting a given area or age group is toward people who are transgender. In a less accepting environment, we would expect people to be less open about it.

Our understanding of what it means to be transgender has evolved and expanded over time. On what it means to be transgender, Dr. Julia Serano, biologist and transgender woman, notes that it is, at its heart, about gender nonconformity:

> *The word transgender historically refers to people who defy societal expectations regarding gender. Trans activists of the 1990s who championed the term left it purposely open-ended—it may refer to transsexuals (i.e., people who transition, who I'll get to in a minute), people who identify outside of the gender binary, crossdressers (i.e., people who identify with their birth-assigned gender, but sometimes dress and/or express themselves as the other gender), people whose gender expression is non-conforming (e.g., feminine men, masculine women, people who are androgynous, etc.), and possibly others. Not everyone who falls under this umbrella will self-identify as "transgender," but are all viewed by society as defying gender norms in some significant way.*
> *—Detransition, Desistance, and Disinformation: A Guide for Understanding Transgender Children Debates, Medium 2016*

Another lesser-talked-about part of the transgender umbrella is nonbinary gender identities. People who are nonbinary describe their gender as neither man nor woman. They may identify with some or no aspects of masculinity or femininity, or may move fluidly between them. Some nonbinary people come from a culture where there are more than two socially acknowledged genders. A few examples of nonbinary gender identities are genderqueer, two-spirit, and agender. Gender identity is by definition not binary (this stands in contrast to other aspects of gender—like gender roles, of which we are prescribed only two by society). It refers to the inward experience of gender, which means there are potentially as many identities as there are human beings.

More than Two Genders Around the World

In the West, most people conceptualize gender in terms of two: there are men, and there are women. But in other parts of the world, different cultures have conceptualized gender in terms of three or more. These cultures offer interesting insights into the nature of gender.

TWO-SPIRIT (NORTH AMERICA)

The native two-spirit are thought of as a third or fourth gender and have a well-documented history in at least 150 Native American tribes. Two-spirits carry both male and female spirit. They are revered by their tribe and respected as critical components of tribal culture. "Two-spirit" is an umbrella term, and various tribes may use more specific terms. For instance, the Navaho use the term *nàdleehé* while the Sioux refer to two-spirits as *winkte*.

NORTH AMERICA

MAHU (HAWAII)

The Hawaiian mahu are an ancient and revered third gender. Hina Wong-Kalu, an outspoken activist for gender diversity and inclusion in Hawaiian culture, explains that the mahu are individuals who straddle "somewhere in the middle of the male and female binary. It does not define their sexual preference or gender expression because gender roles, gender expressions, and sexual relationships have all been severely influenced by the changing times. It is dynamic. It is like life."

BISSU (SULAWESI)

On the island of Sulawesi in Indonesia, the Bugis acknowledge three sexes (male, female, and intersex) and four genders (man, woman, calabai, calalai). They also acknowledge one more identity that somewhat transcends gender: the bissu. To be bissu is to be both intersex and all genders at once. Bissu is a spiritual gender; because they are simultaneously male, female, man, and woman, they can act as mediators between humans and spirits.

SULAWESI, INDONESIA

INDIA
MADAGASCAR

SEKRATA (MADAGASCAR)

The sekrata of Madagascar are males who are thought to have a feminine appearance and are thusly raised as girls. Over time, the sekrata learn how to speak with a woman's voice and are treated as entirely female. The Sakalavas are entirely accepting of their sekrata and believe that supernatural forces protect them from those who try to do them harm.

HIJRA (INDIA)

India is the largest modern society with more than two genders, and Hijra is the most common of the third gender identities there. Hijra are typically born male but are seen as neither men nor women. Hijra are revered for their spirituality, and are devotees of the Indian mother goddess Buhuchara Mata. Other genders include kinnar, aravani, shiv-shakti, and kothi.

EXPLORING GENDER IDENTITY

by Robert Louie

I didn't learn what transgender was until after high school. I had heard the term floating around, but in the days before social media, it was a much more abstract concept. I didn't understand that transitioning was an option for people outside of sensationalized stories on daytime television. In the long run, not knowing everything about gender identity ended up being an advantage. It allowed me to explore my gender at a slower pace, alongside the rest of my identity. I was driven to explore by the feeling that there had always been some part of me that I couldn't convey properly to the world—at least not until people really got to know me. I had a lot of freedom to experiment and express myself in different ways. My goal wasn't to figure out whether or not I'm trans; it was to figure out what felt most comfortable to me.

If you are questioning your gender identity, don't be afraid to experiment! It may be minor at first, and in private. In my childhood, though wearing dresses was fun, I identified with being male, with male characters, and somehow I felt male. I had the experience of being lucky enough to have friends and family who accepted me as a tomboy throughout my life. Since I normally wore "boy clothes," I tried out a more feminine gender expression in my junior year of high school, to experiment with gender. It didn't last long, maybe a few weeks or a month, but it was really helpful to me. During that time, I made new friends who loved and accepted me for who I was—a gay tomboy. One afternoon while we were out shopping, I spotted a button-up dress that was styled like a long dress shirt. I recalled a similar dress looking very attractive on a previous girlfriend, so I thought I'd try it on. I didn't tell anyone and sneaked off to the dressing room. After switching my cargo pants and T-shirt for the dress, I looked in the mirror. I could not have been more shocked. I felt like a man, and now in a dress. The mirror affirmed a feeling I'd always felt . . . and I'm not sure if I expected that. While gender norms and how I felt deep inside are different things, it was an insightful moment.

At the time, I didn't understand what this experience meant. I didn't see a different person in the mirror. I didn't suddenly feel more like a girl or young woman just because I dressed more feminine. I gave it an earnest try, and I think there's a lot of satisfaction in that—out of love for myself and also out of curiosity. I went on to try wearing women's clothes again a few times. I got compliments from friends who said they didn't recognize me on the street as they passed or while admiring me at the sandwich shop from a distance. I felt pretty cool in these duds, but I still felt oddly out of place. Throughout all of this, my friends were supportive and really didn't make a big deal out of it. I quickly went back to my normal clothes. This is just one of the many moments that helped me find my comfort zone. There's a lot you can learn from just trying.

As you experiment, I'd suggest not worrying about labels. The external world will label you every day of your life and there are a lot of labels that will pass you by on your journey being trans. It's easy to get caught up in it; but to me, it's not about figuring out which label fits; it's about the adventure of self-discovery. Just try to be your happiest self. As Laci discussed quite a bit, it's important to find a supportive community on your journey. It doesn't have to be a big community or even more than a friend or two, but be sure to have people around you that care for you and support you.

One of the first ways I decided to transition was with my name. On the old anime *Cowboy Bebop*, there was a young hacker girl who went by the name of Ed. When I found this show, it rocked my world and inspired me to pick a boy's name for myself. I chose Bob because it was funny enough to pass off as a joke and kind of matched the simplicity of the name Ed. In high school, I asked some teachers to call me by the name. I felt out which teachers were cool enough to not give me a hard time, and the ones I did ask usually only had one earnest question: are you serious? I assured them it wasn't a prank on them, and it was usually kosher after that. By high school, everyone knew that I went by Bob, and some people asked if I was going to change my name legally. I usually replied, "Nah, I don't think so." Being trans never came up, and everyone went with it. I'm sure there were some detractors at school, but it didn't matter because my friends knew it as my name and always called me by it. The name helped my friends understand how I saw myself, and why all the caricatures I drew of myself were of a boy. On the internet, it was easier to be myself. User names and screen names made it easy to present myself how I wanted to. I always registered myself as male, and had male avatars. That was a great time in my life. The internet and games offered me a safe space to explore, to be myself, and to feel seen and heard for who I am. It was a big part of my journey.

I think one of the most important things you can do for yourself is to remember to make loving decisions for yourself on your journey. There's a part of me that makes reckless decisions—usually spurred by some kind of passion. That energy is useful and adds a dash of bravery I need sometimes, but I also try to listen to the part of myself that makes good choices. I know for me growing up, I did have a lot of turbulent feelings inside, separate from gender-related identity issues. I still don't fully understand why. Perhaps it's just being young and trying to grow into a person. It took a lot of learning to be comfortable with myself and, eventually, to love myself.

From that I learned my own boundaries and learned to make smart choices. It can be tough.

Sometimes we want a thing or we have strong emotions, but inside there's always a part of us that knows what the right thing to do is. Be kind to yourself. Don't be too hard on yourself. If you are being hard on yourself, use that energy you feel and redirect it toward positive action.

Positive action doesn't have to be big, and smart choices don't have to be grand. I know you know what's right, so follow your heart, trust yourself, and love yourself.

gender dysphoria ⚠️

WE'VE COME A LONG WAY IN our understanding of gender non-conformity. In the not-so-distant past, being transgender was regarded as a mental illness. In the media, and even the medical establishment itself, transgender people were characterized by psychosis and criminality. Today, experts agree that *being transgender is not a mental disorder.* In fact, most transgender folks are perfectly healthy and lead happy, fulfilling lives!

Unfortunately, some transgender people struggle with gender dysphoria. Gender dysphoria stems from incongruence between the person's anatomic sex and internal sense of gender. This incongruence can cause such a high level of distress that it disrupts functioning in daily life. It is often accompanied by severe distress, anxiety, emptiness, depression, and suicidal thoughts. The difference between transgender people who transition their sex and those who don't is typically the presence (or absence) of gender dysphoria.

Despite panicked cries that gender dysphoria is some kind of ~new, made-up Tumblr illness~ (a claim I occasionally see online), gender dysphoria is nothing new. It has been a subject of psychological research since the 1960s. Today, the *Diagnostic and Statistical Manual of Mental Disorders*, fifth edition, abbreviated as DSM-5, estimates that about 4 in every 100,000 people has gender dysphoria. It is also estimated that those born male are more likely to experience gender dysphoria—about three times more likely than those born female.

Hormones are now one of the most common treatments for gender dysphoria, alongside working with a therapist to transition to living full-time as one's true gender. But sometimes, these treatments are not enough. Some experts argue that gender dysphoria is inflamed by the near-constant stress of living in a culture where being transgender is stigmatized. This stigma likely contributes to a high rate of suicide attempts: 41% (versus 4.6% for the general population). Other risk factors are associated with even higher rates:

Transgender risk factors	% that attempt suicide
Age 18 to 24	45%
Rejected by family	57%
Bullied at school	50 to 54%
Discrimination or harassment at work	50 to 59%
Disrespected or harassed by law enforcement	57 to 61%
Doctor refused to treat them	60%
Disabilities	65%
Suffered physical or sexual violence at school	63 to 78%
Experienced homelessness	69%

Clearly, given the number of challenges for trans folks brought on by other people —rejection, bullying, and harassment—our society has largely not fulfilled its responsibility to ensure the safety and rights of people who are transgender. Social and political improvements are happening, but it's not nearly enough considering the depth of the problem.

transitioning

SOME TRANSGENDER FOLKS WITH GENDER DYSPHORIA decide to transition their sex to help them live their life as their true gender. There are three basic ways to transition: socially, physically, and legally. Some people choose to do one, two, all three, or none at all. It's really important to remember that there is no "right" or "wrong" way to transition, and doing so doesn't make anyone "more" or "less" of a particular gender. It's also perfectly okay *not* to transition or to wait awhile! It's not a decision anyone should feel rushed or pressured into or out of—not by friends, family, therapists, or meanies online.

Social Transitioning and Coming Out

One of the most common forms of transition is socially. That might include coming out, using your proper pronouns, changing your name, or changing your gender expression. Waiting for the perfect time to transition is a fool's errand, but there are some circumstances that can make it easier. Because transitioning can be more emotionally demanding toward the beginning, it's helpful to come into the process in the best headspace you can. That might mean resolving major issues in your life demanding your attention first. It might mean tending to your relationships, or focusing on self-care. Reflect on what you feel and what you need. If you can, enlist a therapist to offer you support and guidance. Identify a few people in your life who you trust and can confide in. This might include a partner, a friend, a sibling, a therapist, a school counselor, a trusted teacher, or a parent. If you are having trouble finding support, look up your nearest LGBT organizations. These organizations may be local nonprofits, or student groups run through a local high school or college. Folks at these organizations can help connect you to community. You can also seek out support in online communities! I'm a pretty big fan of those, myself.

In your own time and on your own terms, initiate conversations with loved ones. Your initial conversations might involve answering their questions, and sometimes those can be unintentionally insensitive or invalidating. Let them know gently and firmly if that is the case, and be clear about how they can support you. It can be helpful to share resources you like (websites, pictures, videos, books, news articles) that you think will help them understand.

People in your life may respond with an array of reactions, some of which may surprise you. Some folks who have transitioned were relieved to find their parents were actually completely cool about it! Others were met with unexpected anger, confusion, or shock. In the unfortunate event that things get very heated, take a step back and take care of yourself first. Anger makes it hard for people to truly listen to each other. It helps me to try to remember that unaccepting responses are typically rooted in fear. Your family may not properly know how to support you through this. They may be genuinely worried about you, even if, in reality, their response makes things worse. Your mom or dad may feel like they've failed as a parent. They may worry that this will make your life harder. They may think the internet brainwashed you. They may only know about being transgender from sensationalized shows like *Maury* and *Jerry Springer.* They may be religious and worry about what this means for your spiritual fate. If a parent or family member is having a hard time processing, it may be helpful for them to see a counselor too.

Through it all, remember that you are not alone. If things get rockier than you can manage, consider contacting one of the crisis lines listed in the resource section. Reach out for support when you need help! It's the most important step you can take to keep yourself healthy.

Medical Transitioning

In addition to transitioning socially, some transgender people transition their sex with medical interventions like hormones, surgery, or both. The decision to transition medically is one that should be made with the help of a healthcare provider and therapist. The benefit of medical transitioning is that it can help bring the physical self and internal self closer together, making the day-to-day challenges of gender dysphoria more manageable.

Your healthcare provider will play a big role in the process of physical transition, and you'll have an ongoing relationship with them for check-ups. Finding a healthcare provider that you trust and is trans-friendly can make a huge difference! If you have the privilege to do so, take some time to find a doctor that you have good communication with, who is knowledgeable about transitioning, and who will be supportive on your journey.

In conjunction with talk therapy, hormones are one of the most common treatments for gender dysphoria. Let's talk a little bit about how it works, should you and your doctor decide it's right for you. Hormone therapy can feminize or masculinize your physical appearance by altering things like fat distribution, muscle mass, and body hair. It's kind of like a second puberty. Different people have different responses to it, and while mild changes usually happen in the first few months, it can take two to six years to produce the full effects. Unfortunately, taking higher doses of hormones than prescribed will not speed up the process, and can actually slow things down! So follow your provider's advice.

For those transitioning to female, there are three main feminizing treatments: (1) estrogen, (2) androgen-suppressing medications, and (3) progestins. They can be delivered with a pill, injection, skin patch, or gel.

ESTROGEN!

Basics	Estrogen is the main hormone involved in feminization. Pills and injections are the most common method, but for people who are at risk of blood clots or heart problems, skin patches and gels are safer forms. There are lots of different formulations of estrogen, but the most common and safest form is called 17-beta-estradiol. Conjugated estrogen and ethinyl estradiol are generally not used because studies have linked them to health problems in cisgender women.
First 6 months	Decreased muscle mass, increased body fat, fat redistribution toward hips and breasts, lower sex drive, softer erection, fewer spontaneous erections, decreased sperm count/fertility*, less ejaculatory fluid
1+ years	Breast growth*, nipple growth*, less facial and body hair, slowed male pattern baldness, decreased testicular size

ANDROGEN-SUPPRESSING MEDICATIONS!

Basics	Medications that suppress androgens are typically paired up with estrogen to block the effects of testosterone. They also reduce the amount of estrogen needed to be effective, which minimizes possible health risks of high doses of estrogen. They work mostly by blocking masculinizing traits (like facial hair and male pattern baldness), but they can also promote mild feminization. The most common in this category are spironolactone and finasteride.

* = irreversible

First 6 months	Lower sex drive, softer erection, fewer spontaneous erections, decreased sperm count/fertility*, less ejaculatory fluid
1+ years	Mild breast growth*, less facial and body hair, slowed male pattern baldness
PROGESTINS!	
Basics	Progestins are the least common feminizing hormone, mostly because their effects on feminization aren't fully understood yet. They can also have some unpleasant side effects, like increased risk of depression and increased fats in the blood. My medical reviewer writes: "We do not suggest [progestins] as part of standard hormonal care for transgender women. It has been associated with excess cardiovascular and breast cancer risk in older postmenopausal women taking conjugated estrogen." Talk to your doctor to figure out what's right for you.
	* = irreversible

For those transitioning to male, testosterone (or "T" for short) is the key masculinizing hormone. It can be delivered with injection, skin patch, gel, or an implant under the skin. Pill forms of testosterone are considered less effective and may also cause liver damage—which is why they are not recommended by the medical community. The injection and skin patch are the most effective methods, but they have different pros and cons. Injection is faster, but it causes hormones to peak right at the beginning and then fade out until the next shot. This can exaggerate side effects, like irritability when it fades. Alternatively, the skin patch and gel are "slow and steady" kinds of methods. The effects are more even, but it takes a little longer to see results. Some people have skin irritation from the patch.

EFFECTS OF TESTOSTERONE!	
First 6 Months	Increased body and facial hair*, thicker hair, increased muscle mass, fat redistribution toward waist, clitoral growth (1–3 cm)*, increased sex drive, vaginal dryness, acne, periods slow and stop, deepening voice*
1+ years	Facial hair, male pattern balding*, possible sterility*
	* = irreversible

Legal Transitioning

Legal transitioning in the United States basically means updating your gender and name in your legal documents, such as:

- Social Security
- Passport
- Driver's License
- Birth Certificate/Consular Report of Birth Abroad (CRBA)
- Immigration Documents/US Citizenship and Immigration Services (USCIS)

It's an important step to protect your rights, but unfortunately it can be a pain in the ass with a lot of paperwork. If it feels overwhelming, break the process into smaller pieces and take it one step at a time.

supporting transgender loved ones

WHETHER YOU'RE CISGENDER OR TRANSGENDER, non-binary, man, woman, both, or neither, we could all go a long way to support each other with a few simple actions. Here are a few ways to do so:

1 *Never Out Someone.*

Duh. If you know someone who is transgender, either because they told you directly or disclosed it in a group setting, never assume that it is safe to tell anybody outside of those settings.

2 *Ask for/Use Proper Pronouns.*

Using someone's proper pronouns is a simple way to affirm and respect fellow humans who happen to be trans. If you're unsure of someone's pronouns, no need to be shy! Just ask. Try something like, "Hi there! Can I ask your pronouns?" or "My name is Laci, and I use she/her/hers pronouns! How about you?" If you can't or would rather not ask, you can always use gender-neutral pronouns, like they/them/their. They apply to everybody. At some point, you might accidentally misgender someone. It happens. Don't beat yourself up about it; just apologize and pay more attention the next time around.

3 *Speak Up if Someone Is Being Mocked or Harassed.*

Another duh. Folks who are LGBTQ+ are disproportionately targeted for mockery and harassment. If you see this happening, say something. A simple: "Hey, that's not cool. Knock it off" or "How would you feel if someone talked about you like that?" can go a long way. If you don't feel safe to say something, get someone involved who can, like a teacher or a friend.

4 *Respect that Body Stuff Is Personal.*

Just like you probably don't want to be asked about your genitals or hormones, neither do people who are trans or gender nonconforming. If someone wants to share with you, they will! Don't ask invasive questions about personal stuff.

5 *Rights! Visibility! Education!*

It's no secret that society is a little uncomfortable with people who are transgender. We can help end stigma by increasing trans visibility in the media, politics, and the classroom. More awareness in the public helps us communicate more openly, to better understand each other, and to accept each other for who we are.

SIX

⋛° BODY IMAGE °⋚

WHEN I WAS IN HIGH SCHOOL, my relationship with my body was...pretty crap. Every morning I'd wake up and drag myself to school for another long day of near-constant insecurity over how I looked. I worried about my frizzy hair, my thunder thighs, my eyelashes that I couldn't stop picking at. I was self-conscious about my breasts, which felt too big to be my own. PE was the worst—especially swimming and dance classes—and tended to increase my body scrutiny tenfold. I tried not to compare myself to other girls, but I couldn't help it. I wasn't athletic, and gym class typically left me feeling much worse about myself rather than better.

At one point, my poor body image started to affect my relationship with food. During lunch breaks at school, I worried that people would judge me for eating. I rarely, if ever, ate much in front of other people. At the time, the only things that made me feel better for a little while were my boyfriend and my friends. Looking back, I chalk some of these insecure feelings up to the general shittiness that is being a teenager. As an adult, people are considerably less judgy than they were as teens, and things are more chill. But I also think it was harder because I cared more about what people thought of me back then.

Why should I care so much about what other people think, anyway?

This is a question I've asked myself a lot, both with regard to body image and life in general. I tend to think that caring about the opinions of others is just in our nature as humans. Humans are social creatures, and whether we like it or not, we really do need each other. Everybody needs to feel loved, accepted, wanted, listened to, all that jazz. So even as I dig in my heels and screech, "I don't care what people think!!!" the truth is . . . I do. But I'm making my peace with it. I've decided it isn't necessarily a *problem* to care what people think. The problem is in caring what irrelevant-ass people think. Also, priorities. Who cares what Random Dude on Twitter thinks about my appearance? And who decided appearance was an important thing about me to begin with?

It's just a face. It's just a sack of skin. It's just a meat suit. It's just a home for my lizard brain.

I think it's important to talk about body image on the road to sex positivity. For so many of us, how we see our body is very wrapped up in how we experience sex.

IN THIS CHAPTER LET'S CHAT ABOUT

— ♡ —

The media
Thirteen ways to improve your body image

---

the media

OF ALL THE LITTLE THINGS THAT shape our self-image, the media is probably one of the most influential. The message in the media about physical appearance is clear: conventionally attractive people are supposedly happier, more popular, more successful, and get laid more.

On Instagram, a stream of posts present filtered and carefully curated images of other people's picture-perfect lives. In YouTube videos, people sell "fit teas" that will magically make you lose weight and find happiness. In TV shows and movies, the conventionally attractive characters are usually beloved, cool, funny, and a gamut of other positive traits. Meanwhile, characters who are considered less attractive often play the bad guy, or the lovable but stupid "fat friend."

Here's what the media's obsession with appearance looks like in numbers:

- In the movies, 58% of female characters had comments made about their looks. Male characters' appearances are discussed about 24% of the time.

- One in every three articles (37%) in women's magazines focus on a woman's appearance.

- While 56% of TV commercials aimed at girls used beauty to sell a product, 3% of television commercials aimed at men did the same.

  —*Teen Health and the Media, the University of Washington*

Another media source that is relevant to body image, especially during sex, is porn. Porn, especially the free access variety that is easily accessible online, presents a nearly endless wonderland of sexual imagery. Porn star bodies are at times cartoonish in their proportions. Asses, breasts, and muscles are big, while waists and labia are small. Porn stars have perfect skin, perfect breasts, and somehow manage not to have stomach rolls even in contorted positions. There's very little about professional porn that's real—strategic camera angles, airbrushing, and plastic surgery are all common in the industry.

The effects of our media environment are real. They create an atmosphere where self-monitoring is considered normal and desirable.

And it starts young; by age nine, many girls have already learned that if they are to be valued and worthy of love, they must look a certain way and take up as little space as possible. A whopping 40% of nine-year-old girls have already tried to lose weight. By age seventeen, 78% of girls say they dislike their body. To measure up, some undergo dangerous weight-loss regimes. Cosmetic surgeries that can compromise sexual pleasure, like labiaplasty or breast augmentation, are on the rise. One in twenty girls and one in thirty boys develop an eating disorder. These problems have complex causes, but they are all related in the context of our image-conscious culture.

Sexually, body image struggles can also present a number of challenges in the bedroom:

- Difficulty relaxing and being in the moment
- Anxiety that your partner will find you gross or unattractive
- Lower sex drive on bad body image days
- Anxiety about sexual experimentation
- Anxiety about having the lights on

If you've experienced any of this junk before, welcome! The good news is that self-image can improve with a little work, and tends to improve on its own as we age. Studies show that women's body image tends to be at its highest when we are in our forties. So hey, even when things are shit . . . better days lie ahead.

Eating Disorder Warning Signs ⚠

In some cases, body image struggles go beyond a little anxiety and begin to seriously affect physical and mental health. Eating disorders can be dangerous and should be taken seriously. Here are some warning signs from the National Eating Disorders Association:

1. Exercising excessively (several hours a day)
2. Extreme calorie cutting (under 1,000 calories/day)
3. Bingeing or hoarding food
4. Constant exhaustion
5. Withdrawal from friends or family
6. Refusing to eat, cooking meals for others but not for self
7. Abuse of laxatives, drugs, or appetite suppressants (like cocaine or Adderall)
8. Extreme mood swings, depression, or suicidal thoughts

If you think you or somebody you know might be struggling with an eating disorder, reach out for outside help. The sooner, the better. You can speak to a parent, school counselor, nurse or doctor, or another person you trust that can offer guidance. You can also Google hotlines and resources in your area. National organizations like the National Eating Disorders Association (1-800-931-2237) or the National Suicide Prevention Lifeline (1-800-273-8255) can offer help and direction in times of crisis. Taking care of yourself is an act rooted in love and strength. There is no shame in reaching out for help when you need it.

thirteen ways to improve your body image

TO ME, BODY IMAGE IS ABOUT the relationship my mind has with my body. Positive body image is a relationship that is nurturing and loving, or neutral most of the time. Negative body image is one with a lot of self-judgment, scolding, and shame. If you find yourself feeling like your body is your enemy sometimes, here are thirteen exercises that helped me develop a better relationship with mine.

1 *Spend More Time Alone Naked.*

I have a complicated relationship with my nakedness. On one hand, being naked is a special kind of liberating. There's nothing like it; every flap and jiggle can fly free in the wind. But it also sends me into an uncomfortable hyperawareness about how my body looks and moves; whether I'm taking a shower, changing my clothes, or stripping down with a partner, the feeling is always the same. It's like my eyes go from watching the world around me to watching and scrutinizing myself. It's more pronounced in sexual situations. Nonsexual nudity during my alone time has challenged me to confront and reflect on my discomforts. Getting more familiar with my nakedness has helped me accept how my body looks, how it moves, and how it feels without coverings.

2 *Practice Gratitude, Every Day.*

The science is clear: taking time out of the day to reflect and be grateful is good for your health. It improves physical and emotional well-being, sleep quality, and even resilience in times of struggle. That's right: a simple attitude of gratitude builds emotional strength. Kind of amazing, right? Gratitude is fairly easy to practice, too. Just take a couple seconds out of every day to feel or express gratitude for some aspect of your body.

3 *Ditch the Habit of Negative Self-talk.*

Another powerful exercise that is backed by some research is positive self-talk. When you're having self-critical thoughts, try to replace them with healthier thoughts as they come up. Those thoughts might pivot toward what you do like about your body, appreciation, forgiveness, or acceptance. Make sure to do it often enough to really break the negative habit. The more you practice, the more effortless those kinder thoughts should become.

4 *Self-care.*

One way to show gratitude toward your body is to nurture it, rather than criticize or punish it. I don't need to tell you that it's important to eat right and exercise. And there's more to self-care than that. Taking care of your body means doing things that make you feel GOOD and ALIVE. That might mean going dancing to let it all out, or hiking on the weekend to get some peace and quiet, or making sure to get enough sleep at night. When it comes to self-care, it helps me to try to make one small healthy change at a time. Avoid sabotaging your efforts with a massive to-do list full of dramatic changes right up front. Small changes add up to big rewards over time.

5 Shake Up Your Beauty Routines Once in a While.

Another exercise that has been positive for me is shaking up my routines. I used to shave every week, wore makeup most days, spent time doing my hair and so on—which is A-okay. It was also helpful to not do those things sometimes, to break the rules I was imposing on myself to get comfortable with my appearance in lots of states: from all dolled up, to going au naturel, to my true form as a ragamuffin. I eventually stopped shaving my legs and armpits regularly ('cept when it's sweaty out), simply because I realized it wasn't necessary and it cost money and time that I didn't personally wish to spend on it. Making time to change my routines up allowed me to explore what truly made me feel my best.

6 Ditch the Scale for a While.

No tool embodies the complicated relationship between my health and body image more than the bathroom scale. I used to keep a scale around to monitor my weight, but at some point I found it had a huge effect on my mood. If the scale ever ticked up, I felt depressed for the rest of the day, if not the week. If the scale ticked down, it was a goooood day. Inevitable fluctuations in my weight around my period became a point of preoccupation and dread. So a couple years ago, I decided to ditch the scale for a while. Instead, I tried to pay closer attention to how my body felt after certain foods, drinks, and activities. I found that taking these cues from my body helped me make healthier choices, and all without letting a number determine how I would feel about myself for the day.

7 Nurture Your Skills and Your Community.

Teaching yourself new skills or dedicating time to developing your talents is a holistic way to naturally build confidence and improve your self-image. It also has practical benefits: get good at shit and help other people. Reflect on what you love or what you're good at—and get involved! If you can't think of anything (and even if you can), seeking out volunteer opportunities is a great way to give back and build a positive community.

8 *Be a Body-positive Friend (or Parent, Sibling, Healthcare Provider, etc.).*

Even if you're having a bad body image day and can't be loving toward yourself, practice being loving toward others. This is especially important when it comes to how parents regard their children, who are in a delicate developmental period. Avoid projecting your own insecurities onto the people in your life, and practice quieting judgmental thoughts and words toward others.

9 *Be a Body-positive Lover.*

If your partner has some body image struggs, romantic relationships can be a reprieve. Open communication will make it easier to talk to you about it if they want to. Since body image is pretty personal, they may not want to, and that's okay too. Don't try to fix a partner who has negative self-image issues. Just keep on loving their body as you always have. Gentle touch of the body (before/after sex, or nonsexually) and words of affirmation can help a struggling partner feel more comfortable and sexy with you.

10 *Remember Who Your Body Belongs To.*

When I was twenty, a guy I had been dating briefly asked me if I'd considered getting a boob job. "They're a good size," he said, looking up at me while I mounted him in my tiny college apartment. "But, they're just so heavy. Maybe you could get them lifted up higher? You would have literally a perfect body then." I don't remember what I said in response, but I remember how I felt: a bit shocked, and devastated. My discomfort being around him had already been increasing before his comment, and in that moment I realized what was right in front of me: this is not a kind or worthy dude. I dumped him the next time I saw him.

Here's my advice: Never stay with someone who treats your body like a project or talks about it in degrading ways. Screw anyone (not literally) who thinks your body exists for their pleasure, and not yours. My breasts, thighs, hips, belly, and booty do not belong to the world; they belong to me.

11 Brush Up on Your Media Literacy.

In today's world of lightning-speed news cycles and social media bombardment into our lives, media literacy is everything. Being media-literate means knowing how to evaluate and think critically about complex messages that are conveyed in the media. For instance:

- Who is this media or message targeting?
- What techniques are used to persuade me of a particular message?
- What does the maker of the media want me to believe or do?
- What aspects of this media might be biased? Toward what or whom?
- Is there anything being left out of the picture or story?
- How does this media make me feel about myself or others?

And when it comes to body image:

- What kind of body types, hair types, skin colors, and facial features are applauded in the media you consume? Who is left out or missing?
- How are beauty standards applied differently based on gender, race, class, or ability?

While it's definitely impossible to render ourselves immune to the negative influences of certain media, practicing critical thinking helps mitigate its effects.

12 Support Body-positive Media.

Thanks to the internet, it is now easier to supplement our media diet with healthier messages. Bloggers, YouTubers, Instagrammers, and online magazines are all creating more body-positive content these days. Body-inclusive shops and products are also popping up online, better serving a range of people who may not have the best luck at department stores. (My favorite finds are DD+ bras and thigh bands that help prevent chafing.) Body-positive media creates a more positive mindset without much effort. On the flip side, if you find yourself feeling worse with certain types of media—cut that media out. Unfollow the Instagram account or cancel your subscription to the magazine. Good vibes only.

13 Don't Beat Yourself Up.

It bears repeating that it's OKAY to have bad body image days, or weeks, or months, or years. It's OKAY to hate this thing, or that. It's OKAY to want to change parts of your body. The journey toward better body image shouldn't be approached as another unreachable goal in the pursuit of perfection. It's a lifelong practice, a commitment to nurturing yourself even when the world is a bit shit. Be kind to yourself, be gentle, be curious, and keep moving forward.

If I could tell myself only one thing when I was younger, it would be: you are enough.

SEVEN

⇒∘ MASTURBATION AND ORGASM ∘⇐

ROLL UP YOUR SLEEVES, BECAUSE IT'S about to get sexy.

More often than not, our very first sexual experience is with our very own hands. I'm referring, of course, to good ol'-fashioned masturbation. In America, masturbation is still a pretty stigmatized practice. The roots of our negativity toward masturbation run deep, right down to the word itself. The root of the word "masturbation" means to "defile with the hand." DEFILE! As in, desecrating yourself. As in, damaging yourself! I mean, come on. There's nothing damaging about a nice little orgasm with yourself before bed.

As it turns out, antimasturbation sentiment was a large part of the reason that circumcision became so popular in America in the early 1900s. To stop the supposed evils of masturbation, circumcision was introduced as a cure. In his famous work *Plain Facts for Old and Young*, John Harvey Kellogg (the guy who invented cornflakes) pushed for circumcision—without anesthetic. Because he was apparently a lunatic. Various contraptions were invented to stop children from touching their genitals.

Kellogg also suggested that females who masturbate should have pure carbolic acid applied to their clitoris, to burn and blister it, making them unable to orgasm. So . . . uhhh, yeah. Today, we no longer burn people's clitorises off for masturbating (#progress) but we're still a little weird about it. In this chapter, we'll explore various aspects of masturbation and orgasm.

Ready? Let's gooooo.

IN THIS CHAPTER LET'S CHAT ABOUT

Self-pleasure
Ask Laci: On self-pleasure
The big O
Male multiple orgasms
Ask Laci: On orgasms

---

self-pleasure

THE BEST PART OF MASTURBATION IS that it is completely safe. No STIs. No pregnancy. Also fewer feelings and less emotional business to work through with another partner. It's also a completely normal instinct. Most of us begin masturbating in childhood.

Child Sexual Development and Masturbation

Sexuality and child development experts universally regard masturbation as a healthy and normal behavior. It's so normal, in fact, that fetuses have been captured masturbating in the womb before they're even born. Most infants discover their genitals before they are one year old, perhaps during a diaper change or while taking a bath. By age five, many children rub their genitals on a regular basis. They may rub themselves, or rub their genitals up on other objects (like stuffed animals or sofas). Masturbating may leave them flushed in the face and out of breath. Don't freak out. It's normal. They've just made a very basic realization: "Hey! That feels pretty good." There's typically nothing to worry about, unless it is interfering with their well-being, or it seems to be distressing them. If a child's behavior has you concerned, consider talking to a nurse, doctor, or child psychologist about it. But in general, keep it cool.

It's also normal for kids to be curious and want to "play doctor" to find answers to their questions about their bodies. So long as they aren't touching other kids without permission, there's no cause for alarm. These are some of the first experiences kids have with their own sexuality. Parent overreactions and shaming teach kids to feel embarrassed about it for no reason. It also tells the kid loud and clear that they can't talk about sexuality with their parents. Ideally, a sex-positive parent's role is to guide their kid toward healthy behavior and to create a nonjudgmental atmosphere so kids feel safe asking questions and being open about sexuality issues.

Why Masturbation Is G-R-E-A-T

Contrary to the memes, God probably doesn't kill a kitten every time you masturbate. In fact, there are some pretty substantial perks to masturbating. My early experiences with self-pleasure were some of the most transformative experiences I've had with my own sexuality. Self-pleasure helped me get comfortable with my body and learn what feels good; it also helped me figure out how to have an orgasm.

SELF-PLEASURE IS . . .
NORMAL. YEPS.

Safe. In a relationship, masturbating together (a.k.a. mutual masturbation) is a way to be sexual without the risks of infection or pregnancy. Observing can also help folks learn what feels nice for their partner, if you're comfortable with that sort of thing.

Pleasurable. Similar to kissing, masturbation unleashes a cocktail of neurotransmitters. Like serotonin, which boosts your mood. Or oxytocin, which promotes relaxation and bonding. Or prolactin, which helps you feel sexually satisfied and sleepy.

Healthy. Masturbation (or more frequent ejaculation) has been linked to a reduced risk of prostate cancer.

Self-directed. Self-pleasure puts you in the driver's seat, and you can drive wherever your little heart desires. During self-pleasure, everything that happens sexually is on your own terms. This is why therapists will sometimes suggest it as an exercise for those recovering from rape, sexual assault, and other forms of sexual trauma.

Self-pleasure can also help you get comfortable with your body. If you feel awkward and embarrassed about sexual pleasure, doing it on your own is one way to dip your toes in the water.

It can relieve sexual tension. I dunno about you, but it helps me calm the heck down and focus sometimes. It's especially useful before a hot date, so I can keep my head on straight.

It can teach you what feels pleasurable. By experimenting on your own, you can figure out what type of touch feels good and what doesn't. Self-pleasure is an opportunity to learn about and listen to your body, without the distractions of another person. If you are still figuring out how to orgasm, self-pleasure offers time to experiment and explore without pressure to perform. And by knowing what feels good, it is easier to communicate that to a partner.

THAT SAID, IT'S OKAY NOT TO MASTURBATE. Maybe it's not your thing, it stresses you out, you don't have a very high libido—whatever the case. There's nothing unsafe or unhealthy about not masturbating—just do you!

How to Have a Healthy Relationship with Porn

At the end of each year, massive porn distribution site PornHub releases their "Year in Review" detailing their website's analytics. During the years of 2015 and 2016, they reported that over 9 billion hours of porn was consumed on their website. When you do the math, that translates to over *one million years* that humans spent watching porn—in just two years, on just one of the thousands of porn websites online. So, uh . . . that's pretty crazy.

If you masturbate to pornography, it's important to maintain a healthy relationship with it. Scientists are still researching how pornography affects us, so we don't have a ton of objective (ahem, unbiased) guidance on what "healthy porn usage" really means. But hey, we do have common sense. Here are some things to think about.

Masturbate without Porn, Too.

If you can't masturbate without porn, you may be conditioning yourself to only respond to certain types of sexual imagery. While it is only anecdotal, some people have told me they feel watching too much porn made it harder for them to become aroused in real-life situations, with real people. Shake your routines up once in a while.

Don't Use Porn to Deal with Your Feelings.

Most people watch porn because it's entertaining and they're horny. But in some cases, people use porn as a distraction when they're upset with a partner, when they're feeling lonely, or even when they're angry. In other words, porn is a coping mechanism. It's good to do a self-check-in about porn usage, and how you feel when you use it. If you find you are using porn as a distraction, be proactive about finding healthier ways to deal. Talk to a friend, vent it out in some writing, or seek out a counselor.

Remember that Pornified Sex Isn't Necessarily Good Sex.

The most common complaint I hear about porn is about partners who try to reenact porn sex in real life. But porn doesn't always keep it real—and it isn't always the best model for good sex.

In chapter 6, "Body Image," we talked about how the bodies seen in porn don't always reflect a typical body. In porn, you are more likely to encounter actors who change their bodies with supplements, drugs, or surgeries. Their bodies may not only look different, but move differently during sex. In commercial porn, bodies are also movie-magicked with flattering angles, fluffers (people on set who help keep a male porn star erect), and editing.

A common unreality of porn is that the sex depicted usually centers on male pleasure and entertainment. IMO a big part of the reason for that is that porn is more often directed by men, and assumed to be for other men to watch (women don't like sex, 'member?). Lesbian porn is a notable example. My favorite is when they rub boobs together or suck on a dildo for ten minutes (lolwut?), both acts that generally aren't very stimulating for women. In straight porn, this happens too—hence the proliferation of "money shots" and blow jobs that would make the average person gag.

Another notable unreality in porn is rushing through outercourse and other types of sex—or leaving it out entirely—and going straight to penetration. Obviously, it's hard to say "That's bad sex!" because everyone's preferences are different. But in most cases, skipping everything but penetration *is* bad sex. In gay porn, rushing to penetration happens too, skipping over other types of sex and the preparation required to make sex safe and pleasurable.

The sex positions that are popular in porn are usually meant to maximize visual stimulation, not pleasure or comfort. You don't usually need to hang upside down or have your feet wrapped back around your head to have a good time—and despite its prevalence in porn, most women don't like having their face ejaculated on.

In a similar vein, porn often neglects safety. WHERE ARE THE FREAKING CONDOMS? And while we're asking, where is the freaking consent? You might argue that consent is meant to be implied (it is porn after all), but some porn clips I've stumbled upon really disturbed me. In some clips, it's not clear that the person in the video is actually okay with what's happening, nor are they aware they're being recorded. For all I know, these clips may be a live filming of sexual assault and rape. It's dark, but it's real, and it poses difficult ethical questions about pornography. It is not ethical to participate in the sexual exploitation of others. But how do you know what porn is ethical and what isn't? One way to cut down on sexual exploitation is to actually pay for porn, from companies that have a good reputation and take care of their performers. Check out the resources section for more ethical, sex-positive porn sources.

Ask Laci: on self-pleasure

? Is there such a thing as masturbating too much?

If your masturbation habits aren't interfering with friends, family, school, work, etc., then you're fine. It also should not cause damage to your body (like chafing, bleeding, etc.). If it starts to cause problems, scale it back. If you are having difficulty scaling back, talk to a health-care provider that you trust.

? Is it weird if girls masturbate?

Definitely not. But for some reason, girls are much more likely to feel bad for doing it.

If you wanna put a number to it, girls report three times as much shame as boys for masturbating. In my own experience, some of the shame I felt masturbating was connected to broader shame about my vagina. When I was younger, the message was loud and clear that my vagina was gross and probably smelly or otherwise unattractive. I was legitimately scared of it. This was reinforced by high school friends who joked about "fish vaginas" while companies pushed ~feminine prod-ucts~ to make my vagina "cleaner"—as if it's dirty by default. As we've already discussed, it's not disgusting, and this stuff is BS. There's also a weird gender-y thing going on here; there's this sort of understand-ing that sex and masturbation are "boy things," that boys are horny, they have strong sexual desires—but girls don't. Some churches, media sources, and abstinence-only classrooms around the country tell girls it is their job to remain chaste and "pure." If they don't, they are "sluts."

As a result of this negativity, our vagina becomes a site of someone else's pleasure—not our own. It's there to look or smell a particular way for *someone else*, to arouse *someone else*, to pleasure *someone else*. This can create a sense of fear and detachment from our own bodies. For women, there's an extra sense of taboo attached to masturbation—and with it, shame. The many ways that we tell girls that our bodies, our pleasure, *don't belong to us* is one of the more messed-up attitudes our sexual culture instills in us. The effects are huge, and shaming masturbating is just the tip of the iceberg.

SO BASICALLY . . . go to town, girl. Screw the haters.

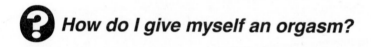 ## How do I give myself an orgasm?

Well now, I'm glad you asked.

the big o

LOOK, I'M NOT GONNA LIE: ORGASM is the jam. To me, it feels like a powerful swell in the body that can feel like the earth is literally shattering (in a sexy way, not an oh-god-an-earthquake way). Orgasm produces a wave of pleasurable contractions, leaving the body in a relieved, slightly loopy state of relaxation. Whether you're giving an orgasm to yourself or to someone else, there's nothing quite like it.

That said, orgasm has occupied a somewhat troubling place in our cultural psyche. It is sometimes treated as a requirement to experience sexual pleasure and satisfaction, the hallmark of "good sex." In reality, it's more of a bonus than a mandate.

Let's take a closer look at what orgasm is:

Throughout the history of sex research, several models of sexual response have been proposed. The first was a linear model proposed in 1966 by the iconic William H. Masters and Virginia E. Johnson. Their research provided the basis on which more complex models were built in the coming decades. Masters and Johnson proposed that our bodies respond to sexual stimuli in four phases.

SEXUAL RESPONSE CYCLE

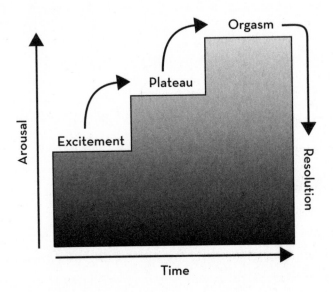

Phase 1: Excitement

Excitement can last a few minutes to several hours. Tension in the muscles, increased blood flow. Vaginal and penile lubrication. Breasts and testicles swell slightly.

Phase 2: Plateau

Excitement continues. The clitoris becomes more sensitive; the testicles pull up. The vagina (internal) turns a darker purplish color. More muscle tension and spasms, a.k.a. myotonia, may occur in the face, hands, feet.

Phase 3: Orgasm

Orgasm is a series of involuntary, rhythmic muscle contractions of the vagina, uterus, or penis. Contractions start out faster and occur closer together, then occur more slowly and space out further apart. The contractions vary in number and intensity, indicating the intensity of the orgasm. During orgasm, blood pressure, heart rate, and breathing reaches a peak. The brain floods with feel-good oxytocin. Some people also get a "sex flush," where the body (especially face and chest) turns a bit rosy. Muscle tension is released. Ahhhh.

Phase 4: Resolution

Following the sexual relief of orgasm, most experience calm in the mind and body. Resolution is marked by heightened feelings of intimacy, and perhaps some fatigue. Swollen body parts return to their normal shape, size, and color.

After resolution, females can typically go back through plateau and orgasm again several times, until they'd like to stop. Males typically require a break before going at it again, which is also known as the refractory period. The length of the refractory period varies by individual, and tends to get longer with age.

As a very basic guide, the Masters and Johnson model of the sexual response cycle works. However, it doesn't fully account for the wide variations we see in sexual response, especially among females. Before it was commonly accepted that females may have different sexual response patterns, doctors and psychologists suggested women who deviated from these steps were abnormal, perhaps requiring medication or therapy. Later research suggests that many females do not move through the phases in a linear order, and it may be more fluid (multiple orgasms being one example of that). The Masters and Johnson model has also been criticized for leaving out, or at least oversimplifying, the role that environment and context plays in shaping sexual response. It's now well known that variables like relationship satisfaction, body image, and previous sexual experiences all shape our sexual response.

The model I find most useful is a nonlinear model proposed by Dr. Rosemary Basson in 2000. It incorporates the role that culture and environment play in our sexual response. Rather than framing sexual response as a series of steps to orgasm, Basson's model is circular, with several points of potential entry and exit.

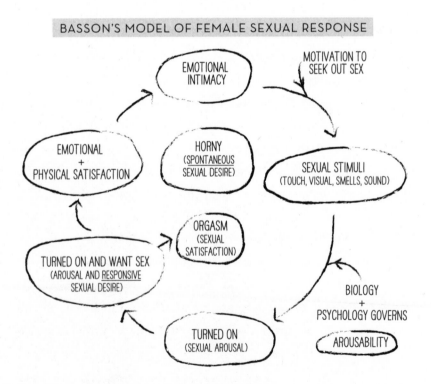

BASSON'S MODEL OF FEMALE SEXUAL RESPONSE

EMOTIONAL INTIMACY

MOTIVATION TO SEEK OUT SEX

EMOTIONAL + PHYSICAL SATISFACTION

HORNY (SPONTANEOUS SEXUAL DESIRE)

SEXUAL STIMULI (TOUCH, VISUAL, SMELLS, SOUND)

ORGASM (SEXUAL SATISFACTION)

TURNED ON AND WANT SEX (AROUSAL AND RESPONSIVE SEXUAL DESIRE)

BIOLOGY + PSYCHOLOGY GOVERNS

AROUSABILITY

TURNED ON (SEXUAL AROUSAL)

Rather than a purely biological, somewhat sanitary progression of steps to orgasm, Basson's model shows that sexual response is a complex interplay of physical/biological stuff, alongside psychological and cultural stuff. Here are a few takeaways from this model.

Sexual Arousal Can Be Spontaneous or Responsive.

Spontaneous sexual arousal, which manifests as a passionate or urgent horniness, is more common at the beginning of a relationship. Responsive sexual arousal is more common later in relationships, when the honeymoon phase has waned. Even though you might not feel urgently horny, being open and willing to be sexual with a partner can generate desire when paired with stuff that turns you on. This shows how desire may sometimes come after physical arousal, as opposed to always coming before it. Sexual arousal can be physical, psychological, or both.

State of Mind During a Sexual Encounter Plays a Large (If Not the Largest) Role in Sexual Desire.

Context is everything! Typically, the context of sexual arousal is a relationship of some kind. If the vibe in your relationship is positive and supportive, with trust and passion and flirtation—the stage is set. On the flip side, conflict, resentment, distrust, and insecurity in the relationship can pose serious roadblocks to arousal.

People Have Lots of Different Motives for Having Sex, and It's Not Always Orgasm.

People have sex for many reasons. We usually chalk it up to physical pleasure—but sex can also be motivated by emotional intimacy, a desire to enhance your connection with a partner, or to express affection, attraction, and love. Understanding motive is useful in understanding our own and our partner's sexuality. Because we have sex for many reasons and experience pleasure in many different ways, having good sex doesn't necessarily require following the linear path that ends in orgasm. Orgasm can be great, and if you want it, get it! But bear in mind that it isn't always the defining characteristic of good sex.

Good Sexual Experiences Will Lead You to Want More of Them.

It might sound obvious but . . . good sex motivates us to have more good sex. On the flip side, a pattern of negative or unfulfilling sexual experiences will lead to decreased motivation and desire. This means that one-sided sexual pleasure and unacknowledged problems in the bedroom should be addressed early on to keep things healthy.

How to Give Yourself an Orgasm

Having trouble figuring out how to orgasm? That's okay! Orgasm is a skill that's learned—it doesn't always come natural to us. This is especially the case for women and vulva owners, whose pleasure has been sidelined throughout history in porn, in sex ed classrooms, and well . . . pretty much everywhere.

As usual, everyone's body is different. But it all starts with arousal. Maybe it's a particularly hot fantasy, erotica, pictures of a crush or lover, porn, dirty talk, etc. Unless you're asexual or recovering from sexual trauma, this part usually comes the easiest.

If you have a vulva, the clitoris is the source of a lot of pleasure. Your clitoris may be very sensitive or not very sensitive at all—and that determines the type of touch and pressure you'll need to bring yourself to orgasm. Some people enjoy hands-free clitoral stimulation through something called syntribation—which is basically squeezing the thighs together, sometimes by crossing the legs and rubbing the thighs. For those who enjoy touch, many people enjoy a gentle, lubricated touch that is consistent and repetitive. Use lube, or saliva in a pinch. You can stimulate the clitoris with your hand, a shower head or bath faucet, or a vibrating toy. Experiment with different strokes! Try gentle rubbing up and down across the clitoris, rubbing around it in a circular motion, or gently tapping it. Every touch or stroke will slowly heighten your pleasure. If direct rubbing of the clitoris with your fingers is too intense, try sliding your fingers along the side of the clitoris in a "V" shape between your labia.

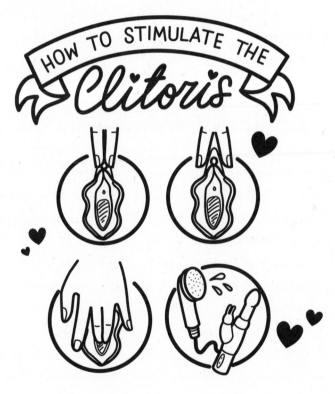

HOW TO STIMULATE THE Clitoris

You can pinch your fingers in this "V" formation to heighten the sensation. Try out different pressures, speeds, and levels of lubrication to figure out what feels good. In porn, I sometimes see people mashing and rubbing into a clitoris aggressively—but this can dull the sensation, especially at first. Proceed with caution.

For many people, consistency is key: when you find what feels good, keep doing it for a while. Find a pace and rhythm that works for you and listen to your body. As you get closer to orgasm, you will feel your muscles starting to tense. Clenching your PC muscles a bit (the same muscles you use to stop a stream of pee) can heighten the sensation even more and make it easier to orgasm.

Stimulating the back of the clitoris can also enhance pleasure. Recall from before that about one to two inches inside the vagina, on the upper wall, you may find a pleasurable little area known as the g-spot. Make a gentle "come hither" motion toward the belly button to feel it out. You can also stimulate the outside of the clitoris while you finger yourself by positioning the bottom of your palm over the clitoris. Some people like both external and internal clitoral stimulation at the same time; some just like one or the other.

During masturbation, orgasm takes an average of four minutes of clitoral stimulation. But that's just the average—it could very well be a shorter or longer amount of time for you. When you're new to it or when you're not very aroused, it will likely take longer than four minutes, perhaps even much longer. Relax, and don't stress about it! The idea is to have fun and enjoy yourself. If it feels good, you're doing it right.

Obviously, you have everything you need at your fingertips (literally). But hey, if you're looking for a way to spice things up, sex toys can be a lot of fun and produce powerful orgasms. I think of them as power tools; they do the job faster, and sometimes more efficiently. Vibrators and masturbation sleeves are the most common sex toys used during masturbation. We'll talk more about sex toys in the next chapter. Experiment, explore, and find what works for you! It's all a part of the journey.

The Orgasm Gap

The first time I had an orgasm, I was eleven, and it was a complete accident. After a sweaty summer day in Sacramento, I had hopped in the shower for a cool-off, and unassumingly pointed the shower head between my legs for a while. Let's just say, I have been a fan of detachable shower heads ever since. At first, I didn't realize what had happened was an orgasm. I had no idea what the clitoris was, or its role in sexual pleasure—and I wouldn't for several years. Which, frankly, is tragic.

Having chatted with a lot of people online about their sex troubles, one of the recurring themes for women is difficulty having an orgasm. Large-scale studies paint an interesting picture: during sex, straight ladies have an average of one orgasm for every three that a straight guy has. About one in three straight ladies *never* has an orgasm during intercourse . . . at all. This is sometimes called "the orgasm gap." What the heck?

Historically, female orgasm has been thought of as an ~elusive and unknowable~ mystery. Female pleasure has been deemed much more complicated than males'; our sexual desires much more muted, our bodies too finicky and uncooperative to orgasm easily. Sometimes, the orgasm gap is chalked up to evolution. After all, female orgasm isn't necessary for conception. But there are a few holes in this theory. The first is that there is no orgasm gap between straight men and lesbian women—they have roughly the same number of orgasms as each other. This suggests that there's something about heterosexual relationships specifically that creates an orgasm gap. Any guesses?

In my opinion, a large part of the gap comes from the fact that our sexual culture tends to center penis-in-vagina sex (PIV) as "real sex," while every other form of sex is relegated to the land of "foreplay" or "extra stuff." This is a problem, because for many women (and some men too), sexual play besides PIV is pretty critical to orgasm. In fact, only 18% of women can orgasm from vaginal penetration alone. This statistic is a little mind-blowing. If porn or Hollywood were any indication, you'd think that penetrative sex is the key to Kingdom of Orgasms. But the real MVP is clitoral stimulation and other forms of outercourse—and it's too often ignored during heterosexual sex.

Another part of the orgasm gap may come from the contexts in which the sex is taking place. Take a look at this nifty chart from a study called "Orgasm in College Hookups and Relationships" by Elizabeth Armstrong et al.

Percent of Women Having an Orgasm in Four Sexual Contexts, by Occurrence of Selected Sexual Behaviors

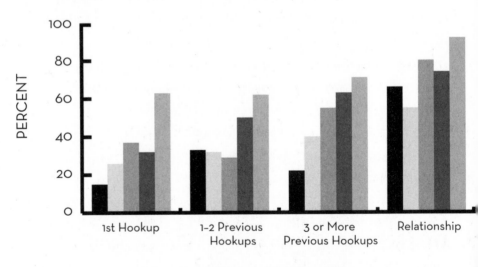

Notice how much higher the orgasm rate is for women when couples engage in penetration, oral sex, AND self-stimulation. And the effect becomes even more exaggerated the better the couple knows each other. In the study, when men and women were in a relationship, they were much more positive about the importance of their partner's pleasure and orgasm. Men said they want to get their lady off, while the women said they expect equal pleasure. But when they are hooking up, things change. Some men in the study expressed the view that her orgasm doesn't matter, put frankly in one quote: "In a hookup, I don't give a shit." On the flip side, the women in the study said they don't expect to get off, and may even feel that expecting an orgasm is rude or imposing on a partner.

I've felt this way before. I guess I sort of assumed that my pleasure didn't matter as much as his, but it's hard to say *why*. Even if it is a hookup, why shouldn't she come, too? It's hard for me to see this as anything more than devaluation of female pleasure and/or laziness. It has echoes of Victorian-era sexuality, when women were regarded as sexless and naive, there only to appease male sexual desires.

The bottom line is basically this: there is a way to close the orgasm gap with more attention to clitoral stimulation and outercourse, as well as more regard for women's sexual pleasure (especially during hookups).

multiple orgasms

IF YOU HAVE A VAGINA: CONGRATS! The ability to have multiple orgasms should come pretty easily once you figure out how to orgasm. You just, uh, keep going. Until you're done, really. If the mood is right, some people even have rapid multiple orgasms and stay in a heightened orgasmic state for over a minute. Woo! Just how orgasmic are we talking? Let's just say: the world record for the most female orgasms in one hour is: 134. Challenge accepted.

If you have a penis, worry not. You can also have multiple orgasms! Maybe not 134, but the world record for males is still a whopping 16 times in one hour. You don't need to get *that* wild to still have a good time. But the point is: it's possible! The key to multiple orgasms for males is to recognize that ejaculation and orgasm are actually two different things. Even though the two usually occur in sync, orgasm doesn't *cause* ejaculation, and ejaculation doesn't *cause* orgasm. Orgasm usually happens just before or during ejaculation. So, to have multiples, you just learn to reach orgasm without ejaculating. Then, you orgasm as many times as you want before you ejaculate. It takes a little dedication and practice, but I know a guy who knows a guy who figured out how to do it in just a few weeks.

Having multiple orgasms won't necessarily make sex better or more pleasurable. An orgasm is a beautiful thing in its own right, and having just one is fine! But if you're curious, here's a roadmap of how to do it. These practices will also make your orgasms stronger—whether it's one, or several!

Strengthen Your Pubococcygeus Muscles, a.k.a. PC Muscles.

The PC muscles are important when it comes to stronger orgasms and multiple orgasms. They are the muscles you can flex to stop a stream of pee when you're peeing. Just like these muscles control your stream of pee, they also control ejaculation. You can feel the PC muscles by placing a finger over the perineum, that small patch of skin between the back of your balls and the anus. Clench, and you will feel the muscles in there contract, lifting your testicles slightly. With strong PC muscles, you will be able to contract for thirty seconds with little effort.

PC muscles are strengthened with an exercise called Kegels. To do Kegels, contract the PC muscles for five to ten seconds, ten to twenty times in a row. Gradually increase intensity and number of repetitions as you get stronger. You can also practice doing Kegels in rapid succession or in different positions. If you're into apps like I am, there are even Kegels training apps to try out on your smartphone.

The more you practice, the stronger your orgasms will get. And strong PC muscles are great for a lot of other reasons, too. They can help you go longer before orgasming; can help with bladder control (which is why Kegels are sometimes used to recover from surgeries), erectile dysfunction, premature ejaculation; AND they can help men have multiple orgasms. They're basically magic.

Be Able to Masturbate/Have Sex for More Than Ten Minutes Without Orgasming.

If you have trouble going longer than ten minutes without orgasming, practice pulling yourself back from the edge before you orgasm. Strong PC muscles can help do the trick. When you feel yourself getting close, clench down as hard as you can and hold. Other things that can help are gently squeezing the head of the penis, taking a deep breath, or changing the rhythm of your stroke. Experiment and figure out what works for you. Pay attention to your grip, pressure, and speed while masturbating or having sex—adjusting these can slow orgasm as well.

Practice Edging.

Now that you know how to stop yourself from orgasming and can go for a little while, practice doing it multiple times in a session. Edging is the practice of getting as close as possible to orgasm before backing down. Edging several times before orgasm can produce very powerful orgasms. It can also be used to train your body to separate orgasm from ejaculation.

Separate the Orgasm.

As you get better at edging, you will get to know your body's physical responses better. Eventually, you will get to the point where you know precisely when you are about to ejaculate. The very moment that you hit "the point of no return," clench down on the PC muscles hard. Your penis may twitch, but you will experience orgasm—without ejaculation. At first, ejaculation may come right after, or you may clench a little too early or late, either stopping the orgasm or allowing the ejaculation. But with a good bit of practice with all the above steps, you will be able to orgasm, delay the ejaculation, and keep going.

Keep at It!

The first few times separating orgasm and ejaculation may be a little lackluster, but the sensation and power of the orgasm will improve as the technique becomes more familiar.

Ask Laci: on orgasms

❓ How can I tell if I had an orgasm?

I don't want to sound annoyingly mysterious here but . . . you'll know if you had an orgasm. Your heart rate and breathing will have risen to a peak, then dropped back to normal. If you place your hand over your vulva or penis, you may be able to feel it pulsing during and after orgasm. These are the contractions that signify orgasm. Most of all, you can tell if you've had an orgasm if you felt a wave of pleasure that lasted at least a few seconds followed by a sense of relaxation and calm. It might have been a teensy-tiny wave or a large wave, but a wave nonetheless!

❓ I've tried everything, and I still can't orgasm. What am I doing wrong?

No stressin'. You may be overthinking it and putting too much pressure on yourself. Try to put less emphasis on having an orgasm and focus on exploring all the things that make your body feel good. Soak up those sensations and be present with them. Practice self-pleasure without a particular goal in mind, beside enjoying yourself. Remember that *it's okay not to orgasm*. It's okay for your body to do _____. It's okay to feel _____. There's no rush! Relax and enjoy whatever your body wants to do today.

❓ Why are my orgasms so weak? I want the big powerful ones everyone talks about.

The strength of your orgasm depends on a number of factors, both psychological and physical. Experiment to figure out things that heighten your arousal alone or with a partner. That might mean more sexual stimulation than you've been getting, reading some erotica, or building deeper emotional intimacy with your partner. Weak PC muscles can also make for weaker orgasms. Practice Kegels every day for stronger muscles. When you're about to orgasm, bearing down on the muscles can create a more intense sensation.

❓ Why is it so much easier for me to orgasm during masturbation than sex?

This is a pretty common concern, and it can stem from any number of causes. Often, it's because you know how to get yourself off better than your partner does. In which case, it might help to offer them some guidance. It might also be that you don't feel as comfortable and able to relax around them. In which case, work on building intimacy and trust by spending some time together and talking openly about your sexual relationship. It might be that you need different types of stimulation during partner sex. In which case, experiment together, or show them how you self-pleasure to get some new ideas.

❓ Is it bad to fake orgasms? I don't want my partner to feel bad.

It's not exactly ideal to fake it, because it basically tells your partner "This is how you make me come!" . . . when it isn't. It's noble to want to make your partner feel good and signal that you're having a good time, but orgasm is obviously not the only way to do that. There's a lot of pressure to orgasm, and that creates a lot of pressure to fake it. Talking to your partner can take the pressure off. It might help to talk about what is and isn't working for you or how you'd like to end sex when you're done and are not going to orgasm. Be honest and gentle, and a sense of humor never hurts either.

EIGHT

SEX TOYS

ONE OF MY VERY FAVORITE PARTS of sexploration is sex toys! In the past few decades alone, hundreds of new toys have flooded the market to offer you new sexual sensations and possibilities for pleasure, both alone and with a partner.

> **IN THIS CHAPTER WE'LL TALK ABOUT**
>
>
>
> Vibrators: Then and now
> What's your toy made of?
> Visiting the sex shop
> Cleaning sex toys

Vibrators: Then and Now

Legend has it that the first vibrator was invented by the infamous Egyptian queen Cleopatra. In a fit of sexual tension, Cleopatra is said to have hollowed out a gourd and stuffed it full of . . . angry bees. Because why not, I guess? She then used the vibration generated by the bees as a vibrator. It's unclear how much truth there is to this story, but it still gives me a chuckle.

Since the Victorian era, there have been dozens of whirring gizmos and vibrating gadgets designed to help women get off. Back then, these gadgets were prescribed by doctors to treat an ominously vague condition called "female hysteria." We now know that they were referring to *clinically high* levels of horniness.

To treat female hysteria, one method was "hydriatic massage"—basically spraying water on the clitoris until orgasm was achieved. Doctors also helped their patients out manually, with their hands *ahem*. Later, newfangled devices were invented to help all those hysterical ladies out. One of the first of these was "The Manipulator" (yes, that's its real name), invented in 1869 by George Taylor, an American doctor. The Manipulator was steam-powered and also the size of a table, like a freaking boss. It contained a cut-out area where the woman's pelvis would go, which had a rotating sphere for stimulation. The steam engine was in another room, where the doctors would operate the machine. Dr. Rachel Maines, author of *The Technology of Orgasm*, noted: "Doctors didn't like [The Manipulator] because you couldn't move it and take it with you on a house call, and they also didn't enjoy shoveling coal into it."

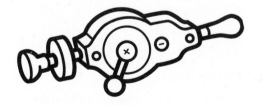

Another notable OG vibrator is the Pulsocon. I mean, just look at this thing.

That's right, folks: it was HAND-CRANKED. I mean, at least they didn't have to worry about batteries. This particular gadget was readily available in the Sears catalog, marketed as a device to help women "loosen their joints and increase the circulation of blood." It was invented by Dr. Gerald Macaura, who was later sentenced to three years in prison and a $600 fine for "vibratory massage fraud." A series of stag films had revealed, to the shock and horror of the public, what his instrument was *really* for. As it turns out, he also was not a doctor. But I'll be darned if our buddy Gerald didn't know what he was doing. The device still vibrates like a charm, nearly one hundred years later.

Of course, the vibrators of today aren't steam-powered or hand-cranked. There are a bazillion different choices on the market, and as technology advances, sex toys are only getting more sophisticated. There are now vibrators that you can control from an app (long-distance lovin', anyone?) and vibrators that slip on the pads of your fingers and masturbation sleeves that simulate a blow job. And don't even get me started on sex robots and VR headsets. The future is here.

While all this fancy new stuff is pretty cool, my personal favorites are toys that are simple in form and function. I also favor toys that are made of high-quality materials and are rechargeable. (Who wants to pay for batteries every month? Or every few days if you're really getting busy. . . .) Unfortunately, toys that fall into this category are often the most expensive. But in the world of sex toys, you get what you pay for. The high-quality toys in my drawer have lasted me over ten years, while the cheapies usually die after a few months. That said, cheapies aren't useless. If you aren't sure a certain type of toy is gonna be your thing or you just don't have the funds, getting a cheaper model first gives you a flavor without the high investment.

Why vibe in the first place? To be blunt, the most powerful orgasms I've ever had were with a vibrator. I mean, it's basically a power tool. It gets the job done faster and more efficiently than my hand ever could. In that sense it's sort of ~dangerous~. It feels so good I might never get out of bed again. Bye-bye, productivity.

What's Your Toy Made Of?

Fun fact: sex toys aren't regulated in the United States, which is why many toys have a "novelty only" disclaimer on the packaging. A lack of regulation means pretty much anyone can make anything and sell it to you, regardless of its safety or the chemicals it may contain—and they cannot legally be held responsible if it causes harm. This means it's on us to be extra vigilant about what our sex toys are made of. After all, we use these devices on some of our most sensitive bits!

There are two main things to pay attention to when you're buying toys: phthalates and porous materials.

Phthalates are substances that are added to plastic sex toys to make them soft and squishy, and to extend the life of the plastic. However, the EPA has designated phthalates as potentially cancer-causing. They have been banned in many countries, as well as banned from use in children's toys in the United States. So, obviously, avoid them. This is tricky because even toys marked "phthalate free" can technically contain phthalates without consequences. How do you know if a toy has phthalates then? Well, ya don't. But you can avoid the materials that phthalates are often added to, such as:

- PVC
- Rubber
- Jelly
- Vinyl
- Cyberskin
- UR3

With these materials, it is safer to pop a condom on the toy. Not only to avoid phthalates, but because these materials are also porous, allowing bacteria to get trapped in them, increasing your odds of infection. Porous sex toys can't be 100% sterilized. Luckily there are several nonporous, phthalate-free options!

Look for sex toys made out of:

- 100% medical-grade silicone
- Glass
- Metal
- Ceramic
- Hard plastic
- Acrylic

Visiting the Sex Shop

These days, a lot of people order their sex toys online, but sex shops can give a more accurate look at what you're buying. They're usually staffed by people who are passionate about pleasure and can help you figure out a toy that fits your needs. Roll right on in with that confident swagger, and don't be afraid to ask questions. If you're intimidated, bring a friend along, or a partner. It can make for a spicy date, so long as you are old enough. In most places in the US, you must be eighteen or older to visit a sex shop. If you're unsure, Google your state's laws or look for signage posted on the storefront.

Some sex shops are better than others. It makes a big difference when they have an informed staff. Personally, I look for shops that are brightly lit, clean, and well kept. I don't dig shops that give off a "porny" vibe and are plastered with posters of scantily clad women. One of my very favorite sex shops is Good Vibrations, founded by a true sex-positive pioneer and friend of mine, the late Joani Blank. Good Vibes has multiple locations in the Bay Area in Northern California and an online store. My experiences there have always included enthusiastic and very knowledgeable staff that helped me find pleasure treasures. Another sex-positive favorite is The Pleasure Chest in Los Angeles. I can't speak to East Coast shops because, well, I'm a California girl. Do some Googling, and support your local sex-positive sex shops! They work hard to keep you satisfied and to cater to *everyone*— including women and queer folks. Hell yeah.

Types of Sex Toys

DILDOS

A dildo is a fake penis or phallic toy that is used in vaginas and butts. Some are shaped like realistic penises, while others take on a more discreet appearance. Some people also use household items as dildos, because it turns out that a lot of things are shaped like a dick. Popular choices seem to include vegetables, hairbrush handles, makeup brush handles, candlesticks . . . you get the idea. If you're going to use a household item, consider its safety first. Because these items can contain pesticides, germs, and bacteria, always cover them in a condom first. Consider whether or not it could break inside you, or scratch you up with pokey bits. If you're sticking one in your butt, make sure that it has a flared base to avoid getting stuck.

VIBRATORS

Dildos and other toys that vibrate fall under the umbrella of vibrators. They are pretty versatile and can be used on butts, clitorises, vaginas, nipples, and anywhere else that feels good. There are a million different kinds in lots of different shapes and sizes, with various levels of vibration. Some are quiet, some make a buzzing noise. Cheaper vibrators tend to be battery-operated, while higher-end vibrators are rechargeable.

RABBIT

Rabbits are vibrators that have a second little arm coming off the top to stimulate the external clitoris while the dildo stimulates the vagina. They're great for people who like internal and external stimulation at the same time.

G-SPOT VIBRATOR

A vibrator with a curve for easier access to the g-spot.

BULLET

Small, handheld vibrating devices that are held over the clitoris, or wherever a little vibration feels nice. If privacy is an issue, bullets tend to be very discreet, and some models are disguised as lipstick.

MAGIC WAND

The modern descendant of the infamous Pulsocon, the magic wand has been a sex toy staple for decades. The most famous model is the Hitachi Magic Wand, but there are dozens of re-creations these days. The magic

wand is somewhat discreet because it looks a bit like a back massager—but that also means it's pretty bulky. It delivers a high-intensity vibration. Which is good for people with less sensitive clitorises, but can be too much for people who are really sensitive. I have heard anecdotal stories of people temporarily going numb after using these bad boys. It doesn't seem to be dangerous and sensation always comes back, but it's something to be aware of.

MASTURBATION SLEEVES

With some of the most popular iterations sold by Fleshlight and Tenga, there are a lot of different kinds of masturbation sleeves. Sleeves are an

alternative to hands that can offer a more realistic and pleasurable sensation on the penis. Some sleeves create a gentle, pleasurable suction as well.

Masturbation sleeves have another sneaky benefit besides pleasure, too—they can help retrain those who have been gripping too hard during masturbation (a.k.a. "the death grip"). Gripping too hard can desensitize the penis to the more typical sensations of sex, making it harder to get off with a partner. By using a sleeve, it will emulate more typical sensations that come from vaginas, mouths, or butts.

PROSTATE MASSAGER

Prostate massagers are specially crafted little gadgets to stimulate the prostate. Some stimulate directly on the prostate, others stimulate the prostate indirectly by applying pressure to the perineum. Some do both! Some vibrate, some don't, and they come in lots of different sizes. Beginners should start small before movin' on up.

BUTT PLUGS AND ANAL BEADS

Butt plugs and anal beads are toys that are put in the butt. Some people remove them just before or during orgasm for extra pleasure. The sensation of pulling them out (and putting them in) is pleasurable because it stimulates the nerve endings around the anus.

COCK RINGS

Cock rings are worn around the base of the penis, or sometimes the penis and the testicles, and restrict blood flow. Some are made of stretchy material to accommodate many sizes; other rings are inflexible and single-size. Cock rings are typically worn to make an erection stronger. Some rings have clitoral stimulators that stimulate the clitoris during penetrative sex, making orgasm stronger for the partner. Cock rings with vibrators can also be worn upside down to gently vibrate on the scrotum or perineum during sex. They are typically safe to wear for up to a half hour. If you feel any tingling or numbness, take it off, as you may be restricting the blood flow too much. This can be caused by a ring that is too small or worn too long.

STRAP-ONS

Strap-ons are dildos that are held on to the pelvis by straps, or sometimes by underwear with a specially designed hole to hold the dildo. There are two pieces of a strap-on: the straps and the dildo, making it easier to mix 'n' match. Strap-ons are great to free up your hands for other types of stimulation.

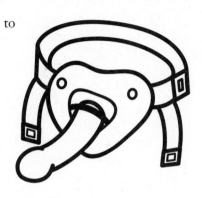

THE SEX TOY OPTIONS AND FUN don't stop here—these are simply the most popular. There are SO many different types of toys to try, and new kinds are coming out all the time. Get sexplorin'! And hey, don't forget the lube!

CLEANING SEX TOYS

Sex toys gotta be cleaned after every use. They can transmit bacteria and irritate your bits. To clean your toys, wash with mild hand or dish soap. You don't want to use anything that's going to leave a residue. Make sure not to submerge battery-operated/buzzy/rechargeable toys in water unless they explicitly state that they're waterproof (and even then . . . eh). You can also buy specialty sprays or wipes if you don't wanna take your toy to the kitchen or bathroom to clean. With glass and stainless steel toys, you have the option to boil them or pop them in the dishwasher. You can also pop a condom on phallic-shaped sex toys for quick cleanup. Easy peasy.

NINE

⋺° YOUR SEXUAL DEBUT °⋳

MY FIRST TIME HAVING SEX WAS cute. Also exciting. Also nerve-racking. Also awkward. The summer before I turned sixteen, one of my best friends had a pool party. All the community theater kids came out, and that's where I met Mitch. He was a year older than me, a fellow musician with a dorky sense of humor and a pretty nice head of hair. I was smitten. We spent that first summer hanging out at local parks, making out until our lips were chapped. We ended up dating two years, making him my first Official Relationship. In the earlier days of the relationship, I was convinced I would marry him. (Spoiler alert: I didn't.) After dating for a few months, we decided we were ready to get sexy. I was full of paranoia, and hormones. I felt ready to have sex, but I wanted to make sure not to screw up. To prepare, he got tested for STIs since he'd had a previous partner. We also stocked up on condoms and spermicide, and we decided he'd also pull out. I figured—that oughta cover us. Then one night in November, during a thunderstorm, we were all cuddled up in his room listening to music and it just seemed right. It felt like something out of a cheesy teen flick. It was perfect. Ish.

But it wasn't perfect because of the sex itself. The condom broke (more on that later), and it was pretty uncomfortable. I remember thinking to myself, "Ummmm, this is what everyone is making a big deal about?" We had no idea what we were doing, and I was miles away from an orgasm that I ended up faking. Yet it was still a lovely and memorable experience. I have nothing but warm feelings about our first experience together—in large part because we had a trusting relationship that made me feel safe, and because we had taken precautions beforehand. We didn't really know what we were doing, but it wasn't really about that the first time anyway. It was about *us*.

So hey, if you're reading this and you've never had a sexual relationship before: woo! It's always helpful to learn as much as you can about sex before becoming sexually active, and hopefully this book helps you cover some bases. Even if you have had sex, there's always more to learn.

**IN THIS CHAPTER WE'LL
TALK ABOUT**

♡

Virginity in the media
Myths about virginity
How to know if you're ready for sex

---

virginity in the media

THERE'S A WHOLE LOT OF HULLABALOO about virginity out there. In my experience, people make a big deal out of who is and isn't a virgin, and what that supposedly says about them. These attitudes are reflected in the media. Teen dramas often feature episodes or plotlines about a character losing their virginity. Male characters who are virgins are usually portrayed as awkward-but-lovable nerds who don't get women, as seen in movies and TV shows like *Weird Science* (1985), *American Pie* (1999), *The 40-Year-Old Virgin* (2005), *Superbad* (2007), and *The Big Bang Theory*. Occasionally the virgin is a woman, like in *Superstar* (1999) and *The To Do List* (2013). She's usually nerdy as well, and perhaps a little desperate. On the flip side, male characters who get laid a lot are often portrayed as cool, attractive, charming, and funny. This trope is reflected in beloved characters like Danny Zuko in *Grease* (1978), Will in *The Fresh Prince of Bel-Air*, and Barney in *How I Met Your Mother*. The message: For guys, being a virgin is the epitome of uncool. It means he's awkward or a "pussy." Part of how society perceives a man's value (and how some men see their own value) is if a girl wants to sleep with him. And so, for dudes, losing their virginity is a positive thing.

For female sexuality on-screen, things are a little more complicated. One common message is that Good Girls wait for true love, like Topanga did in *Boy Meets World*, Bella in *Twilight* (2008), and Jane in *Jane the Virgin*. Girls who wait to have sex are generally depicted as kind, smart, and self-respecting. Girls who have sex aren't usually so charitably regarded. In teen dramas, female characters who have sex are often portrayed as troubled or misguided. See also: *The Vampire Diaries*, *Everwood*, and *The Secret Life of the American Teenager*. Having sex with the wrong guy (because all women are straight, obviously) will land you pregnant, diseased, socially shamed, or heartbroken. In the horror genre, women who have sex (or are sexually alluring) fare even worse. They quite often wind up dead, like in *Psycho* (1960), *Texas Chainsaw Massacre* (2003), *Nightmare on Elm Street* (1984), and *Halloween* (1978). So, uh, that's . . . a little loaded.

The good news is you probably aren't gonna die in a motel shower by a knife-wielding maniac if you have sex. The bad news is that our culture makes us feel a lot of anxiety about our first sexual experiences. There are some weird, confusing, or just plain inaccurate messages floating around out there about the first time you have sex.

This calls for some good old-fashioned myth bustin'.

myths about virginity

● ●

MYTH BUSTED:
It's okay to be a virgin.

First things first: it's okay to never have had sex.

It's okay to not want to have sex, whether that's just for now or always.

It's okay to want to wait until you're in love or married.

It's okay not to feel ready yet.

It's okay if you're the last of your friends to have sex.

It's okay if you haven't had the opportunity to have sex yet, or if haven't found the right person.

Lather, rinse, repeat. It's. All. All right.

Just like shaming people who have sex is pretty dumb, shaming people who don't have sex is also pretty dumb. People shouldn't feel pressure one way or another. Most often I hear from people who are teased or bullied for having sex, but occasionally it's the opposite. Perhaps it's an overcorrection on sex negativity, but sometimes I hear from people who are judged for not having sex, too. Some people call this "prude shaming," and it can lead to social pressure to have sex. We should each take care not to put pressure on each other, intentionally or not. Which should be obvious but, hey, it still happens. **Given all the sex stuff within these pages, I want to emphasize that sex should never feel like something you *have* to do.** ♥

• •

MYTH BUSTED:
It's okay to wait until you want to.

If you're not ready to have sex and your partner is, it's important to communicate that to them. Be honest about how you feel, and let them know where your mind is at. Decide what you are and aren't comfortable with, and let them know.

For example:

💬 "I really like making out with you, but I don't want to do other sexual stuff right now."

💬 "I think you're awesome, but I don't want to be sexual together."

💬 "I need some time before I'm ready for that."

If someone is upset about you saying no or setting boundaries, that's a warning sign. A partner worth keeping around will always respect your feelings and limits. It's okay to say no, no matter what the situation is. ♥

• •

MYTH BUSTED:
You don't "lose" anything.

TBH, the concept of "losing your virginity" is super weird to me. I mean, why do we describe having sex for the first time as literally losing a part of yourself? What do you lose, exactly? Does virginity float up out of your body when you have sex? At what point during sex is your virginity officially "lost"? For girls, the story goes that you tear your hymen the first time you put a penis in you and suddenly you're not a virgin anymore. This confused me growing up. Lots of women use tampons when they start their period . . . so . . . why would a penis change anything? Like we discussed in chapter 1, the hymen doesn't even "tear." There are no permanent physical changes that happen to your body when you have sex.

We tend to define "sex" and "losing your virginity" as penis-in-vagina (PIV). But, as we will soon discuss in way too much detail, there is way more to having sex than PIV. In lots of circumstances, the definition falls flat. For instance, the PIV definition of "virginity" implies that a lesbian who has never had PIV sex with a penis owner is a virgin forever. And for those of us with vulvas, orgasm usually entails stimulation of the clitoris, which PIV doesn't always do. Defining sex solely in terms of PIV is hetero- and male-centered, and tends to erase LGBTQ+ and female sexual experiences from the equation. We could all benefit from thinking a little more deeply about "virginity."

You'll notice this chapter refers to your sexual debut. Personally, I prefer to think of first-time experiences as "sexual debuts" rather than as "losing your virginity." It's more comprehensive and accounts for different types of sex besides PIV. I loosely define "having sex" as acts that can transmit sexual infections. That includes not just PIV, but oral sex, anal sex, and rubbing genitals without clothes on. Not only that, but "sexual debut" doesn't define us in terms of what we've "lost." My first time having PIV sex, I didn't lose anything—no body parts or parts of my soul either. My sexual debut was a new experience. It was memorable, a bit clumsy, but otherwise nothing worth kicking up too much dust for, especially since my first partner and I had already been sexual in other ways without PIV sex beforehand. ♥

MYTH BUSTED:
Sex can intensify feelings, but it's not the end of the world.

Sex can make you feel new things for a partner. It's a highly intimate act, and that can generate a special type of closeness. I mean, you're usually naked, and you're getting up close and personal with someone's genitals. Intimacy is to be expected. I have noticed that feelings of intimacy are sometimes used to fearmonger about sex. "Oxytocin," I was told, makes you feel intensely attached to anyone you have sex with—FOREVER. If you ever break up, you will be left feeling empty and used. Check this bit that has made its rounds on the internet for years:

> *There is a chemical in girls' brains which is only released three times in her lifetime: when she has sex, gives birth, and when she breastfeeds her child. It's called oxytocin. This chemical emotionally connects her to the other person for the rest of her life. Men only release the chemical when they bond with their children. Even if you are lucky enough to stay friends with a girl after having sex, a girl will always have feelings for you, because of the chemical.*

Oy. It's true that sex can create feelings of attachment. This is thanks in part to the chemical cocktail that is released in the brain and body during sexual touch and orgasm. One of those chemicals is the aforementioned oxytocin, which is a hormone that promotes bonding. Oxytocin feels all warm and loopy and lovey. Its effects can last a few hours to a few days. There's a reason pop singers have compared sex and love to "a drug" in a bazillion songs. Oxytocin isn't just released during sex, birth, and breastfeeding, though—it's also released while cuddling (it's sometimes even referred to as the "cuddle hormone"), hugging, masturbating, and nonsexual things like petting your dog.

The upside of this chemical cocktail is that it feels good. The downside is that it feels good. When attraction or a relationship starts to fade, it's an unpleasant feeling—and losing the connection that is sometimes generated through sex has the potential to make that feeling worse. So that's a thing to be aware of. But to be honest, in my experience, breaking up sucks pretty badly either way. Part of being ready for any sort of relationship, sexual or not, is acknowledging that you could wind up with complicated feelings or a broken heart. That's part of relationshipping. We'll talk more about how to deal with broken hearts in chapter 15. ♥

● ●

MYTH BUSTED:
Your First Time (and Every Time) Should be Safe.

All sex carries the risk of contracting an STI or getting pregnant (if there's a peen + vageen)—even the first time. It's important to understand the risks and be prepared before becoming sexually active! We'll talk all about this in the next couple of chapters. But when it comes to basics, here's what you need:

how to know if you're ready for sex

SOMETIMES, PEOPLE ASK ME WHAT THE "right" age is to have sex. Legally, there are age-of-consent laws that determine how old a person must be to have sex consensually (typically around age eighteen), so that's something to be aware of depending on where you live. But emotionally, I think it's difficult to put an exact number to "readiness." Emotional maturity is more important than an exact age. Here are some signs that you are emotionally mature enough for sex:

- You are able to communicate about sexuality with your partner.
- You are able to reflect on where your feelings come from, and healthy ways to deal with them.
- You are able to understand and respect your partner's boundaries.
- You know the differences between healthy and unhealthy relationships.
- You know how to take responsibility for potential outcomes of sex (including pregnancy or STIs).

My experience suggests that around sixteen years old, emotional readiness starts kicking in, but it really varies. We'll talk about most of the above throughout this book, but beyond these pages, these are life skills that you will continue to strengthen as you get older and gain more experience.

In addition to emotional maturity, I think it's important to wait until you've found the right person. The traditional advice is to "wait until you're married," but I feel it's more realistic to wait until you really want to have it. Wait until you not only desire, but feel close and connected to your partner. My experience is that sex is most fulfilling when it's with someone who you feel comfortable and safe with, who respects you, and who you enjoy spending time with (duh). The right person won't pressure you, wants you to feel good too, and will be there for you if a problem comes up. There is no rush. The right person is worth the wait. If you're horny in the meantime, just masturbate.

Lastly, part of being ready for sex is fully understanding the risks and how to stay safe and healthy when you're sexually active. This means understanding sexually transmitted infections, birth control, and sexual consent. I don't wanna freak anyone out, but I do feel like a lot of people don't take enough time to understand this stuff before diving in. Sex is great and fun and positive, but it's also something that requires safety and responsibility. It only takes one time to get pregnant or contract a disease.

But hey, I gotcha, boo. No worries. The coming chapters in our journey cover all the basics (and more than basics).

TEN

⊰° SAFER SEX °⊱

OKAY, WHO REMEMBERS THE BLUE WAFFLE? When I was in high school, there was this photoshopped picture of a bluish pearly vulva passed around seemingly everywhere online. It was ghastly. Shocking. Terrifying and grody. And underneath it all, a warning of what STIs (formerly called STDs) can do to you. I still carry the mental scars, so do yourself a favor and DON'T Google it. This pretty much sums up the only things I remember learning about sexually transmitted infections as a teenager: (1) they are nasty as hell, and (2) they can kill you. I remember sitting in class, staring at shocking pictures of diseased genitalia, overcome with panic that this could happen to me and ruin my life.

In retrospect, fear is generally not a healthy way to learn about sexuality. It makes us scared of our own bodies and stigmatizes the important practices that keep us safe. STI fearmongering doesn't stop people from having sex; it just makes them feel anxious and paranoid. Shock pics might scare people into using condoms more often, but it also makes people scared to talk about sexual health with their partners and hinders them from getting tested regularly. It's a misguided tactic that does not work. More than half of people who are sexually active contract an STI in their lifetime, and there are almost 20 million new infections every year in the USA alone. While STIs are a fact of life that can't be completely eliminated, ideally . . . that number should be smaller. The antidote to fear, stigma, and health problems is, of course, information! Obviously, STIs aren't Pokémon. You don't wanna catch 'em all. But if you do happen to get one, it's not the end of the world. Life will go on, and you will continue to have happy and healthy relationships.

Most STIs are curable, and all are treatable, which is why sex educators call them STIs, which stands for sexually transmitted infections. STI is typically a more medically accurate term than "sexually transmitted disease." A disease is what happens when a constellation of symptoms occur in the body. A disease can be caused by infection, and communicable diseases are those that are caused by infections passing from person to person. To that end, we describe someone as having an infection if a virus or bacteria has invaded a part of their body with or without sequel of disease. Most of the bugs and viruses transmitted through sex are not diseases, and will not turn into diseases if they are treated. Not only that, but it's critical to note that STIs *usually do not have any symptoms*, and symptoms are a defining characteristic of "disease."

As usual, it's important to think critically. In this case, about the stigma associated with STIs. Like I mentioned before, widespread fear about STIs sometimes winds up causing more harm than the actual virus or bacteria itself. The bottom line is that STIs aren't especially different from any other class of germs, bugs, parasites, bacteria, and viruses that humans get from each other. The only difference is that they are contracted through sex. And I mean, people don't worry that their life will be over if they catch a cold. People don't scoff in judgment and call people "dirty" when they catch the flu. We don't shame people when they get a wart on their fingers or toes, even though hand warts are often caused by the same virus that causes genital warts. (Both are

caused by HPV, human papillomavirus. It's just different strains.)
What gives? By reducing some of the stigma around human sexuality in general, we reduce stigma around STIs, which helps keep everyone healthier.

**LET'S UNPACK. IN THIS CHAPTER
WE'LL TALK ABOUT**

— ♡ —

Bacterial and parasitic STIs
Viral STIs
What to do if you contract an STI
How to have safer sex
Safer sexting

---

bacterial and parasitic STIs

GOOD NEWS! INFECTIONS CAUSED BY BACTERIA and parasites are typically curable. The infections that are the most common are noted.

Trichomoniasis (Most Common Curable STI)

Type of infection: Parasitic

Trichomoniasis, a.k.a. "trich," is a parasite that infects the genitals. It is one of the most common sexually transmitted infections in the United States, with an estimated 3.7 million or more people infected (both men and women). Bacterial vaginosis, yeast infections (both discussed in chapter 3), and trichomoniasis are the three most common types of vaginitis. They are often confused with one another. It is also possible to have more than one type of vaginitis at a time.

You can get it by: Skin-to-skin contact.

How to prevent it: Using condoms and dental dams (see section 4 on how to have safer sex for more information). Trichomoniasis generally infects the vagina or penis.

Symptoms: *Trich usually has no symptoms, especially in men.* When there are symptoms: itching genitals; frothy, yellowish, or greenish discharge; pain peeing; swelling of vulva.

Curable? Yes.

How it's tested: Traditionally trichomonas was diagnosed by looking under a microscope for the swimming parasites. This is still very commonly done, but your doctor may also send a nucleic acid amplification test—basically a fancy way of testing for trichomonas's genetic material. For females, this typically requires a vaginal swab with or without a pelvic exam. You can ask for a test when you get a pap smear. For males, it typically requires a urethral swab or urine sample.

How it's treated: Trich is treated with antibiotics, typically metronidazole and tinidazole. Generally this is a one-day/one-dose treatment. It is important to take your entire dose of antibiotics according to your doctor's directions; otherwise the infection may not be entirely wiped out. Wait until you (and your partner, if applicable) finish antibiotics, or seven days (whichever is longest), to have sex again. Reinfection with trich is common. Any partners you've had within the past sixty days need to be notified and tested.

Possible complications if untreated: Pregnant women with trichomoniasis are at an increased risk of preterm birth or a baby born with low birth weight. Trich also increases the risk of contracting other STIs.

Pubic Lice (a.k.a. Crabs)

Type of infection: Parasitic

Pubic lice are itty bitty parasites that hang out on the skin and hair around the genitals. They survive by living off a person's blood and are sometimes called "crabs" because, up close, they look just like tiny crabs. The bad news is that they are very contagious—about three million people in the USA get pubic lice every year. The good news is that these insects are pretty harmless and easy to get rid of!

You can get it by: Skin-to-skin contact. Pubic lice typically live in pubic hair, but can crawl into other patches of hair, like beards, chest hair, armpits, or eyebrows. Less commonly, they are contracted from clothing or bedding that have pubic lice on them. However, pubic lice can't live long when they are away from a human body and they can't cling to smooth surfaces like toilet seats. Pubic lice aren't caused by bad hygiene, either: you can be squeaky clean and still get them!

How to prevent it: Crabs are very contagious and unfortunately can still spread with condom usage. The only definite way to prevent them is not to have sexual contact.

Symptoms: Itchiness around the genitals.

Curable: Yes.

How it's tested: Visual inspection. In some cases, you can see the lice or their eggs (nits) at the base of the pubic hair with the naked eye. But they are tiny, so a magnifying glass may help. If you are unsure, see a nurse or doctor to check it out.

How it's treated: Most cases of pubic lice can be treated with over-the-counter pubic lice treatments like Nix. Follow the product's directions closely, and make sure anyone you've had sexual contact with recently does the same. It is also important to wash all bedding, clothing, and towels after treatment to avoid reinfection. If you still see pubic lice after a week or two, repeat the treatment or talk to your healthcare provider. Make sure to avoid sex until you are all clear! These medications are the only way to kill pubic lice. Shaving and waxing will not get rid of crabs, as they can still cling to microscopic hairs and your skin.

Possible complications if untreated: Intense scratching can inflame the skin and cause other skin infections. If the pubic lice are on the eyelashes, they can cause eye infections like pink eye. Pale bluish dots can be left on the skin from repeated bites (this is not a medical issue, just a cosmetic one).

Chlamydia (Very Common)

Type of infection: Bacterial

You can get it by: Contact with sexual fluids. Usually, it is transmitted when infected sexual fluids (pre-cum, semen, vaginal discharge) make contact with the cervix, urethra, or mucous membranes of the anus or mouth. These fluids can be transmitted between partners of any gender by genital-to-genital contact, genital-to-anal contact, or more rarely, by using hands to transmit infected fluids. You can also transmit chlamydia to the eye this way.

How to prevent it: Using condoms and dental dams (see section 4 on how to have safer sex for more information). Chlamydia can infect the vagina, penis, urethra, rectum, eyes, mouth, or throat.

Symptoms: *Chlamydia usually has no symptoms.* When there are symptoms: unusual discharge, pain or burning when you pee, swelling of the testicles. When chlamydia spreads to the cervix and uterus it can cause pelvic pain and pain during sex.

Curable? Yes.

How it's tested: Pee in a cup. A nucleic acid amplification test will test your pee—it's basically a fancy way of testing for chlamydia's genetic material. You may also be tested by swabbing the male urethra, back of the throat, anus, or cervix (this is sometimes done during a routine pap smear).

How it's treated: Because chlamydia is a bacterial infection, it is treated with antibiotics. Often this is a one-day/one-dose treatment. It is important to take your entire dose of antibiotics according to your doctor's directions; otherwise the infection may not be entirely wiped out. Wait until both you (and your partner if applicable) finish antibiotics, or seven days (whichever is longest), to have sex again. Otherwise, you may be reinfected. Any partners you've had within the past sixty days need to be notified and tested.

Possible complications if untreated: Pelvic inflammatory disease, or PID, which is when bacteria moves into the uterus or other reproductive organs. PID can cause infertility by causing scarring in the fallopian tubes, which prevents eggs/sperm from being able to meet and travel together into the uterus. Chlamydia is the leading cause of preventable infertility. A history of PID also puts you at increased risk of an ectopic pregnancy (a pregnancy outside the uterus), which can be life threatening. It also increases the risk of contracting other STIs. PID can spread into the abdominal cavity, causing inflammation of the liver capsule. Chlamydia can be transferred to infants of infected mothers, causing infections in the infant's eyes or lungs.

Gonorrhea (Common)

Type of infection: Bacterial

You can get it by: Contact with sexual fluids. Usually, it is transmitted when infected sexual fluids (pre-cum, semen, vaginal discharge) make contact with the cervix, urethra, or mucous membranes of the anus or mouth. These fluids can be transmitted between partners of any gender by genital-to-genital contact, genital-to-anal contact, or more rarely, by using hands to transmit infected fluids. You can also transmit gonorrhea to the eye this way.

How to prevent it: Using condoms and dental dams (see section 4 on how to have safer sex for more information). Gonorrhea can infect the cervix/vagina, Bartholin's glands, penis, urethra, rectum, mouth, throat, and eyes.

Symptoms: *Gonorrhea usually has no symptoms.* When there are symptoms, they include unusual discharge, pain or burning when you pee, swelling of the testicles, bleeding between periods. When gonorrhea spreads to the cervix and uterus it can cause pelvic pain and pain during sex.

Curable? Usually, but not always. In recent years, a strain of gonorrhea has emerged that is resistant to many of our go-to antibiotics.

How it's tested: Pee in a cup. A nucleic acid amplification test will test your pee—it's basically a fancy way of testing for gonorrhea's genetic material. You may also be tested by swabbing the male urethra, back of the throat, anus, or cervix (this is sometimes done during a routine pap smear).

How it's treated: Because gonorrhea is a bacterial infection, it is treated with antibiotics. Often this is a one-day/one-dose treatment. It is important to take your entire dose of antibiotics according to your doctor's directions; otherwise the infection may not be entirely wiped out. Wait until both you (and your partner if applicable) finish antibiotics, or seven days (whichever is longest), to have sex again. Otherwise, you may be reinfected. Any partners you've had within the past sixty days need to be notified and tested.

Possible complications if untreated: Pelvic inflammatory disease, or PID, which is when bacteria moves into the uterus or other reproductive organs. PID can cause infertility by causing scarring in the fallopian tubes, which prevents eggs/sperm from being able to meet and travel together into the uterus. A history of PID also puts you at increased risk of an ectopic pregnancy (a pregnancy outside the uterus), which can be life threatening. PID can spread into the abdominal cavity, causing inflammation of the liver capsule. It can also spread to the joints and blood. It increases the risk of contracting other STIs. Gonorrhea can be transferred to infants of infected mothers, causing infections in the infant's eyes or lungs.

Chancroid

Type of infection: Bacterial

Chancroid is a highly contagious infection. It is not very common in the United States.

You can get it by: Skin-to-skin contact through microabrasions in the skin of the recipient.

How to prevent it: Using condoms and dental dams (see section 4 on how to have safer sex for more information). Chancroid can infect the vagina, penis, urethra, rectum, mouth, and eyes.

Symptoms: Chancroid sometimes has no symptoms, especially in females. When there are symptoms, chancroid can cause a deep, painful, pussing ulcer on the genitals with swollen lymph nodes in the groin.

Curable? Yes.

How it's tested: Most clinics do not have the ability to test for chancroid. Diagnoses are made in the presence of ulcers.

How it's treated: Because chancroid is a bacterial infection, it is treated with antibiotics. It is important to take your entire dose of antibiotics according to your doctor's directions; otherwise the infection may not be entirely wiped out. Wait until both you (and your partner, if applicable) finish antibiotics, or seven days (whichever is longest), to have sex again. Otherwise, you may be reinfected. Any partners you've had within the past sixty days need to be notified and tested. Partners within ten days of outbreak should be treated. Blisters should be drained by a medical professional. Abstain from sex until the blister has completely healed.

Possible complications if untreated: Tissue around the sores can die and lead to more serious infection. Chancroid also increases the risk of contracting other STIs.

Syphilis

Type of infection: Bacterial

You can get it by: Contact with sores during sex. Sores can be on or around the penis, vagina, anus, in the rectum, on lips or mouth. Can also be passed from mother to infant in the womb. After a period of decline, syphilis is again on the rise in the United States.

How to prevent it: Using condoms and dental dams (see section 4 on how to have safer sex for more information).

Symptoms: Symptoms of syphilis depend on which stage the infection is in.

Stage 1 (primary syphilis)—A single 1–2 cm ulcer that is small, round, firm, and painless. The sore is where syphilis entered the body. This sore is called a chancre.

Stage 2 (secondary syphilis)—The chancre goes away. Most people do not have symptoms, and any symptoms may be mild. Symptoms include a faint skin rash on hands or feet, swollen lymph nodes, fever. Can also have a rash on your torso or lesions inside the mouth. Occasionally hair loss. These symptoms often self-resolve without treatment, and syphilis goes dormant.

Stage 3 (latent syphilis)—No symptoms. This can last from one to thirty years.

Stage 4 (tertiary syphilis)—Severe medical problems. Not all syphilis advances to stage 4, and it typically takes 10–30 years to develop after initial infection. There can be severe symptoms affecting the heart, skin, internal organs, or brain.

Neurosyphilis—It was once thought that syphilis affecting

the nervous system could only occur after many years. Now it seems that neurologic symptoms can happen at any time in the course of the disease. Symptoms can vary greatly but they all require prompt treatment.

Curable? Yes.

How it's tested: Blood sample. Occasionally lesions may be swabbed and examined under a microscope.

How it's treated: Early-stage syphilis is treated with an injection of penicillin or with a round of antibiotics. Syphilis that has gone over a year without treatment will need a stronger course of antibiotics, usually in the form of a weekly injection for three weeks. Neurosyphilis needs intravenous antibiotics daily for two weeks to be appropriately treated. It is important to take your entire dose of antibiotics according to your doctor's directions; otherwise the infection may not be entirely wiped out. Wait until both you (and your partner, if applicable) finish antibiotics, or seven days (whichever is longest), to have sex again. Any partners you've had within the past sixty days need to be notified and tested.

Possible complications if untreated: Tertiary syphilis can cause brain, heart, eye, and nervous system damage, blood infection, and death. Pregnant women with syphilis are at risk of passing syphilis to their babies, causing them to be born with congenital syphilis—a wide array of significant birth defects and medical problems. It also increases the risk of contracting other STIs.

viral STIs

Human Papillomavirus
(HPV, a.k.a. Genital Warts—the Most Common STI)

Type of infection: Viral

You can get it by: Skin-to-skin contact, which is part of why warts are incredibly common and easy to spread. There are over two hundred strains of HPV, which can pop up in different places on the body.

How to prevent it: Get vaccinated, which protects against some of the most harmful strains of HPV. Using condoms and dental dams helps as well, but they aren't 100% effective because the virus can hang out on uncovered skin. You usually can't see HPV with the naked eye, and warts do not need to be present for the virus to spread. If warts are present, abstain from sex until they have completely gone away and always use protection.

Symptoms: HPV usually has no symptoms, and most people who are infected don't know it. This is especially the case for cancerous strains, because they don't have warts. When there are symptoms, the warts look like flesh-colored cauliflower-like growths on genitals, anus, or mouth. There may be one or a few; they may be flat or raised, small or large.

Curable? No, but in many cases the virus goes dormant (undetectable) within a couple years.

How it's tested: Swab during your pap smear. HPV testing is not done for women and trans men under thirty unless their pap result comes back abnormal. Over age thirty, an HPV test with a pap smear is routine. Currently, there is no HPV test for throats or penises. Anal pap smears with HPV testing are used in some high-risk populations.

How it's treated: The strains of HPV that cause warts are different than the strains that cause cancer. Strains that cause warts are deemed *low-risk*, while strains that cause cancer are deemed *high-risk*. Genital warts/low-risk HPV can be removed from your skin by a doctor (via medication, freezing, or burning), or you can wait them out if they're not troublesome or painful. You can also apply topical prescription medications to warts to help them dissolve faster. For high-risk HPV, cancerous cells are monitored and removed if they start growing.

Possible complications if untreated: HPV that causes warts is not dangerous, but raises the risk of being infected with high-risk HPV at the same time. High-risk HPV can cause a range of cancers, including cervical cancer, throat cancer, penile cancer, and anal cancer.

Herpes Simplex Virus (HSV—Very Common)

Type of infection: Viral

You can get it by: Skin-to-skin contact, which is part of why herpes is incredibly common and easy to spread.

How to prevent it: Using condoms and dental dams helps, but doesn't always 100% prevent transmission because the virus can hang out on uncovered skin. You usually can't see herpes with the naked eye, but if sores are present, abstain from sex until they have completely gone away (and consider taking antivirals to prevent transmitting them to someone else).

Symptoms: Herpes usually has no symptoms, and most people who are infected don't know it. When there are symptoms, herpes sores may look like a single, small blister or a cluster of blisters on genitals, anus, or mouth. HSV-1 typically lives on the mouth (also known as cold sores), while HSV-2 typically lives on the genitals or anus. However, both strains of herpes can live in either location and can be transmitted from mouth to genitals through oral sex—and HSV-1 cases on the genitals are on the rise. HSV-1 is much more common, infecting over half of the population, and tends to be less aggressive than HSV-2.

Curable? No.

How it's tested: Blood test or swab and culture of lesions.

How it's treated: Because there is no cure, treatment is only required when someone has symptoms. Outbreaks are more likely to happen when you are stressed out or your immune system is compromised. Outbreaks are typically the worst at the beginning and become more mild and more spaced out over time. The virus may even go dormant, causing outbreaks to go away completely. For those who have repeat outbreaks, antiviral drugs can be used to suppress symptoms and prevent transmission to a partner.

Possible complications if untreated: In most cases, none. Herpes isn't dangerous unless it affects the eyes; it's just a pain in the ass and can hurt. Herpes that is transmitted to your eyes (by rubbing genitals/mouth then eyes, for instance) can cause blindness if left untreated. Very rarely people can have problems with the nerves in their pelvis. Pregnant women who have herpes may pass it on to their infant and usually take suppressive therapy during the end of their pregnancy.

HIV/AIDS (Human Immunodeficiency Virus and Acquired Immune Deficiency Syndrome)

Type of infection: Viral

You can get it by: Contact with sexual fluids, blood, and breast milk. It can also spread by sharing needles, through birth, and blood transfusions.

How to prevent it: Condoms are a highly effective way to prevent HIV, as well as dental dams (see section 4 on how to have safer sex for more information). Don't share needles. Those at increased risk of HIV exposure should ask their doctor about a once-a-day pill to prevent HIV called PreP (pre-exposure prophylaxis). There is also an emergency pill that can be taken if you think you may have been exposed to HIV. Ideally this medication should be started within two hours but can be initiated for up to three days after. It's called PEP (post-exposure prophylaxis).

Symptoms: Initial HIV infection usually has no symptoms. When there are symptoms, the initial HIV infection may start with what feels like a mild flu. Other symptoms are highly varied, from lesions to fever to blurred vision. Because HIV destroys immune system cells, as infection worsens, it is harder and harder for the body to defend itself from illness. Those who have contracted HIV and aren't being treated get sick more easily.

Curable? No.

How it's tested: Blood test or cheek swab.

How it's treated: Antiviral drugs can help to suppress HIV, sometimes to the point where the virus becomes undetectable. Other treatment for HIV is for the side effects, like the illnesses and opportunistic infections that can happen when the immune system is compromised.

Possible complications if untreated: HIV may advance to AIDS without treatment, which can be deadly. AIDS is the same virus as HIV; it is the point at which HIV becomes a disease caused by chronic infection that has gone untreated. When HIV has managed to destroy 80% of your immune system cells or when you acquire certain illnesses that are evidence of severe immune system compromise, it is classified as AIDS. HIV also makes it easier to contract other STIs.

Hepatitis B

Type of infection: Viral

You can get it by: When mucous membranes make contact with infected sexual fluids, pus, or blood, usually during sexual activity or IV drug use. Hepatitis B spread through birth is the most common cause of chronic hep B worldwide. Rarely, it can be passed by body piercing, organ transfusion, or sharing toothbrushes or razors.

How to prevent it: Always practice safer sex. The hepatitis A and B vaccines are typically given to toddlers, and are the easiest way to stay safe. Unfortunately, the hepatitis B vaccine did not become available until 1984, and the hepatitis A vaccine until 1996. Adults today may or may not have received this vaccine. A preventative shot if you think you've been exposed is available. Avoid sharing personal items that make contact with body fluids.

Symptoms: Hepatitis B initially usually has no symptoms. When there are symptoms: joint pain, rash, fatigue, loss of appetite, dark urine, jaundice.

Curable? No, but only 5–10% of those with hepatitis will develop chronic hepatitis.

How it's tested: Blood test.

How it's treated: Because there is no cure, treatment is for symptoms that hepatitis B can cause.

Possible complications if untreated: Liver cancer, liver damage (cirrhosis), death.

Notes on other strains: Hepatitis A can also be transmitted sexually through oral-anal sex, since it may be present in fecal matter. The CDC has recommended the hepatitis A vaccine for men who have sex with men. Hepatitis C can also be transmitted sexually, but this is less common. There is no vaccine for hepatitis C, but it has recently become curable.

what to do if you contract an STI

CONTRACTING AN STI CAN BE A scary experience, and it might low-key feel like the end of the world. But I promise you, it's not. The stigma is often scarier than the reality of having an STI. Most STIs are curable, and all of them are treatable. Your life will go on. You will continue to have love and sex. You'll also need to make a few changes to your sexual practices.

If you have a bacterial STI, you'll need to abstain from sex for a few weeks while you are treated with antibiotics. Call each partner you've had since you were last tested (and in the last two months) to let them know they may have been exposed to an STI and need to be tested. Many health clinics and doctors' offices will call past partners for you, anonymously. After the infection has cleared, it's critical to be more careful next time. Bacterial infections can evolve to resist treatment the more we use antibiotics (as is the case of untreated "super gonorrhea"). Antibiotics are also hard on your body.

If you have a viral STI, you'll need to do all of the above, plus a few more things. Viral STIs, like HIV and sometimes herpes, may require daily treatment throughout your life. You'll also need to begin disclosing your status to new partners.

Regardless of your current status, it's important to talk about it before you get sexy with someone. The goal of the conversation should be to openly discuss your sexual health status and to plan to get tested.

Here are a few conversation starters:

 "So, when was the last time you were tested?"

Q "Have you ever had an STI?"

Q "I was thinking we should get tested together first. What d'ya think?"

When it comes to disclosing a viral STI, be honest and frank. Let them know that they can stay fairly safe during sex when you are on antivirals and by using protection every time. Be real about it, and let them know the risk is there no matter what—just like with all sex. People come to these conversations with a lot of preconceived notions and often misinformation, so be prepared to answer questions. Having resources on hand (videos, articles, etc.) can come in handy. My sense, just from talking to people who have viral infections, is that their partners are generally level-headed and accepting, but it will likely be an ongoing conversation. It's important that everyone involved be informed, and to feel free to do what makes them comfortable. Discuss boundaries with each other, and respect them.

If someone discloses to you, same dish, but vice versa. However you feel about it is okay. Be compassionate, ask questions, get informed, and discuss what you're comfortable with.

how to have safer sex

YOUR ODDS OF DEALING WITH AN STI go way down if you . . .

- **Get vaccinated for HPV.** The CDC recommends that everybody, regardless of sex, be vaccinated at age eleven, and no later than age twenty-six. This helps protect against the majority of cancers that can be caused by HPV. For more information about the vaccine, see chapter 3.

- **Get tested regularly.** Serious consequences to your health can be avoided by detecting an STI earlier rather than later. STIs usually do not have any symptoms, so the only way to know you have one is to get tested.
- **Use protection every time.** There are two main forms of protection against STIs: condoms and dental dams. You can also use finger cots or gloves for your hands. These should be paired with the proper lubricant. The use of condoms and dental dams can't completely eliminate the risk of contracting an STI, but does *dramatically* lower it.
- **Ask your healthcare provider about preventative measures,** like PreP and PEP to prevent HIV.

While it's not the only relationship style out there, when it comes to sexual health, monogamous sexual relationships tend to be the safest. The more sexual partners you have, the higher your exposure to potential infection, and thus the higher your potential risk. That said, even monogamous couples can transmit infections to each other, and it is entirely possible to stay safe with multiple partners with vigilant safer-sex practices. Regardless of your relationship style, it's important to take measures to protect your sexual health.

Getting Tested

Getting tested for STIs can seem daunting, but it's a pretty straightforward process. Schedule an appointment at your doctor's office, or Google health clinics that offer STI testing. Some clinics are even free. Make an appointment (or figure out their walk-in hours) and get it done. You'll pee in a cup and either have your finger pricked or your cheek swabbed. You may also have a vaginal or urethra swab, or blood drawn. My experience has been that it's fast and pretty painless. If you're sexually active, get tested before each new partner and at least once a year. If you think you've been exposed to an STI, wait at least two weeks to get tested to avoid a false negative.

Condoms

Condoms are an easy (perhaps the easiest!) way to have safer sex. You can get them everywhere—gas stations, drugstores, department stores, and sex shops to name a few. Many health centers give them out for free as well. Latex condoms are cheap, they prevent most STIs, and they're 98% effective at preventing pregnancy when you use them perfectly. What's not to love?

Well . . . a little bit, apparently.

It's not uncommon for me to hear lamentations about condoms. Usually something along the lines of "Condoms suck!!" My responses to these sentiments are twofold: firstly, infections and unwanted pregnancy suck more. But also, are you using the right kind of condom? To maximize the pleasure and feel of condoms, it's important to find the right kind for you. Condoms should be the right material and the right size, then paired with the right lube. We'll talk more about lube in a sec—but in general, the lube that comes on condoms isn't usually very high quality, and can contain ingredients that irritate sensitive skin. This also goes for condoms that have spermicide, flavored lubes, desensitizing, or "heating" and "cooling" features. To really get the most out of them, I'd suggest pairing your condoms with a high-quality lubricant of your own that is compatible with their material.

There are five different types of materials condoms are typically made of.

Type of Condom	Helps prevent STIs?	Helps prevent pregnancy?	Compatible Lubes	Pros & Cons	Example brands
Latex	Yes	Yes	Water Silicone	**Pros:** Cheap, widely available **Cons:** Can cause allergies Can feel restrictive on larger penises Can leave a latex smell on your hands	All of them
Polyisoprene Polyisoprene is a synthetic material that has removed the latex proteins that can cause allergic reactions.	Yes	Yes	Water Silicone	**Pros:** Good for most of those with latex allergies Thinner material, more sensation Conducts heat better than latex May be slightly more durable than latex (still being studied) **Cons:** Becoming more popular but can be hard to find in some stores, so may need to order online Can still cause allergies in those who are *extremely* allergic to latex	LifeStyles SKYN Durex Latex Free Durex RealFeel
Polyurethane	Yes	Yes	Water Silicone Oil	**Pros:** Will not cause latex allergies Thinner, more sensitive material Conducts heat better than latex Can be used with oil-based lubricants	Trojan SUPRA Non-Latex BareSkin

Type of Condom	Helps prevent STIs?	Helps prevent pregnancy?	Compatible Lubes	Pros & Cons	Example brands
Polyurethane (continued)				**Pros:** (continued) No odor Fit is looser for those who feel latex is restrictive Have a longer shelf life than latex **Cons:** Not as well studied as latex Harder to find in stores, so may need to order online May be slightly less durable than latex (still being studied) Can lose their shape and scrunch up more easily, increasing the odds of them slipping off. This problem can be minimized by using lube.	
Lambskin	Nope. Viruses are tiny and can pass through the large pores of lambskin condoms. Sperm are much larger than viruses, so these still offer pregnancy protection.	Yes	Water Silicone Oil	**Pros:** Some people like the "natural" feel Definitely better than nothing **Cons:** Doesn't protect against STIs May not stay on as well Expensive (about $3 ea.) It's made out of the digestive tract of a sheep ¯_(ツ)_/¯	LifeStyles SKYN Durex Latex Free Durex RealFeel

SPERM

HIV

Type of Condom	Helps prevent STIs?	Helps prevent pregnancy?	Compatible Lubes	Pros & Cons	Example brands
Female Condom (For vulvas and vaginas only. Do not put in butts. Made of synthetic rubber.)	Yes	Yes	Water Silicone Oil	**Pros:** Can be inserted up to 8 hours ahead of time Slightly more protection against HSV and HPV, because it covers more surface area **Cons:** Can take practice to put in (see page 225 for instructions) Can make a plasticky sound if you don't use enough lube	FC2 Female Condom

Once you find the right material, it's important to buy condoms in the **right size**. Just like clothes and bras, the right fit can make a world of difference, offering not only better protection but increased pleasure. Most of the big brands offer both standard and large sizing, but you should also note that those sizes vary between brands. To get a ballpark idea of your size, you can use a toilet paper roll trick.

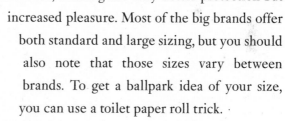

TOILET PAPER ROLL TRICK

Slip a toilet paper roll around your erect penis.

- If there's a bit of extra space, look for "snug fit" condoms (about 35% of guys).

- If it's just right, start with standard-size condoms (about 50%).
- If it feels suffocatingly tight, start with large-size condoms (about 15%).

Don't use a size that's too big, or it could slip off and cause an oopsie! Condoms should fit snugly. But if it's too tight, it will feel restrictive and dig into the skin. After finding the right material and size, the rest is in the bag! Just make sure to use it properly so your efforts aren't in vain.

HOW TO USE A MALE CONDOM

1. Make sure it's not expired and take it out of the wrapper.

2. Pinch the tip of the condom (to leave a small amount of space for the semen) with one hand while you roll it all the way down with the other. Make sure to put the condom on before any penetration—no oopsies!

3. Apply lube. Typical use is applying lube to the outside of the condom, but you can also put a small dab on the inside to increase pleasure. Just don't use too much on the inside, or it won't stay in place!

4. Have awesome safer sex.

5. After sex, pinch the bottom of the condom to pull it off and discard. Don't reuse.

HOW TO USE A FEMALE CONDOM

These baddies can be inserted up to eight hours ahead. Woo.

1. The female condom has two flexible plastic rings, one at either end. Grab the ring on the closed end, pinch to narrow it, and push it up into your vagina. Some find it easier to do this while they're squatting. Make sure to push the ring all the way up in there, against the cervix at the back of the vagina. The other ring at the open end stays *outside* of the vagina, covering part of the labia.

2. Before penetrative sex, make sure the condom isn't twisted for smooth insertion.

3. Apply proper lube to the penis/toy/etc.

4. Have awesome safer sex.

5. After sex, twist the ring (it'll lock the semen in) and pull it out. Discard.

Note: Don't reuse female condoms. Don't use in butts (they could get stuck). Don't use at the same time as a male condom; it can break them. If it's tugging at all or making any plastic noise, apply more lube.

LUBE!

I'm a big advocate of using a high-quality lube during sexytimes. I feel like not enough people use it. BUT WHY?? It improves glide and reduces friction, which not only feels a helluva lot nicer, but also makes your condoms more effective. I think there's a weird stigma to lube sometimes—as if it's strange to use it. But not all body parts lubricate themselves, and vaginas aren't always wet on demand, especially not enough for optimal pleasure and comfort. Vaginal wetness varies by person; it can be affected by age, estrogen levels, stress, and a bunch of other factors. How wet you get varies by encounter too. Super steamy encounters, when you're highly aroused and have a lot of buildup, may be wetter. Vaginas can also be wetter during certain parts of the menstrual cycle, thanks to discharge. There's no shame in using lube to supplement.

There are three basic types of lube: water based, silicone based, and oil based. If it doesn't say which it is on the label, read the ingredients. It's important to know what's in your lube. Personal lubricants, especially those that are mass-produced by big brands, tend to have a lot of crap in them that can be irritating or harmful to the genitals. If you don't have an STI and your lube burns a bit when you apply it, or if it causes irritation, try a different one. I had to try four or five kinds before I found one that felt amazing.

Here are some common ingredients I recommend avoiding:

- Glycerin—it's a form of sugar, which means it can feed/cause yeast infections
- Propylene glycol—can be irritating/burn/itch
- Chlorhexidine—can be irritating/burn/itch
- Petroleum and petroleum derivatives—leaves a coating on skin that can trap bacteria

- Parabens and phthalates—while research has not been able to establish a direct link, there is a possibility that both of these ingredients increase cancer risk
- Citric acid—can be irritating/burn/itch and can be drying

Water Based

PROS: Can be used with all condom/dental dam types. Easy to find. Cheaper.

CONS: Doesn't last as long as other types because water dries more quickly. To rewet water-based lube, apply more water, not more lube.

Silicone Based

PROS: Longer lasting, can be used with all condom types. Waterproof, so it can be used in the shower.

CONS: Can be harder to find and a little more expensive. Can't be used with silicone sex toys. Silicone lube is also flammable and will turn your floor into a slip'n'slide if you spill it.

Oil Based

PROS: Longer lasting. Cheaper.

CONS: Oil will break latex condoms, and many oils are not great for internal use. Oils can feed bacteria and fungi, increasing the risk of infection or worsening an existing one. Oil can also stain your sheets.

Natural Lube Alternatives

Aloe vera is a cheap, water-based lubricant that can be used during sex and masturbation. Because it's water based, it is compatible with latex condoms. Make sure to buy pure aloe vera, not gels with added ingredients like alcohol. Alcohol + vagina or butt = no thanks.

Coconut oil is a cheap, oil-based lubricant that is compatible with nonlatex condoms. Preliminary research shows that coconut oil may have antibacterial and antifungal properties, which would make it a safer natural lube than other oils. Use high-quality coconut oil that is virgin, cold-pressed/unrefined, and organic.

You can also make your own lube!

DIY LUBE: Flax Seed Goo

by Sheri Winston, author of Women's Anatomy of Arousal

THIS LUBE CAN BE USED internally and externally. It's soothing, protective, and hypoallergenic. Plus, when it's fresh, it has hardly any taste or smell. It's also water soluble, so it can be used with condoms.

To make this lube you'll need:
  1 cup whole flax seeds (not ground)
  6 cups water

Combine both in a pot and bring to a boil. Turn down heat, and set timer for six minutes. Turn off heat and let sit for six minutes. Strain the seeds out. Voilà!

Store your lube in the fridge, and keep a smaller amount in a jar or squeeze bottle to keep handy for sex. It will keep for two months in fridge, and two to three days at room temperature. It may be preserved with grapefruit seed extract, calcium ascorbate (or a similar vitamin C compound), vitamin E, potassium sorbate, essential oil of lavender, rosemary, or sandalwood oil.

Sheri's recipe makes several cups of lube. If you don't want a buttload of lube (frankly, I don't know why you wouldn't), you can reduce the recipe; just keep a ratio of 1 part flax seed to 6 parts water.

Safer Oral Sex

Oral sex can transmit infections, too. Most people don't think of oral sex as something that carries any risk, and using protection is deemed a little weird. It's that darn stigma again. But genitals have mucous membranes, and so do mouths. Generally, it's a little harder to transmit infections between mouths and genitals (as opposed to genital-to-genital), but it still happens. For instance, chlamydia, gonorrhea, and herpes can be transmitted back and forth between mouths and genitals. Occasionally I've had students say to me, "Don't worry, I looked beforehand and my partner was clean!" Thumbs up for trying, but you can't tell if someone has an STI by looking at their genitals.

You can protect yourself during oral sex by getting tested with your partner beforehand and by using a protective barrier. Here are a few barriers that will do the job:

1. Condoms. Unlubricated, or with flavored lube, or whatever you fancy.

2. Dental dams. They're basically just a flat square of latex. You can buy them at sex shops or online. I haven't seen them in drugstores.

3. Male condoms turned into dental dams. If it's last minute and you need a barrier, you can turn a male condom into a dental dam. Follow these steps.

4. Plastic wrap. Works in a pinch.

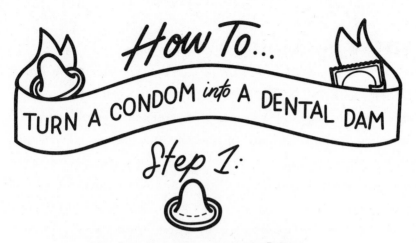

How To...
TURN A CONDOM into A DENTAL DAM

Step 1:

ON A ROLLED-UP CONDOM,
SNIP OFF THE TIP OF THE CONDOM.
YOU WILL NOW HAVE A RING.

Step 2:

SNIP THE RING DOWN THE SIDE.

Step 3:

UNROLL. YOU WILL NOW HAVE
A DENTAL DAM!

safer sexting

SEXTING ISN'T TECHNICALLY SEX—BUT THERE'S A lotta frisky Snapchatting and iMessaging happening these days! And I think it's worth talking about how to stay safe digitally as well. "Sexting" usually refers to sending sexually explicit texts, pictures, or videos over your phone. It's estimated that one in three teenagers sexts. In the sex-edusphere, I have met a few educators who feel caught between a rock and a hard place with how to address sexting. In the right circumstances, sexting is a way to express your sexuality with a partner. It enables couples at a distance to be intimate with each other, and it also allows for a bit of fun without the risks of STIs or pregnancy. But sexting also carries its own complicated and unique risks.

In recent years, scandalous photos have been weaponized by abusive partners. High-profile stories tell tales of abusive exes who used these photos to blackmail and harass their former partners. Sometimes, the photos were shared willingly earlier in the relationship; other times, the photos were hacked and stolen without the owner's knowledge. The phenomenon has become so notorious that it even has its own name: revenge porn. Underground websites have cropped up to name and shame people with their naked photos. Some of these websites have even made millions in advertising and subscription profits. Unsurprisingly, the targets are almost exclusively women.

Revenge porn is a type of abuse that cropped up quickly with the advent of smartphones, leaving lawmakers scrambling to figure out how to address it legally. Today, most states finally have revenge porn laws on the books, making it illegal. But the law is more useful as a deterrent than as a solution to the problem. Once someone's consent and privacy have been violated, it can't be undone.

Outside of legal consequences, we can address revenge porn on a social level by taking care to give abusive people as little power as possible. The most obvious way to do that is to not participate in it. If you find out one of your friends is sharing revenge porn, call them on it, make sure they know what they're doing may be illegal, and let their partner know what's going on. Don't share revenge porn, and discourage others from sharing it as well. If it's at school or work, notify someone who can help you if you need it. When there's a "leak" or a "hack" online, don't open the photos/video. Additionally, do not blame the victim of the leak for taking or sharing the photos. There is nothing ethically wrong with taking a photo or sharing it privately—the ethical violation is in sharing someone else's photos nonconsensually. Avoid blaming the person being targeted, as it only gives more legitimacy to the actions of abusers. If we all refuse to participate in an abuser's attempt to humiliate their victim, the abuser has no power left to exert. People who have been targeted have come up with their own ways to address the abuse as well. There are women who, while they were being threatened, decided to post their photos themselves. In 2017, when she found out paparazzi were selling off her nude photo to the highest bidder, musician Sia decided to post the picture herself on her Twitter. I know two women personally who have taken this approach. Both told me that when it became clear that their ex was definitely going to do it, they felt just slightly more in control by doing it on their own terms. This isn't ideal. Even though it gives the target of the abuse a smidge more control, it is still a form of violation to feel compelled to post the photos yourself because the alternative is for someone else to do it.

In a perfect world, nobody is an asshole who uses the sacred sexiness of scandalous photo swaps against their partner. In a perfect world, people balk at the notion that someone would violate a partner in such a juvenile and sadistic way. And hey, I think most of us do balk at it. But the world is not perfect, and shitty people are out there. Here are some ways to deal.

- Have a conversation with your partner about their comfort levels with sexting.
- Never pressure your partner or expect photos from them.
- Only share photos with people you strongly trust and know well.
- Make sure that your face isn't in it, nor any identifying features in the background or on your body (hair, tattoos, birthmarks, etc.). This will make it untraceable to you.
- Secure your phone and digital devices.
- Use strong passwords that you change regularly.
- Make sure you know where your photos/vids are stored and protect those accounts.
- Don't send pictures through apps and wifi connections that aren't secure.

Of course, it's always okay to take the abstinence route on sexting. Don't ask others for pictures, and don't send them either. If you're under eighteen, this is what I'd suggest. In most places, a minor taking nude photos or receiving nude photos of another minor is actually illegal. Many teen sexting cases are still governed by child pornography laws, and people (including young adults) have actually been sent to jail for it. Know the laws in your area before sexting.

ELEVEN

BIRTH CONTROL

BY NOW YOU'VE PROBABLY FIGURED OUT that there's no stork involved in baby-making (hopefully). Whether you *want* to get pregnant or *don't want* to get pregnant, the key to planning your reproductive future is understanding a bit about how the female reproductive system works. If you are having sex that involves a penis and a vagina and you don't want to get pregnant right now, birth control is a must. And lucky for us, here in the twenty-first century there are several types to choose from!

IN THIS CHAPTER WE'LL GO OVER

Ovulation

Barrier methods

Hormonal methods

Natural methods

Emergency methods

Pregnancy scares

Abortion

ovulation

RECALL FROM CHAPTER 2 THAT THE menstrual cycle lasts twenty-one to thirty-five days on average, and has four basic phases. The relevant phase when it comes to pregnancy prevention is ovulation. Ovulation occurs when one of the ovaries releases an egg to be fertilized. This is the only phase where fertilization can happen, which is why virtually all forms of birth control seek to intervene with it. Ovulation usually occurs about two weeks, or fourteen days, into the menstrual cycle.

There are several signs that indicate ovulation is happening. Around this time, or right before it, testosterone levels peak. As a result, you might notice a spike in your sex drive. When I'm ovulating, I usually feel some very light cramping and bloating. This is normal. It's also normal to have some light spotting or breast tenderness, like a lighter version of period symptoms. It's also normal to have no symptoms at all. I like to use a period tracker app to track ovulation symptoms. The aggregated data helps me predict when I might be ovulating, which is also how Fertility Awareness Methods (FAM) of birth control work. More on that in a bit.

Other signs of ovulation are:

Cervical fluid changes. During ovulation, the consistency of your discharge is similar to egg whites. It's clear and sticks to itself when you pull it between your fingers. You may also produce more discharge and feel wetter as a result.

Basal body temperature (BBT) tends to slowly decline leading up to ovulation. Right after ovulation, BBT jumps up again.

Your cervix changes position. During ovulation, the cervix is higher up in the vagina, softer, and slightly more open.

Unfortunately, avoiding pregnancy is not as simple as avoiding sex during ovulation. While ovulation only lasts one day, sperm can live for up to *five days* inside the body. They're resilient as hell. Sperm vary in the amount of time they take to reach the egg. It is also difficult to determine exactly when ovulation is happening, since everybody's cycle and symptoms are a little bit different.

So, ovulation. That's a thing. Let's talk about all the ways you can intervene with it.

IN THE MOST BASIC SENSE, PREVENTING a pregnancy means preventing one of the hundreds of millions of sperm from reaching the egg. Turns out, that's no easy task. Throughout the ages, humans have come up with all kinds of kooky and creative ways to attempt to prevent pregnancy. In ancient Egypt, women put crocodile feces up into their vagina to kill the sperm. In the 1400s in Japan, ancient condoms to cover the head of the penis were formulated out of tortoise shell or animal horn. Among the more mystical types, European women during the Dark Ages would create amulets out of weasel testicles to ward off pregnancy. So, uh, you could say that times have changed.

These days we have over a dozen different methods to prevent pregnancy that are all much safer, much more effective, and significantly less . . . icky. Each birth control method offers different benefits, and not all methods are suitable for everyone, depending on your medical history. While birth control is sometimes used to prevent pregnancy, it is also used for a wide range of other health issues as well. Some methods may also be used to prevent health problems such as painful periods, cysts in the breasts or ovaries, acne, iron deficiency, bone thinning, and so much more. There are two basic types of reversible birth control: barrier methods and hormonal methods. Let's take a closer look:

barrier methods

BARRIER METHODS WORK BY PHYSICALLY BLOCKING sperm from reaching the egg. There are several different options to choose from, and each has different levels of effectiveness. Below, I've listed the effectiveness rates if you use it *perfectly* and the effectiveness rates in the real world (because, well, in real life we're not always perfect). If a method is listed as 85% effective, that means 15 out of every 100 people end up getting pregnant every year with that method. These effectiveness rates come from Planned Parenthood and the CDC.

Condoms

Perfect use: 98% effective for male condoms, 95% effective for female condoms

Real life: 85% effective for male condoms, 79% effective for female condoms

No prescription required

We already covered male and female condoms in chapter 10, "Safer Sex," so check that out for more in-depth information on this awesome method! Condoms are easy to use, easy to find, cheap, and effective at preventing pregnancy. They are one of the most popular methods out there.

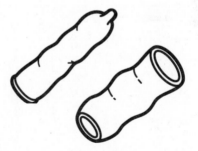

The Sponge

Perfect use: 80–91% effective (it's more effective for those who haven't given vaginal birth)

Real life: 76–88% effective

No prescription required

The sponge is soft and squishy and looks like a small doughnut. You can buy them at drugstores, department stores, online, or at some health centers. In the USA, they're called the "Today Sponge." They're about $10 to $15 for a pack of three. The sponge protects in two ways: it blocks the cervix from sperm getting in, and it contains spermicide to kill sperm that come into contact with it. The sponge can easily be paired with condoms or the pull-out method to increase its effectiveness. Other perks of the sponge are that it's hormone free, it's easily available if it's a last-minute thing, and it doesn't interrupt sex. Drawbacks are that putting it in can be tricky at first, and spermicide is irritating to a lot of vaginas.

Perks of the sponge	Drawbacks of the sponge
• Easily paired with other methods, like condoms	• Putting it in can be tricky
• Available over the counter	• Needs to be inserted before sex, every time
• Hormone free	• Spermicide is irritating to a lot of vaginas
• Disposable	• Spermicide increases the risk of contracting an STI like HIV
	• May increase risk of bladder infections
	• Can't use during your period

HOW TO USE THE SPONGE

Wash your hands, then open the wrapper and wet the sponge with clean water. Squeeze gently until the spermicide in the sponge foams. Don't squeeze the spermicide out; you want it nice and foamy when you put it in. You can put it in up to twenty-four hours before sex.

Gently push the sponge *all the way up* inside the vagina with the indented side going in first. The indentation is where your cervix will sit, and the fabric loop should face you for easy removal. Some find squatting, sitting on a toilet, or putting one leg up on a chair makes it easier to push the sponge in. Gently feel around the edges of the sponge to make sure it's properly placed and all the way in there.

IMPORTANT: leave the sponge in for at least six hours after sex. That way it can kill any sperm. You can leave it in up to thirty hours total. When it's time to remove it, simply tug the fabric strap and pull it out. If your fingers are short or you're having trouble reaching it, squat during removal and/or push a little bit through your vagina, like you're going to poop.

Das it. Throw away. Don't reuse.

DON'T USE THE SPONGE IF . . .

- you're on your period; it can increase the risk of toxic shock syndrome (TSS).
- you're sensitive to spermicide (Nonoxynol-9) or polyure-thane. If you find the sponge makes your vagina feel sore or irritated afterward or you start getting more UTIs, you may have a sensitivity to spermicide. Try a different method.
- you have an infection in/around your vagina.
- you've had an abortion, miscarriage, or given birth in the last six weeks.

Your nurse or doctor can help you decide if this method is a good fit for you.

The Cervical Cap

Perfect use: 80–91% effective (it's more effective for those who haven't given vaginal birth)

Real life: 71–86% effective

Prescription required

The cervical cap is a small cup made of soft silicone that sits over the cervix. This helps stop sperm from reaching the egg. It is more effective when you use it with spermicide to kill the sperm as well. Your healthcare provider will help you find the right size cap for your body. They run about $90 without insurance, but are usually covered by insurance, or some state programs.

Perks of the cervical cap	Drawbacks of the cervical cap
• Easily paired with other methods, like condoms • Hormone free • Reusable • Only needs to be replaced once a year	• Putting it in can be tricky • Needs to be inserted before sex, every time • Spermicide is irritating to a lot of vaginas • Spermicide increases the risk of contracting an STI like HIV • May increase risk of bladder infections • Can't use during your period

HOW TO USE THE CERVICAL CAP

Wash your hands. Squirt ¼ to ½ teaspoon of spermicide in the cup and on the other side in the groove around the dome. Using your finger, spread the spermicide around the brim as well. You can insert the cervical cap up to two hours before sex. Any earlier than that, and it won't work as well.

Feel for your cervix with a finger so you know where to aim for. Using one hand, spread your labia. Using the other, gently squeeze the brim and push it up into the vagina. The removal tab should face you, while the opening to the dome and brim face up into the vagina. This allows the cap to sit around the cervix.

Make sure to leave the cap in place at least six hours *after* sex, up to forty-eight hours total. To remove it, squat and push against the top of the dome to break the suction. Hook and pull the tab on the cap to remove.

Wash and dry your cap with soap and warm water, air dry, and store in a clean place away from extreme cold or sunlight. Give it a good visual inspection now and then to make sure there are no tears or cracks. You can test for leaks by putting water in it.

DON'T USE THE CERVICAL CAP IF . . .

- you're on your period; it can increase the risk of toxic shock syndrome (TSS).
- you're sensitive to spermicide (Nonoxynol-9). If you find the spermicide makes your vagina feel sore or irritated afterward, or you start getting more UTIs, you may have a sensitivity to spermicide.
- you have cervical cancer or other cervix issues.
- you've had an abortion, miscarriage, or given birth in the last six weeks.

Your nurse or doctor can help you decide if this method is a good fit for you.

The Diaphragm

Perfect use: 94% effective

Real life: 88% effective

Prescription required

The diaphragm is a soft cup that covers the cervix, to help prevent sperm from reaching the egg. It is paired with spermicide to kill sperm. It's similar to the cervical cap, just larger.

Your healthcare provider will help you find the right size diaphragm for your body. They run about $75 without insurance, but are usually covered by insurance, or some state programs.

Perks of the diaphragm	Drawbacks of the diaphragm
• Easily paired with other methods, like condoms • Hormone free • Reusable • Only needs to be replaced twice a year	• Putting it in can be tricky • Needs to be inserted before sex, every time • Spermicide is irritating to a lot of vaginas • Spermicide increases the risk of contracting an STI like HIV • May increase risk of bladder infections • Can't use during your period • May need to be resized if you lose or gain ten or more pounds

HOW TO USE THE DIAPHRAGM

Wash your hands. Squirt a tablespoon of spermicide in the cup and spread the spermicide around the brim with your finger as well.

Using one hand, spread your labia. Using the other, gently squeeze the brim, folding the diaphragm in half, and push it all the way up into the vagina—as far as it can go. The top of the dome should be facedown to properly make space for the cervix.

Make sure to leave the diaphragm in place at least six hours *after* sex, up to twenty-four hours total. To remove it, squat, then hook your finger over the top of the brim to pull it out.

Wash and dry your diaphragm with mild soap and water, air dry, and store in a clean place away from extreme cold or sunlight. Give it a good visual inspection now and then to make sure there are no tears or cracks. You can test for leaks by putting water in it.

DON'T USE THE DIAPHRAGM IF . . .

- you're sensitive to spermicide (Nonoxynol-9). If you find the spermicide makes your vagina feel sore or irritated afterward, or you start getting more UTIs, you may have a sensitivity to spermicide.
- you have cervical cancer or other cervix issues.
- you've had an abortion, miscarriage, or given birth in the last six weeks.

Your nurse or doctor can help you decide if this method is a good fit for you.

hormonal methods

The Intrauterine Device (IUD)

Perfect use: Over 99% effective—the most effective method available

Real life: Over 99% effective

Both hormonal and nonhormonal versions are available

Prescription and insertion required

The IUD is a small, flexible, T-shaped device that sits in your uterus to prevent pregnancy. IUDs cost around $850 without insurance, but are usually covered by insurance, or some state programs. Even though there is a high up-front cost, IUDs usually end up being one of the cheapest methods because they last three to twelve years. While IUDs have been gaining popularity as a birth control method again in recent years, they were also pretty popular in the 1970s. These days, IUDs are very safe, they're reversible (not permanent!), and effective—the most effective reversible method, in fact, at over 99%! There 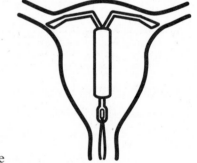 are other perks too. IUDs don't require paying any attention to daily or before sex, and they last for years. These are a few of the reasons why the IUD has been my personal method for ten years.

There are two basic types of IUDs: the copper IUD (which is nonhormonal) and hormonal IUDs. Both types prevent pregnancy in part by forming a barrier for the sperm and causing a little bit of inflammation—enough to be a hostile environment for conception. The copper coil on the nonhormonal IUD also alters the biochemical environment of the uterus, which inhibits sperm's ability to move and makes it hard for them to survive very long. These changes are safe, and stop once your provider takes it out. The copper IUD lasts twelve years, the longest of the five types that are available.

Perks of the copper IUD	Drawbacks of the copper IUD
• Easily paired with other methods, like condoms • Hormone free • Extremely convenient—don't need to think about it • Lasts up to twelve years • Over 99% effective • Cheap method over time ($650 for five to twelve years)	• Insertion can be uncomfortable • May make periods longer, heavier, and crampier, especially the first three to six months • High up-front cost without insurance

Hormonal IUDs work a little differently because they don't have a copper coil. Instead, they release the hormone progestin to prevent pregnancy. The hormones in IUDs are released locally at very low doses, the lowest dose of all the hormonal methods. There are four different types of hormonal IUDs available in the United States currently: Mirena, Kyleena, Skyla, and Liletta. The hormones work by thickening the mucus of the cervix, which helps trap sperm. They can also thin the lining of the uterus, making it impossible for an egg to plant itself there. The lining of the uterus is what is shed during your period, which is why hormonal IUDs often give you lighter periods or eliminate them altogether over time. If there's no lining to shed, there's no period to be had. Ovulation can also be affected by hormonal IUDs. Once an IUD is removed by your provider, the uterus goes back to normal and your period resumes.

Perks of the hormonal IUD	Drawbacks of the hormonal IUD
• Easily paired with other methods, like condoms • Extremely convenient—don't need to think about it • Lasts up to six years • Over 99% effective • Cheap method over time ($650 for three to six years) • Lighter or no periods	• Insertion can be painful • High up-front cost without insurance

A popular misconception about IUDs (that I also thought was true for a while!) is that they increase the risk of pelvic inflammatory disease while you have it in. Research on the topic has found there is only a *very small* risk of infection (0.1%) at the time an IUD is put in place, and for a couple weeks after that. The risk is about the same for those who have an STI when the IUD is put in as those who don't. Your healthcare provider will test you for STIs during your visit.

GETTING THE IUD PUT IN (AND TAKEN OUT)

The most common question I get when I tell someone I have a copper IUD is "Did it hurt??? Do your periods suck??" The answer is yes and yes, though both were manageable and temporary. Also: hella worth it not to worry about pregnancy, and if you don't want sucky periods, there's always the hormonal IUD. It's worth noting that online, horror stories about IUDs seem to get the most traction even though they only represent a very small portion of overall experiences. I think this is because of the way search engine algorithms work, and it can create a lot more fear than is necessary. Just be mindful and critical while perusing the internet for more information.

As far as getting it put in, here's a bit about my experience. I've had two copper IUDs put in. The first time was great, and the second time it was more painful. The first time, it was at Planned Parenthood. They told me to take ibuprofen before I came to help with cramping, and it did help quite a bit. During the appointment, I stripped off my bottoms and lay back on the table with my legs in stirrups while the practitioner inserted the IUD. It's a bit like getting a pap smear, and took maybe five minutes. The IUD is inserted with a thin tube, like a straw, that helps the practitioner slip the IUD through your cervical os. This is what makes it painful—the cervical os is sensitive. It's part of why child labor hurts so bad—that thing dilates to let through a HUMAN HEAD. I'd describe the pain of IUD insertion as similar to a really bad period cramp that lasts for about five minutes. Then, afterward and for the next few days, I had cramping that came in waves. It's the worst right after and slowly improves. If you can, plan to take it easy after getting an IUD put in. Take ibuprofen and whip out your heating pad. I took hot baths and ate hot soup, which helped soothe my achy uterus. After a few weeks, I was all better and didn't think about it again for six years. The second time I had the IUD put in, I was very sore for almost a week after, and I was in an almost blinding amount of pain the night after. My partner at the time took great care of me, but it was pretty miserable for a couple weeks. I believe this happened because the doctor I saw was very rough during insertion and obviously rushed. The moral of the story? Going to a provider that is experienced, that cares about you, and that you trust can make a huge difference in the experience.

As far as periods go, because I have the copper IUD, my periods are slightly heavier and longer with it in—even a few years into it like I am now. Without an IUD, my periods are about four days. With the IUD, they are seven days, and the first two days are a lot heavier. But it's nothing unmanageable. The hormonal IUD is a better method for people who have painful periods or a low pain tolerance.

Removal was simple. I went back in, legs in stirrups, and the nurse removed it by locating and gently tugging on the strings. It hurt for about ten seconds, and then cramping eased off within the hour. I spotted the next day, and that was it. Removal was much easier on my body than the insertion was.

The Pill

Perfect use: 99% effective

Real life: 91% effective

Prescription required

The pill was the first form of hormonal birth control to hit the market in the United States, in 1960. It was a feat of science that dramatically changed the sexual landscape—especially for women. For the first time, the pill offered women in the 1960s the ability to reliably plan their reproductive futures on their own accord, and to have sex for pleasure without worrying about accidental pregnancy. Since then, the pill has come a long way in terms of effectiveness and safety, as well as social acceptance. There are now dozens of different types of pills with different hormonal formulas. Figuring out which pill is right for you may take a little patience and experimentation.

Most birth control pills are "combination pills," meaning they contain a combination of both estrogen and progestin. They may come in a pack of twenty-one, twenty-eight, or ninety-one pills.

Twenty-one-day packs contain three weeks of hormones. You then take no pills for seven days to have your period—set your calendar alarm for seven days so you don't forget. You can also move on to the next pack to skip your period.

Twenty-eight-day packs are the same deal, but they contain seven days of filler pills (no hormones) while you have your period. Some people like taking the filler pills so they stay in their daily habit and don't forget to restart. You can also skip the filler pills and move on to the next pack to skip your period. If you decide to skip filler pills and go straight to the next pack, you may have a little spotting the first few months around the time of your period. If you have any questions about skipping periods with pills, talk to your doctor. It's also worth checking on your insurance coverage, because sometimes insurance only covers one pack per month (to skip periods you need an extra week).

Ninety-one-day packs offer three months of pills and then one week of filler pills while you have your period. With ninety-one-day packs, you only get your period every three months.

REGARDLESS OF THE BRAND OR FORMULATION, all the pills (and all hormonal methods, really) prevent pregnancy in basically the same way: by stopping ovulation and by thickening the cervical mucus so it's difficult for sperm to swim through it on the way up to the uterus. Birth control pills can cost up to $113 a month out of pocket, but they are usually covered by insurance, or some state programs.

HOW TO USE THE PILL

Using the pill is easy. The hardest part is that it needs to be taken once a day *at the same time* to prevent pregnancy. Setting an alarm on your phone or using a birth control app makes it easier to remember. If you forget, follow the package instructions or search "I missed my pill" on Planned Parenthood's website—and use a backup method until you're back on track. Taking the pill at a different time every day makes it less effective, especially for progestin-only pills. When you stop taking the pills, you can get pregnant again.

When you first start taking the pill, continue to use another prevention method, like condoms, for a week or two to give it time to kick in. Using a backup method is also a good idea in general—more protection!

Perks of the pill	Drawbacks of the pill
• Easily paired with other methods, like condoms	• You have to remember it every day
• Hormones can have positive side effects (reducing cramps, reducing or preventing cysts in breasts and ovaries, clearing acne)	• Hormones can have negative side effects (nausea, headaches, sore breasts, bloating and weight gain, mood issues)

Your nurse or doctor can help you decide if this method is a good fit for you.

The Ring

Perfect use: 99% effective

Real life: 91% effective

Prescription required

The vaginal ring is a thin plastic ring that hangs out in your vagina. The ring slowly releases hormones that are absorbed by the vaginal lining. It contains both estrogen and progestin and works like all the other hormonal methods of this sort: by stopping ovulation and by thickening the cervical mucus so it's difficult for sperm to swim through it on the way up to the uterus. The ring can cost up to $75 a month out of pocket, but is usually covered by insurance, or some state programs.

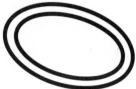

Perks of the ring	Drawbacks of the ring
• Easily paired with other methods like condoms • Only have to think about it once or twice a month • Easy to insert • Hormones can have positive side effects (reducing cramps, lighter periods, reducing or preventing cysts in breasts and ovaries, clearing acne, etc.)	• May have spotting between periods for the first few months • Hormones can have negative side effects, especially the first few months (spotting and irregular bleeding, nausea, headaches, sore breasts, bloating and weight gain, mood issues, etc.)

Wash your hands.

Squeeze the ring together and gently push it into your vagina, like a tampon.

If you want to have a period, leave it in for three weeks, and take it out for one week. If you don't want to have a period, leave it in for four weeks and then switch immediately.

To remove the ring for your period, hook your finger around the ring and pull to remove. Set an alarm to remind yourself when to put it back in!

When you first start using the ring, use a backup birth control method for a week while the ring gets to work. You can leave the ring in during sex, period, everything. It's fine if it moves around, as long as it's inside. If you want to remove it for sex, just make sure to put it back in after you're done. Once it has been out for two days (not including the days it's out for your period), you can get pregnant again.

Your nurse or doctor can help you decide if this method is a good fit for you.

The Shot

Perfect use: 99% effective

Real life: 94% effective

Prescription required

The shot is an injection that is administered every three months to prevent pregnancy. It contains only progestin, and works like other hormonal methods: by stopping ovulation, and by thickening the cervical mucus so it's difficult for sperm to swim through on the way up to the uterus.

The shot can cost up to $120 a month out of pocket, but it is usually covered by insurance, or some state programs.

Perks of the shot	Drawbacks of the shot
• Easily paired with other methods like condoms	• It's a shot, and some people hate those
• Only have to get it every three months	• There may be soreness at the injection site for a few days
• Very discreet—nobody will know you have it	• You have to schedule ahead with your nurse or doctor to get your injection on time
• Progestin only, so safe for those who cannot take estrogen	• In addition to typical hormonal side effects like nausea and weight gain, the shot can also cause temporary bone thinning and migraines while it's in use. It helps not to smoke or drink, to work out, and to get enough calcium. The shot also elevates risk for depression, so try another method first if you have mental health struggles.
• Hormones can have side effects (reducing cramps, lighter periods, reducing or preventing cysts in breasts and ovaries, clearing acne, etc.)	
	• It can take up to ten months to get pregnant again after using the shot

DON'T USE THE SHOT IF . . .

- you've had breast cancer.
- you have a bone disease (the shot may decrease calcium in the bones).
- you drink or smoke a lot.

Your nurse or doctor can help you decide if this method is a good fit for you.

The Patch

Perfect use: 99% effective

Real life: 91% effective

Prescription required

The transdermal patch is a plastic adhesive (kind of like a square Band-Aid) that you stick on your belly, butt, arm, or back to prevent pregnancy. The patch works like other hormonal methods: by stopping ovulation, and by thickening the cervical mucus so it's  difficult for sperm to swim through on the way up to the uterus. The patches run up to $80 for a month's supply without insurance, but are usually covered by insurance, or some state programs. Use a backup method your first week on the patch, if it comes off, or if you forget to change it on time.

Perks of the patch	Drawbacks of the patch
• Easily paired with other methods like condoms	• Have to remember to change it the same day, every week
• Only have to change once a week	• Hormones can have negative side effects, especially the first few months (spotting and irregular bleeding, nausea, headaches, sore breasts, bloating and weight gain, mood issues, etc.)
• Hormones can have positive side effects (reducing cramps, lighter periods, reducing or preventing cysts in breasts and ovaries, clearing acne, etc.)	

HOW TO USE THE PATCH

Open the package and remove the plastic to reveal the adhesive side of the patch. Try not to touch the adhesive with your fingers so that it stays sticky.

Stick patch to your back, upper outer arm, belly, or butt. Don't stick it to your boobs.

Wear it for one week and then switch patches the same day every week. After three weeks, go patchless for one week to have your period. If you don't want to have your period, just go to the next patch.

To remove the patch, pull it off and fold it in half. Throw it in the trash, not the toilet (this helps keep hormones out of our water and dirt).

IF THE PATCH FALLS OFF . . .

It's unlikely, but it happens. Restick it if it's been two days or less. Apply a new patch if it won't stick. Stick to your normal patch-change day.

If it has been more than two days, put on a new patch—and this will be your new patch-change day. Use a backup method for a week.

DON'T USE THE PATCH IF . . .

- you're over thirty-five and smoke cigs.
- you're on certain antibiotics or antifungals (ask your nurse or doc).
- you have problems with migraines or high blood pressure.
- you have had breast cancer, a heart attack, severe diabetes, or blood clots.

Your nurse or doctor can help you decide if this method is a good fit for you.

The Implant

Perfect use: Over 99% effective

Real life: Over 99% effective

Prescription and insertion required

The subdermal implant is a matchstick-sized rod that is inserted into your arm and releases progestin to prevent pregnancy. The implant works like other hormonal methods: by stopping ovulation, and by thickening the cervical mucus so it's difficult for sperm to swim through on the way up to the uterus. Implants run up to $850 without insurance, but are usually covered by insurance, or some state programs. Even though there's a high cost up-front, they do end up being one of the cheaper methods because they last four years. Use a backup method your first week with the implant. You can get pregnant again as soon as you take it out.

Perks of the implant	Drawbacks of the implant
• Easily paired with other methods like condoms	• High up-front cost (though cheaper long-term)
• Lasts 4 years	• Hormones can have negative side effects, especially the first few months (spotting and irregular bleeding, nausea, headaches, sore breasts, bloating and weight gain, mood issues, etc.)
• Extremely effective at over 99%	
• Progestin only, so safe for those who cannot take estrogen	
• Hormones can have positive side effects (reducing cramps, lighter periods, reducing or preventing cysts in breasts and ovaries, clearing acne, etc.)	

GETTING THE IMPLANT
INSERTED AND REMOVED

At your appointment, the nurse or doctor will give you an exam to make sure the implant is safe for your body. Then, they will give you a small shot to numb the area of insertion on your arm. This means you won't feel much when it's inserted, except perhaps a mild pinch. Then they use a special insertion tool to slide the implant under the skin. It takes about five minutes. After the numbing medicine wears off, your arm may feel a little sore for a couple days. There may be a bruise, especially for those who bruise easily. You'll need to wash and care for the insertion site afterward according to your provider's directions. Make sure to use a backup method for the first week with the implant.

Similar to insertion, removal takes only a few minutes. The nurse or doctor will again numb the area, which will feel like a mild pinch. Once you're numb, they'll make a small incision to remove the implant. You won't feel much. Once the numbing medication wears off, you may feel a little sore or bruised, just like with the insertion. Keep it clean and covered while you heal.

natural methods

The "Pull-Out" Method (Withdrawal)

Perfect use: 96% effective

Real life: 78% effective

The pull-out method is exactly as it sounds: the partner with a penis pulls out before ejaculating. This helps keep sperm away from the egg. This method gets a lot of flak and is the source of debate among some sex educators. Some feel that this method shouldn't be taught because of its high failure rate. Per usual, I think more information is better, including information on how to more effectively use the pull-out method.

Because, as it turns out, the pull-out method can actually be incredibly effective at preventing pregnancy—freaking 96% if it's done perfectly! But that's a MAJOR IF. The problem is that this method is usually not done correctly every time, and not everyone is a candidate to do it well. Knowing when to pull out relies on the person knowing their body *very* well. They need to pull out early enough, have great self-control, and not have any accidents (which are pretty common—hence the high failure rate). They also need to be careful not to ejaculate anywhere near the vulva since that can still cause pregnancy. Rule of thumb: on is better than in! Ejaculating on the tummy, breasts, butt, etc., is okay—just not inside. But in the heat of the moment, this is a lot to ask, and a lot of people overestimate themselves. This method tends to work better when paired with condoms and/or very experienced partners who know each other and know their own bodies well.

HERE ARE A FEW WAYS TO make the pull-out method more effective:

- Get to know your sexual response/ejaculation time better with masturbation.
- *Make sure to pee before using the pull-out method.* If the male partner has masturbated recently and didn't pee afterward, sperm can hang out in the urethra and get into the vagina via pre-ejaculate fluid (pre-cum).
- Wipe the penis clean of any pre-cum before vaginal sex.
- Pair the pull-out method with condoms or another birth control method.

- Use sexual positions that make it easier to pull out, like missionary or doggie.
- Withdraw *completely* from the vagina before ejaculation.
- Use emergency contraception if withdrawal fails.

Perks of the pull-out method	Drawbacks of the pull-out method
• Easily paired with other methods like condoms • Don't need any supplies—can be used anywhere, anytime • Free	• High failure rate, especially for younger or more inexperienced guys

Fertility Awareness Methods (FAM)

Perfect use: 76–88% effective

Real life: 76–88% effective

Fertility awareness methods, a.k.a. "the rhythm method," refer to various methods of tracking your cycle so you know when you're ovulating. Once you figure out when you're ovulating, you can either avoid sex leading up to and during your fertile days, or you can use another method of birth control. Like the pull-out method, I suggest FAMs as secondary methods, not primary. Pair them up with condoms, the pill, or any other method to increase their effectiveness!

Perks of fertility awareness methods	Drawbacks of fertility awareness methods
• Easily paired with other methods like condoms	• Need to collect a lot of data first
• Don't need any supplies—can be used anywhere, anytime	• Requires high level of commitment to the method from both partners
• Free	• Not foolproof—can only provide an approximation of ovulation

HOW TO USE FAMS

Successfully using a fertility awareness method will require you to reaaaaally get to know your cycle. Honestly, I think it's kind of cool and puts me in touch with my body, so I tend to keep tabs on my fertility even though this isn't my method. Figuring out FAMs can be a little tricky, so it helps to enlist the guidance of a healthcare provider, especially as you're first getting started.

Here are the basics. There are about seven days out of the roughly twenty-eight-day menstrual cycle that carry a higher risk for pregnancy: the day of ovulation (duh), the day after ovulation (because the egg may still be alive), and the five days before it (because sperm can survive up to six days in the vagina). To figure out which days are your fertile days, you gotta track your cycle and identify when you're likely to be ovulating.

THERE ARE FOUR DIFFERENT WAYS TO track ovulation, and they should ideally be used together:

1. Calendar Tracking

The calendar method can help you estimate when you are fertile and may be ovulating. It's not foolproof, but it is a pretty good rough estimate. To use the calendar method, you'll first need to track your cycle for at least six to twelve months on a calendar or app (you could get away with three to six if your periods are super regular). The longer you track, the more accurate it will be. The goal is to figure out how many total days each of your cycles is. Many apps will tell your fertile days automatically, but you can also calculate it yourself.

First, figure out your cycle length by tracking the first day of each period, every month. One cycle length is the first day of your period to the day before your next period starts. Your cycles must be at least twenty-seven days to use this method. Once you've got your data over several months, roll up your sleeves and do some math.

Next, identify your shortest cycle. Let's say your shortest cycle on record was twenty-nine days. Subtract eighteen from your shortest cycle length (29-18=11). Then, count that many days from Day 1 of your cycle, including Day 1. Remember, Day 1 of a cycle is when you start your period, so in this case, you would count eleven days into the cycle, including the first day of bleeding. This is the first fertile day of your period.

To find when your fertile period ends, identify your longest cycle. Let's say your longest cycle was thirty-two days. Subtract eleven from your longest cycle length (32-11=21) and count that many days from Day 1 of your cycle. Remember, Day 1 of a cycle is when you start your period, so in this case, you would count twenty-one days into the cycle, including your first day bleeding. This is the last fertile day of your period, when pregnancy risk drops.

Now you have a good estimate of your fertile period! These are the days to avoid sex or continue to use a backup method.

2. Temperature Tracking

The temperature method can help you estimate when you are fertile using body temperature. Body temperature drops one to two days before ovulation, and then starts to rise for a few days after ovulation. To use this method, you'll need to track your temperature every day for at least three months first, using a FAM chart like the one below.

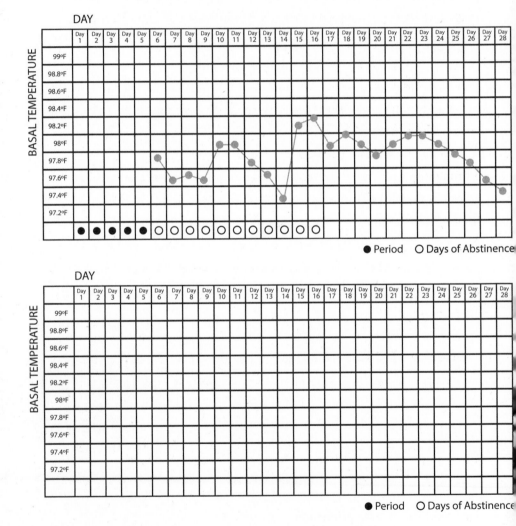

It's important to track your temperature every morning, before you do anything else—talk, walk, drink water, or get out of bed. To track your temperature, you'll need a good-quality thermometer that can accurately detect slight differences. These are usually used through the mouth or your butt. The rectal thermometers tend to be more accurate, so if you don't mind popping it in every morning, give it a go.

Once you've tracked your temperature for several months, you'll be able to identify your fertile days by temperature. Fertile days start as soon as your temperature starts to drop (toward the beginning of the cycle), and end once your temperature has been rising for a few days, signaling the end of ovulation.

3. Cervical Mucus Tracking

Throughout your cycle, vaginal discharge changes a bit. The cervical mucus method seeks to track changes in discharge to identify ovulation. It can be a bit imprecise since everybody is a little bit different, and many things can impact your discharge (like sex, illness, breastfeeding, hormonal birth control, douching, STIs, and more). Identifying the changes in discharge can also take some practice. Per usual, track for at least six months before relying on this method.

Here are the basics for each part of your cycle:

- During your period, there will be blood. These are safer days.
- Right after your period, there are typically a few "dry" days with little to no discharge. These are usually safe days, unless you have a short cycle.
- Before ovulation, the body starts to make more discharge. It's thicker and may feel somewhat tacky. It is cloudy, and whitish or yellowish in color. You may notice it in your

underwear or hanging out in the crevices of the vulva when you wipe. These are fertile days.

- During ovulation, the most discharge is made. Ovulation discharge turns clear and feels slippery. It's stringy, similar to raw egg whites, and can be stretched between two fingers. This lasts four to five days. These are fertile days.
- After four to five days of slippery discharge, it will change back to a tacky consistency and a cloudy white or yellow.
- Then, before your period, back to no discharge. These are safer days.

4. Tracking Standard Days

The standard days method is similar to the calendar method, but differs slightly because you avoid sex on the same days of your cycle every month. In order to use this method effectively, your cycle can't ever be shorter than twenty-six days or longer than thirty-two days. Track your cycle for at least six months first. Then, avoid Day 8 through Day 19 of your cycle, which are your fertile days. Remember that Day 1 is the first day of your period.

HERE ARE A FEW WAYS TO MAKE FERTILITY AWARENESS METHODS MORE EFFECTIVE:

- Pair them with condoms or another birth control method.
- Consult the guidance of a nurse or doctor, especially in the beginning.
- Use tracking apps to collect all your data.

Breastfeeding (a.k.a. Lactational Amenorrhea Method, or LAM)

Perfect use: 98% effective

Real life: Varies

You already know nature is magical at this point, but holy crap! Breastfeeding can act as a highly effective form of birth control if it's done properly. This is because breastfeeding can stop ovulation. No egg, no pregnancy. While this isn't a method for those who aren't already parents, it's another option for new mamas.

But there are a few (somewhat demanding . . .) caveats in order for it to work:

- You must breastfeed exclusively (meaning no supplemental foods or formula, which is not possible for everyone).
- Nursing must happen at least once every four hours during the day and every six hours at night.
- It only works for the first six months after giving birth.

You can increase the effectiveness of LAM by using other methods.

Perks of LAM	Drawbacks of LAM
• Safely paired with other methods, including condoms and hormonal methods	• Breastfeeding can be challenging, especially doing it exclusively
• Free	• Only works for six months
• Very effective	
• Breastfeeding is good for baby too	

emergency methods

SOMETIMES, OOPSIES HAPPEN. WHETHER YOU GOT lost in the heat of the moment or your condom broke or you forgot to take your pill, emergency contraception has your back.

How Emergency Contraception Works

When semen is first ejaculated into the vagina, pregnancy doesn't happen immediately. First, the sperm have to swim all the way up into the uterus and find the egg. The sperm have about six days to do this before they die, and they must reach the egg while it's actually there—which is only during the twelve- to twenty-four-hour period of ovulation. This little time lapse between ejaculation and conception (that is, sperm meeting the egg) is where emergency contraception comes in. Because emergency contraception intervenes before sperm meets the egg, it is *not* an abortion—it's just a very last-minute intervention. If the sperm has found the egg before emergency contraception kicks in, you will still be pregnant and it won't harm the existing pregnancy.

There are two main forms of emergency contraception: a pill and the copper IUD.

Emergency Contraception Pill (a.k.a. "The Morning-after Pill")

75–88% effective if taken within the first seventy-two hours, depending on which pill *

No prescription required

The emergency contraception pill can be found at pharmacies or

---

*The effectiveness of emergency contraception is not measured on a per-year basis like other methods because it's not made for regular use.

online. It contains hormones that work to prevent pregnancy by temporarily halting ovulation. If the egg hasn't been released yet, the pill can stop it from being released. However, if ovulation has already started, you can still get pregnant with emergency contraception. For that reason, the pill should be taken ASAP. The sooner you take it, the more effective it will be. The emergency contraception pills that are available at pharmacies need to be taken within seventy-two hours to be most effective, but can be used up to five days after unprotected sex. They cost about $50.

There are different types of pills. The most common is *Plan B*, but the most effective is *ella*.

Plan B	ella
Available at pharmacy, $40 to $50	Available at pharmacy or online, $60 to $70
Doesn't need prescription	Might require prescription (depends on state)
Most effective in the first seventy-two hours	Works just as well for five days, no matter when you take it
Not as effective for those who are overweight	More effective for those who are overweight
Very safe—side effects sometimes include spotting, cramping, or having your period at a different time	Very safe—side effects sometimes include spotting, cramping, or having your period at a different time

The Copper IUD as Emergency Contraception

99.9% effective if inserted in the first five days after unprotected sex

Prescription and provider insertion required

Interestingly, when the copper IUD is inserted after unprotected sex, it provides the most effective form of emergency contraception currently available. It works immediately to prevent implantation of the egg. After the copper IUD is inserted, it can be left in for up to twelve years afterward to continue providing protection against pregnancy. To read more about the copper IUD, check out the Hormonal Methods section.

pregnancy scares

THE FIRST TIME I HAD PENETRATIVE sex, the condom broke. Well, shit. The good news is that it was right at the beginning, and we noticed it immediately. The bad news is that I was already freaked the hell out before it broke so . . . that was fun. By the next morning, I had managed to convince myself that I must be pregnant, with twins, and that my whole future would be ruined. It was exactly what *Mean Girls* had warned me about. I peed on three pregnancy test sticks that morning, and one of my friends took me to Planned Parenthood to get emergency contraception that afternoon (this was before you could buy it at the pharmacy). As my whole world flashed before my eyes, I decided that condoms and spermicide weren't enough—I needed more peace of mind. So while I was at Planned Parenthood, I also got on the pill. It's a funny memory now, in a kind of sad way. My fear was driven more by paranoia than by a real risk.

If you're having a pregnancy scare, try not to freak yourself out. It's going to be okay. No matter what happens, you will pull through it. **If it has been five or fewer days since the incident, your first priority should be to get emergency contraception, a.k.a. the morning-after pill.** You can also take a pregnancy test. Unlike I did, you shouldn't take it the next day because it won't detect a pregnancy that early. The best time to take a pregnancy test is when you're late for your period, though with some tests you can take it before that. To understand the differences between the at-home pregnancy tests that are available, it helps to know how they work. After conception, the body starts to produce hCG, or human chorionic gonadotropin. This hormone is detectable about a week after the egg is fertilized—at the earliest. This is the hormone that pregnancy tests are looking for, and different tests vary in sensitivity. The more sensitive the test is, the earlier you can take it, but they tend to be more expensive too. Studies have revealed that the most sensitive pregnancy tests on the shelves right now are made by First Response (6.3 mIU/mL) followed by Clearblue (25 mIU/mL). Most other brands clocked in at a less sensitive 100 mIU/mL or greater. The most sensitive and accurate test available is a blood test, which must be done by a healthcare provider.

Other than these steps, a pregnancy scare is a waiting game for your period to come. If you aren't late or haven't missed a period yet, try not to get ahead of yourself with a premature freakout. A nurse or doctor can help you evaluate your risk pregnancy based on what happened and when. If you engaged in unprotected sex where sperm could have gotten on the vulva or in the vagina, then there is always at least a small risk of pregnancy. Obviously the risk is lower if there was no ejaculation, if ejaculation was outside the vagina, or if you were not in the fertile part of your cycle (see the Fertility Awareness Methods section for more on that). The risk of pregnancy also tends to be lower right before, during, and right after your period.

If you decide to tell your partner you're concerned you might be pregnant, they should be there and support you through the experience. Just like it takes two to have sex, it takes two to deal with the potential consequences. If your partner is having a scare, ask them how you can support them and what they need. Depending on the person, they may want more emotional support, or they may prefer space. Friends or family members can also be a good source of support through a pregnancy scare.

If the pregnancy test is negative ➤ Close one. Time to get on birth control.

If the pregnancy test is positive ➤ Time to evaluate your options.

If there's a plus sign, you're pregnant (unless it's a false positive, which is rare—false negatives are much more common). A positive pee stick can be a shock. Take some time to collect yourself, and then come up with a game plan. You can talk to a healthcare provider about your options, which are to carry the pregnancy to term or to have an abortion.

While partners, friends, or siblings (or whomever you decide to tell) may be able to offer guidance or perspective in your decision, ultimately it's your body, it's your life, and it's your choice. I know it's cheesy, but you have to listen to your heart and do what feels right to you. The physical and emotional experience of pregnancy is a broad subject that goes beyond the scope of this book. Check out my suggested reads in the resource list.

abortion

IN APPROXIMATELY 10 TO 25% OF cases, the body spontaneously terminates a pregnancy, also known as a miscarriage. The Guttmacher Institute, a leading research institute focused on reproductive health, notes that in 2014, approximately 20% of pregnancies were terminated with induced abortion, making it a fairly common procedure in the United States. The abortion rate in the USA has been falling steadily the past few years, an effect that has been linked to increased access to birth control, especially long-acting reversible contraceptives like the IUD or the implant. In the United States, abortion is a safe and legal procedure, and according to polling data from the Pew Research Center, most Americans support abortion rights. But . . . it's no secret that not everyone does, and abortion is an especially charged word in politics. The procedure is heavily stigmatized, and while about one in four women have an abortion by age forty-five, most keep it a secret.

Like a lot of sexuality issues throughout history, abortion wasn't always as polarizing as it is today. In the United States, abortion was legal until the late 1800s, when it was first criminalized. Before that point, it was a fairly open practice, and abortions were performed before quickening (the first signs of fetal movement, which happens at about four months) without anyone batting an eye. Abortion was out in the open. Midwives and naturopaths provided herbal concoctions that acted as abortifacients, and eventually commercial products were available to purchase at stores. Physicians of the time openly marketed themselves as abortion providers, touting special pills or procedures. The clinical abortions performed by midwives and physicians were done with some . . . pretty primitive equipment. The abortifacients available were sometimes lethal, and many women wound up with deadly infections from unsanitary conditions. Some of the first regulatory laws around abortion were laws that targeted poisons that were being sold to induce abortion, not abortion itself.

What changed?

The initial push to criminalize abortion in the United States came at the hands of physicians. The medical establishment was in its infancy and seeking to establish its authority over midwives, who had traditionally presided over pregnant women. The American Medical Association portrayed midwives as kooks and quacks without a real education. They sought to restrict midwives' ability to provide abortion—perhaps to make it safer, or perhaps to eliminate their biggest competition.

The medical establishment's campaigns also promoted fear about the dangers of abortion, though not for the reasons you might assume. At the time, immigration to the USA was increasing while white Protestant women were having fewer babies than before. Physician Horatio Storer asked on the record if Americans wanted their country to "be filled by our own children or by those of aliens? . . . This is a question our women must answer; upon their loins depends the future destiny of the nation." Abortion, and women who didn't want to have many children, were framed as threats to the racial fabric of United States. By 1910, all but one state had criminalized abortion, except when it was necessary to save a woman's life.

But making abortion a crime didn't stop abortion from happening. Regardless of available technology or the legality of abortion, women throughout history have taken tremendous risks to control their reproductive future. Historians estimate that in the early 1900s, about two million abortions were performed per year in the United States. Today, around 900,000 are performed per year, and our population is much larger. That makes the abortion rate in the early 1900s roughly seven times the rate of today. The abortion rate dropped dramatically not when the procedure was made illegal, but when birth control was made widely available.

The period of time in America when abortion was illegal was an ugly and traumatic one for women. Driven underground, abortions were expensive, dangerous, and difficult to come by; this time period is where the "back alley abortion" began. Many women attempted to induce their own or each other's abortions with coat hangers, knitting needles, or pens. Women would use harsh abrasives like drain cleaner or bleach, or attempt to blow air into the uterus—resulting in serious injury, infection, chemical burns, organ damage, or worse. Fearing criminal charges, women were rarely honest if they were brought into a hospital, making it harder for their nurses and doctors to properly care for them. Thousands of women died, at least five thousand per year, and many more suffered serious consequences to their health. Hushed horror rocked families and communities throughout the country as women mysteriously died from unnamed causes. Among those who suffered most under these draconian rules were women of color and the poor. Wealthy women, who were usually white, could sometimes find private doctors who would perform "therapeutic abortions" in secret. But as doctors faced increasing pressure and stigma for performing abortions and threats to their professional reputation, abortion became even more difficult to find, even for the very wealthy. In some cases, wealthy American women would fly to London for an abortion, where it was legal. Poor women and women of color were left to fend for themselves.

In the 1960s, a movement began to grow, led by grassroots activists, lawyers, and doctors. Seeing firsthand the horrors that criminalizing abortion had caused, doctors became vocal advocates for change. The history here is a little ironic of course, considering that the AMA had been a large driver in making the procedure illegal to begin with. This movement came to a head with the 1973 Supreme Court case *Roe v. Wade*. With a stroke of the pen, *Roe v. Wade* saved millions of women's lives. The ruling affirmed women's right to privacy and legalized abortion until the age of viability, which is the point that a fetus could survive outside the womb. *Roe v. Wade* also posited that state restrictions on abortion must not jeopardize women's health. It was an incredible victory for women's rights and autonomy, and remains so today.

Well, kinda.

Today, we find ourselves in yet another curious historical evolution. Since 1995, the number of anti-choice laws has been steadily growing in the United States. In 2014, there were well over eight hundred anti-choice measures enacted throughout the country. Most of these laws fall under the umbrella of "TRAP" laws (targeted regulation of abortion providers), mandatory waiting periods, and insurance coverage bans. As of 2017, 89% of counties in the United States had no abortion provider. It would seem that the pendulum is attempting to swing back to the days when abortion was a crime.

Caught in the middle of these politics are women. The political assault on abortion rights has come with an onslaught of violence. In 2016, abortion providers endured the highest levels of violence in twenty years. Murder, attempted murder, bombing and arson, vandalism, and anthrax are just a few weapons of terror that have been lobbed at American healthcare providers. Women going to clinics that offer abortion are so routinely harassed that large-scale efforts to train abortion clinic escorts have been launched. Outside of the physical violence, "crisis pregnancy centers" have cropped up all over the United States; these centers have been documented promoting pseudoscience, political propaganda, and lies to guilt pregnant women out of having an abortion. These tactics are reprehensible, of course. While we are all entitled to our own beliefs, we are not entitled to use violence, coercion, harassment, and emotional manipulation to impose those beliefs on others.

Where to Get Help Making a Decision

As you seek out sources of information and guidance in your decision, make sure it is from a trusted healthcare provider. An unbiased resource will offer medical facts and information, rather than resources that seek to push political propaganda or pseudoscience. Beware of resources that use emotionally loaded language, show a clear bias toward one particular decision, or attempt to make you feel ashamed. I'd suggest seeking out resources that rely on the latest research. If you find yourself in need of emotional support, ask your nurse or doctor for recommendations. Hit up a counselor or trusted friend to talk to about it. There are also nonprofits devoted to listening to those who have had an abortion, such as Exhale Pro-Voice. There is no "right" experience or feeling about having abortion—and reactions may range from relief to grief. Despite the stigma, most women who decide that an abortion is right for them report feeling positively about their decision a few months later. Take care of yourself. You're #1.

MY ABORTION EXPERIENCE

by Anonymous

When I found out I was pregnant, I was shocked. I was overjoyed. I was terrified. Like other women who have accidentally become pregnant, a huge part of my distress was because of where I was at in my life. I was barely able to support myself at the time. I was living alone in a new town, all my friends had moved away to other colleges, and I was in a new relationship. I was also fighting my way through an advanced graduate program that was moving at twice the pace of a regular program. I wanted to finish school, build my career, and become financially stable before starting a family. It was difficult to manage all the emotions that came up when I found out I was pregnant. My body was going through so many changes so quickly, and I could feel it. I had to remind myself many times that I was allowed to feel a range of emotions. It is so important to surround yourself with support during an unplanned pregnancy for this reason. It is a lot to handle alone.

While the emotions that came up were difficult, I knew immediately that I could not carry the pregnancy. Politically, I have always been pro-choice and I believe that a woman must be free to make critical health decisions about her body. I still feel this way, but it didn't make the decision any easier. I felt a deep sense of loss, which only intensified when my nurse told me that it was most likely twins. I burst out into tears. She informed me that she couldn't move forward with the procedure until I was able to give her consent that didn't come between long, drawn-out sobs. I felt absolutely awful. I was so confused in my heart. I had no intentions of carrying the pregnancy, so why now did I feel so heartbroken and upset in moving forward? I sat by myself in the room in silence for a few minutes. I lay back on the treatment table and closed my eyes.

One thing I have learned as I have gotten older is that our gut instincts must be listened to. So often we ignore our instincts—sometimes because we learn to ignore them, sometimes because we are in denial. My intuition was calling out to me, screaming the answer. Though I want to be a mom one day, I knew that I couldn't be one at that moment. And so, I decided to go through with the abortion. I hoped that one day I could forgive myself for having an abortion, and that I would be able to keep moving forward in my life. As soon as he was finished, the doctor inserted an IUD to protect me from going through this again. For a while afterward, I sat in a waiting room with other women who were in recovery. There was a movie on, and crackers on the table. I looked around, feeling disgusted with myself. "Am I a bad person?" I couldn't shake the guilt. That was one year ago.

As you may have noticed by my anonymous pen name, I still keep my abortion a secret. I am not quite ready to be open about it yet. So many people pass judgment and shame onto women who have an abortion, when they have no idea how difficult the experience was for me. The lack of empathy for the lives and complicated realities of women is disturbing to me. I have struggled to accept that I am not a bad person. That I just made a birth control mistake. That my future matters. That my needs are valid. But through it all, I know without a doubt that I made the right choice. I am learning to forgive myself with each passing day, and I refuse to let myself believe that I am a bad person for having an abortion. I don't believe that we should feel bad about doing what is right for ourselves. Women are often tasked with making difficult decisions, and so we do. We fight through it, just as we always have.

What Can You Expect if You Have an Abortion?

There are two ways to have an abortion: a prescription abortion pill, and an in-clinic abortion. The abortion pill can be taken up to ten weeks after the first day of your last period. After that, the abortion must be performed in a clinic.

THE ABORTION PILL

To be prescribed the abortion pill, you should first make an appointment with your healthcare provider or a local health clinic that offers abortion services. They will confirm you are definitely pregnant, and discuss your options with you.

The abortion pill is actually two pills: mifepristone and misoprostol. In some states, you have to go to the clinic twice in order to get your medications because of the restrictive laws we discussed above. At your first appointment, you will also be given an antibiotic to prevent infection. Before you take the pills, your healthcare provider will give you an exam and lab tests. The first pill, mifepristone, is taken at the nurse or doctor's office. The second pill, misoprostol, is taken the next day at home. The first pill works by stopping the production of progesterone (which is needed for a pregnancy), while the second pill causes cramping and bleeding to prompt the uterus to empty. It is normal to have large clots of blood and tissue, similar to a miscarriage.

The abortion pill feels like a very heavy, crampy period and sometimes causes nausea or vomiting. Most of the tissue passes in five to six hours, but cramping and bleeding can continue for a couple days. Stock up on pads (no tampons), grab a heating pad, and give yourself enough time to relax and take it easy. You can take ibuprofen for the pain; just avoid aspirin, as it can cause more bleeding. Plan to give yourself a day off your feet if possible, and definitely avoid any physical exertion for a few days. Any fever, chills, dizziness, or nausea should go away shortly, and if they don't, give your provider a call.

For aftercare, follow your nurse's or doc's instructions. It's crucial to go to your follow-up appointment because medication abortions are unsuccessful about 2–8% of the time. If you continue to have retained pregnancy tissue you could become extremely sick. When all goes smoothly, you may spot for a few weeks. Your period will go back to normal in a month or two. You can start taking birth control right afterward, too.

IN-CLINIC ABORTION

Rather than being prompted by a pill, an in-clinic abortion uses gentle suction to empty the uterus. While medication abortion takes twenty-four hours, in-clinic abortion takes five to twenty minutes.

Before the procedure, the nurse or doctor will perform an exam and lab tests to ensure you're good to go. They may also insert small sticks called laminaria into the cervix a few hours before the procedure. These sticks absorb moisture and slowly swell to dilate the cervix. You will also be given antibiotics to prevent infection, and a shot to numb the cervix. Using a thin tube through the cervix and a small suction device, your nurse or doctor will gently remove the contents of the uterus. A small metal tool called a curette is occasionally needed to ensure the tissue is completely emptied. The procedure can cause anything from mild to strong period cramps, depending on the person. Afterward, you'll stay at the doctor's office or clinic for about an hour to make sure you're doing A-okay. Most people stay about an hour. You may have a bit of cramping for twenty-four hours, and most people are back on their feet the next day.

After having an abortion, it's important to protect your sexual health in the future. Be proactive and find a reliable birth control method that works for you to prevent another unplanned pregnancy.

TWELVE

CONSENT AND COMMUNICATION

CONGRATULATIONS! YOU'VE OFFICIALLY MADE IT FAR enough to reach the very heart and soul of sex-positive sexual ethics. The most basic aspect of being a sexually ethical person is to **do no harm to others**—and it all starts with consent!

IN THIS CHAPTER WE'LL DIVE INTO

Affirmative consent

The limits of consent

Consent culture

Ask Laci: On consent

Communication basics

Sexual communication

affirmative consent

WITH GREAT PLEASURE COMES GREAT RESPONSIBILITY. Perhaps the most basic and important form of sexual communication is affirmative consent. It's pretty simple: consent is a verbal check-in before sexual contact to make sure your partner is into it. Despite its simplicity, affirmative consent is not yet the norm in our culture. More often, the default is to assume sexual consent is implied, usually based on body language. We operate on the assumption that someone is consenting so long as they don't say no. And even then, "no" is sometimes interpreted as being open to persuasion. This is a huge mistake to make when it comes to something as intimate as sex. Assumptions are simply not a suitable stand-in for consent, and forgoing consent runs the risk of sexually violating someone. There is a long list of reasons why assuming is ineffective, most of which come down to the fact that we simply aren't always as great at reading each other as we think. Body language varies from person to person and culture to culture. It's an imprecise measure of someone's boundaries in sexual situations because everyone expresses themselves differently. What one person might read as passive interest could in reality be how that person expresses polite discomfort. It is also easy to read desires, thoughts, and feelings into a sexual situation that aren't actually there—especially when one person is very hopeful. This is particularly true for people we are still getting to know (for instance, during hookups or in the early stages of a relationship).

This is why enthusiastic, verbal agreement is the gold standard. The only way to get clear on consent is with words. Of course, this also means accepting that sometimes those words might include "no."

Consent Is . . .

YES!
An agreement.

ENTHUSIASTIC
Authentic and freely given.

VERBAL
Out loud, with words.

NONTRANSFERABLE
Not implied based on past sexual exchanges.

REVERSIBLE
Retractable at any point.

SPECIFIC
Consent to one act isn't consent to all acts.

SOBER
Given of clear and conscious mind.

The perks of practicing good consent (beside not violating someone) are that it is good communication, shows respect, builds trust, embodies good ethics, and is also very hot.

Here Are a Few Ways to Ask for Consent:

"What do you want to do tonight?"

"Want to fool around a little bit?"

"Are you into this?"

"Can I kiss you?"

"Can I touch you here?"

"Do you like that?"

"Do you want me to keep going?"

"How does that feel?"

"Wanna _____?"

Here's What Consent Might Sound Like:

"Yes please."

"Gimme more."

"That feels amazing."

"I'm down."

"Keep going."

"Right there."

"Fuck, I like that."

"I want you to _____."

💬 "I'm down for _____."

If consent kinda sounds like dirty talk, that's because it often is. The language of consent is a language of desire. Hence, as the old sex ed adage goes, "Consent is sexy."

Here's What Nonconsent Might Sound Like:

💬 *Silence*

💬 "Ummmm."

💬 "I don't like that."

💬 "I dunno."

💬 "Can we hold up for a second?"

💬 "I'm not feeling this."

💬 "I changed my mind."

💬 "I'm not sure."

💬 "Please stop."

💬 "No."

Getting rejected sucks. But choosing to proceed without someone's consent is sexual assault, which is a serious crime, not to mention very shitty.

Here What Pressuring and Guilting Might Sound Like:

- "C'mon, I thought you liked me."

- "Just do it for me."

- "If you really loved me you'd _____."

- "Stop making such a big deal out of it."

- "I know you want it."

- "I don't think I can control myself."

Pressuring people is creepy. Be aware of how you come off.

On Saying No

Should you find yourself in a sexual situation where you feel uncomfortable, remember that it's always, always

always

ALWAYS

LITERALLY FOREVER AND ALWAYS okay to say no.

"No" is a complete sentence.

"No" doesn't require justification or elaboration.

"No" isn't an invitation for negotiation or persuasion.

It's a definitive statement—and you are allowed to say it whenever you feel uncomfortable. It's also okay to say, "I changed my mind," "I'm only okay with _____," or "I'm not feeling this." You may be as gentle or firm as you like. Either way, your sexual boundaries should *always* be respected.

But, as you may have noticed in other contexts, enforcing boundaries can be a strangely difficult thing to do. Think about it: Has there ever been a time you weren't fully okay with something, but you went along with it anyway? A lot of people struggle with guilt or hesitance in saying no, especially in sexual situations. Because of gender role socialization, women in particular tend to experience higher levels of anxiety about saying no. I have been in situations in the past where I felt curiously indebted to someone because I had flirted with them earlier and didn't want to disappoint. The pressure to go along with it, even when I'm uncomfortable, is sometimes exaggerated when I do feel some interest in them, or that they're a nice person. They may even be offering to buy me a drink or pay for my meal. But obviously, it should go without saying that buying someone dinner isn't a ticket for a trip Down Under. Give yourself permission to assert your boundaries and communicate what you need. It does not make you a bad or mean person, I promise! You're the boss of your own body. The more you practice, the easier it will become. Some folks I know have found greater confidence and self-empowerment in reclaiming their right to say no without apologizing for it.

(I'm one of them. 10/10 would recommend.)

the limits of consent ⚠️

NOW THAT WE'VE GOT THE BASICS down, it's important to discuss situations where affirmative consent doesn't apply. The first of those situations is where there is an imbalance of power.

Paying attention to power dynamics is a really important part of practicing good consent. When there is a power imbalance, one person may feel like they can't (or shouldn't) say no out of fear of repercussions. Imbalances of power can also create situations where consent cannot ethically be obtained, such as between adults and minors. This is why age-of-consent laws exist to protect young people from sexual exploitation. Here are some examples of power imbalances that can compromise consent:

- When one person is a minor and the other is an adult (this is statutory rape—age-of-consent laws vary by state)
- When one person relies on the other for shelter or food
- When one person is too ill or senile to understand what's happening
- When one person is an authority figure over the other (such as teacher/student or boss/employee)
- When one person holds a lot of social status or power (celebrities, famous musicians, athletes, actors, coaches, etc.)
- When one person threatens or blackmails the other
- When one person has a history of violence or aggression

Another situation that compromises consent is when someone is drunk or on drugs. This is because their decision-making faculties have been compromised. The legal standard when it comes to alcohol is that sexual contact with an "impaired individual" is sexual assault. However, what constitutes being "impaired" depends on the jurisdiction. Outside of the law, a good rule of thumb when it comes to alcohol and consent is that if *someone is too drunk to drive, they are too drunk to consent.* The legal limit for drunk driving in the United States is a blood alcohol content (BAC) of .08%. At this level of drunkenness, a person's coordination and decision making becomes impaired.

CONSENT AND ALCOHOL

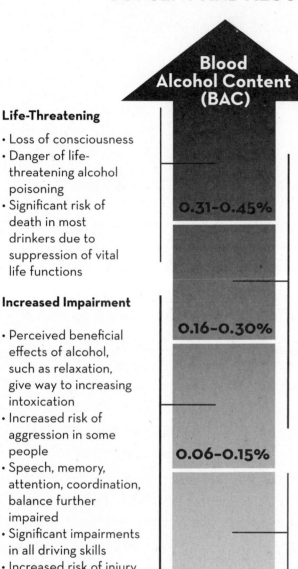

Blood Alcohol Content (BAC)

Life-Threatening

- Loss of consciousness
- Danger of life-threatening alcohol poisoning
- Significant risk of death in most drinkers due to suppression of vital life functions

Increased Impairment

- Perceived beneficial effects of alcohol, such as relaxation, give way to increasing intoxication
- Increased risk of aggression in some people
- Speech, memory, attention, coordination, balance further impaired
- Significant impairments in all driving skills
- Increased risk of injury to self and others
- Moderate memory impairments

Severe Impairment

- Speech, memory, coordination, attention, reaction time, balance significantly impaired
- All driving-related skills dangerously impaired
- Judgment and decision making dangerously impaired
- Blackouts (amnesia)
- Vomiting and other signs of alcohol poisoning common
- Loss of consciousness

Mild Impairment

- Mild speech, memory, attention, coordination, balance impairments
- Perceived beneficial effects, such as relaxation
- Sleepiness can begin

0.31-0.45%

0.16-0.30%

0.06-0.15%

0.0-0.05%

Can still consent:	Too drunk to consent:
Able to clearly communicate	Slurred or nonsensical speech
Actively participating	Nonparticipation, "dead fish"
Clearly aware of what's going on around them	Loss of coordination and situational awareness

Sex is sexual activity that happens *together*.

Sexual assault is sexual activity that one person does to another.

When in doubt, wait until they have sobered up. If you're into each other, neither partner should need to be shit-faced drunk to have some fun together. Cuddle them, tuck them in, and leave your phone number. If it's meant to be, it'll happen.

consent culture ⚠

IN 2017, A DRIP TURNED INTO a waterfall as women around the world came forward with their stories of sexual violation on social media under the hashtag #MeToo. The hashtag was started by activist Tarana Burke way back in 2006 during the Myspace days, but was amplified when actress Alyssa Milano encouraged Twitter users to tweet "me too" if they had experienced sexual harassment or assault. Within the first twenty-four hours, Twitter reported that #MeToo had been tweeted 1.7 million times, while Facebook reported more than 12 million posts. The highest-profile allegations came against men in Hollywood, beginning with Harvey Weinstein—which were perhaps foreshadowed by the more than fifty allegations that had come out in previous years against Bill Cosby. In the following months, #MeToo stories continued to flow from not only Hollywood, but from sports, to academia, restaurants, the hospitality industry, and retail, to music, news media, and politics. No industry was immune.

For many of us, hearing millions of stories come out into the open around the world was a bit of a shock. It's one thing to hear statistics about sexual violence; it's quite another to suddenly become aware of the private suffering and abuses of power taking place all around us for decades. The #MeToo flood is a powerful reminder of the very real experiences of sexual violence and exploitation that lurk beneath the surface in our culture. It is a reminder that power dynamics and sexual exploitation continue to shape the lives, psyches, careers, and futures of many women and men. It's above all a reminder of how much work there is left to do to change our sexual culture—to ensure that all sexual exchanges are consensual, rather than coercive or exploitative.

As I mentioned in the prologue, the defining characteristic of sex positivity is *consent*. I believe we can all work to cultivate a new sexual culture where consent and mutual respect are at the heart of our experiences with sexuality. We'll call this "consent culture"; it refers to communities where open communication, respect, and consent are the bedrock of sexual and romantic interactions. Sex positivity really only works in the context of consent culture. Sex positivity is a "do no harm" type of philosophy; it allows us to own and enjoy our sexuality, so long as nobody gets hurt. What happens between consenting adults in the bedroom is nobody else's damn business. However, what happens between nonconsenting adults is absolutely our business—and it won't be tolerated.

Sex positivity and consent culture are natural bedmates. Because the sex-positive philosophy posits sexuality as a normal and healthy part of being a human, people are encouraged to speak openly and frankly about their desires rather than try to navigate turbulent waters of poor communication. Consent culture also makes it safer and socially acceptable to say no; sexual or romantic rejection are met with acceptance rather than retaliation. Rejection is not internalized as personal failure, an injustice, or an obstacle to be overcome. If I'm rejected, I accept it and move on. In social situations, those who don't practice good consent are not tolerated, and intervening is the normal course of action if someone is being a creep. Bad behavior is met with rigorous accountability and conversation; there are no excuses or victim blaming to be had. These practices are upheld regardless of the person's gender, race, sexual orientation, or ability.

I think consent culture is beautiful. And it does exist, in a subsubculture-y sort of way. I have encountered consent cultures in some communities as a college student, at events put on by sex educators (surprise, surprise), and at conferences or festivals where sex geeks have a strong presence and influence. I have also found consent cultures cultivated at some BDSM clubs and queer-friendly bars. I have surrounded myself with friends who also cultivate consent culture during our group outings and parties. It's a noticeably safer environment. I am better able to relax and connect with people knowing that my boundaries will be respected and supported by the people around me. I believe that with a lot of work, our mainstream sexual culture may become more of a consent culture. But for now, it's not.

Consent culture stands in contrast to what I'll call coercion culture. Rather than centering mutual desires and personal boundaries in sexual or romantic situations, a coercion culture is one in which sexual violation is commonplace, and coercive behaviors are often written off as "unavoidable" or "normal." In casting coercion as normal, it closes the door to any type of change. No matter how fervently some corners of our culture may tolerate it, coercive and exploitative sexual behaviors are *not* normal. They are only the norm because we allow them to be. I know this because, as I mentioned, I live most of my life in spaces that are much more sex-positive.

What does coercion culture look like? Here are a few examples.

COERCION CULTURE IS "I WON'T TAKE NO FOR AN ANSWER"

It's a familiar scenario: you might be out at a party, wind up having a good conversation with a cute stranger, and a little bit of flirting ensues. The stranger invites you back to their place, but you aren't really feeling it. You don't know them well enough to feel comfortable being alone with them in private. You give them a gentle "not tonight." Instead of accepting your answer (consent culture), the stranger tries to convince you (coercion culture): "C'mon, it'll be fun!"

"No, really, not tonight," you say again. The stranger gets offended and accuses you of being uptight.

In a coercion culture, persistence and hostility after being told no is considered normal in sexual situations. Once, at a party, I ran into an unfortunate man who jokingly told me, "Three nos and a yes is still a yes!" WTF? When someone's no isn't respected, especially after saying it THREE TIMES, that means they aren't being given an actual *choice* in the situation. With regard to sexual contact, this is sexual harassment and/or assault.

Consent culture alternative: No means no, and only a yes means yes. Accept it. Respect it. Lather, rinse, repeat.

COERCION CULTURE IS WHEN CREEPY BEHAVIOR IS DEEMED "ROMANTIC"

Twilight's vampire hunk Edward Cullen crept his way into hearts and minds with his undying adoration for his beloved Bella. But when you take a closer look, much of Edward's behavior is ethically questionable, like sneaking over to her house without her knowledge to watch her sleep and never letting her out of his sight. Obsessive, stalkerish behavior in romance films is often used to convey the message of devotion that "love conquers all." And hey, sometimes it does. But sometimes it doesn't. When someone's behavior violates another person's space, compromises their privacy, or makes them feel uncomfortable, that behavior shouldn't be celebrated or normalized.

These attitudes run deep and start early. When I was a kid, I found myself in a situation at school with a boy who simply would not leave me alone. He followed me around at recess, waited for me outside the bathrooms; he sat next to me every day on the bus home from school; he wrote me notes of affection and insisted on being in my group during every class project. Every time I tried to tell an adult that I was uncomfortable I was met with the same lines: "He likes you!" or "Take it as a compliment." Yet it didn't feel anything like a compliment. Compliments are supposed to make you feel good. It felt like a violation of my boundaries and personal space, and it made me feel helpless and anxious. I'll never forget how relieved I felt when fifth grade finally ended.

The whole "being mean or creepy is romantic" mentality dismisses harmful sexual and romantic behaviors. If a kid is acting out in ways that make another uncomfortable because they have a crush or otherwise, that behavior should be addressed, not encouraged. Children must learn the importance of respecting other people's boundaries. To do the opposite normalizes what should be seen as warning signs of stalking, harassment, or abuse. It also dismisses personal accountability for harmful actions.

Consent culture alternative: Teach young adults that respect, trust, and kindness are healthy ways to express love. Unwanted advances and controlling behavior are not what love looks like.

COERCION CULTURE IS "BOYS WILL BE BOYS"

I've encountered a lot of situations with a worrying pattern: a guy will behave in an inappropriate or aggressive way; then people dismiss that behavior as normal. "What do you expect?! Boys will be boys." To be frank, I expect boys to be held to the same standards of decency as girls.

While it's true that males outrank females in expressions of aggression, it's not true that this means men can't control their behavior (and that predatory behavior should be excused). The "boys will be boys" line has been used to write off an array of sexual misconduct, from harassment to sexual assault.

Consent culture alternative: We are each responsible for our own actions. No more excuses for harmful behavior and choices.

COERCION CULTURE IS ASSUMING GUYS ARE ALWAYS DOWN FOR SEX

When someone is pursuing a guy, there is often an assumption that he should *always* be down for sex. As a result, I've seen coercive behaviors from both men and women that range from making fun of guys who aren't down to invading a guy's privacy and personal space to get him to have sex. If the situation were a guy doing this to a woman, it would be more readily understood as unacceptable.

This reveals a disturbing mentality about sexual violence against men. People tend to think it's less serious when a man is violated, on the assumption that deep down he probably wanted it—or he was at least more okay with it than a woman would have been. It is assumed that sexual abuse and trauma are less harmful to men, minimizing the experiences of male abuse survivors. It's an extension of those pesky gender roles, where guys are supposed to be unfeeling and "tough" in order to be masculine.

One of the more horrific ways that this type of coercion plays out is with the smattering of female teachers who have violated male students—and gotten away with it. While a male teacher raping a female student is readily regarded as wrong, when the victim is a male, it is trivialized and perhaps even treated as a joke. This is a confusing message to send to young men; it implies that they are supposed to be sexually available at all times, even to authority figures who exploit them. This message also plays into the idea that men simply can't be raped—a falsehood that stigmatizes and isolates male rape survivors. Not only do male survivors have to deal with being violated, they also have to deal with people making a joke out of it.

Consent culture alternative: Abandon stereotypes and assumptions about male sexuality. Apply the same ethical standards to everyone, regardless of gender.

COERCION CULTURE IS "SHE ASKED FOR IT"

In response to allegations of sexual assault, one of the first questions that tends to pop up on social media is "Well, what was she wearing?" A slew of other interrogations ensue to determine whether or not the victim of the crime is responsible for their rapist's actions. The idea that clothing can "invite" sexual violation is so pervasive that it has served as legal reasoning to dismiss dozens of rape cases in court. Take a 2011 case in Manitoba, Canada, where a rapist who forced himself on a woman in the woods was dismissed because the victim and her friend were wearing "tube tops with no bra, high heels and plenty of makeup." Judge Robert Dewar wrote that "they made their intentions publicly known that they wanted to party. This is a different case than one where there is no perceived invitation." The implication being that clothing is an invitation to have sex, and thus excuses the perpetrator raping her.

This is ridiculous nonsense, of course. The only thing that causes rape is someone choosing to violate another person. You could wear dark eye makeup, flirt and dance sexily, get drunker than your liver would like, run around naked—and you still wouldn't be asking to be raped. In fact, nobody ever *asks to be raped* because that is literally the opposite of what rape is. This is called victim blaming. We'll talk more about it in chapter 16: "Dating Violence."

At the heart of victim blaming is the destructive idea that some-times sexual violation is the responsibility of the victim rather than the perpetrator. In some situations, especially when a woman is improper, a.k.a. "slutty," she deserves to be violated. Obviously, she surrendered her right to respect and consent when she decided to show a little too much thigh. This mentality asserts that only certain kinds of women are worthy of respect; respect depends on how long your skirt is, or how dark your makeup is.

Here's the truth: the only person responsible for sexual violation is the person who makes a deliberate decision to violate someone else. Period.

Consent culture alternative: No slut shaming, no victim blaming. Those who commit acts of violence are held accountable for it. People are free to dress as they please. Personal expression, even if sexual in nature, is not used to dismiss acts of violence.

COERCION CULTURE IS STANDING BY WHILE IT HAPPENS

In 2012, a female high school student in Steubenville, Ohio, was raped by two high school football players out in the open during a house party. The case was unique at the time in that people stood around and recorded what was happening on their phones, mocking the victim and posting the footage on social media. The pictures and videos eventually led to the conviction of Trent Mays and Ma'lik Richmond for rape. There was so much about that case that was deeply disturbing: the public's vitriolic response blaming Jane Doe because she was drunk, the school officials who tried to cover it up (and who were later indicted), as well as the apparent willingness of everybody at the party to film it and mock her rather than stop what was happening. In one of the videos posted by a partygoer, one young man attempts to speak up, pointing out that it is rape. His concerns are laughed off by the others in the video. One has to wonder what would have happened if people had listened to him, and if more people had spoken up to support him. Perhaps then, Jane Doe's life wouldn't have been torn apart that night.

The reluctance of people to speak up when they witness violence is a well-documented phenomenon called the bystander effect. The more people that are present during the situation, the less likely any particular person is to feel responsible for intervening. The best way to combat the bystander effect is to (1) be aware of it and (2) commit to not being complicit.

Consent culture rewards both of these intervening behaviors, making it a safer place for people to be. But even so, let's be realistic—any environment, even consent cultures, can harbor predatory behavior. The strength of consent culture is that when the majority of individuals have good sexual ethics, it tips the scales. In theory, there are enough bystanders willing and prepared to intervene if things go awry.

Consent culture alternative: Don't stand by and do nothing. Consider your safety and options in the situation, then act. Most bystander intervention programs suggest three ways to intervene:

DIRECTLY

If you feel safe to do so, directly intervene with what's happening. You can check in with the victim, or give direct commands to the perpetrator.

> "Hey, are you okay?"

> "Hey, you need to back up."

DELEGATE

If you don't feel safe intervening, find someone who can. That might be a friend, a bartender, a bouncer, or anyone else in charge. They can intervene alone, or you can strategize as a group.

DISTRACT OR DIVERT

If there's nobody to delegate to and you feel unsafe interfering directly, create a distraction or diversion from the situation. This might be getting the victim away from the conversation ("Hey, can you show me where the bathroom is?"), or by distracting the perpetrator so the victim has an out ("Hey, haven't we met before?").

A Note about the Language of Rape Culture

—♡—

Some academics refer to these aforementioned norms as "rape culture." Having used this term myself to teach for a few years, I have found it is sometimes confusing. The term "rape culture" can also feel pretty loaded and alienating. For some people I've talked to, the notion that we live in a rape culture seems to imply that rape is supposedly acceptable in America—which obviously isn't true. Everyone (well, mostly) knows rape is bad. I believe this understanding is ultimately a misunderstanding of the term "rape culture," thanks in large part to misapplications of the concept on social media.

Academically, rape culture refers to the range of coercive behaviors that can cause sexual violence, and the ways that these behaviors are excused and normalized. This stands in contrast to the interpretation that rape *itself* is acceptable. I think the distinction is one worth making. That said, I use the term "coercion culture" here because I find it is a more concise and accessible description for a general audience.

Toward Consent Culture

The ability to create consent cultures in our communities lies in our hands. It starts with speaking up and acting as role models. It means having difficult conversations with our kids, with our friends, with our lovers. Because many of us don't have spaces to critically explore the tenor of our sexual and romantic norms, it can take a little patience and dialogue to help people understand how certain behaviors hurt ourselves and each other. But in my opinion, these conversations are the only way forward. Coercion has played a central role in our sexual landscape for far too long and has ruined far too many lives. We deserve to enjoy our sexuality safely and without fear. With enough people on board, we can tip the scales of our culture to establish consent as the norm and coercion as unacceptable.

We'll talk more about consent culture and abuse in chapter 16, "Dating Violence."

Ask Laci: on consent

❓ Do I need to ask for consent every time in a long-term relationship?

Once you are more deeply familiar with each other's boundaries and needs, your communication about sex will evolve. When it comes to consent, long-term relationships can create more comfort with saying no. But even in loving, long-term relationships, it's still important to set a respectful stage for sex and any ensuing explorations. Talk to your partner on an ongoing basis about what you both feel comfortable with. Some people who are into kink rely on safe words to delineate consent and boundaries (more on that in chapter 14, "Kink"). Others mutually agree that A, B, C is okay while we need to have a discussion first before X, Y, Z. Whatever you decide on, check in about it once in a while to make sure it's still working for both of you.

❓ *What if both partners are drunk? Is it still sexual assault?*

If one partner was active during the exchange while the other partner was not (because they were wasted and out of it, for instance), that is sexual assault. Legally, charges are often brought against the person who initiated the encounter. "I was drunk" is a common excuse that perpetrators use to dismiss or minimize their actions. But a drunk perpetrator is responsible for committing a crime regardless of intoxication—whether they made the choice to sexually assault someone, to drive drunk, to cheat on a partner, or to start a bar fight. Being drunk does not negate responsibility or consequences for actions. If both partners initiated sexual contact and are *actively participating*, that is not sexual assault—but it is also not ideal in terms of sexual ethics and consent. If you want to have drunk sex with a partner, get clear on consent and boundaries beforehand.

❓ *What if I feel like I need to be wasted to have sex?*

It's normal to feel some anxiety about having sex, especially with a new partner. Social pressures to get laid can definitely add to that. Even for the more experienced among us, a drink can take the edge off sometimes. But all things in moderation; the relationship between sex and alcohol should be a healthy one. If your anxiety is so high that you feel you need to be wasted to have sex, you are not emotionally ready to have sex. You can read more about emotional readiness for sex in chapter 9, "Your Sexual Debut." Getting to the bottom of what's causing you anxiety will help you take control of your sexuality and sex life. If your anxiety about having sex is driven by past experiences or trauma, it's healthiest to work through it with a counselor rather than with booze. Be real with yourself and take care of yourself.

Is consent culture really possible?

Yes.

communication basics

CONFESSION: I USED TO FIND TALKING about sex painfully awkward. Still do, sometimes. It was one thing to actually *do* the sex; it was quite another to actually talk about it. Out loud. With words. It can be hard to say what we're thinking or how we feel, to tell a partner what we want sexually, to discuss boundaries, or to have those initial conversations about birth control or STIs. But learning how to communicate well is perhaps the most important sexual skill there is. It has the power to unlock greater intimacy, pleasure, and peace of mind.

You've probably heard the line "Communication is key!" IMO, even that's an understatement. Communication is *e.v.e.ry.t.h.i.n.g.* LITER-ALLY EVERYTHING. It is the lifeblood of all human interaction. We practice communication every day, during every intentional and unin-tentional exchange. We communicate with our words and actions; we communicate with a look; even with silence. But while communication is the lifeblood, *more* communication is not always *better* communication. Sometimes communication is ineffective, or even destructive. With a little practice, we can amp up the good stuff and phase out the bad.

What does "good communication" look like in a relationship? I would characterize good communication as being **open, respectful, effective, and honest**. Open communication means everybody feels comfortable and safe to express how they feel, and the lines are open for discussion as things come up. Part of maintaining that kind of collaborative environment is taking care to communicate respectfully. It should uplift and help you understand each other. Put-downs, constant criticism, or minimizing each other's concerns are all forms of disrespect that compromise open communication. Good communication is also communication that is effective at getting an intended message across: complex thoughts, feelings, and opinions are communicated in a way that is fully understood by the listener. It requires self-awareness about how we express ourselves and how we might come off to someone. And of course, good communication is honest. We all know that "honesty is the best policy!" but let's just acknowledge how hard that can be sometimes. There are a lot of barriers that can make it hard to be honest with each other. Maybe you're worried about being judged. Maybe you're worried about upsetting your partner if you tell them the truth. Maybe you don't quite know how to say it. Maybe you don't even know what to say. The good news is that being open with each other does actually get easier the more you do it. Once honesty is established as the norm within a relationship, you'll start to feel weird about *not* being straight-up with each other. If you struggle to communicate honestly to a partner, try not to overthink things. Just say what's on your mind. Some people like to write their thoughts down first, or practice in front of a mirror. If you don't feel like you are able to communicate honestly, that is a red flag.

Active Listening

As communicators, we take one of two roles: sometimes we are the speaker; sometimes we are the listener. I've found that people tend to struggle the most with the listening end of things. Listening is more than just hearing someone's words. It is the active process of understanding what a person is trying to convey. Emphasis on ACTIVE! To truly listen to someone, firstly, it's important to, well, ya know . . . pay attention. Brains do tend to wander, particularly if you have a lot of things on your mind or you're not especially interested. I find that listening is also challenging when I'm angry. When emotions are running high, my impulse is to focus on what I'm going to say in response rather than on what the other person is saying. But it's important to practice staying focused on the person, to be present and in the moment with them, not consumed with your own internal dialogue. To improve listening prowess, practice focusing on what the other person is trying to get across and taking a beat of quiet to collect your thoughts before responding.

You can signal to your partner that you're ~actively listening~ by
- Making comfortable eye contact
- Leaning into them, facing them
- Offering affirmative body language (like a nod) or verbal cues like "I see," "uh-huh," and "okay" (Don't overdo this one. Lol.)
- Repeating back what they said to you

If you are unsure what your partner means during a conversation, ask questions that will help you understand. You can indicate you have understood someone by paraphrasing what they said back to them. For example: "What I hear you saying is _____, and I feel that _____."

Becoming a good listener will help you hack life in general because, honestly, who doesn't like feeling listened to?! Literally nobody, that's who. Listening builds good vibes in your relationships, establishes you as a comfortable person to talk to, and helps de-escalate conflict.

In a speaking role, it's obviously most effective to be clear and concise. But . . . it doesn't always work out that way. Sometimes your head is just full of crap. Have you ever said something and immediately thought to yourself, "Wait, no, that's not what I mean!"? For me it's pretty much always. It can be hard to find the right words for thoughts, especially the more complicated or abstract ones. Be patient with yourself and figure out how you personally express yourself and communicate. Not everybody excels orally (no pun intended). Perhaps you communicate more easily in writing or art. Exploring your own communication style can help increase effectiveness.

Communicating in Conflict

In conflict (and in general, really) I-statements are a particularly effective way to communicate; they signal *ownership* of your words and feelings, which de-escalates conflict. Instead of starting with accusations like "you are," "you did," or "you want," rephrase with "I am," "I feel," or "I want." Even if someone is being unreasonable, try not to dismiss how they feel—it will only invite resentment. Most people become more reasonable and open to compromise when they feel heard.

In this sense, how you talk to your partner is just as important as what is actually said. Good communicators are strategic and cater their communication to the individual. This might mean taking into account language, tone, or preexisting sensitivities. Just as some of us speak in one way to our friends and another to our family, it's helpful to consider what is most productive for a given situation or person.

Disagreements are going to happen, even in the greatest relationships. In these situations, it's also critical to talk it out face-to-face in distraction-free environments. Take a pass on arguing in noisy restaurants, subway trains, and, for the love of all things holy, over text. Ugh, I am so guilty of it even though I know it's TERRIBLE. Texting is the worst medium for conflict resolution, which relies heavily on tone, emotion, and body language. Sometimes it even causes fights that wouldn't have been started in person! A text is much easier to misread than a face-to-face comment. If talking in person is not an option, a video call or a traditional phone call beats texting by a mile. For those who have never actually used the "phone" function of your phone, resolving a disagreement is a great reason to start! If things get very heated and people start raising their voices or shutting down, it's time to take a breather. Clear communication is impossible when brains are fogged with anger. Respectfully close the conversation and set a time to pick it back up after some time to cool off.

In conflict, it's tempting to focus on being right or proving someone wrong. Feeling right is validating, but in the context of relationship maintenance, it is less important to be right than to come to a mutual understanding. Only when there is mutual understanding can you start to work on solutions. In many situations, I've found we can agree to disagree and still find a fix that works for both of us. And in the event I am in the wrong, I suck it up and own up to it. It took me a while, but I've had to get more comfy with admitting fault and being accountable for my mistakes. Not only does this take some strain off of conflicts, but I've found it helps my partner feel like it's okay to admit fault when they've made mistakes, too.

If this sounds like a lot of stuff to pay attention to, that's because . . . well, it is. But with practice, good communication does become more intuitive and natural. So many problems between humans come down to bad communication. If you can hack these skills, you are well on your way to kicking ass at relationships—and life!

sexual communication

MOST PEOPLE KNOW THAT ALONGSIDE relationshipping, good communication plays an enormous role in having good sex. The million-orgasm question is "How the heck do you communicate about sex?"

Here are a few tips to get the conversation flowing.

Set Aside Judgment

One of the most important elements of having an openly communicative relationship is feeling like you can discuss some of the most intimate parts of yourself without judgment. Feeling judged impairs trust, communication, and respect—all the cornerstones of great sex. When both partners work to create a nonjudgmental atmosphere, it creates a powerful foundation for building intimacy. This, my friend, is where the magic happens.

Whether we like it or not, all of us have internalized judgy feelings about sex stuff. It's important to self-reflect and figure out where our own limitations, discomforts, and biases lie. Without self-awareness, judgment can come out in how we respond to a partner during conversations about sex. Here are a few examples:

Your partner discloses that they have had a threesome before.

Your emotional response: uncomfortable and surprised.

Judgmental response to partner: "Wow, I can't believe you'd do something like that."

Nonjudgmental response: "That's surprising. What was your experience like?"

Your partner wants to explore prostate play.
Your emotional response: uncomfortable and grossed out.

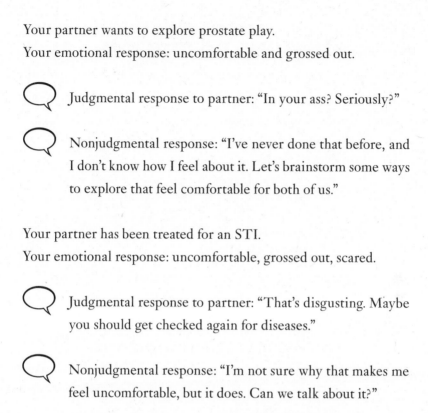

Judgmental response to partner: "In your ass? Seriously?"

Nonjudgmental response: "I've never done that before, and I don't know how I feel about it. Let's brainstorm some ways to explore that feel comfortable for both of us."

Your partner has been treated for an STI.
Your emotional response: uncomfortable, grossed out, scared.

Judgmental response to partner: "That's disgusting. Maybe you should get checked again for diseases."

Nonjudgmental response: "I'm not sure why that makes me feel uncomfortable, but it does. Can we talk about it?"

The shared emotion among nearly all judgy feelings (and subsequent shaming) is discomfort. And hey, it's okay to be uncomfortable. Being nonjudgmental is not the same as being comfortable with every thought or idea that you are presented with. Rather, it is a commitment to reacting reasonably and compassionately, instead of out of disgust or shame. By getting to the bottom of *why* something feels uncomfortable, it is easier to parse out and address in a healthy way with a partner.

Establish a Mutual Commitment to Open Communication

We already chatted about how good communication starts with being open and honest with each other. But that commitment has to go both ways—it simply won't work if open communication is a one-way street.

While a lot of sexual communication is fun and comes naturally, some stuff can feel awkward or difficult. Start by establishing a safe space where open communication is understood as an expected part of the relationship. Here are a few conversation starters to communicate about . . . openly communicating:

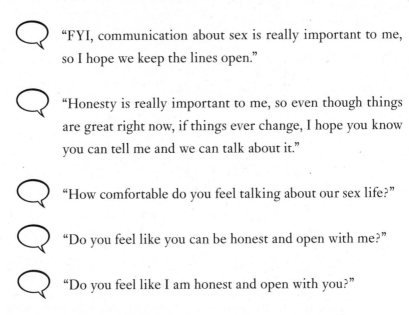

"FYI, communication about sex is really important to me, so I hope we keep the lines open."

"Honesty is really important to me, so even though things are great right now, if things ever change, I hope you know you can tell me and we can talk about it."

"How comfortable do you feel talking about our sex life?"

"Do you feel like you can be honest and open with me?"

"Do you feel like I am honest and open with you?"

Be Open about What You Want and Need

Figuring out what you like and are open to sexually with your partner requires a bit of communication. What are you into? What aren't you into? Is there anything you're curious to try? One way to have this conversation is by filling out a "Yes, No, Maybe" chart together. It can open the airwaves to talk about your interests, fantasies, and boundaries.

Act	Yes	No	Maybe
Marks/hickeys			
Lingerie			
Tribadism (naked genital rubbing)			
Frottage (clothed genital rubbing)			
Food play (whipped cream, chocolate, etc.)			
Temperature play (ice, hot wax, etc.)			
Oral sex			
Facesitting			
G-spot play			
Prostate play			
Pegging			
Being restrained			
Biting			
Tickling			
Hair pulling			
Spanking			
Nipple play			
Sex in public			

Act	Yes	No	Maybe
Sex outdoors			
Cam sex			
Grooming/shaving			
Fisting			
Watching porn			
Dirty talk			
Partner swapping/swinging			
Voyeurism			
Exhibitionism			
Sensory deprivation			
Cross-dressing			
Cosplaying			
Roleplaying			
Wrestling			
Impact play (flogs, whips, canes)			
Vibrators/dildos			
Cock ring			
Butt plug			

Act	Yes	No	Maybe
Anal beads			
Strap on			
Nipple clamps			
Blindfold			
Handcuffs			
Ropes/ties			

Provide Loving Feedback

Unfortunately, humans are not mind readers (usually). Which means that if you need something that you're not getting, you gotta say it. Maybe your partner is being a little rough with your clitoris or rushing to penetration too quickly. Maybe you like it gentler, rougher, faster, slower—whatever the case, the only way they'll know what you need is if you tell them!

So, how to do that? My experience is not to overthink it; just say what's on your mind. Obviously, feedback about sex should never come off as telling someone what to do or making demands. Whatever you're requesting of a partner should also be comfortable and nonburdensome to them. Be gentle and supportive, and turn up the humor when you can.

If you have negative feedback, it helps to cushion it with positive feedback:

"I love it when you _____, but I'm not a huge fan of _____."

Be as specific as possible with your feedback, and ask how they feel about it.

Q "I like it more on the rough side sometimes. Spanking, hair pulling, and biting turn me on. Are you into that?"

When you receive feedback, it's okay to ask questions to clarify.

Q "Like this?" "How's that?"

And when it comes to topics that take more discussion (for instance, how often you'd each ideally like to have sex in your relationship), it is best to talk about these things outside of the bedroom to take the pressure off. Maybe over lunch, while the people at the table next to you take some notes.

Positive Affirmation

Who doesn't like to be told "You're sexy" or "You make me feel good" by a romantic partner? It's affirming to be told when you're doing something that your partner enjoys. It also helps build intimacy and trust. In a healthy relationship, the vast majority of sexual communication should be positive and loving, not critical or demanding. If you are only communicating when there's something wrong, you're missing out on the best part!

THIRTEEN

⋛∘ SEXPLORATION ∘⋚

WHAT DOES IT MEAN TO HAVE "good sex"? I have often asked myself this question while burning the midnight oil and sleuthing around sexy websites at night. Is good sex sexy moves? Is it a hot partner? Is it the buildup? Is it the climax? I eventually came to the realization that what makes for "good sex" is all of the above and more—and what truly, deeply satisfies us as sexual people really depends on the individual. There is no formula for good sex. And actually, the opposite can be useful! Creativity can help you discover what ignites you, what feels good to you, and how to bring that same pleasure to a partner. All of this gets a little easier by understanding how your body works and how to communicate with your partner.

Having good sex also requires thinking of sex as more than just body stuff. A lot of us have anxiety about our sexual performance, and so we seek out guides and articles that claim to reveal special moves and techniques for sexual success. But in my experience, there are no special moves that work across the board. Instead, we should listen to each other's bodies. Listen to the slightest moves and wriggles, to how the breath changes, getting shorter or faster. Pay attention to the tenor of your lover's kisses, smiles, and words. That information has been more helpful than anything I have found tucked away in a book or magazine.

I also feel it's a disservice to separate the sensations of sex from the intimacy that it requires. At the risk of sounding a bit like a grandma (or a New Age hippie), I think there's sometimes too much focus on the physicality of sex, and it can numb us to the greater experience of mutual connection and vitality. Sure, sex is physical, but it's also a form of intimacy and connection with another person. It is a disservice to think of sex (and each other) as a mishmash of body parts and formulas.

So uh, that said, in this section we are going to take a look at some of the more physical aspects of sexual pleasure, with tips and tricks to help you explore. Avoid taking it as a set-in-stone how-to; think of this chapter as a creative launch pad to help you figure out what works for you!

IN THIS SECTION WE'LL TOUCH ON

—♡—

Making out

Hand sex

Oral sex

Vaginal sex

Butt sex

Sex on the margins

---

making out

SOMETHING ABOUT KISSING IS JUST UTTERLY magical to me. A good kiss makes me feel warm inside and quiets my thoughts like nothing else. It's exciting and romantic. Why does kissing feel so heckin' good?

Erogenous Zones, a.k.a. Your Hot Spots

When it comes to pleasure, genitals tend to take the spotlight. But to focus on only the genitals during sexytimes would be a shame. Our bodies are covered in erogenous zones. Erogenous zones are areas that have heightened sensitivity to touch. They can be stimulated in a ton of ways: with the mouth, kissing, licking, biting, gentle touch, rubbing, or using implements like a feather or ice.

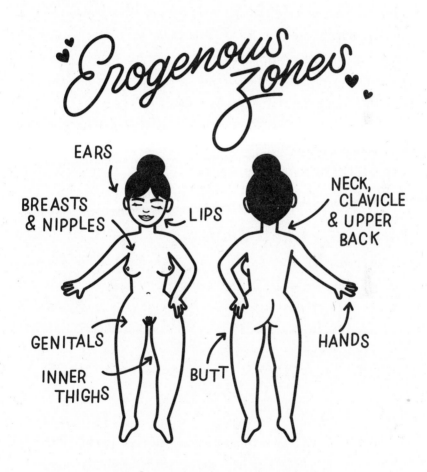

Erogenous Zones

EARS

BREASTS & NIPPLES

LIPS

NECK, CLAVICLE & UPPER BACK

GENITALS

INNER THIGHS

BUTT

HANDS

✳ MOST IMPORTANT—THE MIND!

Lips are the most exposed erogenous zone on the human body, and neuroscientists say they are one of our most sensitive (along with our hands). They are sensitive to even the slightest of touches, and to changes in temperature. When we kiss, signals from touch receptor cells in the lips pass information to the sensory cortex of the brain, setting off pleasure-producing neurotransmitters and hormones in the process. Adrenaline makes the heart beat faster in anticipation. Oxytocin makes us feel a deeper sense of intimacy and bonding, while dopamine deepens our craving and desire. It's an intoxicating brain cocktail that feels pretty nice. So there's that. But kissing is nice for another reason too: it's usually the first physically intimate exchange that happens between a couple. A first kiss is the closest we've been to them, bringing us literally face-to-face and nose-to-nose. When we see them up close, smell them, and taste them, all of these cues help us learn about them (usually subconsciously). Part of the information we process while we're kissing may influence our attraction to them. Kinda cool, right?

How to Kiss Like a Champ

The singer Betty Everett once told us, "It's in his kiss," and she wasn't alone in feeling this way. Artists from every genre, in every decade, can be found singing about the joys of kissing a lover. Obviously, the key to a good kiss is the person you're kissing! But beyond that, there are a few things that can make a kiss extra memorable.

LIPS

Soft lips are where it's at. It's not always possible because of the weather, so obviously keep expectations realistic. Staying hydrated helps when it's dry outside.

Soft Lip Hack

~♡~

Apply a lip moisturizer and let it sit for a few minutes. You can use anything from Carmex to coconut or olive oil. I use O'Keeffe's Lip Repair Lip Balm.

With a soft toothbrush and a little water, gently brush your lips, lifting up dead skin and particles.

Wipe lips clean with a washcloth.

Apply your favorite non-sticky lip balm.

MWAH!

BREATH

Brush yo' teeth! IMO, nothing ruins a good kiss like bad breath or grimy teeth. Oral hygiene is a must when you're breathing in someone's face (and, y'know, generally). You can test your breath by breathing into your hand from the back of your mouth. You can also use a spoon to test your breath. Scrape some of the gunk from the back of your tongue and take a whiff. If it smells, your breath smells. Tongue scrapers work well to get funky gunk off the tongue.

In a pinch, gum can help generate saliva and wash away some of the bacteria that causes bad breath. I like to chew gum and stay hydrated to keep my breath fresh throughout a date.

TONGUE

Deep kissing often involves a bit of tongue. The right usage of tongue goes a loooong way. Wield it gently during kissing, to convey affection or passion. Lips and jaw should feel comfortable and loose. Here are a few common faux pas I've experienced or heard about from friends over the years:

Being too aggressive with tongue (like shoving it down their throat)

Darting in and out of their mouth

Probing around their mouth and teeth

Kissing with a wide-open mouth, effectively eating their face.*

RHYTHM/PACE/PRESSURE

Making out is a bit like dancing, but instead of listening to the music, you are listening to your partner's body. Listen to their movements and the heaviness of their breath, to their pace and the pressure. Passionate and urgent kisses tend to have a quicker rhythm and pace, with slightly more pressure. Slower, gentler kisses tend to communicate a more romantic and loving vibe. Throw in a little pressure to express urgency, or ease off and linger softly on their lips for a few seconds to end a kiss gently. When in doubt, go slow.

HANDS

My first kiss started with an awkward poke in the eye with my partner's nose. Somehow, he had missed where my lips were by about four inches. Then, when we finally found each other's lips, I caught his hands

---

*Permissible if you're a zombie.

moving up and down through the air out of the corner of my eye. He had no idea where to put them. It was so awkward, but also so freaking adorable. I still laugh about it. Where do you put those hands, anyway?

My advice is to rest them wherever it feels natural to you. For me, that's usually on my partner's waist, resting on the small of their back, or wrapped around their shoulders in an embrace. It can also feel nice to have a hand gently rubbing the back or running through their hair.

NIBBLING AND SUCKING

Sometimes, you may well be so overcome with passion that you just want to eat them. But given the non-zombie bit, some well-placed nibbling and sucking will do the trick. It feels amazing and can really heighten pleasure and sensation. This is the case with the lips, but also other sensitive bits like the crook of the neck, clavicle, or nipples. Listen to your partner's body cues to make sure your suction isn't too hard or intense. If they are pulling back, that means TOO MUCH. If they are pulling you in, that means hell yeah. If they seem unsure, it's a good time to check in and make sure they're into it. Many people enjoy having their erogenous zones stimulated before and during genital stimulation.

When it comes to necking, it's important to be mindful not to leave marks that are unwanted. Sucking too hard on the same spot for a while can create small reddish/purple spots, a.k.a. hickeys. Hickeys are basically small bruises from broken blood vessels. You can avoid leaving marks by avoiding sucking too hard and moving around more. If your partner likes a little love mark, consider going for areas that can be covered by clothing. As always, check in with your partner about their preferences.

Hickey Hacks

———— ♡ ————

Hickeys can take up to a week to heal. In the meantime, try these hacks to make them less noticeable.

- Icing it. A hickey is a bruise. Ice packs (or other cold things) can help reduce swelling and constrict the vessel, making it less colorful.
- Color-correcting concealer.

Drug- and makeup stores carry a variety of color correctors that will help cancel out the color of the hickey. They come in green, peach, yellow, orange, and a variety of other colors! If you're unsure of which color to use, Google the right color for your skin tone.

These tones will help cancel out the color of the hickey. Use a thicker, drier concealer to avoid creasing and pat it in rather than rubbing. Then apply a concealer in the proper tone for the skin on your neck on top. Set with powder.

To me, the prelude to a first kiss sometimes feels a bit like a game of chicken. We're having fun, trying to read each other, trying to gauge the perfect moment to place a gentle smooch. Is it too early? Should I do it or should they? Who will go in first? I'M NERVOUS EEEEEEeeeeee.

If you're getting signals that they're into you, but aren't sure how to go about it, here are two approaches that have worked pretty well for me.

Ask if you can kiss them. Simple, to the point. A flirty, confident ask can be pretty hot.

Come in closer to their face and linger. If they're feeling it, they'll come in the rest of the way to kiss you. If they aren't feeling it and you misread the situation, they'll pull back or look away. To smooth over some awkwardness, handle misreads with humor.

hand sex

IF YOU'RE LOOKING FOR WAYS TO be sexual with a partner without the risks of STIs or pregnancy, you're in luck! Using your hands for stimulation, rather than mouths or genitals, keeps sex almost entirely risk-free. This is because there are no mucous membranes on your hands. The only risk is if you have a cut on your fingers or hand, and even then, the risk is relatively small. If you have a cut, refrain from contact, or use a finger cot or glove to protect transmission of STIs through blood.

Mutual Masturbation

Masturbating together is an intimate experience that can offer a lot of excitement and pleasure without the risks of pregnancy or STIs. Make sure to keep your genitals and fluids away from each other to keep it risk-free.

FINGERING

If your partner has a vulva, you can help bring them to orgasm with your hands by gently stimulating the clitoris. Since you are basically copying how they would masturbate, you may find the tips in the self-pleasure section useful. It's also important to ask your partner what feels good, and to take cues from their body responses. It's A-okay to ask them to show you what they like. Everyone is a little different!

Most of my experiences with fingering when I was younger involved my partner aggressively thrusting a couple fingers in and out of my vagina hoping that I'd orgasm. On some occasions, they had nails that scraped my insides (cut those nails!). It did not feel good. It's important to remember that the clitoris is the orgasm center. So while vaginal penetration may feel good, it is less likely to result in orgasm on its own. Before anything else, take ample time engaging your partner's erogenous zones first—caressing their thighs, breasts, butt, and vulva will help them gently ease into clitoral stimulation. When and if your partner is ready for more, lubricate your fingertips (using saliva or lube) and *gently* rub their clitoris. G e n t l y. Don't mash it in—keep strokes light and repetitive. Try a circular motion or moving your fingertips back and forth over the clitoris. Ask your partner what feels good and listen to their body.

You can switch things up by inserting a finger or two inside. Instead of moving your fingers in and out of the vagina, try a more fluid "come here" motion up toward their belly button. Gently curl your fingers inward to press on the back of the clitoris, pulling downward and massaging the vagina as you move in and out. To heighten stimulation even more, stimulate the external clitoris by positioning your palm over it, or with your other hand. Your partner may also enjoy gentle caresses or kisses as you go, particularly on sensitive parts of their body—like lips and nipples.

As your partner's breathing quickens and the sensation builds, you may increase your pace a bit—just don't go crazy unless they ask you to. Building up the pleasurable sensation typically requires consistent, repetitive stimulation. Going too fast or hard can cause a loss of sensation rather than increasing it.

HAND JOBS

If your partner has a penis, you can help bring them to orgasm with your hands. Apply lube to the penis or to your hands, then firmly but gently wrap your hand around the penis and stroke up and down. If you partner is uncircumcised, this will gently tug the foreskin back and forth over the head of the penis. As you may recall, the ridge around the head and the frenulum are the most sensitive bits, so make sure you touch these parts and give them plenty of attention.

Ask your partner how much pressure they enjoy or what pace feels good. As they heat up and build toward orgasm, they may wish for increased intensity. You can enhance the sensation by twisting your hand across the corona as you come up and down over the head. With your other hand, you can caress their body, paying attention to the inner thighs and testicles. Some people like *gentle* stroking or tugging of the testicles to enhance sensation. Your partner may also enjoy gentle massaging of the perineum, which can indirectly stimulate the prostate gland.

oral sex

ORAL SEX IS A TYPE OF outercourse that can be a fun and pleasurable part of sexual play. Compared to penetrative sex, oral sex is less risky for STIs (though you can still contract them), and you can't get pregnant. Oddly, when I was growing up, none of my friends considered oral sex to be "real" sex. Which I don't really understand. I mean, not to be overly crass here, but your genitals are literally in your partner's mouth. And for some people, oral is even more pleasurable than penetration.

Since you can contract STIs from oral sex, here are some ways to reduce your risk:

- Use a barrier like condoms, dental dams, or plastic wrap. Add a dab of lube to the inside of the condom/back of the dental dam to enhance pleasure.
- Don't brush your teeth right beforehand. Sure, you want your mouth fresh AF, but toothbrushes can leave micro-tears in your gums, which make it easier for bacteria and viruses to infect you. For the same reasons, don't eat "sharp" foods like chips right before oral sex.
- Avoid oral sex while either partner is having a herpes or genital warts outbreak. This includes herpes on the lips, also known as cold sores.

The Pubic Hair Question

Pubic hair, like the rest of our body hair, is subject to the whims of current trends and social norms. The proper pubic "hair style" has evolved throughout history and different parts of the world. These days, there is sometimes the perception that removing pubic hair is cleaner and more hygienic, but cleanliness is more about personal hygiene practices than the presence of hair.

So . . . what should you do with your pubic hair before sexytime? The answer is really a matter of personal preference. Some people go all out on the bush, some trim it, while others prefer the look and feel of bare skin. Per usual, just do you. And let your partner do whatever they like, too. At the end of the day, pubic hair management is a matter of what feels most comfortable. I mean, YOU gotta live with it all day.

It's worth noting that pubic hair serves some pretty cool/important functions. There's evidence to suggest that pubic hair traps pheromones to ~attract a mate~. It also offers a range of protections, like providing a little extra cushiness to ease friction on your genitals during sex. Some scientists think that pubic hair may also help keep bacteria and particles out of our sensitive bits, and recent studies have found that shaving may increase STI risk. Because shaving can leave micro-tears in the skin, it increases the risk of herpes, syphilis, and warts. Health-wise, it is safest not to shave, or to trim instead. If you shave, it helps to wait to have sex for a couple days after to let the skin completely heal. I would also caution against shaving around the anus, as it is very delicate and difficult to reach. Obviously, cuts and tears by your butthole HURT. If you want to remove hair around the anus, consider having a professional at a medical spa do it instead.

When it comes to hair removal, a little extra care and caution goes a long way. The main issue I've come up against with hair removal is itchy skin and ingrown hairs. Ingrown hairs are hairs that grow back into the skin or get trapped in their follicle after being shaved off. This causes a bump, pain, redness, and inflammation. Sometimes people mistake ingrown hairs for pimples or for herpes.

There are a few tips to prevent itching and ingrown hairs:
- Trim hair very short before shaving.
- Exfoliate with an exfoliating cloth before shaving to remove dead skin cells.
- Use a mild lubricating gel or soap on the hair to shave (keep the soap away from the urethra or vagina as it can be irritating or upset your pH balance).
- Use a new, sharp razor to minimize the number of times you have to shave over a particular area to completely remove the hair.
- Pull the area taut with one hand while you shave.

- Shave in the direction the hair is growing rather than against it.
- After shaving, apply aloe vera, witch hazel, or hydrogen peroxide to soothe the skin.
- Avoid "aftershave" products, which usually contain irritating fragrances and alcohol.
- If you are in pain because of razor burn, cortisone cream or an oatmeal bath may help soothe the area.

Oral Sex to a Vulva (a.k.a. Eating Out)

Of all the silly "hot tips" I've read on eating someone out, the advice that stands out to me as the most ridiculous is to do the alphabet with my tongue on my partner's vulva. It still makes me laugh. Like . . . what?! Is this really the level that our collective vulva-pleasuring knowledge is at? If you want a hot tip, as usual, the key is to ask your partner what feels good, to take cues from their body responses, and to experiment until you figure out what really gets them going.

At its most basic, oral sex to a vulva is stimulation of the clitoris with the mouth. When you go down on your partner, the clitoris is where it's at, so make sure you have properly identified where it is. If you're not sure, ask! Remember from before that the clitoris is a small nub covered by a hood at the top of the labia minora (inner lips), and may be tucked behind the labia majora (outer lips).

The most common position for oral sex is both partners lying down, but you may also find it more comfortable to position your partner at the edge of a bed or couch. Begin by touching your partner's body, caressing and kissing their thighs. If you want to give yourself better access to their clitoris, gently spread the labia with your fingers. If you don't see it immediately, as you lick or stroke upward from the vagina, you will feel a little bump—that's the clitoris. Gentle licks with the flat of your tongue, and generating a gentle suction with your mouth, will stimulate the clitoris. Once you figure out what is working for your partner, try to keep it relatively consistent unless they specify otherwise.

To increase pleasurable feels, you can run your hands over their body, and especially their erogenous zones like thighs and nipples. Perhaps make soft eye contact once in a while or let them know you're enjoying yourself. This can help a bunch if your partner is feeling self-conscious.

To rev up the sensation, many people enjoy a finger or two in the vagina to massage the back of the clitoris at the same time. Using a gentle "come here" motion with your fingers, knead the back of the clitoris as you eat your partner out. If your mouth needs a break, you can use your fingers to keep the sensation going. Keep your jaw loose and relaxed so that you are comfortable.

If your partner is getting close to orgasm (you'll know because they tell you, or because their muscles begin tensing) and you want to help them come, just keep doing what you're doing—steady and consistent. For some people, it helps to suck *ever-so-slightly* harder as they get closer to the edge, but avoid being too aggressive unless specifically requested. Sucking too hard can dull sensation rather than enhance it, bringing their arousal back down. Your partner may get close to the edge a few times before actually orgasming—that's normal! Don't stress. Just enjoy yourself, take your time, and focus on making them feel good.

If you are on the receiving end, let your partner know what feels good to you and don't forget to give a little love for all their hard work down there afterward. :o)

Oral Sex to a Penis (a.k.a. Blow Jobs)

I had no idea what a "blow job" was until I started watching porn. But... porn probably wasn't the best place to learn about it. Turns out that you don't have to swallow someone's penis whole to make them feel good.

Before you begin, make sure you are both in a comfortable position. One common position is one partner lying down while the other hovers over, or having one partner sit or stand while the other kneels. You can begin by using your hands or your mouth, but whichever it is, make sure it is well lubricated. Work up some saliva in your mouth and lick your partner's penis to lubricate it up. If you aren't a very saliva-y person, you can also use flavored lubricants or an edible lubricant like coconut oil.

The most sensitive part of the penis is the head, so this is the star of the show. Using your mouth with your tongue flat, gently lick and suck the head of the penis. You can use your hand to simultaneously stroke the base of the penis. Using your hand in tandem will increase the surface area that you can stimulate at once. Work your head up and down the penis (as far as is comfortable for you) to generate a gentle suction with your mouth. Make sure to avoid rubbing your teeth against sensitive skin. To prevent teeth contact, some people wrap their lips under a bit. As you suck, you can enhance pleasure for your partner by flicking the flat of your tongue against their frenulum, swirling your tongue around the corona, or twisting your hand around the base and up over the head to give your mouth a quick rest. Listen to your partner's body and ask them how they want it if you're unsure. Go at your own pace and experiment with different movements, pressures, and speeds to figure out what they like. Some people find some soft eye contact is sexy. They may also enjoy gentle rubbing or tugging of the testicles.

If your partner is getting closer to orgasm (you'll know because they tell you or because their muscles begin tensing up) and you want to help them come, stay consistent with your rhythm and speed unless they direct you otherwise. Some may enjoy slightly harder sucking to put them over the edge. Right before your partner comes, you may feel a pulse through their penis—and a polite partner will let you know when they're about to come as well. If you don't want their ejaculate in your mouth (STI-wise, it is safest to avoid their fluids), finish them off with your hand.

If you're the one who's getting oral, guide your partner to let them know what feels good, and don't forget to give some love for their hard work down there afterward. :o)

Prostate Massage

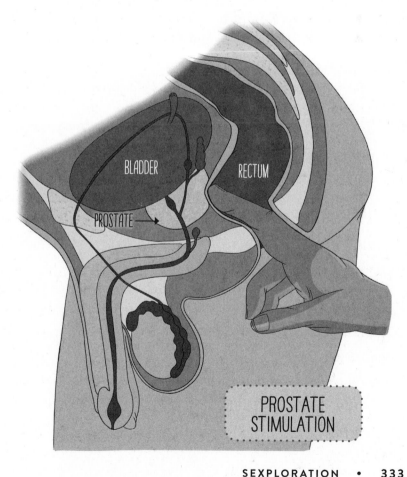

BLADDER

RECTUM

PROSTATE →

PROSTATE STIMULATION

Some folks also enjoy a cheeky finger in the bum during oral sex (or on its own) to stimulate the prostate. Prostate stimulation can feel amazing and send someone over the edge, if they are receptive to it. But this is *not* something to surprise your partner with unless you know they're open to it! Your partner should feel relaxed and receptive; otherwise it will be uncomfortable or painful. Before embarking, make sure you have clean hands and short nails, or use a latex glove for a smoother texture. With lube (Important!! Do not forgo the lube here as the butt doesn't make its own), gently rub the anus to warm your partner up as you stroke their penis. When they're ready, gently insert a finger inside and find the prostate with your partner's guidance. It is a soft, walnut-sized bulb a few inches in. Gently create a "come here" motion to stimulate the prostate with the pad of your finger. You can also rub in a circular motion (a flat circle, not up and down); just ask them what feels good! In general, avoid poking or being too aggressive, as this can irritate the prostate's delicate membrane.

Prostate massage can create lots of pleasure and orgasms of its own—including mind-blowing full-body types. These have been described to me as different from the sensation of penile orgasms. During prostate massage, it's normal to feel like liquid is moving through the urethra or for a milky whitish fluid to come out. Prostate orgasms themselves are typically dry (no ejaculate). We'll talk more about prostates in the butt sex section.

Oral Sex to an Anus, a.k.a. Rimming

Some people enjoy rimming as part of their sexual stimulation and activities. This is because the anus is very sensitive and full of pleasurable nerve endings. The technique is fairly straightforward. Just lick.

The main concern with rimming tends to be sanitary. Most of these issues are eliminated by showering beforehand or using a baby wipe to clear any bacteria. Just like any other type of sex, you can contract STIs from rimming even after cleaning up, so it's important to use a dental dam for protection.

vaginal sex

VAGINAL SEX IS OFTEN REGARDED AS the Official Definition of "sex." But as you've probably figured out by this point, it's just one of many sexually pleasurable acts. I'm sure I don't have to tell you that putting things in your vagina is fun. It's a magical hot pocket that is soft, warm, and wet, and can facilitate lots of orgasms. What's not to like? But doing it properly, with some basic knowledge of how vaginas and clitorises work, can make it muuuuuch better.

Reminder: always use protection and lube. Put condoms on strapons and penises, and/or get on birth control if you're having sex that can get you or your partner pregnant. Using lube on the vulva as well as on your partner's genitals or toys will help eliminate friction and improve glide. Niiiiice.

Types of Clitoral Stimulation

The science is clear: the key to good sex when vaginas are involved is clitorisclitorisclitoris!!! Let's take a closer look at what people say feels good. According to a study in *The Journal of Sex & Marital Therapy* on women's experiences with orgasm:

- 9% of women said they cannot orgasm during vaginal sex.
- 18.4% said they can orgasm from vaginal sex on its own.
- 36.6% say they need clitoral stimulation *during* vaginal sex to reach orgasm.
- 36% say they don't need clitoral stimulation during vaginal sex to orgasm, but it greatly enhances the sensation.

WHAT TYPES OF CLITORAL STIMULATION FEEL GOOD?

- 66% of women reported preferring direct clitoral stimulation.
- 75% of women prefer light-to-medium pressure on the clitoris.
- 16% say all pressures feel good.
- 10% prefer firm pressure on the clitoris.
- Most reported enjoying stimulation around the clitoris (e.g., on the sides along the labia).
- Most reported enjoying stimulation of the clitoris in an up-and-down or in a circular motion. A third enjoyed side-to-side.

WHAT IMPROVES THE QUALITY OF THE ORGASM?

- Most say it's crucial to spend time building arousal.
- Most say being familiar with their partner and having emotional intimacy improves the quality of sex.
- 75% of women say clitoral stimulation enhances or is necessary for orgasm.
- Less than 20% women say that having sex for a long time improves quality.

POSITIONS FOR CLITORAL STIMULATION

Sex magazines are all "Check Out These 365 Sex Positions for Each Day of the Year!!" And I'm over here like, "Can we not?" I'm tired just *thinking* about trying 365 positions. But hey, that's me, and I guess you could call me a pragmatist when it comes to sex positions. I tend to stick to my favorites. That said, trying new positions is fun and can help you find new and exciting forms of pleasure. Whatever you try should be comfortable (and safe!) for both you and your partner. For vaginal sex, different positions can stimulate the clitoris internally and externally in different ways. Here are a few popular ones.

Missionary. An oldie but a goodie, for a reason. Face-to-face creates more intimacy and connection. By pulling your knees up a bit, you can pull your partner in closer to bump up against your clitoris while they thrust.

Hop on top. Lean back while on top and hold your partner's thighs while you grind to better hit the g-spot. Since your partner has two free hands, they can stimulate the external clitoris. You can also stimulate it yourself by spreading your knees apart enough and grinding.

Scissor. Stack your legs to interlock with each other. This offers lots of skin-to-skin friction for more external clitoral stimulation. It also offers pretty good access to the internal clitoris, depending on the angle you are positioned in.

Doggy, but with your hips popped up. If it's uncomfortable on all fours, you can also throw a couple pillows underneath your hips. Popping your hips up offers pretty deep and intense stimulation of the g-spot. For extra zing, have your partner reach around and stimulate the external clitoris too.

Front-facing embrace. Face each other and cross your legs around their back. Or perch on top on your knees, and rock back and forth for g-spot stimulation. Pull in close and grind up on your partner for external clitoral magic.

Spooning. While you're on your side with your legs on top of each other, gently rock back and forth on your partner's penis or strap-on. The pressure of your legs combined with their penis inside can stimulate both the internal and external clitoris. It's also easy for a partner to reach around and stimulate the clitoris or for you to stimulate it yourself with this one.

Reverse spooning, with your partner's leg between yours. Same benefits as spooning, but instead of relying on the pressure of your own legs, you can grind up against your partner's.

QUEEFS

Sometimes during sex, you or your partner might queef. A queef is sometimes referred to as a vagina fart or "vart," and they are caused by air being expelled from the vagina. It's not stinky like a fart because it isn't caused by the breakdown of food and bacteria. It's just trapped air. Nothing to stress about. And c'mon, is there a better word than "queef"? I'm a grown-ass woman, and the word still makes me snicker.

SQUIRTING

Did you know "squirting" is one of the top searched terms on porn websites in the United States? It's right up there alongside "lesbian." People can't get enough of it. But squirting in real life is sometimes a little different. IRL, most people's vaginas don't blast like a garden hose when they orgasm. Let's talk about what's up with squirting (a quick review of those anatomy bits may be helpful here).

Stimulating the front wall of the vagina (a.k.a. the g-spot) is thought to be responsible for female ejaculation and squirting. This is because g-spot stimulation massages the urethral sponge, which is tissue around the urethral tube that fills with blood when you're aroused. The urethral sponge includes paraurethral glands (a.k.a. Skene's glands), which are a network of small glands that produce a milky fluid that is typically a creamy white color and chemically similar to male ejaculate—but without sperm. The body typically produces no more than a teaspoon of it. In the case of female ejaculation, some of that fluid drains out of two ducts on either side of the vagina. Recall that not everybody has Skene's glands, which means that not everyone can ejaculate. Ejaculation is not always super noticeable, except for increased wetness. It is more common than the similar (but slightly different) phenomenon known as squirting.

Unlike ejaculation, squirting tends to draw a little more attention. In porn, it's often faked and shows *a lot* more liquid than is normal. But IRL, a small number of people "squirt." The clear fluid being "squirted" comes out of the urethra. The research on this function of the female body is still relatively minimal, but a small study in the *Journal of Sexual Medicine* about the nature and origin of female squirting found that squirting may be made up of dilute urine that contains prostate-specific antigen, or PSA. PSA is found in male ejaculate as well, but in higher quantities. So while it's not exactly pee, it does have a similar chemical makeup.

Either way, squirting is just something some bodies do and others don't. It's not really a party trick that can be learned, and often sneaks up on people in the throes of pleasure. The More You Know.

PERIOD SEX

Most vagina owners have to deal with periods during sex at one point or another. It's not a huge deal. And hey, it can even have its perks. Some people find period sex feels a little better than usual, thanks to the extra lubrication and engorgement of the vulva when you're on your period. The endorphins released during orgasm can help with cramping and pain, and may even make your period a teensy bit shorter. This is because orgasm causes cervical contractions, which can help expel menstrual fluid from the uterus. That said, if you aren't a huge fan of period sex, you're not alone. Periods can be crampy, bloaty, and can feel like crap. Sometimes I'd just rather curl up with a heating pad and Netflix.

A number of concerns arise when it comes to sex during menstruation, particularly about messiness and safety. The messiness can be no joke. I've had period sex that made my bed look like a crime scene. Oops! To keep things a little neater, I typically lay down a towel when I'm on my period. I also like to put in a disposable soft cup beforehand when my flow is heavy. It holds back the blood while we have sex, making for easier cleanup.

As far as safety goes, just like other sexual fluids, menstrual blood can carry all the same viruses and bacteria, so use protection. Pregnancy risk goes down during menstruation, but it is still possible. The later in your period that you have sex, the higher the risk of pregnancy.

PAINFUL SEX?

If sex is painful, that is a message from your body to listen to. There are a number of different potential causes. Here are a few things to look into:

- Are you warming up enough before penetration? Take your time.
- Are you using enough lube? Excessive friction can tug on delicate skin and cause pain.
- Are you allergic to latex? Try nonlatex condoms and see if that helps.
- Do you have a yeast infection? Yeast can cause pain and soreness during vaginal sex. Though it is not common, it can

also transmit to your partner. (See chapter 3.)

- Do you have a bacterial infection? Having sex before a bacterial infection has cleared up can be very painful, and can transmit the infection to your partner. (See chapter 10.)

- Do you have very painful periods? If so, the pain may be caused by endometriosis. Ask your nurse or doctor for more information.

- Is your vagina uncomfortably dry? You may have a hormonal imbalance contributing to the pain. This is more common among those going through menopause and those who are breastfeeding. Ask your healthcare provider for more information.

- Have you recently given birth or had surgery? The tissue in the vagina may still be healing. Ask your healthcare provider for more information.

- Is the pain caused by muscle spasms? Survivors of sexual trauma sometimes develop involuntary spasms during vaginal sex. There is also a condition called pelvic floor dysfunction, where people carry stress and anxiety in the muscles around the vagina and anus. Ask your healthcare provider for more information.

- Are you up-to-date on your cancer screenings? Ask your healthcare provider to make sure more severe conditions are not underlying the pain.

- For uncircumcised males experiencing painful penetrative sex (or masturbation), the culprit may be phimosis, or a tight foreskin. There are creams that will increase the elasticity of the skin. Ask your healthcare provider for more information.

butt sex

IF THERE IS A GOD, SHE must have a sense of humor, considering the male g-spot is in the butt. Prostate stimulation can produce orgasms that I've heard described as "powerful," "full-body," and "holy %$#!" For vulva owners, although we can't orgasm with our butts, the anus is a sensitive body part that can enhance pleasure, and the fact that it is taboo is part of the turn-on for some people.

First let's talk about how to approach butt stuff safely and pleasurably!

The Essentials

Two supplies are critical before you go through the back door: condoms and lube. The anal cavity is highly susceptible to STIs because the tissue tears easily. So . . . Wrap! It! Up! Additionally, the anus doesn't produce lubrication like the vagina does, so it's really important to use lubricant. Reapply as needed.

Things that are okay to put in the butt:

- Fingers
- Penises
- Toys with a flared base

Things not to put in the butt:

- Veggies
- Cacti
- Baseball bat
- Mom's antique figurines
- ANYTHING THAT DOESN'T HAVE A FLARED BASE

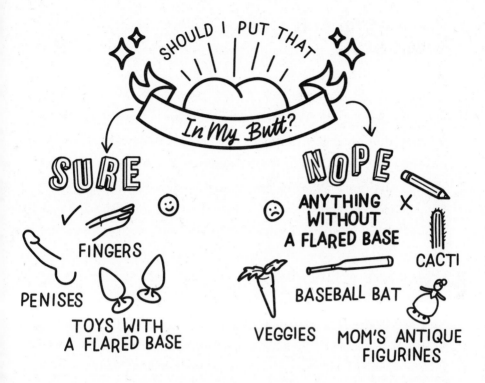

SHOULD I PUT THAT In My Butt?

SURE
✓ FINGERS ☺
PENISES
TOYS WITH A FLARED BASE

NOPE
☹ ANYTHING WITHOUT A FLARED BASE ✗
CACTI
BASEBALL BAT
VEGGIES   MOM'S ANTIQUE FIGURINES

Whatever goes into the butt must have a flared base. Unlike the vagina, the anal cavity doesn't have a cervix at the top to prevent things from getting lost. Vigorous play or orgasmic contractions can cause toys to get stuck in there. Whoops! This mistake causes thousands of trips to the emergency room each year. No, I am not kidding. Nobody wants to be that person in the ER, so flare them bases.

Other important butt sex things:

Go sloooow. Going too quickly or aggressively can tear the anal lining, causing a fissure that requires medical attention.

Don't move from butt to vagina without changing condoms. This will transmit all of the bacteria from the bum to the vagina. Ahhhh!

Listen to your body. If it hurts at any point, that's your body's warning sign. Stop and troubleshoot before continuing.

Prepping for Butt Stuff

The main question I get about butt stuff is a squeamish "um . . . what about the poo??"

Here's the good news: as long as you don't have to take a poop while you're having sex, you don't need to worry. If you do have to go, just do it beforehand or let your partner know you're ~not available~ at the moment. The rectum tends to be cleanest right after you poo. Occasionally particles are hanging out in there, but it's typically not enough to be noticeable. This is less of an issue if you eat a healthy diet with plenty of fiber. Hygiene-wise, rinse your bum with warm water, and if you wish, a mild fragrance-free soap beforehand. That's really all you need. Shaving or waxing isn't necessary, and can cause irritation and cuts since this is a very sensitive area. This can make you more susceptible to STIs.

People who are worried about anal hygiene sometimes use rectal douches (also called enemas) to clear out the rectum. There is a lot of debate about the practice, and I personally don't recommend it. It really isn't necessary and can irritate the delicate lining of the anal cavity, making your bum more susceptible to STIs and bowel issues.

If you want to douche, try to keep it to no more than once a month or so. The safest and easiest type of douche to use is a bulb. Fill the bulb with room-temperature or lukewarm water—but *no soap or cleansers* unless you want an ouch in your bum. Then apply some silicone-based lube around the tip and on your anus. (Water-based lubes wash away more easily.) Gently insert the nozzle and squeeze the water into your bum. Don't squeeze in the entire bulb—this can cause discomfort and a mess. Also, pull the nozzle out *before* letting go of the bulb or you'll suck the dirty water back into it. Once the water is in, you'll feel a bit like you have to poop. Sit on the toilet and expel the liquid. Some people do this process a couple times. I'd suggest doing it a few hours before sex to allow all the liquid time to expel (sometimes it gets trapped in little nooks and crannies).

If you do encounter poo, don't stress. Shit happens. It's part of having a human body. Bring your sense of humor and some baby wipes.

How to Have Butt Sex

Before beginning, both partners—and their butts!—should feel relaxed and at ease. The anal cavity has two sphincters: internal and external.

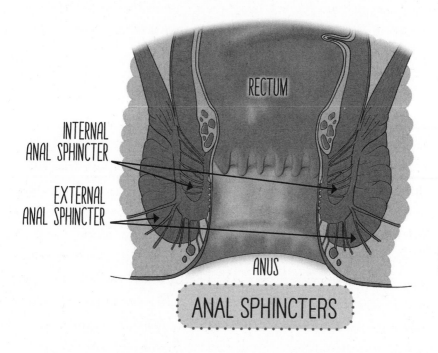

RECTUM

INTERNAL ANAL SPHINCTER

EXTERNAL ANAL SPHINCTER

ANUS

ANAL SPHINCTERS

The external sphincter is the one that clenches when you clench your butt. To relax it, relax the muscles around the bum. The internal sphincter is controlled by the central nervous system, which means that if the receptive partner is feeling tense or anxious, the sphincter can tighten. This will make butt stuff painful and unenjoyable. It can also increase the chance of injury. To ensure it feels nice, it's important to warm up with other types of sex first and make sure you're very aroused before putting anything in the anus. Just like with the vagina, start small; use a finger or small flared-base toy before using larger toys or a penis. Breathe deeply and relax.

Like I mentioned before, because the anus doesn't produce lubrication, it's also important to use plenty of lube. Silicone-based lubricant tends to be the best for anal sex because it lasts the longest. Reapply lube as you need it, and take it nice and slow. The sensation can feel a bit like you have to poo—so don't stress yourself out that you're about to poo all over your partner. Like most sexy stuff, most people I've talked to say the first time wasn't the greatest sex they've had, and that it felt better with practice.

Butt Sex and Homophobia

Anal sex occupies an interesting place in our sexual culture and psyche. It's pretty taboo, relegated to "dirty," "gross," and "deviant," especially for men who enjoy receiving it. But like a lot of sexual taboos, the forbidden nature of anal sex seems to drive our fascination with it. Where does the taboo come from? I have a few theories. I think it's part hygiene concern, and part homophobia. The hygiene concerns are resolved with the basic measures we've discussed. The homophobia is a little more complicated. I've heard from lots of men over the years who worry that enjoying prostate stimulation "makes them gay." But sexual orientation isn't determined by what types of pleasure you like—it's about *who* you like to share that pleasure with. There is no magical button inside your butt that will change your sexual orientation. Even if part of the appeal is having sex with another man, who cares? It's okay to be curious, or bisexual, or gay, or anywhere in between. Live your truth, and don't let homophobia stop you from experimenting with what feels good.

Butt Sex and Coercion

On the flip side of things, too many women tell me that they are pressured into anal sex by male partners. Some even describe violating situations, where a partner "accidentally" tries to slip it in after being told no. This is sexual assault. Even without attempting insertion, pressuring a partner to have anal when they don't want to isn't cool. WTF?

Studies on attitudes about anal sex among heterosexual young people have made some disturbing findings. A study on the subject in *The British Medical Journal* found that young adults expect anal sex to be:

Coercive. Young men reported that they expect to have to persuade their partner into having anal sex. Participants described repeated and emphatic pestering, "slipping it in" without asking, hoping she won't say anything, and attempting to continue with penetration despite their partner saying no.

Painful. Both men and women believed that anal sex would be painful for the woman, and techniques to reduce pain were not discussed. Interviewees also said anal sex *could* be pleasurable if the woman would "relax" and "get used to it." Women who didn't like anal sex were described as either uptight or secretly into it.

Unsafe. Condoms were not usually used during anal sex, and when they were, it was for hygiene purposes and not for STI prevention. Some participants in the study wrongly stated that you can't get STIs during anal sex, or that it is less risky than vaginal sex.

To make matters worse, the *reasons* that most of the young men in the study cited for trying anal sex had nothing to do with a mutual desire for pleasure or exploration. Instead, porn was often cited as a reason for wanting to try anal sex. Young men in the study also discussed anal sex as a type of competition. Convincing a partner to try it was applauded among their peers. Young women were also applauded, though for different reasons: for being "adventurous" and proving they're not prudes.

Even with the accolades, young women were left to balance them with risks to their reputations—risks that did not affect young heterosexual men.

Yikes.

It's not clear, exactly, to what extent these attitudes affect LGBTQ+ communities. And it should be emphasized that this study doesn't suggest that *all women hate anal sex* while *all men are trying to force it on them*. What it *does* highlight is a disturbing trend in how anal play is being understood by some young people. And I worry that this is made worse by the fact that nobody is willing to talk about consent and safe anal play. Even in sex education classrooms, butt stuff is rarely, if ever, discussed. This leaves students uninformed and increases stigma.

Let's clarify the message, then: while butt stuff can be pleasurable and fun, it is an activity for those who truly wish to experiment with it. Nobody should be pressured to try anything that they're not into or are uncomfortable with. It is okay to say no, and boundaries should always be respected. Doing anything to a partner's body against their will is sexual assault, plain and simple. To combat the normalization of coercion, young people must speak up to cultivate consent culture among their peers. (See also chapter 12.)

sex on the margins

IN ALL OUR SEXY EXPLORATIONS, IT'S important to remember there is a multitude of experiences in the world, each with their own challenges and rewards. To explore the intersection of marginalized identities and sexuality, I invited a couple of my friends to share their thoughts. They'll offer their perspectives and advice on navigating sexual relationships for asexuals and people with disabilities.

SEX WHILE ASEXUAL

by Gaia Steinberg

If there is one thing I have learned in the asexual community, it's that sex isn't obligatory. You can go through an entire life without ever having sex, and it doesn't make you less of a human being. People can *choose* to have sex, but they don't *have* to. A lot of asexuals prefer never engaging in sexual activity, while others choose to have sex for various reasons: some wish to please a romantic partner; some enjoy the physical aspects of sex or the emotional closeness they feel comes with it.

Growing up, I remember the main advice I received about sex was "Wait until you're ready." I was never sure what that meant—the "sexual readiness" concept assumed *everyone* would want to have sex eventually. As an asexual, I didn't know if sex was for me at all. This always made me feel half-baked—as if there was a human sexuality factory, and I was left halfway down on the assembly line. But my asexuality isn't an "undeveloped" sexuality. While I didn't desire traditional sexuality—and therefore, you could say, was not "ready"—I did crave the intimacy I was told is achieved only through sex.

I feel like the "sexual readiness" concept originates in the belief that sexual experiences exist on a ladder of intensity: from kissing to making out to sex (with a bunch of other rungs along the way). In this ladder, sex is seen as the highest point of physical pleasure one can reach with a partner—and in a romantic relationship, you are expected to climb the ladder together. Being told sex is the ultimate physical pleasure can leave asexuals feeling like they can't experience pleasure at all. Moreover, having the expectation to "climb the sexual ladder" with a partner can leave asexuals feeling responsible for their partner's sexuality, potentially depriving them of experiencing such physical pleasure as well. This all adds to the pressure.

I used to feel like I *had* to have sex with partners so they wouldn't leave me. This pressure usually didn't come from my partners, but from myself—I felt morally obligated to sexually please people I was romantically involved with. It took me years to realize my emotions and desires mattered as well. For this reason, I find it very important to emphasize: *when it comes to asexuals dating allosexual people (someone who experiences sexual attraction), the issue at hand is the discrepancy of desire—not the asexuality itself.* This is not unique to asexual-allosexual relationships—even between two allosexual people, there is sometimes a difference of desire regarding the amount or type of sex. There are a variety of ways to deal with such a discrepancy. Each couple is unique, and different solutions work for different individuals. That said, I will give a few ideas and questions to think about that I found useful in my personal journey.

1. Set comfortable expectations from the beginning.

A lot of the time, sex is seen as part of the package deal of a romantic relationship. As an asexual, this always made me feel like I wasn't "living up" to my end of the relationship bargain. One thing I found very liberating was deciding that, for now, sex was off the table completely. This way, if it made sense for me and my partner, we could *add* sexual features to our relationship later on. But it wouldn't be a standard we had to reach or be judged according to. Instead of standing at the beginning of the sexuality ladder, waiting to climb, we would look away from it altogether and ask, "What makes sense for *us*?"

When the assumption is first and foremost *not* sexual, it can actually help asexuals explore what areas of sexuality, if any, they *are* interested in. I used to be afraid that if I decided to experiment with certain types of sexual touch, I would be stepping up to a higher rung of the sexual ladder with my partner, and I wouldn't be allowed to step back down later (or go sideways, away from the sexual script). By going off-script, sexual touch wasn't an expectation that I had to say no to, but I got to say yes to situations where that was wanted. Another thing I feel is important to stress is that *you should not assume that if you are willing to say yes to a sexual situation, your partner desires it as well!*

I used to go into relationships with so much guilt about not being "sexual enough"—which made me assume my partners always wanted sex and I was stopping them from having it. This is, of course, not true—hardly anyone always wants sex. It's important to be attentive to your partner as well as to yourself, and to figure out together what parts of sexuality, if any, make sense to you and when.

Lastly, it's crucial to mention that figuring out sex in a relationship—what types of activities work for you and how often—isn't going to end up at the exact middle between the individuals. Engaging in sexual activities you don't desire can be harmful and even traumatic. Try to keep your sexual explorations emotionally safe—communicate with your partner if you're feeling pressured or if you're afraid your partner might be feeling pressured. Remind yourself that it's okay not to engage at all. Go back to the very beginning.

2. Explore touch.

Figure out what kind of touch you *do* enjoy. This will help you figure out what kind of touch you want as a couple. I have met many asexuals who have said they enjoy different aspects of sexuality—like emotional intimacy, intensity of physical closeness, the joy of pleasuring someone they love, and so on. These aren't inherently sexual features, but can also be experienced through sex. Finding out if there are parts of sex you actually enjoy can really help you understand what you'd like to incorporate into a relationship with a partner. Explore different types of touch as well. Touch can be passionate and filled with desire without necessarily being sexual. Exploring what *you* find pleasurable is just as important, even if that pleasure isn't sexual.

Many asexuals crave touch, but don't know how to create it outside of the sexual script. This is something you can bring up with your partner—have a conversation about what kinds of touch excite both of you, sexual or otherwise. Discuss what you are willing to explore together, and be attentive to each other. It's important to be respectful of the needs and boundaries of everyone involved.

3. Explore relationship structures.

Lastly, I think it's important to think about the type of relationship you wish to build. Monogamy tends to be most people's "go-to" relationship. However, one way to bridge the sexual gap in a relationship is actually to break away from monogamy.

Open or polyamorous relationships can help take off the pressure of pleasing your partner sexually. Having multiple partners can allow an allosexual partner to find sexual gratification with others. This is especially useful if the discrepancy of desires is relatively high (for example, an allosexual person who desires sex on a daily basis, and an asexual partner who prefers not to engage in sex at all). This is what I found most useful in my life—my partners can have sexual experiences in close, intimate relationships, just not the one they are sharing with me. Of course, this doesn't suit everyone, and you should think what type of relationship makes sense to you.

It's also important to remember that not everyone is suited for each other—and that's okay too. Two people who want a monogamous relationship with each other, but also have a large difference in sexual desires, might not figure out a way to both be happy in the relationship. I don't mean to be a downer here, but sometimes if you love each other, the most realistic solution is to break up and not to pressure yourself into sexual situations you don't want.

What do I do if my partner is ace?

Don't assume anything—communicate. Some asexuals would prefer not to engage in any type of sexual activity, and that's okay. If this is the case with your partner, you can both try some of the advice given here: start by taking sexuality off the table, explore different forms of touch if wanted, and consider the relationship structure that fits you. You might find a creative way to meet both of your needs in the relationship. It is also possible you'll end up finding out that your needs are so different they cannot be met with each other.

Other asexuals might desire different aspects of sexuality, so don't assume all asexuals want sex to be off the table completely. Discuss this with your partner, explore together, and be attentive to each other's boundaries.

As you figure things out, don't forget that there's a huge variety in asexual people's experiences and desires. Some crave physical intimacy; some don't. Some are repulsed by sexual activity, some are indifferent, and some might even enjoy it. For others, the line between sexual activity and nonsexual intimacy doesn't really matter. All these experiences are meaningful and valid.

SEX WITH DISABILITIES

by Olivia Dean

In high school I was teased a lot because I was different. I had severe scoliosis that caused me to bend over while sitting, with my head arching backward so that I could see. I compensated by being the outspoken disabled girl who was extremely flirtatious. I was teased for this, mostly by fellow students, but there were one or two times when a teacher joined in. I wanted to "slut it up" just like everyone else, but was instead laughed at and shushed. This is my experience as a disabled person growing up. We are not seen as sexual beings; instead we are infantilized or viewed as asexual.

My sexual awakening began in college. I took a class on human sexuality, and that's when I discovered that I am a sex geek. My professor was an amazing person who taught me the difference between gender and sex, about the g-spot, the Kinsey Scale, and much more. Around this time, I also started dating my first boyfriend. It was a validating experience that helped me let go of the stereotypes that society was feeding me. This was the catalyst that set me off on my journey to not only grow as a sexual being, but as an open-minded and confident person. I joined *The Vagina Monologues* and performed a four-person piece on menstruation while wearing lingerie in front of a live audience. It was one of the most liberating things that I had done. I also joined the sexual health education program at my school, where I handed out condoms and discussed sexual health with other students. Through this program, I facilitated two peer-led classes. One was on human sexuality, and one was a class that I created myself, called "Intro to Sex and Disability."

The class had eight students, most without disabilities. We talked about how people with disabilities are portrayed by the media through popular TV shows and movies. How do disabled characters and their stories on-screen influence and reflect our perceptions of people with disabilities in real life? Take Artie, a character in *Glee* who has a spinal cord injury. In one episode, he is at the mall with his love interest and tells her that all he wants to do is dance. He jumps out of his chair, and a giant flash mob ensues with awesome dance moves done to the song "Safety Dance," by Men Without Hats. Artie wows the audience with his moves as people in the crowd dance along. The performance is awesome and, dare I say it, lit until . . . BAM. Artie falls back into his chair, and he is crushed when he realizes that he had hallucinated the entire performance. As viewers, we are left with a sinking feeling. One you might call pity.

Artie's plot line is something we call "inspiration porn," a common theme in the media. Inspiration porn is when you put a disabled person on a pedestal just for existing. If I had a dollar for every time someone told me I was inspirational, I could afford to shop at Whole Foods every week. And I kind of get it: the fragility of life is shoved in your face when you see us. We are a reminder to everyone in the world that their life is not that bad. Because hey, at least they are not in a wheelchair. But let me set the record straight: people with disabilities aren't here to make everyone else feel better. There is nothing sad or pitiful about our lives. We are individuals with value and purpose and meaning to our existence, just like everyone else. Should you see a disabled person outside living their life, and you feel inspired by them inhaling and exhaling, please check yourself before you wreck yourself. Devaluing our life and invalidating our humanity takes away our dignity. You're allowed to call me brave and a hero if I stand up to a cop who is harassing someone for no reason. But if you call me brave because I am waiting for the bus, prepare for me to glare at you until you walk away.

This characterization of people with disabilities also affects perceptions of our sexuality. One stark example of this happens every spring during prom season. On social media, those who ask people with disabilities to prom are often applauded—for all the wrong reasons. In one case where a popular football player asked a young woman with Down syndrome to prom, the majority of people didn't even consider the girl's perspective on the situation. Instead praises were heard all around for the guy doing something so noble and honorable. What, exactly, is so "righteous" about including someone with a disability in a routine high school tradition? Disabled people should be included anyway, in all aspects of a relationship—whether it be platonic or romantic. This pity-based narrative leads people with disabilities to doubt their own self-worth, and to see themselves as less valuable than everybody else.

What should people with disabilities know about their sexuality?

I can't speak for everyone, but I can speak for myself. I want people with disabilities to know that they are perfect just the way they are. I know it sounds like a cheesy Hallmark card slogan, but it's true. Know your worth; know that you are enough—all on your own. We don't need to have another person to make ourselves whole.

I also want people with disabilities to explore their sexuality freely without judgment. Get creative with exploring your sexuality. If you can't hold a vibrator, try a lightweight long pen to help you reach clitoral climax. If you have a penis, wear pants with a large fly for easier access to yourself. Be open to your sexuality; don't let it scare you or oppress you. Learn to have a relationship with yourself, and love yourself. It is the most important relationship that you will ever have.

Remember that being sexual with ourselves and with others is a beautiful thing. If someone turns you down, it's their loss. They don't know what they are missing, because having a disability redefines what being sexual is. Erogenous zones can be relocated and reinvented! Hoyer lifts can go from being used just for lifting to being used as a sex swing! The possibilities are endless.

How can able-bodied people be good lovers to partners with a disability?

The partners of someone with a disability need to be open. Communication is lubrication! Don't be afraid to ask questions.

The person with a disability is probably as nervous as you are.

The best way to show interest in a person with a disability is to see them as a person. Don't walk on glass when you are around them. Show that you are comfortable around them. I know that at least for me, I can easily pick up on people who are uncomfortable around me, and it makes me uncomfortable. We are as human as you are; to view us as an "other" would be quite insulting. Treat us like anyone else. Don't pull our hair (unless we ask you to ;]), don't insult us, and don't make stupid remarks about how fast our chair can go or if we enjoy hitting people with our cane. Don't make assumptions about our disability. Leave us room to talk about what we can and cannot do, on our own terms. Ask questions, in a respectful way, and accept what we say.

Have fun, everyone.

FOURTEEN

≳∘ KINK ∘≲

BY NOW YOU'VE PROBABLY CAUGHT A glimpse of how thoroughly zany and mysterious human sexuality can be. To add another layer to the cake, let's take a walk through the colorful world of kink, fetishes, and BDSM.

> ## IN THIS CHAPTER
> ⌣♡⌣
> Overview
> Stigma
> The essentials

overview

WHAT IS KINK? MOST OFTEN, I hear the word "kinky" used to describe sexual practices or interests that are unusual or less common. It stands in contrast to more "typical" or "vanilla" practices. The number of kinks in the world are nearly endless. Here are a few examples:

- Nipple play—playing with the nipples via licking, sucking, touching, squeezing, etc.
- Erotic massage—massage that stimulates genitals, breasts, and sexy bits
- Roleplay—playing out different scenarios, typically involving a dominant and submissive role
- Cuckolding—having sex with someone while their partner watches
- Edging—getting close to orgasm and then pulling back to keep going
- Furries—dressing up as animals or pretending to be an animal/pet
- Being watched while having sex or masturbating
- Having sex in public
- Having sex with a stranger
- Group sex
- Anal sex

Depending on who you are, you might classify some of these kinks as typical interests and preferences. I mean, is nipple play really that kinky when a lot of people enjoy it? The line between a kink and a nonkink is blurred, and that's because, outside of nonconsent, there is no clear boundary on what constitutes a "normal" sexual interest. It's estimated that about one in three people has a kink of some kind. A study about BDSM in *The Journal of Sexual Medicine* found that the vast majority of kinks that people think of as "unusual" are actually fairly common.

For some people, kink is central to their experience of sex, and perhaps even to their identity. However, kinks are not considered a sexual orientation (like being gay) because they describe a preference for particular acts, rather than a particular sex or gender. There is a vibrant kink community in the United States, made up of people of all genders and sexual orientations, from many different backgrounds and walks of life.

Under the banner of kink are two broad categories: fetishes and BDSM.

Fetishes

Fetishes are a subcategory of kink. The word "fetish" is often tossed around in pop culture to refer to any random sexual interest. But if you wanna get technical, a fetish is a fixation on a nonsexual object or body part that is so intense, the person can't get off without it, or at least thinking about it, during sexual play. A fetishist typically needs to touch, smell, or wear their fetish to get off. This is how fetishes are different from most kinks—they go beyond a mere sexual preference to a requirement for gratification. Fetishes are thought to be formed through conditioning that causes the person to make a strong association between the fetish and sexual arousal. Most experts believe they are formed in childhood, but occasionally a fetish may be formed after that. Some fetishes qualify as a paraphilia, or an "atypical" sexual interest. Strict definitions of what counts as a paraphilia have historically been flawed, given the somewhat subjective nature of what's "normal." The DSM-5 classifies a paraphilia as a type of disorder when it "causes mental distress to a person or makes the person a serious threat to the psychological and physical well-being of other individuals." There are some psychologists and psychiatrists who help rehabilitate people with harmful paraphilias.

That said, most fetishes are fairly innocuous and do no harm. Here are a few of the more common examples:

- Feet
- Stomachs

- Leather
- Corsets
- Heels
- Knee-high/thigh-high stockings
- Rope
- Piercings and tattoos

BDSM

BDSM refers to a set of sexual practices that focus on intense sensations or power play (domination and submission) to achieve sexual release and gratification. The controlled setting in which BDSM is practiced is called a scene. A scene doesn't always involve sex. As an acronym, "BDSM" refers to the following:

B—Bondage

D—Discipline, Domination

S—Submission, Sadism

M—Masochism

Some examples of BDSM:

- Tying someone up (with rope, scarves, neckties . . .)
- Holding someone down
- Hair pulling
- Blindfolding
- Spanking
- Flogging
- Whipping
- Roleplaying
- Biting
- Scratching
- Electrical stimulation

- Hot wax
- Wrapping body parts tightly with fabric, plastic wrap, etc.
- Giving orders
- Topping or dominating
- Bottoming or submitting

There's a pretty wide spectrum of practices that fall under BDSM. Even folks who consider themselves "vanilla" may find themselves practicing BDSM Lite in the bedroom sometimes. Why? The answer is fairly straightforward: for a lot of people, it feels good. BDSM can rev up the excitement and intensity of an erotic situation. Taking control or giving yourself over to someone you trust and feel safe with can be powerfully erotic.

For my fellow science nerds out there, researchers have found that there's something verrrrry interesting going on in the brain during BDSM play. A 2009 study in *The Archives of Sexual Behavior* found it releases a number of endorphins, which scientists have compared to a runner's high. John Mellencamp wasn't kidding when he claimed it "hurts so good." But even more interesting are the mind/body effects that BDSM appears to create. Researchers found that for the bottom, the stress hormone cortisol slowly increased over the course of the scene. For female bottoms, testosterone also increased. But even though the body was under more stress, psychologically, participants perceived themselves to be *less* stressed. This puts some data to the idea that physical stress on the body can act as an emotional release.

Another interesting study from 2016 in *The Journal of Sex Research* found that BDSM practitioners tend to be, well . . . a little less harmful. BDSM practitioners reported significantly lower levels of benevolent sexism, rape myth acceptance, and victim blaming than the control group (college students and adult participants from Amazon's Mechanical Turk, a crowdsourcing website for businesses). This isn't that surprising. In the kink spaces I've been a part of, there is a very serious and explicit expectation of consent and respect for people's boundaries. Breaking the rules, even mildly, is grounds for being kicked out. That means no physical contact whatsoever without consent first. In other words, many kink communities cultivate consent culture. And this study (along with many others) suggests that consent culture actually works. We can, in fact, lower rape-supportive beliefs and behaviors by cultivating consent culture and curating our social environments to reject nonconsensual sexual behaviors. Kink subcultures may be better at doing this than the mainstream is. Even for those who aren't into BDSM, there is much to learn from this sexual subculture.

And yet, the opposite tends to happen: stigma, shame, and repulsion.

stigma

BDSM HAS BEEN WIDELY MISUNDERSTOOD AND stigmatized throughout history, and remains so to this day. In media settings, representations of BDSM are overwhelmingly dark and sinister, with its participants unwaveringly portrayed as damaged or abusive characters. Perhaps the most popular example is *Fifty Shades of Grey*, which, for better and worse, thrust kink into the mainstream in 2011. While *Fifty Shades of Grey* succeeded in removing some of the stigma for the average person who's interested in exploring kink, it also succeeded in reinforcing stereotypes about the practice.

One of the more pervasive stereotypes is that kinksters are deeply broken, or even mentally ill. Why would you want someone to hit you?

You've gotta be fucked up to like that, right? Freud certainly thought so; he asserted that those who practice BDSM are mentally ill and in need of psychological help. Today, experts generally disagree with Freud's interpretation in light of a lack of evidence for his claims. The truth is that kinksters are just like everyone else; most folks are healthy, while some struggle with mental health issues or past trauma. No different than the general population.

Another stigmatizing stereotype is that BDSM is an abusive and violent practice—devoid of love, intimacy, and pleasure. In some sense, I understand why people sometimes confuse abuse with BDSM. Both BDSM and abuse involve power, both involve physical or psychological pain. But . . . that's where the similarities end. BDSM is fundamentally different than abuse because it is practiced (1) consensually, (2) with a trusted partner, and (3) in an environment where the submissive has complete control of the situation. This is pretty much the opposite of abuse.

- BDSM requires clearly negotiated consent, while abuse is nonconsensual.
- BDSM requires that boundaries always be respected, while abuse violates boundaries.
- BDSM can build trust, while abuse breaks trust.
- BDSM is the mutual pursuit of sexual pleasure, while abuse is the one-sided pursuit of power and control.
- BDSM gives the submissive complete control over the situation, which can be stopped with a safe word. Abuse is out of control and cannot be stopped by the victim.
- BDSM makes participants feel good about themselves and their partner afterward. Abuse drives couples apart, destroys relationships, and corrodes the victim's self-esteem.

It's important to challenge the "BDSM is abuse" narrative because it makes people feel shame to express or fulfill their desires. It also leaves consent out of the picture, negating its protocols and importance, which is a broader problem in our sexual culture. BDSM can be loving and tender, and can build intimacy so long as it's practiced properly.

That said, situations that are abusive should not be written off or excused as "BDSM." In a disturbing email I received once, a mother wrote me that her daughter had come home with a black eye after her boyfriend had "surprised her" during a sexual exchange. After the instance, he claimed he just wanted to try BDSM and that she should get over it. This, of course, is not BDSM. This is abuse. Nobody should suffer serious injury, nobody should be surprised, and problems are not written off as "No BD, just BDSM!" We must identify and hold accountable those who choose to abuse and use BDSM as an excuse for their actions.

Given my penchant for feminism, I've met some folks who shame BDSM for an entirely different reason: it's not feminist. BDSM, it is said, is normalized violence against women. But in my opinion, this argument is flawed for a few reasons. Those who espouse this argument typically cherry-pick situations. For instance, when a man is the dominant and a woman is the submissive and they are engaging in a practice like slapping. But this is only one practice, and one gender arrangement. The fact that the BDSM scene is so much more diverse, varied, and complex suggests that diagnosing the practice as "oppression in the bedroom" is dramatically oversimplified. It also ignores the fact that it does the very opposite of oppress a lot of people, offering new heights of liberation and pleasure. That shouldn't be ignored. Pleasure is a feminist issue. The shared undercurrent of BDSM practices is erotic intensity and pleasure, but it can mean other things to people as well. In their book *Queer BDSM Intimacies: Critical Consent and Pushing Boundaries*, researcher Robin Bauer found that BDSM can create "queer playgrounds" where there is more freedom for folks to safely explore gender and sexuality. For others, it isn't even about sex; it creates a space for fun and recreation, operating as a hobby. With practice and mentorship, you can master implements, form, and technique. BDSM is sometimes practiced by abuse survivors to heal from traumatic experiences and regain control over their sexuality. It can be used to help someone who is struggling with their sexuality to feel safe, loved, and whole. I dunno. Sounds pretty feminist to me.

So hey, it's true that our needs, fantasies, desires, and pleasures are not always politically correct. But our sexualities—and the bedrooms they are ignited in—are a sacred place. They cannot and should not be regulated by politics or religion, but instead by the principles of mutual respect, safety, and consent. These are staples of ethical sexuality.

For all these reasons and more, despite its popularity, many educational settings are still reluctant to acknowledge the existence of kink in the world of sexuality. And as a result, it is harder to find information to stay healthy and safe.

Here's what you need to know.

the essentials

BDSM IS NOT A SPONTANEOUS ACTIVITY. Before anything else, you gotta get on the same page with your partner. For starters, you should discuss these five things at minimum:

Discuss what each of you wants out of the experience.
- My kink is _____ .

- I want to take the role of _____ .
- I want to feel _____ during our scene.

Discuss what you will or won't do during the scene.
- What kind of pain are you okay with? What kind of pain aren't you okay with?
- What sex toys are/aren't okay?
- Will we have sex? What kind?
- What kind of STI and/or pregnancy protection will be used?

Discuss any physical or health limits.
Discuss psychological limits, trigger words, or trigger actions.
Discuss a safe word.

Safe words communicate consent. They can be used by either party during BDSM play to slow things down or to stop completely. Safe words are critical since pushing limits is often part of play. They act as a way to press the pause button while giving partners flexibility to push limits, resist, say things like "no" or "stop," and so on.

The safe word should be something easily recognizable that can't be confused for play. Some examples of safe words are "red," "banana," "mercy," or even "safe word." Some people also like to have a second safe word to slow down rather than stop completely, like "yellow," "slow," or "warm." If someone's ability to communicate verbally will be compromised during play (for instance, if you're using a toy like a ball gag), then nonverbal safe words such as raising a hand or squeezing the top's arm twice should be in place.

It's important to take safe words seriously. They are not a joke or an afterthought; they are a key protection that ensures everyone's safety! A scene should never be initiated without a safe word, no matter how well you know your partner. And obviously, if a safe word is invoked, it should never be ignored. Not only is it assault (and thus illegal) to proceed after consent has been revoked, but you could seriously injure your partner.

Other Health Safety Things to Remember

- No intoxication.

Assuming you are of age, a drink or two ain't gonna kill ya, but nobody engaging in BDSM play should be intoxicated with drugs or alcohol. Negotiation requires a clear and conscious mind, and being intoxicated compromises consent. It also compromises safety, since a person who is intoxicated has less body awareness and coordination.

- Respect limits.

Duh! BDSM should never seriously injure your partner, physically or emotionally. Hurting a partner crosses the line from a little sexual fun to sexual abuse. If you're concerned that you're pushing a partner's limits too hard during a scene, check in with them.

- Study your tools and technique beforehand.

If you're using an implement like rope, a flog, a gag, or whatever else, you must know how to use it safely. If you're engaging in an activity that could cause injury, like breath play, spanking, or suspension, you should know proper technique to make sure you're doing it safely. You can use the internet to search, but books by professional kinksters and sex educators on the topic tend to be better-written resources. Check out the books and websites listed in the resource section at the back of this book to continue your research!

- Don't forget the aftercare!

While it's sometimes relegated to barely a footnote, aftercare is an important part of transitioning out of a scene. Aftercare is downtime to relax and recuperate with a partner afterward, and to tend to each other's physical or emotional needs. Physical aftercare may include things like a glass of water, a massage, or a warm bath. Emotional aftercare may include cuddles, talking about the experience, or discussing any feelings that came up. Take care of each other as you transition back into your day or night.

(And always.)

FIFTEEN

⇒∘ RELATIONSHIPPING ∘⇐

WELP, WE'VE REACHED THE MESSIEST ASPECT of sexuality: PEOPLE! And more specifically, the people we get sexy with. I'll admit I initially felt a little weird putting relationships toward the end of this book, considering that relationships are the crux of it all. Sex is about connection. It is often an expression of love. But love, if you ask me, is usually more complicated than sex. I can figure out sex with the right information, good diagrams, or just an open mind. Figuring out love and relationships, though? Little trickier . . . and also totally worth it.

What does it mean to love someone? Love is what I'd describe as a "big feeling." It is expansive and intense, feeding into other intense feelings. Euphoria, peace, excitement, belonging, worry, grief, heartache—it can all stem from love. Artists of all kinds are often inspired by love, hence the 9,285,347 songs and movies and TV shows that tell stories about love and our feelings. Love can soften you, harden you, challenge you, and teach you.

As for me, I'm still figuring out all this relationship business. I first started dating when I was thirteen or fourteen, around my freshman year of high school. (And by "dating," I mean we hung out with each other while we were at school.) One of the biggest differences between now and then is that I know myself better and am far more confident with who I am. I also know a lot more about what I want in a partner. In my earliest relationships, the highs of love felt higher and the lows felt lower. The extremes were intoxicating. In my twenties, my relationships took on a slightly more mature and even tone. I moved into my own place for the first time, went to university, and found myself with a lot more breathing room. I dated casually and enjoyed a few flings. In my senior year of college, I met a guy I really clicked with. He was soft-spoken and smart, and everything between us flowed pretty effortlessly. After a year of dating, we moved in together. It was the first relationship that deeply satisfied me. We shared five years together before our somewhat catastrophic demise. Our breakup was catalyzed by my decision to move three hundred miles away. It was a decision that I made out of desperation—and in all other aspects of my life, it was the right decision for me. It was something I needed to do for my health and happiness. But I regret that it came at the cost of my greatest relationship. We all have that one person, right? I learned a lot from that relationship, and the ones that I've formed since then.

My experiences have shaped my approach to relationships and the premises that I operate on. Which are:

Sadly (but also happily), there is no such thing as "the one." The idea that there's someone perfect out there is romantic, but also unrealistic. I've found myself happy and fulfilled with multiple people throughout my life. The nature of the connection I share with each person is a little different, and some relationships feel like we "click" a little better, but the core feeling is generally the same: warmth and contentment. I think that if I approached relationships as a search for a perfect person (rather than, say, a particular feeling), it would put undue pressure on me and my relationships.

I also believe that friendships are every bit as important as romantic relationships. It's a familiar scenario for me: my friend gets into a serious relationship and all of a sudden I never hear from them anymore. Sometimes I don't see them again until they have a break-up! Meanwhile I'm out here like (???)UM???? WHERE U GO(????)I MISS U(????????) I've lost a few close friends to their romantic relationships, and I'm still kind of salty about it.

In general, I've noticed there's a weird tendency to place romantic relationships above all other types of relationships. I'm guilty of it myself, and there were points in my life when I definitely focused too much on romance and not enough on friendship. Part of the problem is that the beginning of a relationship comes with a pretty sweet high (honeymoon phase, anyone?). But in terms of overall needs . . . friendships and romantic relationships both rank pretty high up on the list of priorities. Friendship is another powerful and important type of love, just without the sex. (Well, usually.)

I've also learned that good lovin' feels GOOD! Even though they're not always easy, relationships shouldn't feel *hard* either. If a relationship starts to feel like a burden, and that feeling persists for a while, listen to that feeling. Even if someone makes you feel good sometimes, when that good feeling is punctuated by regular bouts of conflict and bad feels, that's a warning sign this person isn't a great fit for you. I've hung on to relationships too long because I couldn't accept what was in front of me, or because I was scared of being single (and really, scared of being alone). Since then, I've realized that being alone isn't as scary as it once seemed, especially with so many other things that give my life meaning, like my friends, my family, and my Twitter trolls.

So heyyyy, relationships! Let's explore some of their quirks in a little more detail.

IN THIS CHAPTER

—♡—

Asking your crush out

Dating apps

Compatibility

How to relationship

Keeping the flame alive

Troubleshooting

asking your crush out

WHEN I WAS YOUNGER, MY LIFE was consumed by a regularly rotating stream of crushes at school. There were boys with adorable dimples, girls with the best sense of humor. And then there was me: an awkward ball of anxiety trying my bestest to be one of the Cool Kids. (Update: never got cooler.) Through it all, my self-consciousness was often the main thing holding me back. That—and my debilitating fear of rejection.

Here's my advice. If you have a crush on someone, feel out the situation first. Dip your toes in the pool and see how things feel. If you get the impression that there's a chance they *might* like you too (because they flirt with you, or invite you to spend time with them, or make eyes at you), don't be a chicken—just ask them out! Yes, it's always possible you'll be rejected, but at least then you know they're not romantically interested so you can move on and eventually stop obsessing. It sucks to put yourself out there, but that's how relationships usually begin. A little vulnerability is par for the course. The key is not to put too much stock in the possibility of being rejected. It doesn't say anything about you, your desirability, or your loveliness as a human. It'll hurt, but I promise you will get over it in time.

Figuring out how to ask someone out doesn't have to be a huge ordeal. Romcoms and Instagram prom-posals can create some lofty expectations, but it's perfectly okay to keep it casual. If you're both talkers, invite them out somewhere that you can chat. Grab coffee or a drink, grab food, visit a museum or art show, or hang out at a mall or a park. If one of you is the type of person that needs a little more warm-up before getting chatty, pick an activity that puts less pressure on the conversation. Movies, arcades, concerts, comedy shows, ice- or roller-skating, local festivals, book readings, or poetry slams can all make for fun outings. If you're interested in someone but want to get to know them a little better in a social setting before hanging one-on-one, invite them to come spend time with you and your friends.

To ask someone out, try to get a good conversation with them going first, and wait for a natural time to interject. Shortly before parting is usually a good time, because you have an easy out if things get awkward. If you're nervous, take a deep breath and summon the angels of confidence from deep within your soul. Even if you're feeling a wave of self-doubt and nerves, confidence (in this situation, at least) is about faking it till you make it. You don't need to actually feel confident, but pretending you do can make things a little easier :P.

> "Hey, do you want to go out sometime? There's a new exhibit at the museum that I thought might be fun to check out."

> "Do you like tacos? I know of an awesome spot!"

"I love ice-skating. Have you ever tried it? We should go sometime!"

And that's it. You got this.

dating apps

IN THE JOURNEY THAT IS RELATIONSHIPPING, there's a special place in my heart for dating. I love the pleasant awkwardness of getting to know someone new; I love the flirtatious banter and trying my hand (/embarrassing myself) at new activities. Strangely, few of my friends share my enthusiasm. Dating, I am told, SUCKS. Which is true. At the very least, dating doesn't necessarily . . . not suck. Modern dating culture can be pretty alienating. And to be honest, I mostly blame dating apps for that.

Dating apps have done more to change how we date and have sex than perhaps any other innovation in history. The significance of swiping right, match percentages, and initiating relationships through screens can't be understated. No longer the last-resort option of lonely introverts, pretty much everyone has a dating profile now. There are dozens of apps with different features, all with the purpose of helping people connect. And connect we do. We now have access to more romantic and sexual options than at any other point in human history. On the surface, tons of options sound like a sweet deal. I mean, if I know what I want in a partner, helping me find that person is a good thing . . . right? I'm not so sure.

Sometimes, less is more. Having an avalanche of options can make things harder rather than easier, and it can make us feel less satisfied with the choice we have made. This phenomenon is called the paradox of choice. Imagine going to a restaurant with a menu that is the size of a textbook. What do you choose? What if it's not as good as another dish you could pick!? The paradox of choice has had an admittedly unpleasant effect on my relationships; it has instilled in me a mild case of perpetual FOMO—on experiences, people, greater happiness, whatever. There's another more sinister side effect, too. With the intoxicating promise of an endless stream of potential matches, dating apps have shaped a dating culture that is underpinned by disposability. If a person doesn't check all the boxes, there's always someone else I can date on the app. In the process, our demands of each other become ever more specific. It's easy to miss out on amazing people when we decide an arbitrary trait is a deal breaker.

This disposability is made worse by the fact that dating apps can amplify our tendency to put physical appearance above every other dimension of attraction. On some apps, a person's picture is the only bit of information you get before messaging them! It basically requires you to be shallow to participate, which encourages some unsavory dating behavior. I suppose to some degree, it's like dating offline. If you were approaching someone at a bar, all you'd have to go off of is their appearance as well. There's nothing wrong with wanting to date attractive people, of course. But I think it is shallow and unproductive to evaluate people in terms of their appearance above every other aspect of who they are.

I also think that dating apps have disincentivized people from making an actual effort at times, which is a really important part of having a fulfilling dating experience. I'm guilty of it myself. In 2017, our depressing tendency to applaud dates who only make a minimum effort became the butt of a string of jokes and stories dubbed "Bare Minimum Twitter." Strangely, even though dating apps seem to be lowering the standards of acceptable dating behavior, they also seem to be raising the expectations through the roof. Dating apps make it disastrously easy to slip from healthy and realistic expectations to chasing a perfect fantasy human who doesn't actually exist.

In a welcome twist, all these seeping feelings of disposability in our modern dating culture have helped me find more meaning in the concept of commitment. Yes, there are a lot of people out there. And yet I choose to be in a relationship with my partner every day because they are *just that awesome.* I've found two fulfilling relationships from dating apps, and a number of other fun nights and friendships—which is why, despite their pitfalls, I'm still a fan.

There are obviously a lot of perks to dating apps. They can cut down on the time it takes to find a quality connection. I can easily identify red flags and incompatibilities with basic profile information or a brief text exchange. Apps also offer a greater level of transparency in communicating what we are looking for. Whether you're seeking someone for the night, for a few months, or to start a family with, apps make it easier to be up-front. In theory, this should cut down on incompatibilities of commitment and relationship style. By putting what you're looking for out in the open, it attracts people who want the same things.

That's my experience. What has your dating app experience been like?

How to Make Apps Work for You

Here are my 3 Bs of making apps work! (Because I'm apparently a kooky motivational speaker now.)

BE OPEN!

Avoid the temptation to get overly myopic or narrow-minded about what you're looking for. You may miss out on some cool people and experiences.

BE DECENT!

Why do so many people seem to forget that there are real human beings on the other end of their text messages? I have seen appalling displays of disrespectful behavior, entitlement, and downright harassment on apps. Little ironic, no? Apps are supposed to be about *connecting with each other*, not stoking a deep hatred of humanity. There are men who have called me a bitch for messaging back too slowly. Men who left me a flood of messages after I told them I'm not interested. Men who thought that a comment about my boobs was a nice way to start a conversation. They stand in stark contrast to the fewer, but infinitely lovelier, gentlemen I've met through apps. I would complain about women, too (I'm equal opportunity, especially when it comes to complaining), but my experience with women has always been respectful and fun. ¯_(ツ)_/¯

Of course, decency is not just an "at the beginning" thing. If you've met up with someone and decided they're not for you, let them know. "Ghosting"—or dropping off the map without notice—leaves people in limbo, and it feels like shit. Unless the situation is threatening or abusive, be an adult and tell someone if you decide you don't want to hang out or chat anymore. If you find yourself being ghosted, my general rule of thumb is three messages. If they don't text back after a third follow-up to a conversation, it's time to move on. This is usually a signal that they are not interested and don't know how to communicate like an adult. It sucks. But that's life.

BE YOURSELF!

It's cliché, but worth repeating: be who you are! Use pictures that are up-to-date and look like you, and write your profile for the type of person you're hoping to meet. Try to bring your best self to the table.

Avoid the temptation to exaggerate or be someone you're not. Faking it will only result in fake relationships.

Safety

We are long past the era of stranger danger that seemed to have a grip on every suburban mom in the early 2000s. Back then, if you were talking to someone online, they were probably a pedophile serial killer with twenty bodies in their closet. These days, we know better. It's just other people! Normal, nonmurdery, human peoples! With the OCCASIONAL serial killer. Which is why it's still wise to take basic safety precautions. The first few times you meet someone, don't meet at a home or in private. Choose a public place. Let a friend know when you're going out, and what time you plan to be back. Check in when you're back home. If you meet someone and feel uncomfortable, it's okay to let them know you're not feeling it and end the date.

Troubleshooting

The main complaint I hear about dating apps is that, well, they don't work. They take a bunch of time and nothing good comes of it. To some degree there's no getting around this one, because dating and relationships do take time. And sometimes, nothing good does come of it. But don't give up too quickly. If the return on investment feels a little low, here's my advice:

- Be strategic with messaging people. Write a boilerplate intro message that is friendly and personal, but is *customizable* to tailor to the profile. It's obvious when someone has sent you a mass message, and you definitely want to avoid sounding spam-y because your message will end up in the trash. The first message is a good place to say hi, express what you like about their profile, and ask an approachable question to get the conversation started. Humor is always a good idea too.

- If you're getting flooded, restrict your inbox to a higher match percentage, or add another filter to wade through the sea of profiles more efficiently. This means finding matches that have a better chance of turning into a date.

- Don't talk for ages before asking them out. Personally, I like to have a little conversation before meeting in person. Nothing serious, maybe a little more about ourselves, what's in our profiles, or some witty banter. Everyone's a little different in their chat preferences. But in general, the conversation needn't go on forever. I like to invite someone out after an initial conversation that is enjoyable. Some people like to talk for a little while before to get comfortable. That's okay too; just make sure that's communicated in the conversation. If someone seems to be dragging their feet for a long time without any explanation, that's a sign that they may not be interested in meeting or are keeping you on the back burner.

- Don't waste time on people who suck. Love yo'self.

First Date Conversation Starters!

—♡—

Want to add a little zest to keep the conversation rolling? Here are some ideas from my goofy-ass friends.

"What Hogwarts house are you in?"—Katherine

"What are your top three favorite foods?"—Rob

"If you could travel anywhere, where would you go?" —Breezy

"What's your idea of success?"—Tim

"Who's your best friend? Tell me about them."—Tyler

"What's the weirdest food you've ever tried?"—Laci

"What's your favorite type of music?"—My uncle

"What do you think about astrology?"—My aunt

"Tell me about the best taco you've ever eaten."
—Rosie

"What makes you laugh?"—Kevin

"Would you rather fight a hundred duck-sized horses, or one horse-sized duck?"—Ben

"Is the universe fully deterministic?"—Jason

"What's your favorite place that you've traveled to?"
—Suzie

"How do you feel about the possibility that the universe is a hologram?"—Brian

"What are your thoughts on capitalism?"—Scott

"What's your favorite meme?"—Courtney

"What are your favorite colors in a sunset?"—Gail

"What's your favorite childhood memory"—Sima

"What's the funniest thing that has ever happened to you?"—Robert

"What's your biggest pet peeve?"—Carolyn

"Have you ever had a lucid dream?"—Olivia

"How do you like the new *Thriller* album? Sorry, I haven't done this in a long time."—Bill

"Why did you think this was a good idea?"—Zoe

"Do boneless chicken wings count as wings, or are they just big nuggets?"—Also Zoe

"Are there any albums that have changed your life?" —Sam

"Where's the first place you would hide a dead body?"—Devlin***

***Do not recommend.

One of my favorite resources for conversation starters with a partner/potential partner is the "36 Questions That Lead to Love." Google it! Researchers found that the list of 36 questions, combined with sustained eye contact, can create emotional intimacy between perfect strangers.

compatibility

WHEN I WAS SEVENTEEN, MY SISTER did my horoscope. In meticulous detail, she explained to me the type of person I needed to be with (an Aries—fiery!) and why I would be attracted to them. The subsequent ten years proved to be a little bit messier. If only compatibility were so simple as finding someone with the right birthday.

When I think about compatibility, I mostly think about what characteristics of theirs mesh well with mine, and where we butt heads. Do we work well together? Do our qualities complement each other? Do we bring out the best in each other? There have only been a couple times in my life when I felt truly compatible with the person I was dating. Most of the relationships I've ended were because of incompatibilities between our personalities and lifestyles. I've found that one of the more helpful questions to reflect on in a relationship is who I am with them. Every person I date brings out different parts of me, of my personality. Usually, it's for the better—they make life a little goofier or challenge me intellectually. But sometimes, it's for the worse—I've had partners who made me feel stressed or bad about myself. Paying attention to how you feel around someone can be an important indicator of compatibility.

Here are a few dimensions of compatibility to think about:

- Values, beliefs, and philosophies
- Attachment style
- Relationship style
- Communication style
- Sexuality
- Goals and ambitions
- Personality and introversion or extraversion
- Temperament
- Intelligence
- Sense of humor
- Interests
- Marriage or family plans

Let's talk in more detail about those first three on the list.

Your Values, Beliefs, and Philosophies

Sharing values, beliefs, and philosophies about life is kind of a biggie for the long-term success of a relationship. IMO, this goes a step beyond having different opinions—values shape how we actually *go about our lives*. They inform our view of the world, the things that matter to us, and who we are as people. Which is why it's not surprising that research suggests sharing values with a partner is pretty important. Being somewhat similar to your partner, in general, seems to have positive effects. This suggests that even if it's true that "opposites attract," it may not be ideal for long-term success. The Legacy Project at Cornell University, which documents the advice of elders, has some wisdom to share:

> *The research findings are quite clear: marriages that are homogamous in terms of economic background, religion and closeness in age are the most stable and tend to be happier. Sharing core values has also been found to promote marital stability and happiness. So the elders are in the scientific mainstream when they urge you to seek a partner who is similar to you in important ways.*

So . . . does this mean couples who are very different from each other are doomed? Not necessarily.

Those who are happily married for decades (and social scientists) don't tell you unconditionally to avoid marrying someone who is different from you even though you're deeply in love. They just want you to recognize that if you marry someone with values very different from yours, you are much more likely to face complex challenges in married life. According to the elders, in the face of objective differences (such as culture or economic background), shared values and outlook on life go a long way to promote both the quality and stability of a marriage.

The takeaway: being somewhat alike is the path of least resistance, but being different can work too, with a healthy mindset. A healthy mindset here is one that accepts that your partner probably won't change their beliefs over time—they are who they are, they believe what they believe, and they need to be accepted as such. Secondly, partners with whom you have serious differences may take a little more work—on communicating, compromising, and understanding each other. Both people need to be willing to pull their weight to make it work.

When I've found myself with different opinions, beliefs, or values than my partner, I ask myself a few questions to help me navigate it:

- How important is this particular belief to me? To my partner? If it's not that important, to one (or both) of us, it's easier to resolve.
- How important is it to me that my partner and I agree on this? If disagreeing on this particular belief makes me feel less safe, respected, or fulfilled in the relationship, that is a giant red flag.
- Does my partner express their dissent in a way that still makes me feel respected and heard?

Conversations about political differences sometimes get a little heated, but they should *always* feel respectful.

Your Attachment Style

Have you ever noticed how some people need a lot of attention and validation in a relationship, while others need more space? Differences like these may be explained by attachment theory. Attachment theory puts forth the idea that the emotional bond that develops between romantic partners is similar to the bond that develops between an infant and their caregivers. Psychologists have identified three basic attachment styles in romantic relationship. The degree to which our childhood affects romantic attachment as adults is a topic of debate among psychologists.

1. SECURE ATTACHMENT (60% OF PEOPLE)

Securely attached people tend to be emotionally mature. They are comfortable setting and respecting boundaries, they don't feel much anxiety about relationships, and they give and receive expressions of intimacy in a healthy way. They tend to feel comfortable and relaxed when they're alone as well as when they're with their partner. When there is distress or conflict within a relationship, securely attached people feel comfortable going to their partner for support or to talk about disagreements. They are less likely to be controlling and don't play games. They are stable partners and find success more easily with every attachment style.

2. ANXIOUS ATTACHMENT (20%)

Anxiously attached people feel more nervous about their relationships and may have higher anxieties about things falling apart—even when they're great. They are more prone to be suspicious of their partner, and perhaps a little clingy. It distresses them to be alone. Anxiously attached people may be more prone to conflict, and take comfort in the validation and reassurance that resolution after an argument can offer. In more extreme cases, they may even feel more comfortable with the familiarity of high-conflict relationships. For some with this attachment style, they have a history of bad relationships. Anxious attachers thrive with lots of positive reinforcement and outward expressions of love to feel secure. With a securely attached partner and long-term commitment to a healthy relationship with someone, anxious attachers can become secure attachers.

3. AVOIDANT ATTACHMENT (20%)

Those who are avoidantly attached are self-sufficient and highly independent. This style is split into two subtypes: dismissive-avoidant and fearful-avoidant.

Dismissive-avoidant attachers tend to emotionally distance themselves from their partner. They ultimately desire freedom and aren't very drawn to relationships, which they think can feel suffocating. Many have broader struggles with commitment and intimacy, which can translate to more acquaintances and few to no close friends. As people come and go from their life, they easily let go of people. For a dismissive-avoidant attacher, relationships tend to come in last place; things like work, school, or travel take precedence. Some (not all) have troubled backgrounds and have adapted to their harsh environment by dismissing the need for intimacy.

Fearful-avoidant attachers are different from dismissive-avoidant attachers in that they do actually *want* intimacy . . . but they fear it. They may have a troubled background and struggle to trust others because of past pain or trauma. They fear the vulnerability that intimacy requires and may be suspicious that their partner will abandon or betray them if they get too close. Because they have strong feelings and acknowledge their need for intimacy, but also have a high fear of intimacy, fearful-avoidant attachers can seem a bit unpredictable and erratic. It is not unusual for a relationship with a fearful-avoidant attacher to have high-highs and low-lows. They may hold on tighter when they feel rejected, and reject their partner when things become more intimate.

ANXIOUS ATTACHERS DO NOT DO WELL with avoidant attachment types for obvious reasons. It is a road to heartache. While some avoidant attachers prefer to be single, it is not destiny. Securely attached partners can do well with avoidant attachers when they are comfortable with a high degree of independence themselves.

Attachment type is not static or permanent. Anxious and avoidant attachers can become securely attached and have healthier relationships. Part of finding emotionally healthy relationships is processing past experiences to help understand who you are today. This creates more self-awareness and can offer the insight you need to begin healing yourself and your relationships. A counselor can be an excellent asset on that journey.

Your Relationship Style

Another dimension of compatibility is what kind of relationship you want to have. Relationship styles generally fall under the banners of "monogamous" and "non-monogamous." Monogamy is a relationship style where two people mutually agree to be romantically and sexually exclusive to each other. It is the most common and visible relationship style. But not everyone is monogamous; in fact, about 1 in 10 people are non-monogamous! Non-monogamy is an umbrella term for relationships where partners are not emotionally or sexually exclusive to each other.

There is no "right" style here; both monogamy and non-monogamy have their benefits and challenges, and it really depends on how to best meet the needs of you and your partner. I have had both monogamous and non-monogamous relationships, to varying degrees of happiness and success. In my experience, the biggest perk of monogamy is that it offers me a deeper sense of comfort and security within the relationship. The agreement between us is straightforward, and it requires less work to maintain for the simple fact that it's only us. But monogamy can be challenging in its own right, especially when one person is expected to fulfill all the human needs of their partner single-handedly. Expectations can become overwhelming, and some also find it lacks novelty and excitement in the long term.

Polyamory is a non-monogamous relationship style in which partners get their needs met by multiple people. In polyamory, there is typically a primary relationship and a secondary relationship or relationship(s). The primary relationship is where the most time and energy is spent, and it is considered the priority. Secondary relationships vary in terms of how many there are, who dates who, and what boundaries there are. Every poly relationship is different! Polyamory requires excellent communication skills, patience, and a lot of self-awareness to really work. Newcomers to polyamory may find themselves with a number of complex feelings to work through, which can be overwhelming and time-consuming. If you're a busy person, scheduling can be an issue.

At the risk of sounding like a broken record, relationship styles— like all things in the world of sexuality—are a spectrum. The bottom line is that the process of building loving partnerships is much more expansive and creative than we tend to give it credit for. If something isn't working for you, you are allowed to think outside the box and figure out what does.

MANAGING JEALOUSY IN POLYAMOROUS RELATIONSHIPS

by Alaska Harrison

I've been in a non-monogamous (or polyamorous) relationship for three years with my long-term (also known as a primary) partner. The most frequent question I get asked when discussing non-monogamy tends to be "Don't you get jealous?"

The answer is obviously yes. Most people do from time to time. I'm sure either you or someone you know have danced with the green-eyed monster, and to put it lightly, it sucks. Jealousy can bring up a lot of emotions and make you or someone you care about feel like you're not good enough. Sometimes (in my personal experience) it causes a lot of anger, frustration, and confusion. Jealousy is a complex emotion. It's a bit of an "umbrella emotion." Think about it—you're never "just jealous." There are always underlying and contributing feelings, emotions, and causes. You might be feeling upset that, after a bad week, you just received a text message alerting you that your partner has cancelled on your movie date night last-minute to hang out with an old friend of theirs who has just come into town. You might feel angry, annoyed, and admittedly jealous. In this instance things go one of two ways:

1. I get angry, frustrated, and self-conscious as heck, which leads to stress eating or sending a passive-aggressive message. I might even post some photos on Facebook proving I am having a great night without them before stalking their friend for three hours on Instagram.

OR:

2. I sit down and think.

Sounds simple, right? In theory, it is. The problem is that when you're dealing with problems of jealousy, it can be difficult to figure out why you feel the way you do—or to even identify that what you're feeling is jealousy.

But no matter the situation, you cannot work through it without knowing where your feelings come from. Did you have something special planned for that evening? Or after a trash week did you need love and reassurance from your partner? Does being cancelled on last-minute bring up other feelings of self-doubt, self-loathing, or rejection? Does not knowing the third party make you uncomfortable at a time when you're feeling vulnerable? Are you afraid you're going to lose your partner? Being able to identify these emotions and causes is the first step to being able to work through them.

Once you identify where the feelings are coming from, it's time to start communicating with your partner. I find it easier to write everything down before talking. Sometimes, a piece of paper or notes on your phone can be really comforting. Having these conversations is difficult, and it's easy to let other emotions take over, or to let the conversation get derailed. No one *wants* to talk about this stuff, but it's important. Through open communication, you can understand yourself and your partner(s) better.

When it comes time to chat, create a safe and private space and sit down with your partner to discuss your reaction to the earlier event. Be calm and sensitive to the other parties. If you become overwhelmed, say so. (I've even taken multiple breaks during some of my bigger talks with partners.) Explain and discuss why you reacted the way you did, what you were feeling, the reasons you were feeling this, and anything else you wish to share. From there you will be able to come up together with a better mutual understanding for the future. You might both agree that cancellations happen, but to call (rather than text) each other if you do need to change plans. In most cases, jealousy reflects some kind of threat to you or a loved one; this threat can, however, be perceived or assumed rather than real. Through communication, your partner can offer you affirmation and you can work on ways to lower your feelings of threat. Perhaps your partner didn't realize you had anything important planned or didn't know how you were feeling at that time. The only way to find this out is to embrace your feelings, understand them, and then communicate them.

This communication process can be applied to most relationships, sexual, platonic or otherwise. But in non-monogamous relationships it is an especially important tool. When I first began exploring non-monogamy I had a lot of jealousy. New scenarios arose that I hadn't encountered before, and there were more avenues I needed to learn how to navigate. While it was difficult at first, it's now a fantastic tool that allows me to learn from my partners and grow with them.

how to relationship

So, you found yourself a good one and even made it Facebook official. How can you nurture your relationship and keep it healthy?

Relationship

To bake a healthy relationship you will need:
   1 part communication
   1 part trust
   1 part respect
   A heaping teaspoon of healthy boundaries
   Liberally seasoned with passion

Compromise equally until batter is thick and velvety. Bake until internal temperature reaches 69 degrees.

The foundation of every healthy relationship is communication, respect, and trust. We talked about communication earlier on. Respect and trust are just as important. In my experience, respect is a word often used but not often defined. The dictionary says something about respect meaning "admiration," yet that doesn't necessarily work in a relationship context. What does respect really mean? Here are a few ideas:

- Being honest
- Caring for each other
- Making each other feel valued
- Treating each other as equals

- Regarding each other with dignity
- Honoring each other's boundaries
- Honoring each other's independence
- Supporting each other's careers and interests
- Accepting each other's differences
- Empowering each other to make healthy choices

Talk to your partner about what respect means to them, and how you can each show it.

Sometimes, the concept of "respect" is misused. For example, the accusation that it's "disrespectful" for a straight partner to have any friends of the opposite sex when they're in a relationship. Another example is telling a partner what kind of clothes they are allowed to wear, how they should talk to others, or who they can hang out with—all because it supposedly "shows respect." Definitions of respect that involve controlling someone or taking away their choices are the *opposite* of respect. These interpretations often stem from feeling insecure, and this insecurity manifests as jealousy, control, or distrust. We will come back to this in the troubleshooting section.

Trust is another critical facet of a healthy relationship. The feeling of trust runs deep and sets the tone in a relationship in a pretty serious way. Trust is knowing you can be vulnerable and real with someone, without worrying about being judged for it. It is permission to be yourself. Trust is knowing you can say no, disagree, or express your opinions without pressure. Trust is also knowing your partner will be there for you when you need them. A trustworthy person is consistent and reliable. They always come through, especially in the clutch. Trust is built on communication and respect, which connects these basic relationship foundations together. Trust usually takes time to blossom. It can't be rushed or demanded—it has to arise naturally, all on its own.

Healthy boundaries are important as well. Having a healthy amount of space and independence brings couples closer together. Growing up, it wasn't uncommon for a friend's boyfriend or girlfriend to say, "Nope, sorry, you can't hang out anymore." It was immensely painful to lose friends that way, and it is pretty obviously unhealthy. It's important for lovers to maintain their own identities, to maintain their friendships, to have time for their hobbies and for themselves. Setting healthy boundaries starts with a conversation about what you need in your relationship. Boundaries also help communicate what you are and aren't ready for romantically or sexually. Sometimes, a conversation about boundaries starts when they have been crossed. In this case, it is important to bring this up with a partner immediately. Gently but firmly enforce your boundaries by letting your partner know where they crossed a line and why their behavior or words are hurtful to you.

Compromise is another critical aspect of maintaining a healthy relationship. Where boundaries help get your own needs met, compromise ensures that your partner's needs are met too. Compromise is often a routine and boring part of the day-to-day in relationships: we negotiate what to watch on TV, what to eat for dinner, whose turn it is to do the dishes or take the dog for a walk. "It takes two to tango" and alla that. I think it's important for both partners to be aware of how much they are giving and taking in a relationship to make sure it is balanced.

Deeper into a relationship, compromise may become more significant. You may come upon different needs, wants, and goals for the future. When it gets real, it's important to have some idea of where you are and aren't willing to compromise. Compromise entails making reasonable sacrifices toward a shared goal—but it should not include sacrificing core tenets of what you need and who you are. A loving, healthy relationship will never compromise other relationships (like friends and family) or your goals for the future. It will never require that you change who you are, what you value, or what you believe in. Compromise also does not mean settling for less respect or poor treatment. When a relationship demands major compromises to continue functioning, that is a sign that your relationship is not healthy.

Twenty-five Signs Your Relationship Is Pretty Heckin' Good

1. You still make time for friendship. (Have I mentioned this yet? lol.)
2. You maintain your own identity.
3. You feel good when you're together.
4. You're there for each other when things get rough.
5. You respect each other's privacy.
6. Both people make an equal effort.
7. You can talk about anything (including sex).
8. You feel safe with them.
9. You feel respected by them.
10. You trust them.
11. You support each other's goals and passions.
12. You go out of each other's way to show you care for each other.
13. You are both open about your faults, fears, and insecurities.
14. You address problems quickly.
15. You work through conflict to resolve it.
16. You both express gratitude to each other.
17. You have your own friends.
18. You make time for each other.
19. Your family and friends support your relationship.
20. You have shared goals for the future.
21. You split responsibilities and work as a team.
22. You feel confident in your relationship.
23. Your bond feels stable.
24. You both make compromises for each other.
25. They inspire you to be a better person.

Types of Love

Are you in love? Probably! Maybe! Definitely yes! Absolutely not! Yeah, I don't know. All I know is that love is a many-splendored thing. It's all you need, supposedly (presumably alongside food, water, air, and shelter). In an attempt to make sense of lovey feelings and all their nuances, the triangular theory of love was put forth by Dr. Robert Sternberg in the 1980s.

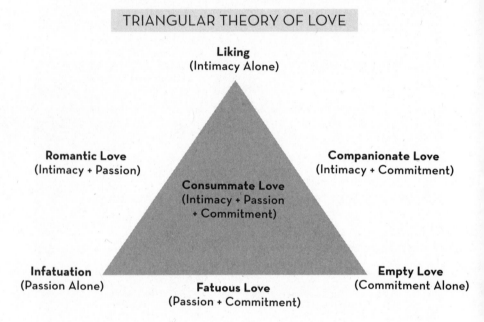

TRIANGULAR THEORY OF LOVE

Liking
(Intimacy Alone)

Romantic Love
(Intimacy + Passion)

Companionate Love
(Intimacy + Commitment)

Consummate Love
(Intimacy + Passion
+ Commitment)

Infatuation
(Passion Alone)

Fatuous Love
(Passion + Commitment)

Empty Love
(Commitment Alone)

The triangular theory of love identifies three components of love:

1. Passion—physical attraction, sexual arousal, the va-va-voom and romance of it all
2. Intimacy—closeness, connectedness, warmth, trust
3. Commitment—dedication, loyalty, the decision to be together

In the triangular theory, these three components interact with each other to form eight types of love.

1. NONLOVE

The absence of all three components. You do not love them, plain 'n' simple.

2. LIKING (INTIMACY)

A type of strong friendship. You like them and enjoy closeness to them, but have no sexy feelings or long-term commitment to them.

3. INFATUATED LOVE (PASSION)

"Love at first sight." It can arise quickly and fiercely, and disappear just as fast. You want to boink their brains out, but don't have feelings of intimacy or commitment to make it last.

4. EMPTY LOVE (COMMITMENT)

In Western culture, empty love can manifest toward the end of a long-term relationship, when intimacy and passion have waned. In societies where arranged marriages are common, empty love may be the first type of love to manifest—you are committed, but that's about it. There is potential for empty love to develop into other types of love.

5. ROMANTIC LOVE (INTIMACY AND PASSION)

Like a close friendship, but with sexual arousal mixed into the picture. Romantic love is physical and emotional, but doesn't embody true commitment.

6. COMPANIONATE LOVE (INTIMACY AND COMMITMENT)

A long-term, committed friendship or romantic relationship where physical attraction, and those frenzied feelings of passion, have died down.

7. FATUOUS LOVE (PASSION AND COMMITMENT)

An intoxicating type of love where intense passion drives commitment, even though there hasn't been enough time for intimacy to develop. Think whirlwind romance and shotgun marriages. It's Hollywood-esque and exciting, but without intimacy for the long haul, it may be an unstable foundation for relationships.

8. CONSUMMATE LOVE (PASSION, INTIMACY, AND COMMITMENT)

"Complete love." It is how many of us picture ideal love. It can be achieved, but is difficult to make last.

—Adapted from "A Triangular Theory of Love" *by Robert J. Sternberg in* Psychological Review, *1986*

Your Brain in Love

The triangular theory of love is just one way to think about the different types of love we feel with different people and over time. Another interesting way to think about love is in terms of what it does to your brain. In nearly every decade of music, artists have compared love to feeling like a drug. And hey, they're not wrong!

Using MRI scans, scientists have observed that the brain in the early stages of a romantic relationship looks like the brain on cocaine. Early on, dopamine, serotonin, and norepinephrine—three neurotransmitters that make you feel euphoric—are all in higher supply than usual. These chemicals generate those obsessive feelings toward a new partner, making it harder to eat, sleep, or think straight. In the psych world, this is sometimes called infatuation, or the honeymoon stage of a relationship. During this period, everything is sexy and wonderful and perfect. You feel amazing—and perhaps a little powerless, in that these feelings are largely out of your control. Infatuation usually peaks at the beginning, then dwindles out over one to three years.

When things start to simmer down in a relationship, we see each other more clearly. And whoops, you might start to notice some of the more annoying things about your partner that were easier to overlook before. Conflict can see an uptick in this stage, as people start to see their differences more clearly. For some people, the end of infatuation is the end of a relationship. But for those who are still vibeing with each other, a new set of hormones kicks in: oxytocin and vasopressin. These neurotransmitters feel good too, but not so much in the euphoric sense. These neurotransmitters are also present during hugging, touching, orgasm, birth, and breastfeeding. They are known to promote social bonding and attachment.

Chemical accounts of love are useful in that they help us make sense of our experiences, but some find it unromantic, if not unsettling. You mean all this goodness is just chemicals in my brain!? SERIOUSLY??

Yup. Seriously.

But look, the same could be said for many (all?) human feelings: fear, happiness, sadness, loss, achievement—you name it. Everything is chemical. It doesn't mean that our human experiences are not real or significant. To me, the chemicals in our brains show how the natural world is a part of everything we do and feel. Nature, and the universe, courses through our veins.

Saying "I Love You"

Using the "L" word is a big deal in our sexual culture. It is considered a major relationship milestone. We obsess over when and how to say it, if it's really love, if the other person feels the same way . . . it's so much pressure!

Interestingly, there is a gender gap in when we choose to say "I love you." On average, heterosexual men say "I love you" after 88 days, while heterosexual women take an average of 134 days. Within the first month, 39% of men say it, compared to 23% of women. Men also report higher levels of joy at receiving a declaration of love. This challenges the narrative that men are stoic, unemotional, and uninterested romantic partners.

Self-help gurus offer long lists of rules and advice for when to say "I love you." Common advice is after ten dates, after two months, or not after sex. But an overly prescriptive approach takes the most important element out of the situation: how you feel. There is no right or wrong time; if you feel it, and you feel comfortable expressing it, it's a fine time.

My personal feeling, after jumping through the "I love you" hoop with a few different people over the years, is that we put too much weight on this issue. Don't be impulsive—but do be expressive and open. I feel that part of the hesitance to express love is that it makes us feel vulnerable. Which isn't necessarily a bad thing. Vulnerability has a time and place in relationships, and it is necessary to build intimacy. Sure, nobody wants to be *too* vulnerable, lest someone rip your heart out and throw it in the garbage. That sucks. But if it feels right, it's okay to put yourself out there. You may be affirmed, bringing you closer together and building intimacy. Or you may not, presenting an opportunity to clarify how you both feel and where you are in your relationship. It's always good to get clear through open communication.

Outside of romance, I tend to feel that people should express their love to those they are close to more openly. Let your care, love, warmth, and light be felt by those around you, in the ways that they are comfortable receiving it. Hug more. Cherish one another. Love heals us.

"The regret of my life is that I have not said 'I love you' often enough."—Yoko Ono

Making Each Other Feel Loved and Appreciated

Remember that awesome relationship I had that I was telling you about? Looking back, I attribute a lot of it to our mutual nurturing of our relationship. We both treated our relationship tenderly, as a sort of living, breathing organism that needed our attention to thrive. We learned a lot together, and I think one of the things that helped our relationship grow over the years was affirmation.

Affirmation is the feeling of being valued, wanted, and loved in a relationship. It's how we communicate love to each other, in a myriad of ways. Dr. Gary Chapman coined a concept known as the "five love languages" to articulate some of the ways that humans affirm each other, within romantic relationships and beyond:

USE YOUR WORDS.

Do: Express your feelings with language, like "I love you," "I appreciate you," "You bring so much joy to my life."

Don't: Use insults, put-downs, or harsh language.

SPEND QUALITY TIME TOGETHER.

Do: Life comes at ya fast. Make sure to designate enough quality "us time" every week to connect and enjoy each other's company. Be present while doing so.

Don't: Flake or be distracted, be on your phone, be in a hurry, etc., during quality time.

DO NICE THINGS FOR EACH OTHER.

Do: Lend a hand and go out of your way to help your partner with acts of service, without being asked. Help with chores, make dinner, run an errand for them, and so on. Be there when things are stressful. Ask what you can do to support them, and do it.

Don't: Make more work for your partner, or say you will do something and don't follow through.

GIVE GIFTS.

Do: Think about tangible, meaningful ways to express love without being prompted. This doesn't necessarily refer to spending money. It may also be things like making a mixtape/playlist for a music lover or making them a treat when they're on their period.

TOUCH EACH OTHER.

Do: Make nonsexual physical contact with each other. That might mean hugs when you see each other, holding hands, a kiss, a back rub, playing with hair, etc. For some, touch helps them feel safe and secure.

Don't: Be rough or smothering with touch, or touch them when they don't want to be touched.

WHILE IT'S NICE TO TRY TO bring all of these things to a relationship once in a while, some are more impactful than others. Everybody receives love and affirmation differently. To one person, quality time says much more than words. It is a vital part of their feeling appreciated. To another, going out of your way to do acts of service is the most affirming and says "I'm here for you" much more than a gift ever could. On the flip side, some forms of affirmation may not be your partner's jam. For instance, some find touchy-feely physical affection awkward. Talking to your partner about how you each receive love, and acting on it, can deepen your connection.

Your Relationship Rights

—♡—

Everybody has rights and responsibilities within a relationship.

You have the right to be respected, to be treated equally, to feel safe, to have privacy, to cultivate friendships and hobbies outside the relationship, to express yourself, to be yourself, to enforce boundaries, and to stay or leave a relationship. In a relationship, you also have the responsibility to respect your partner, to treat them as your equal, to accept them for who they are, to treat them with kindness, to listen, to support them, to compromise when necessary, to respect their independence as a person, and to allow them to leave if they choose.

keeping the flame alive

FOR THE FOLKS I KNOW WHO have done the long-term-relationship thing, or perhaps even the getting-married thing, one of the challenges that always comes up is keeping the relationship sexy, passionate, and fun long after the novelty of a new partner has faded away. In the beginning of a relationship, things are at their spiciest. Even if you haven't figured out how to blow each other's minds yet, merely being in each other's presence is enough to do the trick. In those early moments, your partner is perfect, and you just can't keep your hands off them. Among couples who are sexually active, there is more sex. There is more thinking about sex. Everything is gravy, baby. This type of infatuation is sometimes called the "honeymoon phase," and it typically lasts one to two years. It's accompanied by physiological changes; studies have found that those in the throes of the honeymoon phase have higher levels of the stress hormone cortisol, as well as higher levels of nerve growth factor (NGF), which may contribute to feelings of euphoria. But as a relationship rolls on, and routines fall into place, it's normal for that euphoria (and stress) to fade. Sometimes it fades a little. Sometimes it fades a lot. This can usher in feelings of boredom or indifference toward a partner.

One psychological theory put forward to further explain this phenomenon is known as hedonic adaptation. Basically, it's the idea that with repeated exposure, we get used to the stimuli that make us happy and we have a natural tendency to drift back toward a baseline neutral state. It can happen with a lot of stimuli: think of friendships, activities, or material items that have lost their luster over time. In romantic relationships, researchers suggest that hedonic adaptation can happen in two ways: one is by getting too comfortable in a relationship and taking for granted what you have. You start to feel indifferent, and then drift apart. This is called the "bottom-up" hedonic adaptation route. The other route is "top-down." In this scenario, a partner who is bored seeks out more stimulation in the relationship to stay interested. They may become too demanding of their partner in order to recapture those euphoric feelings, thus putting pressure on the relationship. They may also seek out other *people* to restore euphoric feelings—which is how some folks wind up cheating. Oh boy. What's a couple to do to keep things passionate and healthy? Here are a few ideas that are scientifically backed.

Spend Time Apart

As the old saying goes, "Absence makes the heart grow fonder." And it's true. Spending time apart from each other and maintaining a healthy sense of independence gives you space to reflect on how nice it is to be around your partner. (Should you find you feel *better* when you're apart, that is an important feeling to listen to as well.) Having a healthy amount of space from each other also gives room for sexual desire and longing to grow. Fire needs air to breathe.

Don't Put It All on Your Partner

When you think of traits that turn you on in a partner, "needy" probably isn't at the top of the list. There are points in every relationship where one partner will need more than they typically do, and part of being supportive is meeting them there and addressing those needs. But when one partner's needs are exceedingly high, it can shift the relationship from lover to caretaker. Women in particular are often expected to assume the caretaking role in their marriages, with the modern woman expected to lead both a successful career and a thriving home life. Needless to say, being disproportionately bogged down with responsibilities is not hot. It suffocates erotic desires and passion. We can rekindle eroticism by keeping expectations and demands of a partner reasonable, as well as by taking equal responsibility in relationships.

I think it's wise to consider getting some of our basic needs outside the relationship, too. In American culture, we are often taught to believe that our lover should be able to fill every role in our lives and be able to satisfy our every want and need on their own. But hey, that's a lot of pressure. Discuss what needs you hope are met within the relationship versus needs that might be better met through our broader social networks, like family and friends.

Embrace Impermanence

In her book *Mating in Captivity*, psychotherapist Esther Perel explores the tension between our need for security in relationships and our need for eroticism and passion. At times, these are conflicting needs, and the challenge is in striking a comfortable tension—one that keeps you feeling secure when you need it, and on your toes when you need it, too. But how?

Every day that we are in a relationship, we choose to be with that person and they choose to be with us. At any point, that could change. Keeping this in mind can create a little anxiety—but combined with trust and love, it can also create passion and desire. It's important to remember your partner could choose someone else at any time, but right now they have chosen you. I've found that being in social situations together often offers this reminder. Seeing my partner in their element—socializing and charming others, being good at what they do—is sexy as hell. When do you find yourself feeling a surge of desire for your partner?

Try New Things Together

If you've ever wanted to try a new activity and never got around to it, doing it with a partner can rev up the spice. Whether it's going on a road trip, trying out a dance class, or taking surfing lessons, trying new things throws you into a learning experience together and allows you to see (and fall in love with) your partner in a new light. Activities that get your heart rate up, or that rely on partner/teamwork, are especially good for bonding. My personal favorite is exploring the area we live in by going hiking together, especially hikes with a beautiful view to reward us for our efforts. It's quiet and peaceful, it's romantic, and you get to come home and shower off together afterward. ;)

Try New Things Together (in Bed)

If sex is a yawn, shake things up. Surprise your partner with a hot date, a hot outfit, a new toy, or new moves. Knowing each other well makes it easier to put aside some anxiety about trying something new that feels a little awkward or silly at first. Some couples enjoy things like watching erotic films together, reading each other erotica, dressing up, roleplaying, or inviting a third (or fourth? fifth?) trusted party to join in the fun.

Embrace the Moment

When there are bumps and blips in a relationship, it can be tempting to become consumed by what's going wrong or to worry too much about the future. Don't forget to enjoy the moment and to enjoy the positive aspects of your relationship that bring you comfort and happiness. Being present and feeling gratitude for what you have is not just a healthy practice for relationships, it's a healthy practice for life.

troubleshooting

IT'S NO SECRET THAT RELATIONSHIPS CAN be tough AF. On Twitter, I asked you guys what your most common relationship struggles were. Here are some of the problems that came up.

Arguing about Nothing

Have you ever found yourself in an argument, only to take a step back and wonder what you're even arguing about? "OKAY, WE BASICALLY AGREE. SO WHY ARE WE STILL SCREAMING????" Been there! In the past, I've found myself arguing over nothing more often when I was under stress. Carrying on disagreements longer than necessary (or pulling them out of thin air) was one of the ways my partner and I would take our stress out on each other. Which isn't exactly healthy. It helps to try to recognize when this is happening, acknowledge it (especially if it becomes a pattern in your relationship), and pump the brakes. If you find yourself fighting *a lot*, and over more serious issues, that's a red flag.

Long Distance

As high school students go to college, and college students start their careers, and professionals shift their careers, there is a lot of moving around that happens. Sometimes, those moves are pretty far away and the other person is not able to come along. It happens a lot, and it can be pretty challenging.

Fortunately, modern technology means that long-distance moves needn't mean the end of a relationship. There are many thousands of success stories of people who manage to make their love transcend the distance between them. To maintain and continue a long-distance relationship, good communication—which was already important!—becomes critical. Technologies like texting, Skype, FaceTime, and Snapchat have all made it easier to stay in touch from afar. As you embark on an LDR, discuss how you'd like to use the technologies available, what your expectations are for communication, and how you can support each other from afar. It is also important to see each other regularly. This can be tough at great distances (airline tickets can get pretty expensive), but making an effort makes all the difference. Having an end date in sight makes things more manageable. With the healthy relationship practices we've discussed, the distance might even bring you closer together.

Mental Health Issues

Throughout most of my life, depression has colored my relationships. It regrettably catalyzed one of my more difficult breakups, and I deeply regret how I've handled some things while in the throes of a serious depression. I have also dated people with struggles of their own. Mental health struggles have created some of the most difficult challenges I've had to overcome in dating. Nothing really fixed it, except getting treated.

Dating people who are compassionate and open about mental health issues helps. When I think about the moments in my life where I felt truly, deeply loved, it was when my partner was loving me through those hard times I felt unable to tame my demons. But even the depths of love and patience are not always enough. No amount of compassion, understanding, and patience can fix things if an untreated mental health issue is constantly putting strain on a relationship.

If you or a partner is struggling with mental health, it's important to take care of it before anything else. Your health is #1. The relationship shouldn't be the only place that mental health issues are being talked about or addressed. To keep the relationship healthy, the person who is struggling needs to reach out for counseling, support, and treatment. This is an act of love for yourself and your partner. Take care of yourself and don't put it off.

Partner Is Still in the Closet

One of you is out and proud, but the other is still in the process of coming out. This can create stress within a relationship and, sometimes, feelings of resentment. It can be hurtful to have to live a double life and feel as though your partner isn't proud of you. It can also hurt to feel like you are holding your partner back or are the source of their frustration or pain. It's a difficult situation for everyone involved. Be gentle with yourself and each other.

Communication really is key here; talk openly and understand how each of you feels. It is especially important to really understand the reasons why your partner isn't out yet. Perhaps they fear retaliation from family, friends, or employers. They may be grappling with their faith, or their own internal sense of shame. For some people, coming out is much more difficult than it is for others. For all of these reasons and more, try not to take their being closeted personally (or, on the opposite end, remind them it is not personal). It is not a reflection on you or your relationship. It's about one partner making their place in a world that can be cruel and unaccepting. In the process, remember that you're teammates! That means making compromises that keep both of you safe and get both of your needs met. Talk about your shared goals for the future. As you do so, never compromise your sense of trust or respect for each other. That obviously means never outing someone who isn't ready and not rushing or pressuring your partner to come out. It needs to happen on their own timeline and at their own pace. Identifying the hurdles that are in their way and supporting your partner in addressing them is sometimes easier with the help of a counselor or a supportive queer community, if either is available to you. Communicate where you are, and what being in the closet about your relationship means for you and your needs. Be open about what you're feeling.

Through it all, remember why this process is important to both of you and why it's worth the work. Focus on the freedom and liberation that is waiting for you on the other side of the process. If you determine that you will be in vastly different places for a while, that is a compatibility point to consider as well. Hang in there.

Fear of Commitment

One person wants to make it official, and the other doesn't. Such is the result of differing needs and goals in a relationship. Communicating about what you want and need in a relationship can help, but at the end of the day if one person wants a committed relationship and the other doesn't, that's not necessarily something you can meet each other halfway on. It's also not something that's healthy to pressure someone into. To me, commitment is an issue that is a reasonable deal-breaker. Different levels of commitment mean we're incompatible; we just need different things. Don't put your life on hold waiting for someone to come around. And don't getcha self into relationships you aren't ready to be in.

Cheating

Cheating can wreak serious havoc on a relationship. It's an act of disrespect, and it violates trust, crippling two of the three key foundations of a relationship. It is often accompanied by poor communication and lying, making it a 3/3 fail in some cases.

And yet, studies on cheating suggest it is relatively common, with 20% of people being unfaithful to a partner at some point, and possibly more. The numbers are hard to nab in part because people have different ideas of what counts as cheating. Is it cheating to flirt with an old flame on Facebook? To sext? To kiss? To have sex? Definitions of cheating vary, which is why it's important to establish a mutual understanding of each other's boundaries and expectations early on.

When a partner cheats, one of the first questions to come up is: why? There are a lot of reasons people cheat, and whatever the case may be—there is no excuse for it, and it is nobody's fault but the unfaithful partner. Cheating is a violation of an agreement that is made between partners. Understanding why someone violated that agreement can help us address the root of the problem. However, it is on the unfaithful partner to restore trust and intimacy to the relationship.

Based on people's stories and the stories of some therapists I know, not getting sexual or emotional needs met in the relationship is the most common reason people cheat. Cheating is how someone might temporarily find validation, novelty, or independence elsewhere—but at a high price to both the cheater and their partner. Another of the more common reasons cited by young adults for cheating is a need for independence. This type of cheater may feel smothered and unable to learn more about themselves within the confines of their relationship. It's okay to need independence, but it should be sought after in a healthy way that is considerate of a partner. If you need independence, break up with them first!

It's controversial to some, but cheating can be worked through, especially if:

- The incident is a one-time behavior. No repeats.
- The cheater feels authentic remorse.
- Both people want to make it work.
- The cheater is willing to work to repair trust and intimacy in the relationship.

A therapist can help couples work through infidelity issues. Many couples can (and do) work through an instance of cheating, but it can be very difficult, and some relationships crumble under the weight.

In some cases, cheating is one of several signs that a relationship has *already* crumbled and is perhaps not worth saving. This is the case with people who cheat repeatedly, who don't change their behavior, or whose cheating is part of a broader pattern of entitled behavior. This type of cheater is not invested in the relationship and doesn't care about their partner. Instead of being honest and pulling their weight to make things work, they may even blame their partner for their own behavior. This is a major red flag, if not a nail in the coffin.

When One Partner Doesn't Pull Their Weight

Relationships are partnerships built on reciprocation and compromise. Part of that is sharing the responsibilities and work that it takes to keep a relationship healthy. In unhealthy relationships, that work is one-sided. The needs of one person are elevated, while the other is left to make all the sacrifices needed to make it work. If you find yourself in a relationship that is off-balance, it's time to talk about it. Let your partner know why you're frustrated, and give them a couple examples of their behavior to help them understand. Let them know what you'd like to change in your relationship and how they can help do that. If you're not sure exactly how to restore balance to your relationship, brainstorm on it together. If, in the coming months, they make an effort to pull their weight, that's a sign your partner cares and wants to do better. But if they don't make any real effort, that's a red flag. Their actions indicate they don't care about the relationship enough to put in the work.

Jealousy and Insecurity

My friend Alaska talked a bit about jealousy in polyamorous relationships earlier on, but the green-eyed monster is a common struggle within monogamous relationships too. The pervasiveness of jealousy is understandable to some degree; it's a normal emotion that is part of being a human being—so normal that jealousy is present, in varying degrees, in pretty much every sexual culture around the world. But it's also a potent emotion that can be very destructive—which means it should be handled with care. Jealousy can feed into behaviors that are anywhere from annoying to unhealthy, to abusive. It can ruin relationships, and it can ruin lives.

In my experience, jealousy usually stems from someone feeling insecure with themselves or their relationship. And at its roots, feeling insecure is a type of fear. It's a fear that we're not good enough and our partner will find someone better, fear of potential rejection, fear that we're frauds, fear that our partner is too good for us. To a highly insecure person, the social world poses a number of threats to their sense of stability and worth.

I find that jealousy is quite often irrational—it creeps up even in healthy and stable relationships where there is very little real threat. But jealousy is occasionally rational—for instance, if someone was cheated on by their partner. Jealousy can also be tinged with other emotions, like resentment or distrust.

Here are some examples of jealous and insecure behaviors:
- Always assuming the worst of a partner
- Making accusations that aren't true
- Calling or texting excessively when you're apart
- Always wanting to know where you are

It's important to check behaviors like this, lest they get out of hand. Jealousy can be quelled by acknowledging when it's happening and getting to the heart of what's causing it. Then, you can implement some solutions to address the problem. Focusing on the affirmative actions of the love languages discussed earlier can help make unstable partners feel more secure.

Whatever the accommodations or resolution, they should not be controlling. That's not healthy, my friend. It may even be abusive. We will discuss in more detail in the next chapter.

breaking up

AS I'M WRITING THIS, I'M GOING through a breakup. Fortunately, it's one of the milder ones I've been through—the result of unfortunate circumstances, not irreconcilable differences. Still, I'm not very good at breakups. I have a track record of handling them poorly. My most vivid breakup memories involve me driving around the foothills near my hometown, trying to soothe myself, taking in the countryside and intermittently breaking out in tears. The first time I was broken up with, it felt like part of me had died. Every breath I took felt labored, every tick of the clock felt like a century. I learned exactly why they call it heartbroken; there was a sinking feeling that started in my chest, pooled in my gut, and dripped down to my toes. The realization that we wouldn't be together was a smack of reality I wasn't ready for, an affront to my fantasies about the future and to my ego.

In relationships where I was the one to initiate the breakup, I tended to drag things on too long, putting undue stress on the relationship and on my partner. Which is ironic, because pain was what I was trying to avoid. I can't bear seeing crying eyes or causing emotional pain. It's . . . the worst. It wasn't just their pain I tried to avoid; it was also my own. I didn't want to face my fear of being alone. Being alone is one of my worst fears, and perhaps one of my most irrational. I mean, there are people everywhere, all over the world, that I could share adventures and partnership with. Why should the ending of this one relationship make me feel like I'm doomed to sadness and loneliness forever?

I've found it can be difficult to know when it's time to move on. But there's one indicator that says it all: Are you happy? Does your relationship generally bring you more joy than stress or pain? It's normal to go through rocky periods, but I take serious note when I find myself happy less than half the time in my relationship. If it's more stress than stress relief to hang out, that's a feeling to listen to. If you've tried putting in a fair shot to fix problems in the relationship and found no improvement, that is an experience to listen to. Maybe your personalities are incompatible; maybe you're in different places in life; maybe you want different things out of the future. Listen to your heart and be honest with yourself.

If you're not sure about how you feel about a relationship, sometimes it helps to take a break. A break is basically putting things on hold so you can have the space you need to reflect on what you want and need. Put aside extra time for self-care, spending time with friends, and exploring your feelings. Some distance can really put things into perspective. People take breaks in lots of different ways, but most involve a period of non-contact (or dramatically reduced contact) with each other. If you and your partner decide to take a break, make sure to get clear on what your expectations are of each other during this period. Sometimes people date or have sex with other people on breaks—I would suggest against this in most situations. It creates more problems and is sometimes unethical. It is almost always not done in a healthy state of mind, and because you're not actually broken up, it can be deeply painful for a partner. Many consider it cheating. In monogamous relationships, if you are interested in starting a relationship with someone else, the respectful course of action is to break up. All that said, it's important for you to discuss and figure out what kind of break will work best for you and your partner. My other suggestion is to set an end date to the break. It might be a week or a month. At that point, it's time to reconvene and communicate about what you want and need.

Breaking up doesn't always mean The End of things. A good chunk of relationships have what it takes to transition to friendship, but it has to be something that you both want (which is . . . harder to come by). It also takes some time and maturity to transition to friendship after a breakup. In my experience, it's best to take a breather after the breakup before initiating friendship. Make sure you're in a healthy enough emotional place to build a different relationship with them, and then ease on in. Ex-partners who didn't work out as lovers can still make amazing friends.

Of course none of these problems is so difficult as going through a breakup itself and getting over someone, which is basically Hell on Earth. Here a few things I've learned that helped me to push through.

ACCEPT THE BREAKUP.

If you are being broken up with, don't deny what's happening. Accept how you feel, how they feel, and accept that this is real. Do not try to convince your partner to feel other than they do, unless you feel there was a serious misunderstanding.

GO COLD TURKEY.

After a breakup, when all you need to say has been said, it's best to cut off communication for a while. This is the hardest thing to do when you are craving the comforting voice of your ex, but I promise it will make things easier in the long term. Talking to your ex only serves as a distraction from processing the breakup, making it harder to move on.

If your partner is the one still texting you, it's okay to let them know if you need space from the relationship.

PROCESS THE BREAKUP IN
A HEALTHY WAY.

Some of the emotional processing about the breakup will happen with your former partner, but a majority will happen without them. Processing happens with friends, family, and on your own. Take enough me-time to work through your feelings. Some people like to write blog/journal entries, write music, take it out at the gym, or uh . . . drink the pain away. Preferably, don't drink the pain away. Channel your feelings—whatever they may be—into something healthy and productive. If there's a hobby you've always wanted to take up but just didn't have the time, a breakup is a window of opportunity.

REMEMBER THAT TIME HEALS. FERREAL.

Even if it feels absolutely unbearable, every day will get just a hair easier. They say you should give at least half the length of the relationship itself to recover from it (so if it was two years long, a year to recover). This, of course, depends on your age and the nature of your relationship . . . but I've found this is somewhat true for me. Although sometimes, it has taken longer.

REMEMBER THERE ARE LOTS OF AWESOME PEOPLE IN THE WORLD.

Another cliché, but it's true. "There are plenty of fish in the sea." There are other people you can (and will!) giggle with, cry with, feel attracted to, fall in love with, have adventures with, cuddle with, have sex with, try new things with, learn new things with. Don't rush it. Let things happen naturally.

OUT OF SIGHT, OUT OF MIND.

It can be painful to be reminded of someone constantly with a picture, or song, or whatever while you're trying to recover. Put reminders away for a while.

RELATIONSHIPS ARE VALUABLE, EVEN WHEN THEY END.

A relationship's value isn't determined by how long it lasted. It's about quality, not quantity. Which means there is no time for regrets. No time to feel sorry for yourself. What did you learn from this relationship? What new experiences did you have? How has it helped you grow as a person and learn about others and the world? Reflect on it, internalize it, grow from it.

IT'S OKAY FOR RELATIONSHIPS TO FAIL.

The end of a relationship is not a sign that you are a failure as a person, a "fuck-up," unworthy of love, or anything of that sort. It's normal and okay for relationships to come to a close. It does not say anything about your worth as a person. It is just a sign that things had run their course, and it's time to keep moving.

YOUR RELATIONSHIPS WITH FRIENDS, FAMILY, AND YOURSELF ARE JUST AS IMPORTANT AS ROMANTIC ONES.

The loss of one relationship is an opportunity to continue to build others. Breakups hurt less when you have a strong support system in place. The feelings of loneliness and isolation after a breakup can be cushioned by the companionship and love of friends and family. Take time to focus on building those relationships instead of romantic or sexual ones for a while.

PRACTICE SELF-CARE.

Mourn. Cry. Mope. Get your aggression out on a punching bag at the gym. Whatever it takes, let it out (in a healthy way). Give yourself a few weeks to feel bad or angry or whatever comes up. Focus on healing, relaxing, breathing more deeply. Spend time with friends, spend time doing things you love, and give yourself a little extra license to self-pamper. Get back on your feet when you feel ready. Don't allow yourself to grovel longer than is healthy.

SAY GOODBYE (ON THE INSIDE).

After you feel like you've had a chance to mourn and heal a little bit, it's time to let go of the relationship. Start picturing your life without them, focusing on the positives: time with friends, time for yourself, no more of that one thing you hated about the relationship, new possibilities with other people. It can take a few weeks to a few years to picture your new future without it hurting, but you will get there. It can help to find a symbol of the relationship to let go of. Maybe it's old concert tickets, a letter, their artwork. I'd suggest picking something that is only significant because it makes you think of them, and not disposing of items you might want later (like pictures).

MOVE ON.

When and if you so choose, get back in the dating game. Or, adopt a puppy. That works, too.

SIXTEEN

⚠

⇒∘ DATING VIOLENCE ∘⇐

WE'VE TALKED A WHOLE LOT ABOUT healthy relationships. But what about the unhealthy ones? In an unhealthy relationship, there may be one-off moments of harmful behavior. These can usually be fixed with things like open communication or respect for boundaries. Unhealthy behaviors cause discomfort and turbulence within a relationship, and need to be addressed as soon as they come up. On the more extreme end of things, abusive behaviors can cause serious distress. Abuse may make one partner feel scared to speak up for themselves, or to feel unsafe in the relationship. While abuse is typically thought of as a straight thing, abuse can occur in same-sex relationships as well.

There are some signs that an unhealthy behavior has become abusive:

1. If the behavior makes you feel unsafe or scared at any time
2. If the behavior is repeated more than once
3. If the behavior limits your ability to go about your life normally

Whatever your relationship style may be, relationships are meant to be a retreat from the world. Being around your partner should offer comfort and make you feel safe. If a relationship stops feeling this way, something is up. Abusive relationships almost never start out that way.

They start off just like any other relationship: happy, passionate, fun, and exciting. Toxic behaviors tend to seep in slowly and escalate over time. For those with a history of abuse or with no point of reference, an abusive relationship might even feel normal . . . except for the fact that, y'know, it isn't.

Abusive relationships are way too common among young adults.

- Nearly 1.5 million high school students nationwide experience physical abuse from a dating partner every year.
- Young women ages sixteen to twenty-four experience the highest rate of dating violence, almost triple the national average.
- One in three young women in the United States is a victim of physical, emotional, or verbal abuse from a dating partner.
- One in ten high school students has been purposefully hit, slapped, or otherwise physically hurt by a boyfriend or girlfriend.
- Nearly half (43%) of dating college women report experiencing violent and abusive dating behaviors.
- One in six (16%) college women has been sexually abused in a dating relationship.

Even worse, abuse in young people's relationships usually goes unseen and unrecognized.

- Only 33% of teens who were in an abusive relationship ever told anyone about the abuse.
- Though 82% of parents feel confident that they would be able to recognize it if their child was experiencing dating abuse, a majority of parents (58%) failed to correctly identify all the warning signs of abuse.

—*Dating abuse statistics compiled by Love Is Respect, loveisrespect.org*

types of abuse

ABUSE IS NOT A ONE-TIME BEHAVIOR. It has a predictable cycle that escalates over time. After an abusive outburst, it is usually followed by making up and a period of calm that can bring feelings of relief and hope. Eventually, the tension starts building again. This feeling is often described as "walking on eggshells," and it usually precedes another incident.

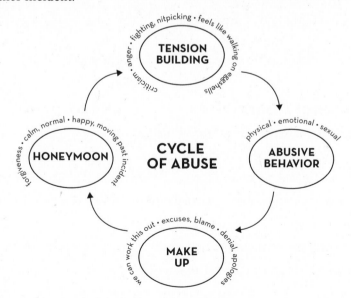

—*Adapted from Lenore Walker,* The Battered Woman, *Harper and Row, 1979*

When people think of dating violence, they typically think of hitting and bruises. Physical abuse is the type of abuse most likely to put someone in immediate physical danger, but it is only one of several types of abuse that can occur in a relationship. Every type of abuse is serious and harmful. Their effects are felt differently from person to person. There is no universal experience of or response to abuse.

Physical Abuse

Statistically, physical abuse that is present in a relationship will get worse over time. Physical abuse is not present in all abusive relationships.

Identifying Physical Abuse

◆ Hitting ◆ Scratching ◆ Strangling ◆ Smothering ◆ Slapping ◆ Pulling hair or clothes ◆ Threatening to use weapons ◆ Blocking you from leaving ◆ Throwing things at you ◆ Destroying property ◆ Touching without permission ◆ Hurting pets ◆

Emotional Abuse

A behavior doesn't need to leave a bruise to be abusive. Creating a threatening environment where you are being berated, threatened, or made to feel afraid is emotional abuse. Emotional abuse wears someone down psychologically rather than physically; the abuser does this by grating down their victim's self-worth and exploiting that vulnerability to exert control over their life. Like physical abuse, emotional abuse can pose a serious danger to the victim's wellness and safety.

Identifying Emotional Abuse

— ♡ —

◆ Constant put-downs ◆ Constant criticism ◆ Yelling and screaming at you ◆ Embarrassing you in front of others ◆ Isolating you from family or friends ◆ Controlling who you talk to ◆ Monitoring who you talk to ◆ Monitoring where you go ◆ Monitoring what you do ◆ Threatening to hurt you or your pet ◆ Threatening to commit suicide ◆ Destroying property ◆ Extreme jealousy ◆ Accusing you of cheating or lying ◆ Blaming their behavior on you ◆ Threatening to out you ◆ Outing you ◆ Starting rumors about you ◆ Hurting pets ◆ Guilting you into sexual activity ◆ Threatening to have your children taken away ◆

A common feature of emotional abuse is gaslighting. "Gaslighting" is a term that was popularized by the 1944 movie *Gaslight*, wherein a woman's husband slowly dims the gaslights in their house over time to drive his wife crazy. When she points out the lights are darker, he insists that she is delusional and just imagining things. Gaslighting is a type of emotional abuse that, over time, destroys a person's sense of their own reality. It causes the victim to constantly second-guess their instincts, their feelings, and their perception of what is happening. Is this really happening, or am I just crazy? This corrodes a person's trust in themselves, redirecting power toward the abuser to affirm to them what is "real" and what they're "just imagining." Victims of gaslighting might find themselves asking if they are being too sensitive, losing confidence in themselves, making excuses for the abuser's behavior, or feeling that something is wrong in their life without a clear cause to point to.

Digital Abuse

Digital abuse is a subset of emotional abuse where technology is exploited to exert power and control.

The digital world is real life. It is increasingly entangled in our social world, jobs, and inner lives. As we have started to socialize online and on our smartphones more, it has become a venue for abuse to be carried out in new ways. Digital abuse is still emerging as an accepted category of "real abuse," and its impact is sometimes underestimated by authorities. This has started to change in recent years, with laws against abusive behaviors online (like "revenge porn") slowly making it onto the books.

Identifying Digital Abuse

◆ **Uses social media or technology to track you** ◆ **Looks through your phone** ◆ **Asks for or steals your passwords** ◆ **Requires you to constantly text them** ◆ **Monitors your digital conversations** ◆ **Pressures you to send explicit pictures** ◆ **Sends you mean, insulting, or threatening messages online** ◆ **Threatens to or shares your sexual pictures** ◆

Sexual Abuse (a.k.a. Sexual Violence)

Sexual abuse is an umbrella term for a range of coercive behaviors. Often, the victim is made to do something sexual that they (1) do not want to do or (2) cannot give informed consent to do, for instance, if they are incapacitated or a minor. Sexual abuse may occur at the hands of partners and spouses, acquaintances, family members, teachers and authority figures, or perfect strangers.

It is important to note that 73% of the time, sexual violence is perpetrated by somebody the survivor knows. This reality is sometimes obscured by the narrow focus on "stranger danger" in conversations about sexual assault. We are taught to fear strangers the most, and we do not learn to recognize or handle sexual abuse from people within our own lives. In a romantic relationship, sexual abuse sometimes includes controlling the reproductive choices the victim is allowed to make about their body. People of all genders and sexual orientations may be victims (and perpetrators) of sexual abuse.

- **Sexual assault:** unwanted touching, kissing, sexual activity; violence during sex; forced participation in degrading sex acts; sexual contact while a person is unconscious, drunk, or drugged
- **Rape** (a form of sexual assault): unwanted penetration of the vagina, anus, or mouth
- **Molestation** (sexual abuse of minors): sexually touching a child's sexual parts, exposing genitals to a child in a sexual manner, making a child watch them masturbate, making a child perform oral sex, taking pornographic photos

People who experience sexual abuse may have trouble accepting that (1) what happened was abusive, and (2) it was not their fault. Sexual abuse is sometimes misunderstood as something that is forceful rather than a situation where the abuser uses manipulation, guilt, and coercion to get what they want from an unwilling participant. To an outsider, the lines of consent and non-consent may look less clear than an overt show of force (such as pinning someone down). This casts a shadow of doubt for victims that ultimately empowers the abuser.

Adults who prey on young people often use a form of emotional coercion called grooming. Grooming is the process of identifying a victim, slowly making the child feel special to gain their trust, and building a relationship with them that is shrouded in secrecy. They may use treats, gifts, special outings, special attention, physical and/or emotional affection to make their victim feel safe. Once they have the child's trust, the abuser will seek out or manipulate opportunities for alone time (like one-on-one coaching, church activities, tutoring, babysitting, etc.). Sexuality is gradually introduced into the relationship with flirting/teasing, sending suggestive texts or pictures, touching, or creating situations where they will be naked or have intimate contact. The abuser often exploits their victim's natural curiosity and sexual confusion, making them feel like they are to blame. This is one of the ways that the abuser maintains control. If the victim expresses discomfort, they may face blame or shame or even threats. Some victims worry that ending the relationship will result in a loss of the love they feel, and that they will end up unwanted.

The emotional consequences of sexual abuse are complicated by the fact that sexuality is the weapon. It employs contact with the body that, in a consensual context, might be pleasurable and loving. Sexual

Identifying Sexual Abuse
—♡—

◆ Refusing to use condoms ◆ "Stealthing"/taking a condom off without consent ◆ Hiding or restricting access to birth control ◆ Refusing to use protection from STIs ◆ Refusing to let their partner choose an abortion ◆ Pressure and threats to participate in unwanted sex acts ◆

violence may involve being physically inside of somebody's body, leaving profound scars of violation. Survivors have a range of reactions to abuse, and there is no "right" response or feeling. Some survivors describe feeling like a stranger in their own body, being disassociated from their genitals or sexuality, having trouble with intimacy and trust, being unable to feel "clean," or being unable to feel anything at all.

Financial Abuse

Like other nonphysical forms of abuse, financial abuse sometimes slips under the radar unnoticed. It is a common manipulation tactic for abusers who are trying to trap somebody in a relationship. By controlling their victim's economic situation, the abuser makes it very hard for their victim to get out.

Identifying Financial Abuse

♦ Forbidding you from having money or a bank account ♦ Deliberately ruining your credit ♦ Hiding/stealing your financial aid • Monitoring what you buy ♦ Running up your debt ♦ Not allowing you to have a job ♦ Getting you fired from or interfering with your job ♦ Hiding family assets ♦ Withholding money for food, rent, medication, and other staples ♦

Stalking

Stalking refers to harassing and monitoring behaviors that keep the victim in a constant state of fear. Stalkers may go to extreme lengths to feel in control of their victim, including threats of or actual violence. Stalkers are often socially isolated people, and they may have various motives. Some are romantically obsessed with their victim and delusional, believing that their behavior will earn their victim's love. Some stalkers do so to exact revenge and regain control when they feel slighted or rejected. Others are just predatory strangers who stalk someone for the sake of sexual gratification.

Identifying Stalking

◆ Sends you unwanted messages, texts, calls, emails, voice mails, or social media ◆ Leaves you unwanted notes or gifts at work, home, or school ◆ References places you've been/things you've done that you didn't tell them about ◆ Calls and hangs up ◆ Surveillance ◆ Exposing their genitals ◆ Graphic phone calls ◆ Spreads rumors about you ◆ Contacts your employer ◆ Shows up unannounced ◆ Tries to learn more about you through others (online or off) ◆ Threatens to commit suicide if you don't talk to them, date them, etc. ◆

causes of abuse

IT'S HARD TO MAKE SENSE OF abusive behavior. How can regular, everyday people be so horrible, especially to their loved ones? How do they justify manipulation, coercion, and violence? On a gut level, I will never, ever understand it. And when I don't understand something, I look to the research (as you may have noticed by now).

Abuse requires an attitude of entitlement and lack of empathy for others. Abusers believe they have a right to control their victim's life or their body. Anybody of any age, gender, race, or sexual orientation can be an abuser. Media stereotypes of abusers are quite narrow; the word "abuser" conjures an image of an angry drunk man in a tank top. It's such a notorious stereotype that some people started calling white tank tops "wifebeaters." While some abusers fit the stereotype, many do not, which spurs doubt and disbelief when the abuser is a regular guy—or a woman. Survivors of relationship abuse often describe their abuser as charming and confident and say they were swept off their feet in the beginning. Abusers may be engaging, benevolent, thoughtful, charismatic, and incredibly sweet outside of their abuse. This ingratiates them to their peers, casts them as sympathetic, and protects them from suspicions or accusations of misconduct.

Another trait that all abusers have in common is a lack of empathy. Regardless of how they may behave, abusers do not see their partner as a whole person or as their equal. They believe they have a right to do whatever they want to others, including hurt them. They may feel like they know what's best for their partner or enjoy a sense of power that abusive behaviors give them. Some abusers may harbor insecurities about their abilities or career and lash out against their partner in order to feel in control. Others abuse when they know that they can get away with it and will face no consequences from friends, family, or law enforcement.

While the vast majority of men are not abusers, around the world, abusers are most likely to be men. One theory that sets out to explain the profound gender gap links abuse to hypermasculine gender roles, a.k.a. "toxic masculinity." Toxic masculinity is an extreme version of masculinity that encourages men to show power, control, and dominance over others—including their lovers—in order to be "real men." Violence and aggression, rather than communication and empathy, are encouraged to solve conflicts: "fight it out like a man," "talking it out is for pussies," and other endorsements of harmful behavior. This is obviously pretty unhealthy for relationships, and it's destructive to men as well; it stokes feelings of shame and guilt in men who aren't unfeeling macho robots. It isolates male victims of sexual abuse, who are accused of being "weak" or "secretly wanting it." They feel more shame about what happened to them, hesitate to come forward, and feel pressure to "toughen up" (that is, to repress their emotions). The expression of emotional vulnerability is generally discouraged in a hypermasculine framework, making male survivors less likely to seek out counseling to heal from sexual trauma.

Whatever the underlying causes of abusive behavior may be, **abusing another person is a deliberate choice that a person makes**. How we choose to treat others is entirely within our own control. Instead of choosing abuse, a person could choose to walk away, to respectfully talk through their frustrations, to take a break from the relationship, or to break up if things are not working. There is simply no excuse for the choice to abuse someone—ever. Not even if:

1. The abuser is intoxicated.

Alcohol is often used to excuse abusive behavior. While intoxication can escalate harmful behaviors at a quicker pace, alcohol itself cannot cause harm without the will to be violent. Hurting others is not a natural side effect of being drunk; many millions of people get drunk every day without abusing others. The decisions we make under the influence of alcohol are our own, and there are no excuses for behaviors that hurt others, intoxicated or not. This applies not just to relationship abuse, but to sexual assault, cheating, drunk driving, and the entire gamut of drunk decisions that hurt others.

2. The victim "provoked" the abuser.

There is a common knee-jerk tendency to blame the victim for their abuser's behavior. This is embodied in claims that "the victim asked for it" or that "they are both in the wrong." Questions about what the victim said or did to cause the abuser to act out, what they were wearing (common in the case of sexual assault), or why they didn't just leave—these all shift responsibility for what happened to the victim instead of the abuser. This is called victim blaming.

Victim Blaming

Here are five problems with victim blaming.

Victim blaming effectively excuses violence. It reframes abuse as something the abuser had *no choice* but to do. It assumes that abusing someone is out of the abuser's control and that stopping the abuse is in the victim's control. Therefore, the victim must always anticipate the things that could "invite abuse." They must take care to talk a certain way, dress a certain way, not be too rude or too friendly, not stay out too late, not get too drunk, not flirt or "give him ideas," not make him mad, obey all his rules—otherwise, in the mind of the victim blamer, the abuse is somehow justified. However, all of these behaviors are freedoms that every person in the United States has. They are in no way an invitation for abuse—they are merely excuses for it.

Victim blaming erases imbalances of power. Claims that "both parties are guilty" suggest that both parties have the same amount of control over the situation. If someone fights back or employs self-defense tactics, that does not negate the abuse or make them a perpetrator. While mutually abusive relationships do exist, there is nearly always one party responsible for continually instigating harmful behavior toward their partner.

Victim blaming re-victimizes victims. (Say that one ten times fast.) Victims of abuse and sexual violence often suffer tremendous shame and guilt about what happened. Like society, they may blame themselves for inviting it. This creates inner turmoil for many survivors of sexual abuse, who may struggle with the feeling that it is their fault.

Victim blaming makes it less likely that a victim will seek out support. When friends, family members, or officials make excuses and do not hold an abuser accountable, it sends a strong message. These words and actions convey support for an abuser's behavior. As a result, people who are experiencing violence doubt their own right to safety or justice. Many do not feel safe coming forward with their story, and abuse stays in the shadows.

Victim blaming causes more violence. On a personal level, no accountability means no change. At an institutional level, no accountability means no deterrent to stop further abusive behaviors or other abusers.

The bottom line is this: Abuse and sexual violence are not (and never will be) the survivor's fault. The only person responsible for abusive behavior is the abuser. Period.

Victim blaming goes beyond the sphere of sexual abuse—it is a common psychological response to crimes of all kinds. Experts have a few theories as to why. The most common explanation is belief in the "just-world hypothesis." Basically, we tend to believe that people get what they deserve. If something bad happens to someone, they must be a bad person. If someone is fortunate, it is because they earned it. Under the just-world hypothesis, the universe is assumed to be fundamentally fair: it punishes evil and rewards goodness. This is the narrative thread of almost every Disney movie—and really, any movie with a bad guy and a hero. Goodness always prevails! It would be great if things were always that simple, huh? The just-world hypothesis serves an important psychological purpose: it helps us feel safe. If we believe that victims of terrible things have done something to deserve it, we are better able to distance ourselves from the fear that terrible things could happen to us (or to our children, friends, lovers, etc.).

Dr. Sherry Hamby, an expert on the psychology of violence, notes that belief in the just-world hypothesis is more common in America. The idea of the American Dream and a belief in our ability to control our own destiny (if we try hard enough, that is) are tremendously popular. These beliefs are an integral part of the American identity and cultural psyche. In war-torn or highly impoverished countries, people more readily accept the reality that bad things can happen to good people, and that we don't always get what we deserve.

A person's moral values also influence how likely they are to victim blame. Dr. Laura Niemi and Dr. Liane Young conducted a series of studies that found that the more strongly a person held "binding" moral values, the more likely they were to victim blame. Binding moral values are those that prioritize loyalty, obedience to authority, and purity. The researchers say these values serve to unite groups of people—for instance, a religious group that does not eat certain kinds of foods. When these particular values are taken to their extreme, however, they can be damaging and can downplay individual injustices for the sake of group cohesion. People with binding moral values are more likely to believe that the victim is a bad person and that the victim was not hurt by the abuse. On the flip side, people with strongly held "individualizing" values victim blame the least often. Individualizing values prioritize the importance of the equality of individual people and the unconditional prevention of harm.

The belief that a victim "asked for it" is one of the most widely held myths about rape in our culture. But . . . there are more.

myths about abuse

LET'S TALK ABOUT SOME OF THE common mythologies about sexual violence and abuse.

Fact: Rape Allegations Are Almost Always True.

According to the FBI, 98% of sexual violence reports are truthful. Of the 2% that are false, they should of course be taken seriously. Lying about sexual violence is a crime with legal consequences, including jail time. However, not all false allegations are malicious. False allegations that go on record include memory errors (identifying the wrong perpetrator in stranger attacks) or dropping a legal case for emotional reasons. The belief that abuse accusations stand a very high chance of being false may be rooted in stereotypes about women: that women are liars, attention seekers, or "gold diggers." This treatment of abuse survivors stands in stark contrast to victims of other crimes. There are no widespread suspicions that victims of auto theft are lying about it, though they are statistically up to five times as likely to make false reports. Reports of auto theft are false about 10% of the time.

Fact: Men Can Control Themselves Just As Well as Women.

The notion that men can't control themselves is not only inaccurate, it's degrading. Just like women, men are not feral animals. And just like women, men can make the decision not to sexually violate others— which is exactly what the vast majority of men do. If men were "natural predators," the majority of men would be rapists, and yet the percentage of men who rape is quite low. A robust 2002 study in the journal *Violence and Victims* found that between 6 to 14.9% of college men self-report acts that meet the legal definition of rape or attempted rape.

While sexual violence and sexual desire are sometimes confused, it's important to make the distinction. Sexual violence is coercive. It is an expression of power; sex is a tool that is used to control someone's body, or to humiliate them. Sexual violence is not caused by being horny, or most teenagers would be rapists (they're not, phew!).

Fact: Rape Is Rape.

The idea that some incidents of rapes are "more real" than others stems from stereotypes about sexual violence.

Rape is rape.

Whether or not there were weapons . . .

Whether or not they fought back . . .

Whether or not it was a stranger . . .

Whether or not they had had sex before . . .

Whether or not they are married . . .

Whether or not the victim said anything . . .

Whether or not the victim reported it to the police . . .

Whether or not the victim _____ .

Fact: Men Can Be Raped, and Are.

Stereotypes about men depict them as animals that are always on the prowl for sex. This leads to the misconception that men can't actually be raped, or that they must have "secretly wanted it." In reality, men are whole human beings with their own desires and agency, and that agency can be violated. At least one out of every ten rape survivors is male, and the odds that a young man will experience sexual violence increases five times if he goes to college.

Fact: Revealing Clothing Doesn't Cause Rape.

In the consent culture section, we chatted a bit about slut shaming. Basically, women are judged and divided into one of two categories: "respectable girls" and "slutty girls." "Respectable girls" dress modestly, they don't sleep around, they don't wear heavy makeup or party hard. They are perceived as good, compliant, and therefore worthy of respect. Slutty girls, however, are not worthy of respect. Because they break our rules, and are therefore subject to shame (ahem, slut shame) from their peers.

Sometimes slut shaming stems from feeling threatened by another woman. Girls are told that we need to be attractive and desirable in order to be worthy of love, and the result of that is sometimes tearing each other down in order to feel good enough. This is, of course, destructive to all girls. The solution is to recognize that sexuality and appearance do not determine your worth, and that there are plenty of romantic partners to choose from. Slut shaming may also stem from double standards. When a man has a lot of sex, he is lauded for it. When a woman has a lot of sex, she is berated for it. During the same sexual exchange, the man might be seen as a "stud," while she's "easy" and "trash." Slut shaming creates a contingency of worthiness and respect for women based on arbitrary measures of sexuality. It is sexist and sex-negative at its core.

Fact: Everyone Copes with Trauma Differently.

In some situations, I have seen survivors of sexual abuse subjected to doubt and ridicule because they weren't "acting like a victim." The truth is that there is no monolithic behavioral response to sexual violence. The research on sexual trauma is clear: everybody copes with sexual trauma differently. A survivor's tone, demeanor, or outward emotions do not indicate the severity or truth of their situation.

"why didn't she just leave?"

WHEN A STORY ABOUT AN ABUSIVE relationship is in the news, a common question that many people ask of the victim is "Why didn't they leave as soon as their partner was abusive?" The short answer is that the process of getting out of an abusive relationship can be tremendously difficult. So much so that, on average, it takes leaving the relationship seven times before they are able to get out for good. There are many reasons why people stay.

1. A big reason survivors may stay is because they are **economically and/or legally bound to their abuser**. Many abusers have financial power over their victim, making it hard for the victim to establish independence to leave. The victim may not have anywhere else to go or may not be able to afford living on their own, especially when children are involved. Survivors face a tremendous uphill climb in escaping and restabilizing their life outside of the relationship. Legal challenges can make things worse; they may be married, they may have children together, and they may fear losing their children if they try to leave.

2. **Isolation** adds insult to injury. Abusers often isolate their victim from their friends and family over time. This leaves some survivors feeling like there is nobody they feel comfortable asking for help. They may harbor shame, embarrassment, and anxiety or may struggle with addiction, furthering their isolation. Isolation is exacerbated when family or friends become judgmental or only offer conditional support as the survivor navigates their situation. To leave, a survivor must have at least one patient, nonjudgmental, empathetic, and proactively supportive person in their life. This is harder to come by than one would hope.

3. **Fear of retaliation** can be a powerful factor for someone trying to leave an abusive relationship. When someone leaves their abusive partner, their risk of violence at the hands of their abuser sharply increases.

A sobering 75% of domestic violence homicides happen when, or after, the victim decides to leave.

4. In some **religions and cultures**, leaving a partner, even if they are abusive, is very taboo. It is viewed as moral failure, or as bringing shame to the family. As a result, a survivor of violence in faith communities may not find support they need or may be met with judgment and condemnation.

5. Survivors with **disabilities** may have additional needs that make it harder to leave an abusive relationship. They may lack the physical, financial, or emotional means to escape. An abusive partner may withhold basic needs like medication, food, and access to the bathroom. A survivor with disabilities may be dependent on their abuser for assistance or critical health insurance and may have few opportunities for privacy to get help. Women with disabilities experience domestic violence at twice the rate of the general population.

6. Perhaps the hardest part for outsiders to accept is that the survivor may **still love their abusive partner**. They may even have a long history together. Leaving a partner can be exceptionally difficult, even in the absence of abuse. To be able to acknowledge that the person you love is also a person who hurts you is a painful thing and takes time to truly accept and process. A survivor may hold out for change even after it is clear that the abuser will not put in the effort to improve. Even in a threatening or painful situation, survivors are still human.

The question of why someone stayed comes up when friends and family (or the public, even) are trying to make sense of the situation. But the question itself is sometimes used in a victim-blaming manner, implying the victim is responsible for what's happening because they haven't left. In these contexts, it is helpful to recenter the question on the abuse rather than on the victim's response to it. If we're going to ask why the victim chose to stay, we should also be asking why the abuser is choosing to harm their partner.

unlearning abusive behavior

ABUSIVE PARTNERS CAN SOMETIMES CHANGE. ABUSE is a learned behavior, and so it can also be unlearned. That said, "change" and unlearning are far more often talked about than actually achieved. Changing abusive behavior requires serious commitment to doing so. Abusive partners must be willing to acknowledge their behavior and hold themselves accountable. They can work toward rehabilitation by seeing a counselor who specializes in domestic violence, undergoing substance abuse programs, taking a batterers intervention and prevention program (BIPP), or some combination of the three. Couples counseling is *not* recommended by experts for abusive relationships because abuse is not a relationship problem that needs to be worked on by both parties. On the contrary, couples counseling can offer new outlets for an abusive partner to manipulate and control their victim, and couples therapy may unintentionally escalate abuse at home.

There are ways to tell if an abuser has actually committed to change (versus just talking about it). Lundy Bancroft, an expert on male abusers, lists the following steps as positive signs.

- Admitting fully to what they have done
- Stopping excuses
- Stopping all blaming of their partner
- Making amends
- Accepting responsibility (recognizing that abuse is a choice)
- Identifying patterns of controlling behavior, admitting their wrongness

- Identifying the attitudes that drive their abuse
- Accepting that overcoming abusiveness will be a decades-long process, not declaring themselves cured
- Not using change as a bargaining chip
- Not demanding credit for improvements they have made
- Not treating improvements as chips or vouchers to be spent on occasional acts of abuse (e.g., "I haven't done anything like this in a long time, so why are you making such a big deal about it?")
- Developing respectful, kind, supportive behaviors
- Carrying their weight
- Sharing power
- Changing how they act in highly heated conflicts
- Changing how they respond to their partner's (or former partner's) anger and grievances
- Changing their parenting
- Changing their treatment of their partner as a parent
- Changing their attitudes toward females in general
- Accepting the consequences of their actions (including not feeling sorry for themselves about those consequences, and not blaming the partner or the children for them)

—*Adapted from the Checklist for Assessing Change in Males Who Abuse Women, by Lundy Bancroft*

Ask Laci: on relationship violence

? How can I help a friend who's in an abusive relationship?

A supportive friend can make a big difference. Here are some tips:

1. Believe them. Victims of abuse are often met with doubt and blame.

2. Let them know you are concerned and care about them. Let them know you are there for them and want to help. Check in with them to see how they're doing.

3. Listen to them. Try to understand what they are experiencing and be supportive.

4. Leave your judgment at the door. It is important to respect the decisions your friend makes about their situation, even if they're not what you'd hope. Avoid victim blaming or minimizing the situation.

5. Offer them resources. Do some research to find a local domestic violence organization that can help. Point your friend to websites, articles, or YouTube videos that you like and think could help educate or uplift them.

6. Take care of yourself too. Supporting a friend who is in an abusive relationship requires a lot of emotional energy. Make sure to recharge by taking breaks from the conversation, having uplifting hang-out time and activities, setting healthy boundaries, and seeking outside help if you need it. Make sure you ask your friend if it's okay before you disclose any personal details to a safe third party like a parent or your partner. Be careful not to put them at any additional risk while taking care of yourself.

❓ What can I do if someone I know is abusing their partner?

Good on you for paying attention and not just turning a blind eye. If you can, it's important to say something. Come in with healthy expectations about what you can really do here—they will only change if they truly want to. You can start a conversation by asking if they're aware of the impact they're having on their partner, or telling them why their behavior is worrying you. They may try to victim blame or minimize what they have done. Do not indulge their excuses. It is important to keep the conversation focused on their actions and the effect they are having.

If they accuse you of turning against them, let them know that you are stepping in because you care about them and the well-being of their partner. Tell them you are there for them and want to support them, but you will not support their behavior. Encourage them to seek out further help for themselves, like counseling. If you are in *any way* concerned that their partner may be in danger, do not delay in contacting the police. Your local domestic violence shelter can offer more resources and support.

❓ What should I do if I think my relationship is abusive?

If any of this stuff has raised a red flag in your brain about your relationship, know that you are not alone and that there is support available if you want it. The first priority is always your safety. Are you safe right now? If not, reach out to somebody you trust to let them know what's going on. Navigating a relationship that has become abusive can be confusing. It's okay to still be in love with your abuser. It's okay to be confused. It's okay to take your time to figure out what you want to do next.

Should you leave the relationship? Well, if you're asking me, yeah. You deserve happiness. Love. Respect. Safety. All the things. But things aren't always so straightforward, are they? Breaking up with somebody who is abusive is a different experience than the typical breakup. Maybe you're worried about retaliation or their reaction. Listen to your gut, and trust what it's saying. If you feel like you need to take precautions before you break up, then do so. If you go to school with your abuser, talk to a school counselor and figure out a safety plan for campus. If you're worried about how they'll respond when you break the news, break up over the phone or in a public place. Keep your friends and/or family in the loop about what's going on, and call on them for support.

After the breakup, it's best to cease contact. Resist the urge to contact them or see them again, at least for a little while. If they are contacting you and/or harassing you, document any text messages, voice mails, and social media posts from them. Should their behavior continue to escalate, documentation will help you if you need to file for a protective order. Depending on the state, a protective order can require your abuser to keep their distance (this would be known as a restraining order), it can require them to relinquish their weapons, it can help evict them from a shared lease, or to institute other measures to keep you safe. Most states offer protective orders to LGBTQ+ relationships as well. However, as of this writing, a few still do not. This does not necessarily mean you won't have success. A local domestic violence center can help you figure out your options and how to proceed.

If you are in a same-sex or queer relationship that is abusive, you may find yourself facing additional challenges to leaving. It is common for people in same-sex relationships to worry about outing themselves, finding support, giving a "bad name" to LGBTQ+ communities, or not being taken seriously. Reach out to your community domestic violence, LGBTQ+ health, or LGBTQ+ rights organizations if you find yourself lacking in support. You deserve safety and you have rights.

❓ How can I enjoy sex again as a survivor of abuse?

It's not uncommon for survivors of sexual abuse to find themselves facing new challenges with relationships and sex. Sometimes those feelings set in immediately; other times they can bubble to the surface months down the road. Everybody deals with trauma differently and on their own timeline. In most situations, I think a counselor can be a fantastic tool to help navigate and heal. If you have access to counseling, I'd encourage you to pursue it. There are also a few general things to keep in mind as you begin to reinitiate sexual relationships.

It's absolutely A-okay to set new rules and boundaries for yourself as you heal (and always). If you don't want to have sexual relationships, or are only okay with certain things, that is perfectly fine. It's important to take your time and go at your own pace. Some people find that safe words (see chapter 14) can help communicate boundaries more easily with new partners.

It's also important to choose partners that you trust and feel safe with. They should be able to communicate with you about your boundaries and needs. Your partner should work with you to accommodate your needs to help you feel your best as you recover. They should never, ever pressure you to move at a faster pace than you are ready to.

Don't pressure yourself, either! There's no onus to "jump back in" or "get it over with." Take care of yourself and do what feels best, on your own terms, for as long as you need.

⇒° WHY WE NEED SEX ED °⇐

HEYYYYY, YA MADE IT! THANK YOU, friend, for joining me on this magical journey. I hope that the information in this book has proven interesting, encouraging, or otherwise useful to you in your life. Of course, this is only the beginning. There is so much more to learn about sexuality, so many more conversations to have, and so many more ideas to explore. I hope you do just that. Enrich yourself and your life with knowledge. Stay curious, and seek pleasure and love and vitality—you deserve it all!

To close the conversation, I wanted to talk a bit about why I believe the information in this book should be commonplace and why sex education is so important to me. The fact that *none of the health information in this book*, some of which is lifesaving, is allowed to be taught in most schools is a tragedy.

It's no secret that the United States doesn't do sex education well.

- As of 2017, only 50% of females and 8% of males aged 15 to 19 reported having received formal instruction about how to use a condom. (Guttmacher)
- Only 55% of young men and 60% of young women have received formal instruction about methods of birth control. (Guttmacher)

- Only 14% of middle school and 21% of high school students know how to ask for consent. (Planned Parenthood)
- One in two young adults contract a sexually transmitted infection (STI) before age twenty-five. (Planned Parenthood)
- Less than a third of students can describe what a healthy relationship looks like. (Planned Parenthood)
- As of 2013, fewer than 5% of lesbian, gay, bisexual, and transgender (LGBT) students aged thirteen to twenty-one reported that their health classes had included positive representations of LGBT-related topics.

—Source: GLSEN

These are the same teenagers who are dating, falling in love, and having sex (though not always in that order). While telling people to wait it out till marriage was the go-to line of the adults in my life, a whopping 97% of people ignore that advice. The reality is that a lot of teenagers have sex. They just do. They always have. Your grandparents had sex as teenagers. Their grandparents had sex as teenagers. And their grandparents had— Okay, you get the point. The sooner we can accept that sexuality is a part of life, the sooner we can focus on how to be safe, healthy, and fulfilled.

A Is for Abstinence-only.

As of this writing, only twenty-four states in the United States, plus DC, require some form of sex education at school. Of the states that teach it, only twenty require that the programs be medically accurate (based on facts). Only eight states require that it be unbiased. Girl WHAT????

The way I see it, many "sex ed" programs in America attempt to deter students from having sex by simply scaring them out of it. Perhaps a pus-oozing herpes outbreak is projected up on the wall, to the disgust of everyone in class. Perhaps students are given an assignment where they write a mock letter to their family to let them know that they have AIDS. Perhaps a shrieking doll wakes a student up four times a night in an effort to instill the horrors of raising a baby.

As a sex educator, I have found myself dealing with the fallout of these fear-based lessons. For instance, when a high school class is shown examples of STIs that are extreme or photoshopped, students don't learn what the average infection looks like. I've met students who believe they can simply "check" their partner for STIs before having sex, under the impression that STIs would be obvious. I have also met adults who didn't know they had an STI and wound up infertile. I have met people who deal with severe depression and anxiety because they've contracted an STI from their long-term partner even when they used protection.

Another common theme in abstinence classrooms is using HIV/AIDS to condemn being gay. Curriculums like Facing Reality teach students that AIDS is a punishment for people who are homosexual. LGBTQ+ sexuality is framed as a "lifestyle choice" rather than as a part of who someone is. And even more often, abstinence-only curricula ignore LGBTQ+ sexuality entirely. In turn, queer and questioning youth are left with even fewer answers than their straight peers are, and may face intensified shame about their sexuality.

In the Words of Abstinence-only Textbooks

Actual things written in books that students and educators are required to read:

"Schools put themselves at great economic risk in regard to liability issues when they teach 'safer sex.' Misleading teens to believe contraceptives will protect them is not sound public policy." (WAIT Training, p. 36)

"Many men and women still prefer to marry virgins, so you don't want to lose out on a future with someone special just because you didn't say 'no' to premarital sex." (Sex Respect, Student Workbook, p. 73)

"Because they generally become physically aroused less easily, girls are still in a good position to slow down the young man and help him learn balance in a relationship." (Sex Respect, Student Workbook, p. 12)

"A guy who wants to respect girls is distracted by sexy clothes and remembers her for one thing. Is it fair that guys are turned on by their senses and women by their hearts?" (Sex Respect, Student Workbook, p. 94)

"Finally, AIDS (Acquired Immune Deficiency Syndrome), the STD most common among homosexuals, bisexuals and IV drug users, has now made its way into heterosexual circles." (Sex Respect, Student Workbook, p. 54)

Of course, no discussion of the fallout of abstinence-only programs would be complete without the infamous virginity pledges. Virginity pledges were popularized in the early '90s by a program called "True Love Waits," a creation of the Christian Sex Education Project. The curriculum is currently in wide use, in both religious and secular settings. Here's one sample pledge:

> *Today I commit to Abstinence as a way to make the Best preparation for my future by Choosing to wait until marriage to have sex, because I want to be free: from worry, guilt, pregnancy, sexually transmitted diseases, and the feeling of being used by another; to control my life, to like myself, to work towards personal goals, to experience healthy relationships, and to enjoy being a teenager.*
> —Choosing the Best LIFE, *Student Workbook*

Virginity pledges aren't necessarily a bad idea on the surface and may even have benefits. Research shows that when taken in small groups—as opposed to big classrooms—virginity pledges can be effective at delaying sex by up to a year and a half (though it does not help delay sex until marriage). Emotionally, pledging may offer some protection from peer pressure, giving the pledger permission to go at their own pace. Pledges might also help promote acceptance of abstinence as a valid choice. So maybe there's a way to incorporate opt-in pledges in comprehensive sex education classes, particularly for younger teenagers who aren't emotionally ready for sex yet.

The problem is that virginity pledges are correlated with riskier behaviors and often rely on shaming to get their point across. As a result, young adults who take a virginity pledge are:

- One-third less likely to use contraception.
- Less likely to use condoms and to get tested for STIs.

- More likely to contract HPV (51% of pledgers vs. 33% of nonpledgers).
- 50% more likely to accidentally become pregnant.

—*Sexuality Information and Education Council of the United States,* The Journal of Marriage and Family

Communities with high pledge rates show significantly higher STI rates overall.

These outcomes are not especially surprising. Students who take virginity pledges often do so in the absence of accurate information about contraception and STI prevention.

Virginity pledges are also troubling in that they are an outgrowth of what's been dubbed "purity culture." Purity culture is a facet of our sexual culture that emphasizes virginity as a highly valuable commodity—particularly for girls. When I was Mormon, purity culture was the only framework I had to think about my sexuality. It promotes the idea that virgins are "pure" and "clean," while nonvirgins are "dirty," "loose," "easy," or otherwise less valuable. A truly impressive array of analogies is used to convey this message at church and in classrooms.

Purity culture has had a tremendous impact on our sexual culture as a whole in the United States, and not for the better. It tells young people that their value and worth as people is determined by their virginity rather than by their character, intellect, or good deeds. It teaches that men have sexual needs and desires which may be "uncontrollable," whereas women don't have sexual desires of their own. It teaches that women's bodies are a site of temptation and shame. It teaches that she is responsible for the predatory behaviors of others; that if she is sexually violated, she "asked for it," "invited it," or "acted like a slut." Purity culture teaches that women who enjoy sex don't "respect themselves," and thus don't deserve to be treated with respect by others. It creates a false hierarchy between women who obey the arbitrary rules ("proper") and women who reject them ("trashy"). It also sends damaging messages to survivors of sexual abuse. Defining someone's worth in terms of their sexual encounters means something very different to those who did not get a say in their first sexual experiences. It tells survivors of sexual abuse that they are unworthy of love or respect, that their bodies are now "dirty" and "used." The damage this can cause was beautifully articulated by Elizabeth Smart. Smart became a household name in the '90s after she was kidnapped at fourteen and sexually abused by her captors for nine months. Years after her rescue, she shared why she did not try to escape:

> I think it goes even beyond fear, for so many children, especially in sex trafficking. It's feelings of self-worth. It's feeling like, "Who would ever want me now? I'm worthless." That is what it was for me the first time I was raped. I was raised in a very religious household, one that taught that sex was something special that only happened between a husband and a wife who loved each other. And that's how I'd been raised, that's what I'd always been determined to follow: that when I got married, then and only then would I engage in sex. After that first rape, I felt crushed. Who could want me now? I felt so dirty and so filthy. I understand so easily all too well why someone wouldn't run because of that alone.
> —"Purity Culture: Bad for women, worse for survivors of sexual assault" by Jill Filipovic for The Guardian

Smart goes on to recall a lesson on abstinence at school, where her teacher compared sex to chewing gum:

> I thought, "Oh, my gosh, I'm that chewed-up piece of gum, nobody re-chews a piece of gum, you throw it away." And that's how easy it is to feel like you no longer have worth, you no longer have value. Why would

it even be worth screaming out? Why would it even make a difference if you are rescued? Your life still has no value.
—*"Elizabeth Smart: Abstinence-only education can make rape survivors feel 'dirty,' 'filthy' by Aliyah Frumin for MSNBC*

Is this really the message we want to be sending to young people?

How Did We Get Here?

The state of sex education in twenty-first century America is all the more puzzling when you consider that a whopping 93% of parents support comprehensive sex education in public schools. That's a huge majority. So why has the United States done the exact opposite for more than forty years? As usual, things haven't always been this way. The United States enjoyed a much earlier era of friendliness toward sex education that has since gone awry.

In the late 1800s, sex education was widely supported and a noncontroversial issue. In 1919, the US government declared its support for sex education as part of the White House Conference on Child Welfare, paving the way for family life programs to be nationally popularized in the 1950s. But by 1960, the winds of change began to blow right as the birth control pill hit the market for the first time. Suddenly, women were able to take a daily pill to prevent pregnancy, revolutionizing sex and vastly expanding American women's sexual autonomy. On the heels of the pill, the sexual revolution of the '60s and '70s rejected the restrictive sexual norms and gender roles of the '50s.

But these winds of change were not welcome by everyone. The pill, abortion, and sex education became the targets of organized campaigns, some of which continue to this day. Groups like Parents Opposed to Sex and Sensitivity Education (POSSE), Christian Crusade, and Mothers Organized for Moral Stability (MOMS) cropped up to fight against the perils of "free love" and birth control. Their efficient organization and steady-handed focus on achieving specific political goals was a tremendous strength. And in 1975, twenty states voted to restrict or abolish sex education. A few years later, detractors of sex education saw a major victory when the first iteration of the Adolescent Family Life Act (AFLA) was quietly passed by Congress. AFLA sought to prevent teen pregnancy—but it did so by promoting chastity. Hence its nickname: "the chastity act."

In the next decades, AFLA was a drip that turned into a waterfall of government funding for abstinence-only programming. Funding has amounted to more than $2 billion since then. At the state level, abstinence programs continue to receive millions of dollars in public funding each year. The height of abstinence funding happened in 2008, when $177 million was spent under President Bush. However, this record is set to be outpaced by President Trump, who proposed $277 million for abstinence programs in 2017. To receive funding, these programs must have as their "exclusive purpose the promotion of abstinence outside of marriage, for people of any age." Translation: Not only is abstinence to be taught, it is the *only* thing that is allowed to be taught. From the get-go, public funds for these abstinence-only programs were controversial. The American Civil Liberties Union (ACLU), a nonpartisan civil rights organization, took AFLA to court early on for violating the separation of church and state, and many years later won.

Outside of the unconstitutional intermingling of church and state, the real failure of abstinence-only is that it has never quite managed to reach its own stated goals of decreasing accidental pregnancy and disease. Over a hundred studies on their impact over two decades found that:

- No abstinence-only program increased condom use.
- No abstinence-only program increased contraceptive use.
- No abstinence-only program increased the rate of abstinence.
- No abstinence-only program raised the age of first sex.

This is a tremendous disservice to America's youth. Why are these programs still being funded by taxpayers?

Sex Ed for All

The two most common arguments I hear against sex education are that it's the parents' job and that sex education encourages young people to have sex. Here's why I feel these arguments are misguided.

IT'S NOT EITHER/OR; SCHOOLS *AND* PARENTS MUST PLAY A ROLE IN SEX EDUCATION.

Getting basic health information at school is merely the start of conversations that should continue at home. Schools should offer up-to-date information about health and disease control, which is an entryway to further discussion about sexuality at home. I also hear from a lot of parents who support public sex ed because they don't feel like they are prepared to tackle all the sexuality issues that come up for young people these days. The media and technology environment is rapidly changing, and sex educators are uniquely equipped to help parents navigate that with their kids. A multipronged approach where educators, parents, and public health organizations *all work together* helps keep young people healthy and safe.

SEX EDUCATION IS ABOUT KEEPING YOUNG PEOPLE INFORMED AND SAFE.

The notion that sex education *causes* or even *encourages* people to have sex might feel intuitive, but is ultimately misguided. Study after study demonstrates that comprehensive sex education actually *raises* the age of first sex. Why? There are likely a number of factors that come into play. For one, comprehensive sex education gives young people a healthy narrative about sex, plus a safe and constructive place to ask questions. This is an incredibly powerful alternative to the extreme narratives about sexuality that come from abstinence-only programs and porn (which currently set the tone of the conversation about sex for most people). Young people are desperate for sex education that is unbiased, factual, and empowering. Another reason sex education may delay sex is by undermining a forbidden fruit effect. When you are told something is forbidden, it makes it more appealing, and may fuel riskier behavior. When sexuality is treated as something that is out in the open and neutral, facts are better able to shape behaviors rather than taboos. On a practical level, sex education gives students tools to communicate their needs and set boundaries. It empowers young people to be confident and informed rather than scared and ignorant. They are better able to understand what they are and aren't ready for, and they learn how to communicate their boundaries with a partner. And hey, that's only the beginning of the magical powers of sex ed.

It can prevent unintended pregnancy.
It can reduce abortion.
It can prevent infection and disease.
It can prevent relationship abuse.
It can prevent sexual violence.
It helps young adults build healthy relationships.
It helps young adults have a healthy body image.
It helps reduce homophobia and transphobia.
It normalizes open communication in relationships and life.
It helps people handle their emotions in healthy ways.

It helps young people discuss STIs or birth control with a partner.

It helps young people communicate about consent.

It gives young people a safe place to ask questions.

It helps young people safely intervene when they witness abuse.

It helps young people to cope with and contextualize sexual abuse.

It helps young people to recover from trauma.

It promotes critical thinking about gender and sex in the media.

It helps people enjoy their bodies and pleasure.

It helps people to feel whole.

If that's so wrong, then I don't want to be right. We can choose to create a healthier, safer world with comprehensive sex education. So what the heck are we waiting for? It's time to get to work.

⋙∘ RESOURCES ∘⋘

For a more up-to-date list with clickable links, visit my resource guide at lacigreen.tv/resources.

Further Sexual Health Info for Young People

Bedsider
bedsider.org

Free STD Testing—American Sexual Health Association
yesmeanstest.org

Go Ask Alice
goaskalice.columbia.edu

Our Bodies Ourselves
ourbodiesourselves.org

Scarleteen: Sex Ed for the Real World
scarleteen.com

Sex, Etc.
sexetc.org

Stay Teen
stayteen.org

Planned Parenthood
plannedparenthood.org

Sexual Health Advocacy and Policy

Advocates for Youth
advocatesforyouth.org

Centers for Disease Control and Prevention—STDs
cdc.gov/std/default.htm

ETR Associates
etr.org

Healthy Teen Network
healthyteennetwork.org

Healthy Women
healthywomen.org/

Power to Decide: The Campaign to Prevent Unplanned Pregnancy
powertodecide.org

Sexuality Information and Education Council of the United States (SIECUS)
siecus.org

The Association of Black Sexologists and Clinicians
theabsc.com

The Center for Latino Adolescent and Family Health
clafh.org

The Center for Sex Education
sexedcenter.org

The Guttmacher Institute
guttmacher.org

The Society for the Scientific Study of Sexuality
sexscience.org

Women of Color Sexual Health Network
wocshn.org

World Association for Sexual Health
worldsexology.org

World Health Organization
who.int/en/

Body Image and Mental Health

Proud 2B Me
proud2bme.org/

National Eating Disorders Association
nationaleatingdisorders.org
Hotline: 1-800-931-2237

National Suicide Prevention Lifeline
suicidepreventionlifeline.org
1-800-273-TALK (8255)

Substance Abuse Hotline
addictioncareoptions.com
1-800-784-6776

Substance Abuse and Mental Health Services Administration
samhsa.gov
1-800-662-HELP (4357)
TTY 1-800-487-4889

National Runaway Switchboard
1800runaway.org
1-800-RUNAWAY (786-2929)

Kink and Sexual Exploration

Feminist Porn Awards
feministpornawards.com/

National Coalition for Sexual Freedom
ncsfreedom.org/

Ethical Porn for Dicks: A Man's Guide to Responsible Viewing Pleasure
by David Ley

Girl Sex 101
by Allison Moon

Mating in Captivity
by Esther Perel

Sex for One: The Joy of Selfloving
by Betty Dodson

SM 101: A Realistic Introduction
by Jay Wiseman

The Ethical Slut: A Practical Guide to Polyamory, Open Relationships, and Other Adventures
by Janet Hardy

LGBTQ+ and Intersex

AIS-DSD Support Group
aisdsd.org

Gay, Lesbian, and Straight Education Network
https://www.glsen.org/

GLAAD
https://www.glaad.org/

interACT: Advocates for Intersex Youth
interactadvocates.org

Intersex Society of North America
isna.org

The Asexual Visibility and Education Network
asexuality.org/

The Trevor Project
https://www.thetrevorproject.org/
LGBTQ+ suicide hotline: 1-866-488-7386

Trans Lifeline
translifeline.org
1-877-565-8860

Pregnancy

Note: *I have not read these books,* in large part because I have not been pregnant. These are suggestions from other sex educators and friends of mine who are parents.

Expecting Better
by Emily Oster

Our Bodies, Ourselves: Pregnancy and Birth
by The Boston Women's Health Collective

Ina May's Guide to Childbirth
by Ina May Gaskin

The Mother's Guide to Sex
by Anne Semans and Cathy Winks

The Birth Partner
by Penny Simkin

Reproductive Rights

NARAL Pro-Choice America
prochoiceamerica.org

Exhale Pro-Voice
exhaleprovoice.org
After-abortion hotline: 1-866-4-EXHALE

American Civil Liberties Union
aclu.org

Sexual and Dating Violence

RAINN
rainn.org
National sexual assault hotline: 1-800-656-HOPE (4673)

Love is Respect
loveisrespect.org
Dating violence hotline: 1-866-331-9474

The National Domestic Violence Hotline
thehotline.org
1-800-799-7233

Know Your IX—Empowering Students to Stop Sexual Violence
knowyourix.org

National Network to End Domestic Violence
nnedv.org

Safe Horizon
safehorizon.org
1-800-621-HOPE (4673)

The Anti-Violence Project (LGBTQ+/HIV+)
avp.org
1-212-714-1141

For educators, I recommend the Center for Sex Education's curricula and resources.
http://www.sexedstore.com/

For children, I recommend Robie H. Harris's books.

⋟∘ BIBLIOGRAPHY ∘⋞

Chapter 1: Your Genitals

"Bulbourethral Gland." *Encyclopædia Britannica.* The Editors of Encyclopædia Britannica, 29 Jan. 2014. www.britannica.com/science/bulbourethral-gland.

"Everything You Need to Know about Your Labia." Women's Health Victoria, 2011. www.labialibrary.org.au/your-labia/.

Farage, Miranda A., and Howard I. Maibach. *The Vulva: Anatomy, Physiology, and Pathology.* Informa Healthcare, 2006.

"Female Anatomy." www.sexualhealthaustralia.com.au, 2010. www.sexualhealthaustralia.com.au/female_anatomy.html.

Haldeman-Englert, Chad. "Congenital Adrenal Hyperplasia." *MedlinePlus Medical Encyclopedia*, National Institutes of Health, 27 Oct. 2015. medlineplus.gov/ency/article/000411.htm.

Heger, Astrid H., Lynne Ticson, Lisa Guerra, Julie Lister, Toni Zaragoza, Gina Mcconnell, and Mary Morahan. "Appearance of the Genitalia in Girls Selected for Nonabuse." *Journal of Pediatric and Adolescent Gynecology* 15.1 (2002): 27–35. Web.

Jannini, Emmanuele A., Beverly Whipple, Sheryl A. Kingsberg, Odile Buisson, Pierre Foldès, and Yoram Vardi. "Who's Afraid of the G-spot?" *The Journal of Sexual Medicine* 7.1 (2010): 25–34. Web.

Jordan-Young, Rebecca M., Peter H. Sönksen, and Katrina Karkazis. "Sex, health, and athletes." *BMJ* 2014; 348:g2926.

"Klinefelter Syndrome—Genetics Home Reference." U.S. National Library of Medicine, National Institutes of Health, 21 Nov. 2017. ghr.nlm.nih.gov/condition/klinefelter-syndrome.

Komisaruk, Barry R., Nan Wise, Eleni Frangos, WenâChing Liu, Kachina Allen, and Stuart Brody. "Women's Clitoris, Vagina, and Cervix Mapped on the Sensory Cortex: FMRI Evidence." *The Journal of Sexual Medicine* 8.10 (2011): 2822–830. Web.

Mautz, Brian S., Bob B. M. Wong, Richard A. Peters, and Michael D. Jennions. "Penis Size Interacts with Body Shape and Height to Influence Male Attractiveness." *Proceedings of the National Academy of Sciences* 110.17 (2013): 6925–930. Web.

"Mayer-Rokitansky-Küster-Hauser Syndrome—Genetics Home Reference." U.S. National Library of Medicine, National Institutes of Health, 21 Nov. 2017. ghr.nlm.nih.gov/condition/mayer-rokitansky-kuster-hauser-syndrome.

Mikkola, Mari. "Feminist Perspectives on Sex and Gender." *The Stanford Encyclopedia of Philosophy* (Winter 2017), edited by Edward N. Zalta. plato.stanford.edu/archives/win2017/entries/feminism-gender/.

"Myths Surrounding Virginity—Your Questions Answered." Vaginal Corona, RFSU, 14 Aug. 2013. www.rfsu.se/globalassets/pdf/vaginal-corona-english.pdf/.

Neves, Walter A., Astolfo G. M. Araujo, Danilo V. Bernardo, Renato Kipnis, and James K. Feathers. "Rock Art at the Pleistocene/Holocene Boundary in Eastern South America." *PLoS ONE* 7.2 (2012): n. pag. Web.

Padawer, Ruth. "The Humiliating Practice of Sex-Testing Female

Athletes." *The New York Times*, 28 June 2016. www.nytimes.
com/2016/07/03/magazine/the-humiliating-practice-of-sex-
testing-female-athletes.html?_r=0.

"Prostate Gland." *Encyclopædia Britannica*. The Editors of Encyclopædia
Britannica, 7 Mar. 2017. www.britannica.com/science/prostate-
gland.

Veale, David, Sarah Miles, Sally Bramley, Gordon Muir, and John
Hodsoll. "Am I Normal? A Systematic Review and Construction
of Nomograms for Flaccid and Erect Penis Length and
Circumference in up to 15,521 Men." *BJU International* 115.6
(2015): 978–86. Web.

"What Does ISNA Recommend for Children with Intersex?" Intersex
Society of North America. www.isna.org/faq/patient-centered.

"What Is Hypospadias?" Urology Care Foundation, 2017.
www.urologyhealth.org/urologic-conditions/hypospadias.

Chapter 2: Periods

"Menstrual Cycle—National Library of Medicine—PubMed Health."
National Center for Biotechnology Information, U.S. National
Library of Medicine, 10 Apr. 2016. www.ncbi.nlm.nih.gov/
pubmedhealth/PMHT0024713/.

Prior, Jerilynn C. "Very Heavy Menstrual Flow." The Centre for
Menstrual Cycle and Ovulation Research, 4 Oct. 2017.
www.cemcor.ubc.ca/resources/very-heavy-menstrual-flow.

Harvard Health Publishing. "Treating Premenstrual Dysphoric
Disorder." *Harvard Mental Health Letter*, Harvard Health
Publishing, Oct. 2009. www.health.harvard.edu/womens-health/
treating-premenstrual-dysphoric-disorder.

"The Link Between Acne & Testosterone." *UPMC HealthBeat*

Dermatology, 9 Oct. 2016, share.upmc.com/2016/10/
testosterone-and-acne/.

United States Congress Office on Women's Health. "Premenstrual
Syndrome (PMS)." Premenstrual Syndrome (PMS), Office
on Women's Health, 12 June 2017. www.womenshealth.gov/
menstrual-cycle/premenstrual-syndrome.

"What Is Premenstrual Dysphoric Disorder (PMDD)?" Premenstrual
Dysphoric Disorder, Johns Hopkins Medicine Health Library,
24 Jan. 2011. www.hopkinsmedicine.org/healthlibrary/
conditions/gynecological_health/premenstrual_dysphoric_
disorder_pmdd_85,P00580.

Chapter 3: The Care and Keeping of Vaginas

Al-Badr, Ahmed, and Ghadeer Al-Shaikh. "Recurrent Urinary Tract
Infections Management in Women: A Review." *Sultan Qaboos
University Medical Journal* 13.3 (2013): 359–367. Print.

Centers for Disease Control and Prevention. Sexually Transmitted
Diseases Treatment Guidelines, 2015. MMWR, 64(RR-3).

"Gynecomastia." Edited by Steven Dowshen, KidsHealth, The
Nemours Foundation, Oct. 2016, kidshealth.org/en/teens/
boybrst.html#.

"HPV and Cancer." National Cancer Institute, 19 Feb. 2015.
www.cancer.gov/about-cancer/causes-prevention/risk/infectious-
agents/hpv-fact-sheet#q4.

Martinez, Rafael C.r., Shannon L. Seney, Kelly L. Summers, Auro
Nomizo, Elaine C.p. De Martinis, and Gregor Reid. "Effect of
Lactobacillus Rhamnosus GR-1 and Lactobacillus Reuteri RC-14
on the Ability Of Candida Albicans to Infect Cells and Induce
Inflammation." *Microbiology and Immunology* 53.9 (2009): 487–95.

"NIH Human Microbiome Project Defines Normal Bacterial Makeup of the Body." National Institutes of Health, U.S. Department of Health and Human Services, 31 Aug. 2015. www.nih.gov/news-events/news-releases/nih-human-microbiome-project-defines-normal-bacterial-makeup-body.

Payam, Behzadi, Elham Behzadi, Hodjjat Yazdanbod, Roghiyyeh Aghapour, Mahboubeh Akbari Cheshmeh, and Djaafar Salehian Omran. "A Survey on Urinary Tract Infections Associated with the Three Most Common Uropathogenic Bacteria." *Maedica (Buchar)* 5.2 (2010): 111–15. Web.

"Self-Exam: Vulva and Vagina." Our Bodies, Ourselves, OBOS Anatomy and Menstruation Contributors, 28 Mar. 2014. www.ourbodiesourselves.org/health-info/self-exam-vulva-vagina/.

Shields-Cutler, R. R., J. R. Crowley, C. S. Hung, A. E. Stapleton, C. C. Aldrich, J. Marschall, J. J. P. Henderson. "Human urinary composition controls siderocalin's antibacterial activity." *The Journal of Biological Chemistry*, 26 June 2015.

"The American Cancer Society Guidelines for the Prevention and Early Detection of Cervical Cancer." American Cancer Society, The American Cancer Society Medical and Editorial Content Team, 9 Dec. 2016. www.cancer.org/cancer/cervical-cancer/prevention-and-early-detection/cervical-cancer-screening-guidelines.html.

"Urinary Tract Infections." UCSF Medical Center, UCSF Health, www.ucsfhealth.org/conditions/urinary_tract_infections/.

"What Are the Symptoms?" Centers for Disease Control and Prevention, Centers for Disease Control and Prevention, 6 Mar. 2014. www.cdc.gov/cancer/gynecologic/basic_info/symptoms.htm.

"Women's Health Care Physicians." *ACOG Revises Breast Cancer Screening Guidance: Ob-Gyns Promote Shared Decision Making—ACOG*, American College of Obstetricians and Gynecologists, 22 June 2017, www.acog.org/About-ACOG/News-Room/News-Releases/2017/ACOG-Revises-Breast-Cancer-Screening-Guidance--ObGyns-Promote-Shared-Decision-Making.

Chapter 4: Sexual Identity

Adams, Henry E., Lester W. Wright, and Bethany A. Lohr. "Is Homophobia Associated with Homosexual Arousal?" *Journal of Abnormal Psychology* 105.3 (1996): 440–45. Web.

Cass, Vivienne C. "Homosexuality Identity Formation." *Journal of Homosexuality*, vol. 4, no. 3 (1979): 219–235. doi:10.1300/j082v04n03_01.

Continuum of Human Sexuality. University of Illinois at Springfield, Student Affairs Office (2009).

Gates, Gary J. "How Many People Are Lesbian, Gay, Bisexual, and Transgender?" The Williams Institute, 2011. williamsinstitute.law.ucla.edu/wp-content/uploads/Gates-How-Many-People-LGBT-Apr-2011.pdf.

Herek, Gregory M. "Beyond 'Homophobia': A Social Psychological Perspective on Attitudes Toward Lesbians and Gay Men." *Journal of Homosexuality*, vol. 10, no. 1–2 (1984): 1–15. doi: 10.1300/j082v10n01_01.

Homosexuality in the Animal Kingdom. Naturhistorisk Museum, 25 Feb. 2009. www.nhm.uio.no/besok-oss/utstillinger/skiftende/againstnature/gayanimals.html.

"Kids Pay the Price." Conversion Therapy Laws, Movement Advancement Project, 9 Nov. 2013. www.lgbtmap.org/equality-maps/conversion_therapy.

Kimmel, Michael S. "Masculinity as Homophobia: Fear, Shame, and Silence in the Construction of Gender Identity." *Theorizing Masculinities*, edited by Harry Brod and Michael Kaufman, 119–141. SAGE Knowledge. Web. Research on Men and Masculinities Series. Thousand Oaks, CA: SAGE Publications, 1994. doi: 10.4135/9781452243627.n7.

Moskowitz, David A., Gerulf Rieger, and Michael E. Roloff. "Heterosexual Attitudes towards Same-Sex Marriage." *Journal of Homosexuality* 57.2 (2010): 325–336. PMC. Web. 6 Dec. 2017.

National Report on Hate Violence Against Lesbian, Gay, Bisexual, Transgender, Queer and HIV-Affected Communities Released Today. National Coalition of Anti-Violence Programs, 2017. avp. org/wp-content/uploads/2017/06/NCAVP_2016_HVReport_ Media-Release.pdf.

Park, Haeyoun, and Iarnya Mykhyalyshyn. "L.G.B.T. People Are More Likely to Be Targets of Hate Crimes Than Any Other Minority Group." *New York Times*, 16 June 2016. www.nytimes.com/ interactive/2016/06/16/us/hate-crimes-against-lgbt.html.

Rochlin, Martin. Heterosexuality Questionnaire. University of Wisconsin–Green Bay, 1977.

Sanders, A. R., E. R. Martin, G. W. Beecham, S. Guo, K. Dawood, G. Rieger, J. A. Badner, E. S. Gershon, R. S. Krishnappa, A. B. Kolundzija, J. Duan, P. V. Gejman, and J. M. Bailey. "Genome-wide Scan Demonstrates Significant Linkage for Male Sexual Orientation." *Psychological Medicine* 45.07 (2014): 1379–388. Web.

Storms, Michael D. "Theories of Sexual Orientation." *Journal of Personality and Social Psychology*, vol. 38, no. 5 (1980): 783–792. doi:10.1037//0022-3514.38.5.783.

The 2015 National School Climate Survey Executive Summary.

GLSEN, 2015. www.glsen.org/sites/default/files/GLSEN%20
  2015%20National%20School%20Climate%20Survey%20
  %28NSCS%29%20-%20Executive%20Summary.pdf.

"The Klein Grid." AIB, 2014. www.americaninstituteofbisexuality.
  org/thekleingrid/.

"The Lies and Dangers of 'Conversion Therapy.'" Human Rights
  Campaign. www.hrc.org/resources/the-lies-and-dangers-of-
  reparative-therapy.

"UC Berkeley Psychologist Finds Evidence That Male Hormones in
  the Womb Affect Sexual Orientation." *ScienceDaily*, 30 March 2000.
  www.sciencedaily.com/releases/2000/03/000330094644.htm.

Wålinder, J. "Transsexualism: Definition, Prevalence and Sex
  Distribution." *Acta Psychiatrica Scandinavica* (1968), 43: 255–258.
  doi:10.1111/j.1600-0447.1968.tb02000.x.

Weinstein, N., W. S. Ryan, Przybylski DeHaan, N. Legate, and
  R. M. Ryan. "Parental autonomy support and discrepancies
  between implicit and explicit sexual identities: Dynamics of self-
  acceptance and defense." *Journal of Personality and Social Psychology*,
  102(4) (2012): 815–832. http://dx.doi.org/10.1037/a0026854.

"Westboro Baptist Church: Homosexuals Should Be Put to Death."
  YouTube, Midweek Politics, 10 Oct. 2012. www.youtube.com/
  watch?v=iqyUU66qNuE.

Chapter 5: Gender Identity

Ashbee, Olivia, and Joshua Mira Goldberg. "Hormones: A Guide
  for FTMs." Trans Care Gender Transition, Vancouver Coastal
  Health, Feb. 2006. apps.carleton.edu/campus/gsc/assets/
  hormones_FTM.pdf.

Bearak, Max. "Why Terms like 'Transgender' Don't Work for India's 'Third-Gender' Communities." *The Washington Post*, 23 Apr. 2016. www.washingtonpost.com/news/worldviews/wp/2016/04/23/ why-terms-like-transgender-dont-work-for-indias-third-gender-communities

Blosnich, John R., George R. Brown, Jillian C. Shipherd, Michael Kauth, Rebecca I. Piegari, and Robert M. Bossarte. "Prevalence of Gender Identity Disorder and Suicide Risk Among Transgender Veterans Utilizing Veterans Health Administration Care." *American Journal of Public Health* 103.10 (2013): n. pag. Web.

Cole, C. M., et al. "Treatment of Gender Dysphoria (Transsexualism)." *Texas Medicine.* U.S. National Library of Medicine, May 1994. www.ncbi.nlm.nih.gov/pubmed/8029771.

"Definitions Related to Sexual Orientation and Gender Diversity in APA Documents." American Psychological Association, 14 Nov. 2017. www.apa.org/pi/lgbt/resources/sexuality-definitions.pdf.

Flores, Andrew R., Jody L. Herman, Gary J. Gates, and Taylor N. T. Brown. "How Many Adults Identify as Transgender in the United States." *Williams Institute.* UCLA, 26 July 2016.

Graham, Sharyn. "Sulawesi's Fifth Gender." *Inside Indonesia,* 30 July 2007. www.insideindonesia.org/sulawesis-fifth-gender-2.

Haas, Ann P. "Suicide Attempts among Transgender and Gender Non-Conforming Adults." The Williams Institute, 2014. williamsinstitute.law.ucla.edu/wp-content/uploads/ AFSP-Williams-Suicide-Report-Final.pdf.

"Interactive Map: Gender-Diverse Cultures." PBS, Public Broadcasting Service, 11 Aug. 2015. www.pbs.org/ independentlens/content/two-spirits_map-html/.

Laframboise, Sandra, and Michael Anhorn. "The Way of the Two Spirited People: Native American Concepts of Gender and Sexual Orientation." Dancing to Eagle Spirit Society, 2008. www.dancingtoeaglespiritsociety.org/twospirit.php.

Olyslager, Femke, and Lynn Conway. "On the Calculation of the Prevalence of Transsexualism." University of Michigan, 6 Sept. 2007. ai.eecs.umich.edu/people/conway/TS/Prevalence/Reports/Prevalence%20of%20Transsexualism.pdf.

Serano, Julia. "Detransition, Desistance, and Disinformation: A Guide for Understanding Transgender Children Debates." *Medium*, 2 Aug. 2016. medium.com/@juliaserano/detransition-desistance-and-disinformation-a-guide-for-understanding-transgender-children-993b7342946e.

Snow, Jade. "What Native Hawaiian Culture Can Teach Us about Gender Identity." *Yes Magazine*, 27 July 2015. www.yesmagazine.org/issues/make-it-right/what-native-hawaiian-culture-can-teach-us-about-gender-identity.

"Transgender Regret Surgery Issues." *Healthline*, Healthline Media. www.healthline.com/health-news/transgender-regret-is-rare-but-real.

"What Is Gender Dysphoria?" Reviewed by Ranna Parekh, American Psychiatric Association, Feb. 2016. www.psychiatry.org/patients-families/gender-dysphoria/what-is-gender-dysphoria.

Zervigon, Andres. "Drag Shows: Drag Queens and Female Impersonators." *GLBTQ: An Encyclopedia of Gay, Lesbian, Bisexual, Transgender, and Queer Culture.* www.academia.edu/595439/Drag_Shows_Drag_Queens_and_Female_Impersonators.

Chapter 6: Body Image

"Body Image and Nutrition." Teen Health and the Media, Washington

State Department of Health. depts.washington.edu/thmedia/
view.cgi?page=fastfacts&section=bodyimage.

Harvard Mental Health Letter. Harvard Medical School, Nov. 2011.
www.health.harvard.edu/newsletter_article/in-praise-of-gratitude.

"Warning Signs and Symptoms." NEDA Feeding Hope, National
Eating Disorders Association, 2016. www.nationaleatingdisorders.
org/learn/by-eating-disorder/anorexia/warning-signs-symptoms.

Chapter 7: Masturbation and Orgasm

"7 Surprising Facts about Female Orgasm." One Medical, 12 July 2017.
www.onemedical.com/blog/live-well/female-orgasm/.

Armstrong, E., P. England, and Alison Fogarty. 2009. "Orgasm in
College Hookups and Relationships. *In Families as They Really Are*,
edited by Barbara Bisman. New York: W.W. Norton and Co.

Basson, Rosemary. "The Female Sexual Response: A Different
Model." *Journal of Sex & Marital Therapy*, vol. 26, no. 1 (2000):
51–65. doi:10.1080/009262300278641.

Herbenick, Debby, et al. "Women's Experiences with Genital
Touching, Sexual Pleasure, and Orgasm: Results from a
U.S. Probability Sample of Women Ages 18 to 94." *Journal of
Sex & Marital Therapy* (May 2017): 1–12. doi:10.1080/00926
23x.2017.1346530.

Jones, Nicola. "Bigger Is Better When It Comes to the G Spot." *New
Scientist,* 3 July 2002. www.newscientist.com/article/dn2495-
bigger-is-better-when-it-comes-to-the-g-spot/.

Kellogg, John Harvey. *Plain Facts for Old and Young.* Heritage Press,
1974.

Kratochvil, S. "The Duration of Female Orgasm." *Cesk Psychiatrie,* vol. 89, no. 5 (Oct. 1993): 296–299.

Masters, W. H., and V. E. Johnson. *Human Sexual Response.* Boston, MA: Little, Brown, 1966.

Viglianco-VanPelt, Michelle, and Kyla Boyse. "Masturbation." Your Child Development and Behavior Resources, University of Michigan Health System, July 2009. www.med.umich.edu/ yourchild/topics/masturb.htm.

Wade, Lisa. "The Orgasm Gap: The Real Reason Women Get Off Less Often Than Men and How to Fix It." *Alternet,* 3 Apr. 2013. www.alternet.org/sex-amp-relationships/orgasm-gap-real-reason-women-get-less-often-men-and-how-fix-it?

"What You Need to Know: Female Sexual Response." Association of Reproductive Health Professionals, Mar. 2008. www.arhp.org/ uploadDocs/FSRfactsheet.pdf.

Chapter 8: Sex Toys

Denning, Burke, and Debby Herbenick. "The Safety Dance: Sex Toy Safety for a New Generation." *Kinsey Confidential,* The Kinsey Institute, 12 Mar. 2014, kinseyconfidential.org/safety-dance-sex-toy-safety-generation/.

Schulz, Bill. "From the Vault of the Museum of Sex: Macaura's Pulsocon." *The New York Times,* 14 Aug. 2015. www.nytimes.com/ 2015/08/16/nyregion/from-the-vault-of-the-museum-of-sex-macauras-pulsocon.html.

Stern, Marlow. "'Hysteria' and the Long, Strange History of the Vibrator." *The Daily Beast,* The Daily Beast Company, 27 Apr. 2012, www.thedailybeast.com/hysteria-and-the-long-strange-history-of-the-vibrator.

Chapter 9: Your Sexual Debut

"About Oxytocin." Psych Central, 17 July 2016. psychcentral.com/lib/about-oxytocin/?all=1.

Chapter 10: Safer Sex

"Chancroid." Centers for Disease Control and Prevention, 4 June 2015. www.cdc.gov/std/tg2015/chancroid.htm.

"Chlamydia." Centers for Disease Control and Prevention, 4 Oct. 2017. www.cdc.gov/std/chlamydia/stdfact-chlamydia.htm.

"Five Kinds of Condoms: A Guide for Consumers." Five Kinds of Condoms: A Guide for Consumers | Go Ask Alice!, Columbia University, 26 Jan. 2001. www.goaskalice.columbia.edu/answered-questions/five-kinds-condoms-guide-consumers-0.

"Genital Herpes." Centers for Disease Control and Prevention, 1 Sept. 2017. www.cdc.gov/std/Herpes/STDFact-Herpes.htm.

"Gonorrhea." Centers for Disease Control and Prevention, 4 Oct. 2017. www.cdc.gov/std/gonorrhea/stdfact-gonorrhea.htm.

"How To: Find Your Condom Size!" Lucky Bloke, 2017, luckybloke.com/pages/find-your-condom-size.

HPV Vaccination Resource Book. Area Health Education Centers, 2017. www.alabamapublichealth.gov/immunization/assets/hpvresourceguide.pdf.

"Human Papillomavirus (HPV)." Centers for Disease Control and Prevention, 23 Aug. 2017. www.cdc.gov/hpv/index.html.

Pinsky, Laura, and Paul Harding Douglas. *The Columbia University Handbook on HIV and AIDS*. Columbia University, 2009. health.columbia.edu/system/files/content/healthpdfs/MS/GHAP_HIV_Aids_Handbook.pdf.

"STDs & HIV." Advocates for Youth. www.advocatesforyouth.org/ storage/advfy/documents/std-brochure.pdf.

"STI Statistics." American Sexual Health Association. www.ashasexualhealth.org/stdsstis/statistics/.

"Syphilis—CDC Fact Sheet." Centers for Disease Control and Prevention, 13 June 2017. www.cdc.gov/std/syphilis/STDFact-Syphilis.htm.

"The Australian Immunisation Handbook," 10th edition. Australian Government Department of Health, Aug. 2016. www.immunise.health.gov.au/internet/immunise/publishing. nsf/Content/ 7372ED840C99FB81CA257D4D0022CB44/ $File/4-6-HPV.pdf.

"Trichomoniasis." Centers for Disease Control and Prevention, 14 July 2017. www.cdc.gov/std/trichomonas/stdfact-trichomoniasis.htm.

"Pubic Lice (Crabs)." *Mayo Clinic*, Mayo Foundation for Medical Education and Research, 30 Dec. 2017. www.mayoclinic.org/ diseases-conditions/pubic-lice-crabs/symptoms-causes/ syc-20350300.

"What Are the Symptoms of Pubic Lice (Crabs)?" Planned Parenthood, 1 Dec. 2017. www.plannedparenthood.org/learn/stds-hiv-safer-sex/pubic-lice/what-are-symptoms-pubic-lice-crabs.

"Viral Hepatitis." Centers for Disease Control and Prevention, 26 Sept. 2017. www.cdc.gov/hepatitis/populations/stds.htm.

Winston, Sheri. "Lube Rules!" Intimate Arts Center, 31 Aug. 2017. intimateartscenter.com/lube-rules/.

Chapter 11: Birth Control

"Anti-Choice Violence and Intimidation." NARAL, 1 Jan. 2017.

www.prochoiceamerica.org/wp-content/uploads/2017/01/
1.-Anti-Choice-Violence-and-Intimidation.pdf.

"Birth Control Patch." Planned Parenthood, 1 Dec. 2017.
www.plannedparenthood.org/learn/birth-control/birth-control-
patch.

"Birth Control Pill." Planned Parenthood, 1 Dec. 2017.
www.plannedparenthood.org/learn/birth-control/birth-control-
pill.

"Birth Control Ring." Planned Parenthood, 1 Dec. 2017.
www.plannedparenthood.org/learn/birth-control/birth-control-
vaginal-ring-nuvaring.

"Birth Control Shot." Planned Parenthood, 1 Dec. 2017.
www.plannedparenthood.org/learn/birth-control/birth-control-
shot.

"Birth Control Sponge." Planned Parenthood, 1 Dec. 2017,
www.plannedparenthood.org/learn/birth-control/birth-control-
sponge.

"Breastfeeding." Planned Parenthood, 1 Dec. 2017.
www.plannedparenthood.org/learn/birth-control/breastfeeding.

Bryant, Amy G., and Erika E. Levi. "Abortion Misinformation from
Crisis Pregnancy Centers in North Carolina." *Contraception*, vol.
86, no. 6 (2012): 752–756. doi:10.1016/j.contraception.2012.06.001.

"Cervical Cap." Planned Parenthood, 1 Dec. 2017.
www.plannedparenthood.org/learn/birth-control/cervical-cap.

Cole, Laurence A. "The Utility of Six Over-the-Counter (Home)
Pregnancy Tests." *Clinical Chemistry and Laboratory Medicine,* vol. 49,
no. 8 (Jan. 2011). doi:10.1515/cclm.2011.211.

Cole, Laurence A., et al. "Sensitivity of Over-the-Counter Pregnancy Tests: Comparison of Utility and Marketing Messages." *Journal of the American Pharmacists Association,* vol. 45, no. 5 (2005): 608–615. doi:10.1331/1544345055001391.

"Condom." Planned Parenthood, 1 Dec. 2017. www.plannedparenthood.org/learn/birth-control/condom.

"Diaphragm." Planned Parenthood, 1 Dec. 2017. www.plannedparenthood.org/learn/birth-control/diaphragm.

Donnelly, Tim. "History's 10 Worst Forms of Birth Control." *New York Post,* 29 Apr. 2014. nypost.com/2014/04/29/historys-10-worst-forms-of-birth-control/.

"Emergency Contraception." Planned Parenthood, 1 Dec. 2017. www.plannedparenthood.org/learn/morning-after-pill-emergency-contraception.

"Female Condom." Planned Parenthood, 1 Dec. 2017. www.plannedparenthood.org/learn/birth-control/female-condom.

"Fertility Awareness." Planned Parenthood, 1 Dec. 2017. www.plannedparenthood.org/learn/birth-control/fertility-awareness.

"Implanon & Nexplanon Information." Planned Parenthood, 1 Dec. 2017. www.plannedparenthood.org/learn/birth-control/birth-control-implant-implanon.

"In Clinic Abortion." Planned Parenthood, 1 Dec. 2017. www.plannedparenthood.org/learn/abortion/in-clinic-abortion-procedures.

"Induced Abortion in the United States." Guttmacher Institute, 20 Oct. 2017. www.guttmacher.org/fact-sheet/induced-abortion-united-states.

"IUD." Planned Parenthood, 1 Dec. 2017. www.plannedparenthood.
org/learn/birth-control/iud.

Kim, Leland. "IUDs Don't Cause Pelvic Inflammatory Disease
in Women." UC San Francisco, 20 Nov. 2012, www.ucsf.edu/
news/2012/11/13157/iuds-dont-cause-pelvic-inflammatory-
disease-women.

Law, Bridget Murray. "Monitor on Psychology." www.apa.org/
monitor/2011/03/hormones.aspx.

"Miscarriage: Signs, Symptoms, Treatment and Prevention." American
Pregnancy Association, 5 Dec. 2017. americanpregnancy.org/
pregnancy-complications/miscarriage/.

"Ovulation 101: What Is It & How Does It Work?" Clue, 24 Nov. 2017.
helloclue.com/articles/cycle-a-z/ovulation-101-what-is-it-how-
does-it-work.

"Testosterone in Women." Public Health and Preventive Medicine,
Monash University, Sept. 2017, www.monash.edu/medicine/
sphpm/depts-centres-units/womenshealth/info-sheets/
testosterone-for-women.

"The Abortion Pill." Planned Parenthood, 1 Dec. 2017.
www.plannedparenthood.org/learn/abortion/the-abortion-pill

"What She Said." *Indian Literature*, vol. 29, no. 1 (111), 1 Jan. 1986,
p. 24.

"Who Decides?" 24th Edition. NARAL, 2015. www.prochoiceamerica.
org/wp-content/uploads/2017/04/2015-Who-Decides.pdf.

"Withdrawal (Pull Out Method)." Planned Parenthood, 1 Dec. 2017.
www.plannedparenthood.org/learn/birth-control/withdrawal-
pull-out-method.

Chapter 12: Consent and Communication

10 U.S. Code, § 47-920 (2016). Print. Rape and sexual assault generally.

"Alcohol Overdose: The Dangers of Drinking Too Much." National Institute on Alcohol Abuse and Alcoholism. U.S. Department of Health and Human Services, Oct. 2015. pubs.niaaa.nih.gov/publications/alcoholoverdosefactsheet/overdosefact.htm.

"Blood Alcohol Concentration." Rev. James E. McDonald, C.S.C., Center for Student Well-Being, University of Notre Dame. mcwell.nd.edu/your-well-being/physical-well-being/alcohol/blood-alcohol-concentration/.

Marsh, Jason, and Dacher Keltner. "We Are All Bystanders." *Greater Good Magazine*. University of California, Berkeley, 1 Sept. 2006. greatergood.berkeley.edu/article/item/we_are_all_bystanders.

"Sexual Assault." The United States Department of Justice, 16 June 2017. www.justice.gov/ovw/sexual-assault.

Chapter 13: Sexploration

Chalabi, Mona. "The Pubic Hair Preferences of the American Woman." *FiveThirtyEight*, 11 Apr. 2014. fivethirtyeight.com/features/au-naturel-or-barely-there-the-data-on-pubic-hair-preferences/.

Marston, C., and R. Lewis. "Anal Heterosex among Young People and Implications for Health Promotion: A Qualitative Study in the UK." *BMJ Open*, vol. 4, no. 8 (2014). doi:10.1136/ bmjopen-2014-004996.

"Myths Surrounding Virginity: Vaginal Corona." Swedish Association for Sexuality Education, 14 Aug. 2013. www.rfsu.se/globalassets/pdf/vaginal-corona-english.pdf/

Osterberg, E. C., T. W. Gaither, M. A. Awad, et al. "Correlation between Pubic Hair Grooming and STIs: Results from a Nationally Representative Probability Sample." *Sexually Transmitted Infections*, 93(2017): 162–166.

Pierce, R. V. *The People's Common Sense Medical Adviser in Plain English; or, Medicine Simplified.* Selections from Dr. Pierce's *Medical Adviser* at MUM. www.mum.org/peopcomc.htm.

Ramsey S., C. Sweeney, M. Fraser, and G. Oades. "Pubic Hair and Sexuality: A review." *The Journal of Sexual Medicine* 2009; 6:2102–2110.

Salama, Samuel, et al. "Nature and Origin of 'Squirting' in Female Sexuality." *The Journal of Sexual Medicine*, vol. 12, no. 3, 2015, pp. 661–666., doi:10.1111/jsm.12799.

Wedekind, C., et al. "MHC-Dependent Mate Preferences in Humans." *Proceedings of the Royal Society B: Biological Sciences,* vol. 260, no. 1359 (1995): 245–249. doi:10.1098/rspb.1995.0087.

Chapter 14: Kink

Ambler, James K., et al. "Consensual BDSM Facilitates Role-Specific Altered States of Consciousness: A Preliminary Study." *Psychology of Consciousness: Theory, Research, and Practice,* vol. 4, no. 1 (2017): 75–91. doi:10.1037/cns0000097.

Joyal, Christian C., et al. "What Exactly Is an Unusual Sexual Fantasy?" *The Journal of Sexual Medicine,* vol. 12, no. 2 (2015): 328–340., doi:10.1111/jsm.12734.

Klement, Kathryn R., et al. "Participating in a Culture of Consent May Be Associated With Lower Rape-Supportive Beliefs." *The Journal of Sex Research,* vol. 54, no. 1 (2016): 130–134. doi: 10.1080/00224499.2016.1168353.

McManus, Michelle A., et al. "Paraphilias: Definition, Diagnosis and

Treatment." *F1000Prime Reports* 5 (2013): 36. Web. 29 Nov. 2017.

Sagarin, Brad J., et al. "Hormonal Changes and Couple Bonding in Consensual Sadomasochistic Activity." SpringerLink, Springer US, 19 June 2008. link.springer.com/article/10.1007/s10508-008-9374-5.

Wismeijer, AA., and M.A. van Assen. "Psychological Characteristics of BDSM Practitioners." *The Journal of Sexual Medicine*, 16 May 2013. onlinelibrary.wiley.com/doi/10.1111/jsm.12192/abstract.

Chapter 15: Relationshipping

Ackerman, Joshua M., et al. "Let's Get Serious: Communicating Commitment in Romantic Relationships." *Journal of Personality and Social Psychology*, vol. 100, no. 6 (2011): 1079– 1094. doi:10.1037/a0022412.

Chapman, Gary D. *The 5 Love Languages*. Chicago, Northfield Publishing, 2015.

Edwards, Scott. "On the Brain." neuro.hms.harvard.edu/harvard-mahoney-neuroscience-institute/brain-newsletter/and-brain-series/love-and-brain.

Fisher, Helen, et al. "Romantic Love: An FMRI Study of a Neural Mechanism for Mate Choice." *The Journal of Comparative Neurology*, vol. 493, no. 1 (2005): 58–62. doi:10.1002/cne.20772.

"I Want to Know Where Love Is." EurekAlert!, Concordia University, 20 June 2012. www.eurekalert.org/pub_releases/2012-06/cu-iwt061912.php.

Lewandowski, Gary W. "What Physiological Changes Can Explain the Honeymoon Phase of a Relationship?" *Scientific American*, 10 Sept. 2013. www.scientificamerican.com/article/what-physiological-changes-can-explain-honeymoon-phase-relationship/.

McLeod, Saul. "Attachment Theory." *Simply Psychology,* 1 Jan. 1970, www.simplypsychology.org/attachment.html.

"One Thing to Look for in a Mate: Advice from Long-Married Elders." The Legacy Project, Cornell University, 4 Feb. 2013. legacyproject.human.cornell.edu/2013/02/04/one-thing-to-look-for-in-a-mate-advice-from-long-married-elders/.

Sternberg, Robert J. "A Triangular Theory of Love." *Psychological Review,* vol. 93, no. 2 (1986): 119–135. doi:10.1037//0033-295x.93.2.119.

Chapter 16: Dating Violence

"Auto Theft Prevention." National Conference of State Legislatures, 2008, Auto Theft Prevention. www.ncsl.org/print/cj/autotheftreport.pdf.

Bancroft, Lundy. "Checklist for Assessing Change in Men Who Abuse Women." Lundy Bancroft, 2007. lundybancroft.com/articles/checklist-for-assessing-change-in-men-who-abuse-women/.

"Dating Abuse Statistics." Love Is Respect. www.loveisrespect.org/pdf/Dating_Abuse_Statistics.pdf.

"Domestic Abuse Perpetrated against People with Disabilities." *NHS Choices,* NHS, 2017. www.domesticviolencelondon. nhs.uk/1-what-is-domestic-violence-/21-domestic-abuse-perpetrated-against-people-with-disabilities.html.

Lisak, David, and Paul M. Miller. "Repeat Rape and Multiple Offending among Undetected Rapists." *Violence and Victims,* vol. 17, no. 1 (Jan. 2002): 73–84. doi:10.1891/vivi. 17.1.73.33638.

"Reporting Rape in 2013." US Department of Justice, 9 Apr. 2014. ucr.fbi.gov/recent-program-updates/reporting-rape-in-2013-revised.

Roberts, Kayleigh. "The Psychology of Victim-Blaming." *The Atlantic*. Atlantic Media Company, 5 Oct. 2016. www.theatlantic.com/ science/archive/2016/10/the-psychology-of-victim-blaming/ 502661/.

Walker, Lenore E. *The Battered Woman*. New York, Harper and Row, 1987.

Epilogue: Why We Need Sex Ed

"A Brief Explanation of Virginity Pledges." SIECUS, Aug. 2005, www.siecus.org/_data/global/images/Virginity%20Pledge%20 Fact%20Sheet%20-%20SIECUS-08.05.pdf.

"ACLU Memo to Interested Persons Regarding Abstinence-Only-Until Marriage Programs." American Civil Liberties Union, June 2005. www.aclu.org/other/aclu-memo-interested-persons-regarding-abstinence-only-until-marriage-programs.

Bearman, Peter, and Hannah Brackner. "Promising the Future: Virginity Pledges and First Intercourse." *American Journal of Sociology*, vol. 106, no. 4 (2001): 859–912. doi: 10.1086/320295.

Bersamin, Melina M., et al. "Promising to Wait: Virginity Pledges and Adolescent Sexual Behavior." *Journal of Adolescent Health*, vol. 36, no. 5 (2005): 428–436. doi: 10.1016/j.jadohealth.2004.09.016.

Brackner, Hannah, and Peter Bearman. "After the Promise: The STD Consequences of Adolescent Virginity Pledges." *Journal of Adolescent Health*, vol. 36, no. 4 (2005): 271–278. doi:10.1016/j. jadohealth.2005.01.005.

Bubala, Mary. "Elizabeth Smart Speaks at Human Trafficking Forum in Baltimore." CBS Baltimore, 2 May 2013. baltimore.cbslocal. com/2013/05/02/elizabeth-smart-speaks-at-human-trafficking-forum-in-baltimore/.

"Choosing the Best PATH and LIFE Summary." Community Action

Kit—Choosing the Best PATH and LIFE Summary, SIECUS, 2008. www.communityactionkit.org/index.cfm?fuseaction=Page. ViewPage&PageID=1178&stopRedirect=1.

Connolly, Ceci. "Federal Funds for Abstinence Group Withheld." 23 Aug. 2005. www.washingtonpost.com/wp-dyn/content/article/2005/08/22/AR2005082201230.html.

Filipovic, Jill. "'Purity' Culture: Bad for Women, Worse for Survivors of Sexual Assault," *The Guardian*, Guardian News and Media, 9 May 2013, www.theguardian.com/commentisfree/2013/may/09/elizabeth-smart-purity-culture-shames-survivors-sexual-assault.

Finer, Lawrence B. "Trends in Premarital Sex in the United States, 1954-2003." *Public Health Reports*, vol. 122, no. 1 (2007): 73–78. doi:10.1177/003335490712200110.

"History of Sex Ed." Sex Education Resource Center, Advocates for Youth, 2008. www.advocatesforyouth.org/serced/1859-history-of-sex-ed.

"History of Sex Education in the U.S." Planned Parenthood Federation of America, Nov. 2016. www.plannedparenthood.org/uploads/filer_public/3e/de/3edec4e8-3604-44f9-998b-6a7cff9d22ad/20170209_sexed_d04_1.pdf.

"'I Swear I Won't!' A Brief Explanation of Virginity Pledges." *SIECUS—Fact Sheet*, Sexuality Information and Education Council of the United States, Aug. 2005, www.siecus.org/index.cfm?fuseaction=Page.ViewPage&PageID=1202.

Martinez, Gladys M., and Joyce C. Abma. "National Center for Health Statistics." Centers for Disease Control and Prevention, 2 2 July 2015. www.cdc.gov/nchs/products/databriefs/db209.htm.

"New Study: Overwhelming Support for Consent Education in

Schools." *Planned Parenthood Action Fund*, 21 Apr. 2016,
www.plannedparenthoodaction.org/blog/overwhelming-support-
for-consent-education-in-schools.

"On Our Side: Public Support for Comprehensive Sexuality
Education." SIECUS, Apr. 2010. www.siecus.org/index.
cfm?fuseaction=Page.ViewPage&PageID=1197.

Paik, Anthony, et al. "Broken Promises: Abstinence Pledging and
Sexual and Reproductive Health." *Journal of Marriage and Family*,
vol. 78, no. 2, 2016, pp. 546–561., doi:10.1111/jomf.12279.

PPFA Consent Survey Results Summary. Planned Parenthood
Federation of America, 2015. www.plannedparenthood.org/
files/1414/6117/4323/Consent_Survey.pdf.

Schroeder, Elizabeth, and Judith Kuriansky. *Sexuality Education: Past,
Present, and Future.* Chicago, Praeger, 2009.

"Sex Education in the United States." Planned Parenthood
Federation of America, Mar. 2012. www.plannedparenthood.org/
files/3713/9611/7930/Sex_Ed_in_the_US.pdf.

"Sex Education Linked to Delay in First Sex." Guttmacher Institute,
24 Feb. 2017. www.guttmacher.org/news-release/2012/sex-
education-linked-delay-first-sex.

Sharpe, Jared. "UMass Amherst Sociologist Finds Abstinence
'Pledgers' Have Higher Risk of HPV, Non-Marital Pregnancies."
News and Media Relations, UMass Amherst, 7 Jan. 2016.
www.umass.edu/newsoffice/article/umass-amherst-sociologist-
finds-abstinence.

"State Abstinence Education Grant Program Fact Sheet." Family
and Youth Services Bureau, 23 June 2016. www.acf.hhs.gov/fysb/
resource/aegp-fact-sheet.

⋛° ACKNOWLEDGMENTS °⋚

IT TAKES A VILLAGE, Y'ALL. I wanted to share some love and gratitude for those in my life who supported me on this adventure.

First, always, my family. You guys, we are a wacky bunch. But I love that we always, always stick together through thick and thin. Dei and KK, you are the best siblings a lady could ask for. I live for your zany humor and I am constantly in awe of your kindness. Even if everything falls apart, I will always be here to help you piece it back together. Mom and Pops, you are my rock in this turbulent world. Thanks for making me, for guiding me, for believing in me, and (let's be real) for enduring all my bullshit as a teenager. You shaped me into the woman I am today, and I am so grateful. I love you down to my toes!

To my far-off family—Grandma and Gramps, Annie and Uncle Dave, Dori and Uncle J, you are my home away from home. Thank you for always helping me find quiet in the chaos, feeding me nomnoms, and making me laugh at the dumbest crap for hours. There's so much love in cowtown.

Of course, there are some family members that we choose. To my oldest pals, Adam and Todd, who have walked many miles in the woods with me, figuring shit out and goofing off. You are brothers to me, and I live for our drives through the countryside when I'm home. Thank you for always bringing me back to my center.

To my Bay Area family, thank you for nurturing me through the wild ride of college and YouTube. You guys believed in me from the start, and I'm not sure where I would have ended up without you! (Hippie commune in Santa Cruz??) Nate, Rob, Alex, Christie, Shani—you are the reason the bay was my home. Tom, Trace, Anthony, Pam, and Jared—you made me laugh more than any team I've worked with. And MANNNN do I miss it! You each hold a special place in my heart, even though we don't see each other very often anymore.

To my LA family, thank you for embracing me with open arms when I stumbled into this city a bit broken and disheveled. I am humbled and inspired by each of you in a myriad of ways: by your kindness, your creativity, your intelligence, your ridiculous humor. Chris, Ted, Melissa, Chris, Sam, Matt, Matt, Rob, Karen, Ali, Carolyn, Amanda, Vierra, Jason, Nicky, Bunty, Tim, and so many others: you each bring so much warmth to my life. I can't imagine this city without you in it (or visiting it)! Here's to our future adventures.

To the partners who joined me at various points on this journey, thank you for seeing me and pushing me and loving me. To N, for encouraging me to pursue this project before I believed I could handle it and loving me unconditionally. To T, for being a gentle springboard for ideas and feeding me the world's best cookies. To C, for helping me laugh all of the stress off and find my way forward.

Thank you to my sex ed family for being my mentors and role models. Mark, Bill, Karen, David, and Sam: I learn so much from each of you. Thank you for inspiring me with your kindness, openness, and curiosity. You make the sex ed world a more accepting and interesting place to thrive!

Also, I owe an enormous, MONSTROUSLY HUMUNGO thank you to my incredible book team. You guys took every vision and hope I had for this book and made it even better. I'm in awe of your smarts, creativity, and (let's be real)—efficiency! Together we've made a timeless resource that will hopefully help many humans in the years to come. To Nyk, Ellen, Ellice, and Sarah: thank you for making the book look so beautiful and helping me to communicate with more than just words. To my lovely contributors, who brought dimension and wisdom to this project: Kimberly, Rob, Gaia, Olivia, Alaska, and those who wished not to be named. Thank you for sharing your stories so openly. Jessica, Gwen, Mitchell, Cindy, Camille, and Ebony: thank you for keeping the project moving forward and getting this baby out into the world. To my whip-smart expert reviewers: Bill Taverner, Kimberly Zieselman, Dr. Elizabeth Sara Rubin, and Dr. Ilene Wong, thank you for bringing your wisdom and critical eye, it strengthened this book SO MUCH! To Eve and Erin: thank you for guiding me through the process and advocating for me through every challenge and victory. And finally, thank you, Sara, for being the most badass editor a lady could ask for! Your mentorship through this process has helped to shape me as a writer in such an enormous way. I'm so grateful we got to work together. We did it!

Lastly, thank you to my YouTube family. To those of you who shared my work, invited me to your schools and homes, participated in the conversation, saw the best in me and believed in my message: there are no words for how humbled I am by your support. I feel so blessed to have connected with new colleagues, new friends, and new perspectives around the world despite the chaos that is the internet. To those of you who I never got a chance to meet: your presence is felt in YouTube comments and Twitter replies and 3AM emails full of love and humanity. In some of the shittiest times, the online community we created offers so many of us a safe retreat from the world. Thank you for the late nights and the lols. I feel so privileged to have experienced this world with you.

x

laci

⋺∘ INDEX ∘⋵

life span of, 238
scrotum and, 20–21
testes and, 22
wet dreams and, 24–25
sponge (birth control), 240, 242
how to use, 241
spotting, 42
squirting, 338–39
stalking, 431–32
statutory rape, 290
Steinberg, Gaia, 349–53
stereotypes
of abusers, 433
sexual orientation and, xii, 97
virginity and, 185
of women, 438
Sternberg, Robert, 398–400
STI. *See* sexually transmitted infection
stigmas
of BDSM, 364–67
gay men and, 106
intersex, 28
of masturbation, 147
menstrual cycle, 51–53
of STIs, 195–96, 217
Storm, Michael, 86
Storm Scale, 86–87, *87*
strap-ons, 182
supporting someone coming out, 94–96
syphilis, 207–8

T

Taylor, George, 173
testes
blue ball myth, 22–23
vasocongestion, 23
36 Questions That Lead to Love, 383
toxic shock syndrome (TSS), 46–47
transgender individuals. *See also* LGBTQ+
community
defining, 117
experimentation, 122
gender dysphoria and, 126–27
gender nonconformity and, 119
Louie on, 122–24
loving decisions as, 124–25
name change, 124
nonbinary gender identities and, 119–21

proper pronouns for, 134
risk factors, 127
statistics on, 118
supporting, 134–35
transitioning, 127–33
violence, 108
transitioning, 127
legal, 133
medical, 129–33
social, 128–29
triangular theory of love, 398–400
trichomoniasis, 197–98
troubleshooting in relationships, 409
arguing about nothing, 410
cheating, 413–15
fear of commitment, 413
jealousy and insecurity, 415–16
long distance, 410–11
mental health issues, 411
partner is in the closet, 412–13
responsibilities and, 415
Trump, Donald, 457
TSS. *See* toxic shock syndrome
Twilight, 185, 295–96

U

urethra
female, *11*, 12, 13
male, 25
urethral sponge, *11*, 12
urinary meatus, 9, 19
urinary system, *64*
urinary tract infections (UTIs), 56–57, 63
antibiotics and, 65–66
coconut oil and, 66–67
IC and, 67
prevention of, 66–67
symptoms of, 65
urinary system and, *64*
uterus, 14–15
UTIs. *See* urinary tract infections

W

vagina, *10. See also* healthcare for vaginas
defining, 3
erection of, 11
reproduction and, 11
scent of, 55